SEQUELS

compiled by

Marilyn E. Hicken

Volume I
Adult books

LONDON
ASSOCIATION OF ASSISTANT LIBRARIANS
(GROUP OF THE LIBRARY ASSOCIATION)

The AAL acknowledge the assistance of
REMPLOY LIMITED
in the production of this publication
1991

1st edition 1922 by Thomas Aldred

2nd edition 1928 by W. H. Parker

3rd edition 1947 by F. M. Gardner

4th edition 1955 by F. M. Gardner

5th edition 1967 by F. M. Gardner

6th edition 1974 by F. M. Gardner

7th edition 1982 by M. E. Hicken

8th edition 1986 by M. E. Hicken

9th edition 1989 by M. E. Hicken

10th edition 1991 by M. E. Hicken

British Library Cataloguing in Publication Data

Hicken, Marilyn E. (Marilyn Enid) 1936—
 Adult sequels.—10th ed.
 1. Literature
 I. Title II. Hicken, Marilyn E. (Marilyn Enid) 1936—
 Sequels III. Association of Assistant Librarians
 011. 7

ISBN 0-900092-18-1

Jacket design by Origin Studios, Stoke-on-Trent
Printed by J. H. Brookes (Printers) Limited, 141-149 Lower Bryan Street, Hanley, Stoke-on-Trent
Bound by Remploy Limited, Newcastle, Staffs.

PREFACE TO THE TENTH EDITION

Although it is only just over two years since the last edition of 'Sequels' appeared, I have added some 1400 new titles in this, the tenth edition. The cut-off date for entries is September 1991.

The overall scheme of the book remains the same, and lists

    a) novels in which the same characters appear
    b) sequences of novels connected by theme
    c) sequences of novels with a geographical or historical connection
    d) non-fiction, mainly autobiographical, which is intended to be read in sequence

The number and variety of paperbacks in sequence continues to increase, and, indeed, forms a large proportion of the market in fantasy and science fiction. Some of the more substantial series are dated, others, as before, are dated when they appear in hardback form.

I would like to thank all the people who have helped in the work; my colleagues in Derbyshire, Martin Underwood in Birmingham, whose lists are invaluable, and the Holt Jackson Book Company, who unfailingly supply me with a weekly collection of new fiction. Thanks as well to the AAL Publications Officers, and to Tina Dunn of Remploy Bookbinding who oversees the smooth running of the operation.

December 1991   Mandy Hicken

ARRONS, E. S.
SAM DURRELL:
1 Assignment disaster 1955
2 Assignment treason 1956
3 Assignment Budapest 1957
4 Assignment suicide 1957
5 Assignment Stella Marni 1957
6 Assignment Angelina 1958
7 Assignment Carlotta Cortez 1958
8 Assignment Cong Hai kill 1958
9 Assignment Ankara 1958
10 Assignment Madeline 1958
11 Assignment Helene 1959
12 Assignment Lilli Lamaris 1959
13 Assignment Mara Tirana 1960
14 Assignment Burma girl 1961
15 Assignment Zoraya 1961
16 Assignment Lowlands 1961
17 Assignment school for spies 1961
18 Assignment Karachi 1962
19 Assignment Sorrento siren 1963
20 Assignment Manchurian doll 1963
21 Assignment the girl in the gondola 1964
22 Assignment the Cairo dancers 1965
23 Assignment Palermo 1966
24 Assignment Black Viking 1967
25 Assignment Moon girl 1967
*Most of these have not yet been
published in the U.K. All dates given
are of U.S.A. publication.*

ABBEY, L.
UNICORN AND DRAGON
1 Unicorn
2 Dragon
3 The green man
Paperback fantasy

ABRAHAM, C.
THE ONEDIN LINE:
1 The shipmaster 1973
2 The iron ships 1974
3 The high seas 1976
4 Trade winds 1977
5 The white ships 1979
6 Turning tide 1980
*Adapted from the TV series. The last
title is by B. Stewart*

ABSE, D.
1 Ash on a young man's sleeve 1973
2 There was a young man from Cardiff
1991
3 A poet in the family 1974
*1 and 2 are autobiographical novels;
3 is autobiography.*

ACHEBE, C.
AFRICAN TRILOGY
1 Things fall apart 1958
2 No longer at ease 1960
3 Arrow of gold 1964

ACTON, H.
1 Memoirs of an aesthete 1948
2 More memoirs of an aesthete 1970
N.F. Autobiography

ADAMS, D.
1 The hitch-hikers guide to the Galaxy
1979
2 The restaurant at the end of the
Universe 1980
3 Life, the Universe and everything 1982
4 So long, and thanks for all the fish 1984
*Science fiction, originally written for
radio*
DIRK GENTLY:
1 Dirk Gently's Holistic Detective
Agency 1987
2 The long dark teatime of the soul 1988

ADAMS, R.
1 Shardik 1974
2 Maia 1984
Fantasy

ADAMS, ROBERT
HORSECLANS:
1 The coming of the Horseclans 1985
2 The swords of the Horseclans 1985
3 The revenge of the Horseclans
4 A cat of silvery hue 1985
5 The savage mountains 1985
6 The patrimony 1985
7 Horseclans odyssey 1985
8 The death of a legend 1985
9 The witchgoddess 1985
10 Bili the axe 1985
11 Champion of the last battle 1985
12 A woman of the Horseclans 1985
*A fantasy series published
simultaneously in hardback and
paperback.*

ADAMSON, J.
1 Born free 1960
2 Living free 1961
3 Forever free 1962
4 Elsa and her cubs 1965
*N.F. Books about a lion cub adopted as
a pet. Republished in one vol. 1966.
'The Story of Elsa'.*

ADDIS, F.
1 The year of the cornflake 1983
2 Green behind the ears 1984
3 Buttered side down 1985
4 Down to earth 1987
5 Taking the biscuit 1989
N.F. Life on a smallholding in Devon

ADLARD, M.
1 Interface 1970
2 Volteface 1972
Science fiction

AGRY, E.
O'REILLY:
1 Assault force O'Reilly 1981
2 O'Reilly: blowtorch 1982

AHERN, J.
THE SURVIVALIST
1 Total war
2 The nightmare begins
3 The quest
4 The doomsayer
5 The web
6 The savage horde
7 The prophet
8 The end is coming
9 Earth fire
10 The awakening
11 The reprisal
12 The rebellion
13 Pursuit
14 The terror
15 Overlord

AIKEN, JOAN
1 The smile of the stranger 1970
2 The lightning tree 1980
Gothic romances set in the 19th century

AIKMAN, A.
BOYET RHODES
1 The caves of Segonda 1985
2 The eye of Itza 1986
3 The brokers of doom 1987

AINSWORTH, P.
1 The flickering candle
2 The candle rekindled
3 Steady burns the candle 1970

AIRD, C.
INSPECTOR SLOAN SERIES:
1 The religious body 1966
2 A most contagious crime 1967
3 Henrietta who? 1968
4 The complete steel 1969

5 A late phoenix 1970
6 His burial too 1973
7 Slight mourning 1975
8 Parting breath 1977
9 Some die eloquent 1979
10 Passing stranger 1980
11 Last respects 1982
12 Harm's way 1984
13 A dead liberty 1986
14 The body politic 1990

ALBANY, J.
S.A.S.
1 Warrior caste 1982
2 Mailed fist 1983
3 Deacon's dagger 1983
4 Close combat 1983
5 Marching fire 1984
6 Last bastion 1984
7 Borneo story 1985

ALBERT, M.
PETE SAWYER
1 Stone angel 1986
2 Back in the real world 1987
3 Get off at Babylon 1988
4 Long teeth 1988
5 The midnight sister 1989
6 The last smile 1989
7 Bimbo heaven 1990
8 The zig-zag man 1991

ALDING, P.
C.I.D. ROOM SERIES:
1 The C.I.D. room 1967
2 Circle of danger 1968
3 Murder among thieves 1969
4 Guilt without proof 1970
5 Despite the evidence 1971
6 Call back to crime 1972
7 Field of fire 1973
8 The murder line 1974
9 Six days to death 1975
10 Murder is suspected 1977
11 Ransom town 1979
12 A man condemned 1981
13 Betrayal by death 1982
14 One man's justice 1983

ALDISS, B.
HELLICONIA TRILOGY
1 Helliconia Spring 1982
2 Helliconia Summer 1983
3 Helliconia Winter 1985
Science fiction

ALDISS, B. W.
1 The hand-reared boy 1970

2 A soldier erect 1971
3 A rude awakening 1978

ALDRIDGE, J.
RUPERT ROYCE:
1 A captive in the land 1963
2 The stateman's game 1966

ALEICHEM, S.
1 The old country 1966
2 Texvye's daughters 1973
The stories on which the famous musical
play 'Fiddler on the Roof' was based

ALEXANDER, D.
PHOENIX
1 Dark Messiah
2 Ground zero
Paperback fantasy

ALEXANDER, L.
CHRONICLES OF PRYDAIN:
1 The book of three
2 The black cauldron
3 Castle of Llyr
4 Taran wanderer
5 The High King
Paperback fantasy

ALEXANDER, M.
THE WELLS OF YTHAN
1 Ancient dreams
2 Magic casements
3 Shadow realm
Paperback fantasy

ALEXANDER, S.
MICHELANGELO BUONAROTTI:
1 Michelangelo, the Florentine 1957
2 The hand of Michelangelo 1965
3 Nicodemus 1985

ALLBEURY, T.
TAD ANDERS:
1 Snowball 1974
2 The Judas factor 1984

ALLBURY, A.
1 You'll die in Singapore 1953
2 Bamboo and Bushido 1955
N.F. War reminiscences

ALLDRITT, K.
BLACK COUNTRY SERIES:
1 The good pit man 1976
2 The lover next door 1978
3 Elgar on the journey to Hanley 1979

ALLEGRETTO, M.
JACOB LOMAX
1 Death on the rocks 1988
2 Blood stone 1989
3 Dead of winter 1990

ALLEN, M.
DET. SERGEANT SPENCE:
1 Spence in Petal Park 1975
2 Spence at the Blue Bazaar 1976

ALLEN, R. B.
VENERA
1 The torch of honour
2 Rogue powers
Paperback fantasy

ALLINGHAM, M.
ALBERT CAMPION SERIES:
1 The crime at Black Dudley 1929
   (Black Dudley murder)
2 Mystery mile 1929
3 The Gyrth chalice mystery 1931
4 Police at the funeral 1931
5 Sweet danger 1933
   (Kingdom of death)
6 Death of a ghost 1934
7 Flowers for the judge 1936
8 The case of the late pig 1937
9 Dancers in the morning 1937
10 The fashion in shrouds 1938
11 Mr. Campion and others 1939
12 Black plumes 1940
13 Traitor's purse 1941
14 Coroner's pidgin 1945
   (Pearls before swine)
15 More work for the undertaker 1948
16 Tiger in the smoke 1952
17 Beckoning lady 1955
18 Hide my eyes 1958
   (Tether's end)
19 The china governess 1963
20 The mind readers 1965
21 Cargo of eagles *(completed by* P. Y.
   Carter) 1967
22 Mr. Campion's farthing *by* P. Y. Carter
   1968
23 Mr. Campion's falcon *by* P. Y. Carter
   1969
The volume 'Mysterious Mr. Campion'
1963, is an omnibus volue with one new
short story. The second 'Allingham
Omnibus' gives the inner sequence of
the story of Campion and his wife,
Amanda, in nos. 5, 10, 13, above and
has one new Campion short story.
'Mr. Campion's clowns' is an omnibus
of 2, 14 and 15 above. 'The Allingham

minibus' 1973, contains some Campion
short stories.
P. Y. Carter was Margery Allingham's
husband and collaborated with her in
many of her books.

ALLIS, M.
ASHBEL FIELD SERIES:
1 Now we are free 1952
2 To keep us free 1953
3 Brave pursuit 1954
4 Rising storm 1955
5 Free soil 1960
*A series of novels about an American
family, beginning with the
revolutionary war.*

ALLISON, E. S.
1 Kiwi at large 1967
2 Kiwi vagabond 1969
N.F. Travel and autobiography

ALLISON-WILLIAMS, J.
THE TABARD:
1 Mistress of 'The Tabard' 1983
2 Simon of 'The Tabard' 1984
*Novels set in a 15th century London
tavern.*

ALLYSON, A.
MARTIN ROSS:
1 Don't mess with murder 1972
2 Do you deal in murder? 1973

ALMEDINGEN, E. M.
1 Fair haven 1959
2 Dark splendour 1961
*Andrew Thorngold of 2 is the son of Hal
Thorngold of 1. Scene is Russia in the 18th
century.*

1 Tomorrow will come 1948
2 The almond tree 1951
3 Within the harbour 1955
N.F. Autobiography

ALVERSON, C.
GOODEY
1 Goodey's last stand
2 Not sleeping, just dead
3 Fighting back

AMBLER, E.
1 Uncommon danger 1937
2 Cause for alarm 1938
*The character Zaleshoff appears in both
books, but not otherwise connected.*
1 The mask of Dimitrios 1939

2 The intercom conspiracy 1970
*The crime novelist, Charles Latimer, is
the principal character in 1 and his
mysterious death is the cause of the
action in 2, but he does not appear.*

ARTHUR ABDEL SIMPSON:
1 Light of day 1962
2 Dirty story 1967

AMERY, L. S.
1 England before the storm 1896-1914
2 War and peace 1914-1929
3 The unforgiving years
N.F. Autobiography

AMES, D.
DAGONBERT BROWN SERIES
1 She shall have murder 1948
2 Murder begins at home 1949
3 Death of a fellow traveller 1950
4 Corpse diplomatique 1950
5 The body on page one 1951
6 Murder, maestro please 1952
7 No mourning for the Matador 1953
8 Crime, gentlemen please 1954
9 Landscape with corpse 1955
10 Crime out of mind 1956
11 She wouldn't say who 1957
12 Lucky Jane 1959

SERGEANT JUAN LLORCA SERIES:
1 The man in the tricorn hat 1962
2 The man with three Jaguars 1963
3 The man with three chins 1964
4 Man with three passports 1967

AMIS, K.
PATRICK STANDISH:
1 Take a girl like you 1960
2 Difficulties with girls 1988

ANAND, M. J.
STORY OF LAL SINGH:
1 The village
2 Across the black waters
3 The sword and the sickle

ANAND, V.
BRIDGES OVER TIME
1 The proud villeins 1990
2 The ruthless yeoman 1991

NORMAN TRILOGY:
1 Gildenford 1979
2 The Norman pretender 1980
3 Disputed crown 1982

ANDERSON, J.
1 Assassin 1972

2 Abolition of death 1974

ANDERSON, J. R. L.
MAJOR PETER BLAIR
1 Death on the rocks 1973
2 Death in the Thames 1974
3 Death in the North Sea 1975
4 Death in the desert 1976
5 Death in the Caribbean 1977
6 Death in the city 1977
7 The nine-spoked wheel 1978
8 Death in the greenhouse 1978
9 Death in a high latitude 1981

PIET DEVENTER:
1 A sprig of sea lavender 1978
2 Festival 1979
3 Late delivery 1982

ANDERSON, O.
GUY RANDOM SERIES:
1 Random rendezvous 1955
2 Random mating 1956
3 Random at random 1958
4 Random rapture 1959
5 Random all round 1960

ANDERSON, P.
EARTHBOOK OF STORMGATE
3 vols. in paperback, without individual titles.
FLANDRY:
1 Ensign Flandry 1977
2 A circus of Hells 1978
3 The rebel worlds
4 Tiger by the tail
5 Honourable enemies
6 Flandry of Terra
7 Commander Flandry 1979
8 A handful of stars
9 Knight Flandry 1980
10 A stone in Heaven 1981
Science fiction

POLESOTECHNIC LEAGUE:
1 The Earthbook of Stormgate
2 The trouble twisters
3 War of the wingmen
4 Trader to the stars
5 Satan's world
6 Mirkheim

THE KING OF YS:
1 Roma mater
2 Gallicenae
3 Dahut
4 The dog and the wolf
Paperback fantasy

ANDERSON, V.
1 Spam tomorrow 1956
2 Our square 1957
3 Beware of children 1958
4 Daughters of divinity 1959
5 The Flo affair 1963
6 The Northrepp grandchildren 1968
7 Scrambled eggs for Christmas 1970
N.F. Autobiography

ANDREWS, L.
ST. BARNABAS' HOSPITAL:
1 The young doctor downstairs
2 The new Sister Theatre

ST. MARTHA'S HOSPITAL:
1 The light in the ward 1984
2 The healing time 1986
3 Front line, 1940 1990

THE GARDEN:
1 One night in London 1980
2 Weekend in the Garden 1981
3 In an Edingburgh drawing room 1983
4 The phoenix syndrone 1987
The story of a London teaching hospital bombed in WW2, and its rebuilding to 1980.

ANDREWS, V.
CASTEEL FAMILY:
1 Heaven 1986
2 Dark angel 1987
3 Fallen hearts 1989
4 Gates of paradise 1989
5 Web of dreams 1990

DOLLENGAGER FAMILY:
1 Garden of shadows 1987
2 Flowers in the attic 1980
3 If there be thorns 1981
4 Petals in the wind 1980
5 Seeds of yesterday 1984
Both series were completed by Andrew Niederman after Virgina Andrews' death.

ANDRIC, L.
YUGOSLAVIAN TRILOGY:
1 The bridge on the Drina 1959
2 Bosnian story 1959
3 The woman from Sarajevo 1956
The history of Yugoslavia in fictional form. Nobel prize 1961.

ANGELOU, M.
1 I know why the caged bird sings 1984
2 Gather together in my name 1985
3 Singin' and swingin' and makin' merry like Christmas 1985

4 The heart of a woman 1986
5 All God's children need travelling shoes 1987
N.F. Autobiography of a black American woman.

ANGELS
1 Angels *by* P. Milne 1975
2 Flights of Angels *by* P. Milne 1976
3 New Angels *by* P. Milne 1978
4 Duty calls *by* V. Georgeson 1979
Based on the TV series

ANGOFF, C.
POLONSKY FAMILY:
1 Journey to the dawn 1951
2 In the morning light 1952
3 The sun at dawn 1955
4 Between day and dark 1959
5 The bitter spring 1961
6 Summer storm 1963
7 Memory of autumn 1968
8 Winter twilight 1970
9 Season of mists 1971
10 Mid-century 1974
11 Towards the horizon 1980
The story of a Jewish family who emigrated from Czarist Russia to the USA, and their life there.

ANSTEY, R.
1 Leopold's Congo 1964
2 King Leopold's legacy 1966
N.F. The history of the Congo.

ANTHONY, D.
STANLEY BASS:
1 The organisation
2 Stud game 1977

MORGAN BUTLER:
1 The midnight lady and the morning 1970
2 Blood on the harvest moon 1973
3 The long hard cure 1979

ANTHONY, E.
1 Imperial Highness 1953
2 Curse not the King 1954
3 Far fly the eagles 1955

DAVINA GRAHAM
1 The defector 1980
2 Avenue of the dead 1981
3 Albatross 1982
4 The company of saints 1983
Spy stories

ANTHONY, P.
1 Chthon 1967
2 Phthor 1970
Paperbacks only in this country.

BATTLE CIRCLE:
1 Sos the rope 1968
2 Var the stick 1971
3 Neq the sword 1971
Science fiction. Also published in one volume.

BIO OF A SPACE TYRANT:
1 Refugee
2 Mercenary
3 Politician
4 Executive
5 Statesman

CLUSTER:
1 Vicinity 1979
2 Chaining the lady 1979
3 Kirlian quest 1979
4 Thousandstar
5 Viscous circle 1981
Fantasy

INCARNATIONS OF IMMORTALITY:
1 On a pale horse 1986
2 Bearing an hour glass 1986
3 With a tangled skein 1987
4 Wielding a red sword 1987
5 Being a green mother 1988
6 For love of evil 1990
7 And eternity 1990

OF MAN AND MANTA:
1 Omnivore
2 Orn
3 Ox

TAROT TRILOGY:
1 God of Tarot
2 Vision of Tarot
3 Faith of Tarot
Paperback fantasy, 1982.

THE APPRENTICE ADEPT
1 Split infinity 1981
2 Blue adept 1981
3 Juxtaposition 1983
4 Out of phaze 1988
5 Phaze doubt 1991

THE MAGIC OF XANTH:
1 A spell for the chameleon 1977
2 A source of magic 1979
3 Castle Roogna 1979
4 Centaur Aisle 1982
5 Ogre, Ogre 1981
6 Night mare 1983
7 Dragon on a pedestal 1985

8 Crewel Lye 1988
9 Golem in the gears
10 Vale of the vole 1988
11 Heaven cent 1989
12 Robot adept 1989
13 The man from Mundania 1990
14 Unicorn point 1990
15 Isle of view 1991

ANTONIUS, S.
1 The Lord 1986
2 Where the Jinn consult 1987

ANTONY, J.
1 Mrs Dale's bedside book 1951
2 Mrs Dale at home
3 The Dales of Parkwood Hill 1959
4 Dear Dr. Dale 1970

1 Wisteria Street will soon be gone 1970
2 The young stranger 1971

APPIGNANESI, R.
ITALIA PERVASA:
1 Stalin's orphans 1982
2 The mosque 1985
3 Destroying America 1987

ARCHER, F.
1 Under the parish lantern 1969
2 Hawthorn hedge country 1970
3 Secrets of Bredon Hill 1971
4 A lad of Evesham Vale 1972
5 Muddy boots and Sunday suits 1973
6 Golden sheaves, black horses 1974
7 When village bells were silent 1975
8 Poacher's pie 1976
9 By hook and by crook 1978
10 When Adam was a boy 1979
11 Fred Archer, farmer's son 1986
12 The distant scene 1987
13 The village of my childhood 1989
N.F. Country life and autobiography

ARCHER, J.
1 Kane and Abel 1980
2 The prodigal daughter 1982

ARDEN, W.
KANE JACKSON:
1 A dark power 1969
2 Deal in violence 1971

ARDIES, T.
CHARLIE SPARROW:
1 Their man in the White House 1971
2 This suitcase is going to explode 1972

ARGO, E.
1 Jewel of the seas
2 The crystal star
Paperback only

ARLEN, L.
THE BORODINS:
1 Love and honour 1984
2 War and passion 1984
A family saga originally published in paperback.

ARMITAGE, A.
EVA BOWER
1 Chapter of innocence 1988
2 Chapter of echoes 1989
3 Chapter of shadows 1990

HAWKSMOOR:
1 Hawksmoor 1981
2 Hunter's moon 1985
3 Touchstone 1987
4 Hawkrise 1988
Novels set in Yorkshire from the 18th century to World War II.

ARMSTRONG. C.
DET. FRANK PAGAN:
1 Jig 1987
2 Mazurka 1988
3 Mambo 1990

ARMSTRONG, E. S.
1 Daughter of Valdoro 1975
2 Valdoro's mistress 1976
Set in South American Pampa

ARMSTRONG, R.
CHIEF INSPECTOR MASON SERIES:
1 Dangerous limelight 1947
2 Sinister playhouse 1949
3 Sinister widow 1951
4 Sinister widow again 1952
5 Sinister widow returns 1953
6 Sinister widow comes back 1956
7 Widow and the cavalier 1956
8 Sinister widow down under 1958
9 Sinister widow at sea 1959

ROCKINGHAM STONE SERIES:
1 Cavalier of the night 1955
2 The widow and the cavalier 1956
2 is also in the previous series.

ARMSTRONG, S.
CLACHAN:
1 A croft in Clachan 1976
2 Clachan days 1977
3 A hotel by Clachan 1978

4 The electrics come to Clachan 1979
5 Jamie in Clachan 1980
N.F. Autobiography, set in the Scottish Highlands.

ARMSTRONG, T.
THE CROWTHER CHRONICLES:
1 The Crowthers of Bankdam 1940
2 Pilling always pays 1954
3 Sue Crowther's marriage 1961
4 Our London office 1966
Edwin Crowther makes a brief appearance in 'A ring has no end'.

ARNOLD, B.
COPPINGER TETRALOGY:
1 A singer at the wedding 1979
2 The song of the nightingale 1980
3 The muted swan 1981
4 Running to Paradise 1983

ARNOLD, R.
1 A very quiet war 1962
2 Orange Street and Brickhole Lane 1963
N.F. Autobiography.

ARNOTHY, C.
1 I am fifteen and I do not want to die 1963.
2 It is not so easy to live 1965
N.F. Autobiography

ARTHUR, F.
INSPECTOR SPEARPOINT:
1 Who killed Netta Maul? (The Suva Harbour Mystery 1940)
2 Another mystery in Suva 1956
3 Murder in the tropic night 1961
4 The throbbing dark 1962

ARVAY, H.
TRIAD:
1 Triad 21 1977
2 Society of fear 1979
Novels about the international drug racket.

ASCH, S.
1 The Nazarene 1939
2 The Apostle 1943
3 Mary 1949
4 Moses 1951
5 The Prophet 1955
First conceived as the 'New Testament' trilogy, and then expanded into a biblical series.

ASHE, GORDON, *pseud, see* CREASEY, J.

ASHFORD, J.
DETECTIVE-INSPECTOR DON KERRY SERIES:
1 Counsel for the defence 1961
2 Investigations are proceedings 1963 (The D.I.)
3 Enquiries are continuing 1964
4 Will anyone who saw the accident 1964
5 Superintendent's room 1965
6 Forget what you saw 1967

ASHTON, H.
WILCHESTER CHRONICLES
1 Tadpole Hall
2 Joanna at Littlefold
3 Yeoman's hospital 1949
4 Captain comes home 1950
5 Half-crown house 1956
There are a few references to Wilchester in an the earlier novel, 'Hornet's Nest'.

ASIMOV, I.
BLACK WIDOWERS DINING CLUB
1 Tales of the Black Widowers 1975
2 More tales of the Black Widowers 1977
3 Casebook of the Black Widowers 1980
4 Puzzles of the Black Widowers 1990
Detective stories

DAVID STARR - SPACE RANGER:
1 Space ranger 1972
2 Pirates of the asteroids 1972
3 The big sun of Mercury 1972
4 The oceans of Venus 1972
5 The rings of Saturn 1973
6 The moon of Jupiter 1973
First published in magazine form; here in three double volumes 1st, 2nd and 3rd 'Issac Asimov Double'.

1 I, Robot 1950
2 The rest of the robots 1967
Science fiction

ELIJAH BALEY
1 The caves of steel 1954
2 The naked sun 1958
3 The robots of dawn 1983
4 Robots and Empire 1985
Science fiction

FANTASTIC VOYAGE:
1 Fantastic voyage 1966
2 Destination brain 1987

FOUNDATION:
1 Prelude to Foundation 1988

2 Foundation and Empire 1952
3 Second Foundation 1953
4 Foundation's edge 1983
5 Foundation 1951
6 Foundation and Earth 1986
Science fiction

ASPINALL, R.
THE MALINSON BROTHERS:
1 Yesterday's kingdom 1961
2 The promise of his return 1962
3 Echo sounding 1965

ASPRIN, R.
MYTH:
1 Another fine myth
2 Myth conceptions
3 Myth directions
4 Hit or myth
5 Little myth marker
Paperback fantasy/humour

ASPRIN, R. EDITOR
SANCTUARY:
1 Thieves world
2 Tales from the vulgar unicorn
3 Shadows of Sanctuary
4 Storm season
5 The face of chaos
Stories by different authors, using the same characters and setting. Paperback only.

ASQUITH, LADY C.
1 Haply I may remember 1950
2 Remember and be glad 1952
N.F. Autobiography

ASTLEY, J.
1 Fall of Midas 1976
2 Copsi Castle 1978
Written by Norah Lofts under a pseudonym.

ASTOR, BROOKE
1 Patchwork child
2 Footprints 1986

ASTURIAS, M. A.
1 The cyclone 1967
2 The Green Pope 1971
3 The eyes of the interred 1974
A trilogy on the relationship between a Central American Republic and the American fruit company that dominates it. The author was awarded the Nobel Prize for literature in 1967.

ATKINS, E.
1 We bought an island 1976
2 Tales from our Cornish island 1986

ATKINS, M. E.
IRIS SERIES:
1 By the north door
2 Palimpset 1981
3 Samain 1977
4 Tangle 1988

ATTANASIO, A.
RADIX:
1 In other worlds
2 Radix

AUDEMARS, R.
M. PINAUD:
1 The two imposters 1959
2 The fire and the clay 1960
3 The turns of time 1961
4 The crown of night 1962
5 The dream and the dead 1963
6 The wings of darkness 1963
7 Fair maids missing 1964
8 Dead with sorrow 1965
9 Time of temptation 1966
10 A thorn in the dust 1966
11 The veins of compassion 1967
12 The white leaves of death 1968
13 The flame in the mist 1969
14 A host for dying 1970
15 Stolen like magic away 1971
16 The delicate dust of death 1973
17 No tears for the dead 1974
18 Nightmare in rust 1975
19 And one for the dead 1975
20 Healing hands of death 1977
21 Now dead is any man 1977
22 A sad and savage dying 1978
23 Slay me a sinner 1979
24 Gone to her death 1981
25 The bitter path of death 1982
26 The red rust of death 1983
27 A small slain body 1985

AUEL, J.
EARTH'S CHILDREN:
1 Clan of the cave bear 1980
2 The valley of horses 1983
3 The mammoth hunters 1985
4 Plains of passage 1990

AUSTEN, J.
'Old friends and new fancies' by S. G. Brinton, is an imaginary sequel to the novels of Jane Austen.
'The Watsons': a fragment, concluded

by L. Oulton.
'The Watsons'. Completed in accordance with her intentions by Edith (her great grand-niece) and Francis Brown 1928.
'The Watsons'. Completed by J. Coates 1958.
'The Younger sister' (a continuation of 'The Watsons') by Mrs. Hubback 1850.
'The ladies', by E. Barrington.
Short stories continuing 'Pride and Prejudice'
'Margaret Dashwood' and 'Susan Price' by Mrs. F. Brown are sequels to 'Sense and sensibility'
'Permberley Shades' by D. Bonavia-Hunt, is a sequel to 'Pride and Prejudice'
'Ladysmead' by J. Gillespie continues the story of two characters from 'Mansfield Park' 1982.
'Teverton Hall" by J. Gillespie is a sequel to 'Pride and Prejudice' 1983.
'The journal of Miss Jane Fairfax' by C. Grey is about characters in 'Emma' 1984.
'Lady Susan' by P. A. Karr is an adaptation of an unfinished novel.
See also **Piper, W.**
'Mansfield revisited' by J. Aiken continues the story of 'Mansfield Park' 1984.
'Miss Abigail's party' by J. Terry is a below stairs view of Mansfield Park 1986.
'Brightsea' by J. Gillespie is a sequel to 'Sense and Sensibility' 1987.
'Mrs. Rushworth' by V. Gordon, 1989 is a sequel to 'Mansfield Park'
'Jane Fairfax' by J. Aiken is a sequel to 'Emma' 1990.

AUSTER, P.
NEW YORK TRILOGY:
1 City of glass 1986
2 Ghosts 1986
3 The locked room 1986

AUSTIN, DEE
1 Reckless heart
2 Wild prairie sky

AUSTWICK, J.
1 Murder in the borough library 1959
2 The county library murders 1962
3 The mobile library murders 1963
4 The borough council murders 1965

AVALLONE, M.
ED MOON SERIES:
1 The tall Dolores 1956
2 The spitting image 1957
3 Dead game 1954
4 Violence in velvet 1958
5 The alarming clock 1962
6 The bouncing Betty 1960
7 The violent virgin 1960
8 The crazy mixed-up corpse 1957
9 The voodoo murders 1959
10 Meanwhile back at the morgue 1964
11 The living bomb 1963
12 There is something about a dame 1963
13 The brutal kook 1965
14 The bedroom bolero 1964
15 The fat death 1966
16 The February doll murders 1966
17 Assassins don't die in bed 1965
18 The horrible man 1968
19 The flower-covered corpse 1970
20 The doomsday bag 1970
21 Death dives deep 1971
22 Little Miss Murder
23 Shoot it again Sam
24 London bloody London
25 The girl in the cockpit
26 Kill her, you'll like it
27 Killer on the keys
28 The hot body
29 The x-rated corpse
30 Blues for Sophia Loren
Not all published in U.K. or in paperback only. Above is author's own arrangement.

SUITE POLICIERE:
1 The passenger on the U 1968
2 The fountains at Marlieux 1949
3 The double death of Frederick Belot 1949
4 Carriage 7, seat 16 1963
This is the author's logical arrangement of the sequence, but they were not written or published in that order. The dates given are of first publication in English. The Suite was the subject of a 40-part TV serial in French.
5 Cat's eye 1972
A Belot story which is set at an earlier date.

AVERY, E.
1 The Margaret days 1959
2 The Marigold summer 1960

AVERY, G.
1 The lost railway 1980

2 The onlookers 1983
*Not direct sequels, but the same
characters appear.*

AVERY, V.
1 London morning 1980
2 London shadows 1981
3 London spring 1982
N.F. Autobiography

AVON, 1st EARL OF, *see* EDEN, R. A., 1st EARL OF AVON

AWLINSON, R.
AVATAR TRILOGY
1 Shadowdale
2 Tantras
3 Waterdeep
Paperback fantasy

AYER, A. J.
1 Part of my life 1977
2 More of my life 1984
N.F. Autobiography

B.B.
1 Tide's ending 1950
2 Dark estuary 1953
N.F. Wildfowling

BABSON, M.
PERKINS AND TATE LTD:
1 Cover up story 1970
2 Murder on show 1972

1 A trail of ashes 1983
2 Death swap 1984

TRIXIE DOLAN:
1 Reel murder 1986
2 Encore murder 1989

BACCHELLI, R.
MILL ON THE PO TRILOGY:
1 Mill on the Po 1952
2 Nothing new under the sun 1956
*Originally published in Italy as three
vols. in one. British edition contains
first two vols. under title 'Mill on the
Po'.*

BACHMANN, L. P.
BEN CLANCY:
1 The legend of Joseph Nokato 1971
2 The ultimate act 1972
*Adventures of a young international
lawyer.*

BADDOCK, J.
CORMACK & WOODWARD
1 The radar job 1986
2 Emerald 1987

BAGBY, G.
INSPECTOR SCHMIDT:
1 Bachelor's widow 1935
2 Murder at the piano 1936
3 Murder half-baked 1938
4 Murder on the nose 1939
5 Bird walking weather 1940
6 Corpse with the purple thighs 1941
7 The corpse wore a wig 1942
8 Here comes the corpse 1943
9 Red is for killing 1944
10 Original carcase 1946
11 Dead drunk 1954
12 The body in the basket 1956
13 Murder in wonderland 1965
14 Corpse candle 1967
15 Another day another death 1969
16 Honest reliable corpse 1970
17 Killer boy was here 1971
18 Two in the bush 1976
19 My dead body 1976
20 Innocent bystander 1977
21 The tough get going 1978
22 Better dead 1978
23 Guaranteed to fade 1979
24 I could have died 1979
25 Mugger's day 1980
26 Country and fatal 1981
27 A question of quarry 1981
28 The sitting duck 1982
29 The golden creep 1982
30 The most wanted 1984

BAGLEY, D.
SLADE SERIES:
1 Running blind 1970
2 The freedom trap 1971

CURTIS AND HARDIN:
1 Flyaway 1978
2 Windfall 1982

BAGNOLD, E.
VELVET
1 National velvet 1939
2 International velvet 1978
*No. 2 is a sequel written by B. Forbes
from his filmscript.*

BAILEY, A.
1 America lost and found 1980
2 England first and last 1985
N.F. Autobiography

BAILEY, HILARY
1 Polly put the kettle on 1975
2 As time goes by 1988

BAILEY, M. and M.
1 117 days adrift
2 Second chance voyage to Patagonia 1978
*N.F. Accounts of the authors' voyages
in a small boat.*

BAILEY, P.
1 The raw pearl 1970
2 Talking to myself 1972
N.F. Autobiography.

BAKER, D.VAL
1 The sea's in the kitchen 1963
2 The door is always open 1965
3 We'll go around the world tomorrow
1966
4 To sea with 'Sanu' 1968
5 Life up the creek 1971
6 The petrified mariner 1972
7 Old mill by the stream 1973
8 Spring at Land's End 1974
9 Sunset over the Scillies 1975
10 A view from the valley 1976
11 A long way to Land's End 1977
12 The wind blows from the West 1978
13 All this and Cornwall too 1979
14 A family for all seasons 1979
15 As the stream flows by 1980
16 Upstream at the mill 1981
17 A family at sea 1981
18 Summer at the mill 1982
19 Down a Cornish lane 1983
20 Family circles 1984
21 When Cornish skies are smiling 1984
22 My Cornish world 1985
23 The waterwheel turns 1983
24 The mill in the valley 1984
25 Cornish prelude 1985
*N.F. Autobiography. Nos. 1-4
published in one volume 'Adventures
before fifty' 1969.*

BAKER, DAISY
1 Travels in a donkey trap 1974
2 More travels in a donkey trap 1976
N.F. Autobiography.

BAKER, DONNA
GLASSMAKERS SAGA:
1 Crystal 1987
2 Black cameo 1988
3 Chalice 1989

BAKER, H.
1 All the gods are dead 1984
2 Alive to the burning 1985

**BAKER, K. see FAMILY AT WAR
SERIES**

BAKER, S.
ASHLU CYCLE:
1 Drink the fire from the flames
2 Firedance

BAKER, W. H.
RICHARD QUINTAIN SERIES:
1 Take death for a lover 1964
2 Strike north 1965
3 Destination Dieppe 1965
4 The dogs of war 1966
5 The inexpendable 1966
6 The rape of Berlin 1966
7 The guardians 1967
8 The girl in asses' milk 1967
9 The dead and the damned 1967
10 The girl, the city and the soldier 1968
11 The dirty game 1968
12 The night of the wolf 1969
13 The Judas diary 1969
14 The charge is treason 1973
Nos. 4-9 in paperback only

BALAAM, *Pseud.*
1 Chalk in my hair 1953
2 Chalk gets in your eyes 1956
N.F. Autobiography.

BALDWIN, A.
MEN AT WAR:
1 The last heroes 1986
2 The secret warriors 1987
3 The soldier spies 1988
4 The fighting agents 1988

BALDWIN, J.
1 Notes of a native son 1955
2 Nobody knows my name 1961
N.F. Autobiography.

BALDWIN, M.
1 Granddad with snails
2 In step with a goat
3 Goose in the jungle 1965
N.F. Autobiography.

BALDWIN, MICHAEL
PATRICK MATSON & THE COMMITTEE:
1 Exit wounds 1988
2 Holofernes 1989

BALHAM, J. *see* **THE SWEENEY**

BALL, B.
1 Timepiece 1970
2 Timepit 1971
Science fiction. Projected as a series of five 'Time' novels.

KEEGAN:
1 The no-option contract 1975
2 The one-way deal 1976
Thrillers.
See also SPACE 1999

BALL, J.
VIRGIL TIBBS SERIES:
1 In the heat of the night 1966
2 The cool cottontail 1967
3 Johnny get your gun 1970
4 Five pieces of jade 1972
5 The eyes of the Buddha 1976
6 Then came violence 1980
I won several awards as the best first mystery novel of the year.

JACK TALLON:
1 Police chief 1982
2 Trouble for Tallon 1982

BALLARD, J. G.
1 Empire of the sun 1984
2 The kindness of women 1991

BALLINGER, W. A.
1 The voyageurs 1975
2 There and back again 1977
Sea stories.

BALMER, E. and P. WYLIE
1 When worlds collide
2 After worlds collide
Science fiction

BALDSON, D.
1 Oxford life
2 Oxford now and then 1970
N.F. Topography.

BANFIELD, E. J.
1 Confessions of a beachcomber
2 My tropic isle
N.F. Autobiography.

BANIS, V. J.
BRUSSAC FAMILY:
1 This splendid earth 1978
2 The earth and all it holds 1980

BANKS, L. R.
1 The L-shaped room 1968

2 The backward shadow 1970
3 Two is lonely 1974
A trilogy about an unmarried mother.

BRONTE SERIES:
1 Dark quartet 1976
2 Path to the silent country 1977

BANKS, O.
AMOS HATCHER:
1 The Rembrandt panel 1984
2 The Caravaggio obsession 1985
Thrillers set in world of art dealing.

BANNERMAN, B.
DAVE WOOLF
1 Orbach's judgement
2 The judge's song
3 Controlling interest
4 The last Wednesday
Paperback thrillers

BANVILLE, J.
1 Dr Copernicus
2 Kepler
3 The Newton letter
4 Mefisto 1986

BARBELLION, W. N. P.
1 Journal of a disappointed man 1956
2 Last diary
N.F. Autobiography.

BARBER, A. V.
1 Days at Wickham 1966
2 Childhood in Egypt 1971
N.F. Autobiography.

BARBETTE, J.
HARVEY BRITTEN:
1 Final copy 1952
2 Dear dead days

BARCLAY, T.
CRAIGALLAN FAMILY:
1 A sower went forth 1980
2 The stony places 1981
3 Harvest of thorns 1983
4 The good ground 1984
A family saga set in the mid-western USA.

TRAMONT SERIES:
1 The wine widow 1985
2 The champagne girls 1986
3 The last heiress 1987
A family saga about the wine trade in France.

CORVILL FAMILY
1 Web of dreams 1988
2 Broken threads 1989
3 The final pattern 1990

BARD, M.
1 Doctor wears three faces 1949
2 Forty odd 1952
3 Just be yourself 1957
N.F. Autobiography.

BARDSLEY, M.
SUPT. DONALD MARTIN
1 Murder on fire 1969
2 Murder for sale 1970
3 Murder on ice 1972
4 Hit it rich 1972

BAREA, A.
THE FORGING OF A REBEL:
1 The track
2 The forge
3 The clash
Autobiography and source book of modern Spanish history.

BARK, C. V. *see* **VOSS BARK, C.**

BARKE, J.
1 The wind that shakes the barley 1946
2 The song in the green thorn tree 1947
3 The wonder of all the gay world 1949
4 The crest of the broken wave 1953
5 The well of the silent harp 1954
A series of novels on the life of Robert Burns.
6 Bonnie Jean 1958
Continues the Burns story with the story of his wife Jean Armour as a widow.

BARLING, M. V. M. (C. BARLING and **P. BARRINGTON** *pseuds.)*
INSPECTOR MARSHALL SERIES:
1 The rest is silence 1951
2 Account rendered 1953
3 Night of violence 1959
4 By some person unknown 1960
5 Motive for murder 1963
6 Afternoon with violence 1963
7 Appointment with death 1964
8 Time to kill 1965
9 Cage without bars 1966
10 Slow poison 1967
11 A game of murder 1967
12 Confession of murder 1967
13 A marked man 1968
This author wrote under the

pseudonyms of Charles Barling and Pamela Barrington, and both series featured Inspector Marshall. Above Nos. 1, 2, 3, 4, 9, 10 and 11 were published under the name of Barrington and 5, 6, 7, 8, 12 and 13 under the name of Barling.

INSPECTOR TRAVERS SERIES:
1 The Mortimer story 1952
2 Among those present 1953
Under the pseudonym of Barrington
3 The gentle killer 1961

INSPECTOR HENDERSON:
1 Accessory to murder 1968
(Barrington)
2 Death of shrew 1968 (Barling)

BARLING, T.
1 The smoke 1986
2 Smoke dragon 1988
Thrillers about drug trafficking

BARNARD, C.
1 The soprano
2 Money and music

BARNARD, R.
SUPT. PERRY TRETHOWAN:
1 Sheer torture 1981
2 Death and the princess 1982
3 The missing Bronte 1983
4 Bodies 1986
5 Death in purple prose 1987

BARNES, G. M.
JONATHAN MARK SERIES:
1 Murder is a gamble 1954
2 Murder walks the stairs 1956
3 Murder is insane 1958

BARNES, L.
MICHAEL SPRAGUE:
1 Bitter finish 1983
2 Dead heat 1984
3 Cities of the dead 1986

BARNES, LINDA
CARLOTTA CARLYLE
1 A trouble of fools 1988
2 The snake tattoo 1989
3 Coyote 1991

BARNES, R.
1 A licence to live 1975
2 Coronation cups and jam jars 1977
N.F. Autobiography of East End family life.

BARNETT, J.
SUPT. OWEN SMITH:
1 Marked for destruction 1982
2 Diminished responsibility 1984

BARNWELL, W.
BLESSING TRILOGY:
1 The Blessing papers 1981
2 The Sigma curve 1982

BARON, A.
HARRYBOY BOAS:
1 The lowlife 1964
2 Strip Jack naked 1966

BARR, P.
1 The coming of the barbarians 1967
2 The deer cry pavilion 1968
The opening of Japan in the 19th century, and the impact of Western society.

ALICE GREENWOOD:
1 Chinese Alice 1981
2 Uncut Jade 1983
Missionary life in 19th C China, based on fact.

BARREN, C.
THE STEMSTON FAMILY:
1 Eighty North 1959
2 Jamestown 1960

BARRETT, A.
1 Lucid stars 1989
2 Secret harmonies 1990

BARRETT, G. J.
CHIEF INSPECTOR BLESSINGAY SERIES:
1 He died twice 1968
2 Guilty be damned 1968
3 A cup that kills 1969
4 His own funeral 1972

BARRINGTON, P. *pseud. see*
BARLING, M. V. M.

BARRY, CLIVE
1 The spear-grinner 1968
2 Fly Jamskoni 1969
Stories of an airline in a newly independent state with one airport and one air hostess.

BARRY, J.
CHICK NOLAN SERIES:
1 Murder with your malted 1942
2 Leopard's cats-cradle 1943
3 Lady of night 1945

BARSTOW, S.
VIC BROWN TRILOGY:
1 A kind of loving 1962
2 The watchers on the shore 1965
3 The right true end 1976

ELLA LINDLEY:
1 Just you wait and see 1987
2 Give us this day 1989
3 Next of kin 1991

BARTH, J.
1 Sabbatical 1982
2 More Tidewater tales 1988

BARTH, M.
MARGARET BINTON:
1 The bag bag clan 1983
2 A ragged plot 1984
3 One dollar death 1985
4 The co-op kill 1986
Thrillers set among drop-outs in New York

BARTLETT, V.
1 This is my life
2 And now, tomorrow, 1962
3 Tuscan retreat 1964
N.F. Autobiography.

BARTON, A.
1 Two lamps in our street 1965
2 The penny world 1969
3 School for love 1976
N.F. Autobiography.

BARTON, J.
WASTEWORLD:
1 Aftermath
2 Resurrection
3 Angels
4 My way
Paperback science fiction

BARUCH, B. M
1 My own story
2 The public years
N.F. Autobiography.

BAR-ZOHAR, M.
JEFF SAUNDERS:
1 The third truth 1974
2 The spy who died twice 1975

BASS, T. J.
1 Half-past human
2 The god-whale
Paperback science fiction

BASSANI, G.
1 A prospect of Ferrara 1965
2 The gold-rimmed spectacles 1965
3 The garden of the Finzi-Continis 1965
4 Behind the door 1973
*'In a sense they are all part of one book
—the protagonist, the 'I' is recognisably
the same character. The city described
is always the same one, Ferrara in the
time of Signor Bassani's youth.
Moreover the same characters appear
over and over again, sometimes as
major personages, sometimes as
background figures. This may give the
impression the Signor Bassani is
engaged on a 'Roman Fleucve'. This is
not so since his books have no
consistent sequence.' Times Literary
Supplement.*

BASSET, R.
MARGERY FAMILY:
1 Witchfinder general 1967
2 Amorous trooper 1968
3 Rebecca's brat 1969
4 Kill the Stuart 1970
*The story of an English family from
Cromwellian times to the '45.*
★★★
1 Tinfish run 1977
2 Pier head jump 1978
3 The Neptune landing 1979
*A series about the Royal Navy in World
War I.*

BASSO, H.
1 Light infantry ball 1959
2 Pompey's Head 1954 ® The view from
Pompey's Head ⅜
*The connection is the town of Pompey's
Head. Some characters in 1 are
ancestors of those in 2.*

BATCHELOR, D.
DET. INSPECTOR JOHNSON SERIES
1 The man who loved chocolates 1962
2 On the brink 1964
3 The sedulous ape 1965

BATCHELOR, R.
SERGEANT FENWICK:
1 The murder game 1970
2 Murderer's row 1970

BATES, H. E.
1 The vanished world 1969
2 The blossoming world 1971
3 The world in ripeness 1972
N.F. Autobiography.

LARKIN FAMILY SERIES
1 The darling buds of May 1958
2 A breath of French air 1959
3 When the green woods laugh 1961
4 Oh! to be in England 1963
5 A little of what you fancy 1970
*Published in one volume 1991, as 'The
Larkin Chronicles'.*
★★★
1 My uncle Silas 1953
2 Sugar for the horse 1957

BATESON, D.
LARRY VERNON SERIES:
1 It's murder, Senorita 1954
2 The man from the rock 1955
3 The big tomorrow 1956
4 The Soho jungle 1957
5 The night is for violence
6 I'll go anyware 1959
7 I'll do anything 1960

BAUMAN, J.
1 Winter in the morning 1986
2 A dream of belonging 1988
N.F. Autobiography of a Polish girl

BAX, C.
1 Evenings in Albany
2 Rosemary for remembrance
N.F. Autobiography.

BAXT, G.
1 A parade of cockeyed creatures 1968
2 'I!' said the demon 1969

BAXTER, A.
1 Flat on my back 1974
2 Up to my neck 1975
3 Out on my ear 1976
4 Upside down under 1977
N.F. Humorous autobiography.

BAYER, O. W.
1 Paper chase
2 No little enemy

BAYLEY, B.
1 Collision with Chronos
2 The fall of Chronopolis
3 The knights of the limits
Science fiction

BAYLEY, B. J.
JASPERODUS:
1 The soul of the robot 1974
2 The rod of light 1984
Science fiction.

BAYNHAM, E.
1 From the lower deck
2 Before the mast
N.F. Life at sea in the 19th century.

BEAR, G.
1 Infinity concerto 1988
2 The serpent mage 1988
Science fiction.

1 Eon 1988
2 Eternity 1989

BEARDSWORTH, M.
CHARLES I:
1 The king's friend 1968
2 The king's endeavour 1969
3 The king's servant 1970
4 The king's adversary 1972
5 The king's contest 1975
6 The king's victory 1978

BEARE, G.
VICTOR STALLARD SERIES
1 The bloody sun at noon 1970
2 The very breath of hell 1971
3 The bee sting deal 1972

BEATON, C.
1 The wandering years, 1922-39 1964
2 The years between 1939-44 1966
3 The happy years, 1944-48 1972
4 The strenuous years, 1948-55, 1976
5 The restless years, 1955-63 1976
6 The parting years, 1963-74 1978
N.F. Autobiography.

BEATON, M.C.
1 Death of a gossip 1989
2 Death of a cad
*Detective stories set in rural Scotland.
The author writes historical romance as
M. Chesney.*

BEAUVOIR, S. DE
1 Memoirs of a dutiful daughter
2 The prime of life 1963
3 Force of circumstances 1965
4 All said and done 1974
N.F. Autobiography.

BECKER, J.
1 The keep 1967
2 The union 1971
*Part of a projected trilogy on South
Africa. The characters are Simon and
Josephine Leyton, descendants of
Russo - Jewish immigrants.*

BECKER, S.
1 The Chinese bandit 1975
2 The last mandarin 1979
3 The blue-eyed Shan 1982

BECKETT, S.
1 Molloy 1955
2 Malone dies 1956
3 The unnamable 1958
Later published in one vol, 1959

BECKWITH, L.
1 About my father's business 1971
2 The hills is lonely 1959
3 The sea for breakfast 1961
4 The loud halo 1964
5 A rope in case 1968
6 Lightly poached 1973
7 Beautiful just 1975
8 Bruach blend 1978
9 The bay of strangers 1988
*N.F. Autobiography.
This is in chronological order of
reading. 1 is about childhood, 2-9 about
retirement in the Hebrides*

BEDFORD, S.
1 Compass error 1968
2 A favourite of the Gods 1967
*The two books are continuous in time,
but the central character in 2 is the
daughter of the heroine in 1.*

BEEBEE, C.
THE HUB:
1 The hub 1987
2 The main event 1989
Science fiction

BEEBY, O.
TONY SPENCER SERIES:
1 Blank cheque for murder 1968
2 The faceless men 1969
3 No profit in dying 1970
4 Too many innocents 1972

BEERE, P.
TRAUMA 2020:
1 Urban prey

2 The crucifixion squad
Paperback fantasy

BEHAN, B.
1 Borstal boy 1959
2 The confessions of an Irish rebel 1965
N.F. Autobiography

BEHRMAN, S. N.
1 The Worcester account 1968
2 Tribulations and laughter 1972
N.F. Autobiography

BELL, A.
1 Corduroy 1930
2 Silver ley 1931
3 The cherry tree 1932
4 Apple acre 1942
5 Sunrise to sunset 1944
ROLAND PACE SERIES:
1 The balcony 1934
2 Young man's fancy 1956
3 The mill house 1958

BELL, J.
DR DAVID WINTRINGHAM SERIES:
1 Murder in hospital
2 Fall over cliff 1956
3 Death on the Borough Council
4 Death at half-term
5 From natural causes
6 All is vanity
7 Death at the medical board
8 Death is clairvoyance
9 Summer school mystery 1950
10 Bones in the barrow 1960

***

1 To serve a queen 1971
2 In the King's absence 1973
Historical novels about the Civil War
CLAUDE WARRINGTON-REEVE, Q.C.:
1 A well-known face 1960
2 A flat tyre in Fulham 1963
JACOBEAN TRILOGY
1 Jacobean adventure 1969
2 Over the seas 1970
3 The dark and the light 1971
*The story of two Scottish emigrants to
the first settlement at Jamestown*

BELL, V.
1 The Dodo 1950
2 This way home 1951
N.F. Autobiography
DR. BAYNES SERIES;
1 Death under the stars 1949
2 Two by day and one by night 1950

3 Death has two doors 1950
4 Death darkens council 1962
5 Death o' the night watches 1959
6 Death walks by the river

BELLAIRS, G.
DET. INSPECTOR LITTLEJOHN SERIES:
1 Littlejohn on leave 1941
2 Four unfaithful servants 1941
3 Death of a busybody 1942
4 Dead shall be raised 1942
5 Murder of a quack 1943
6 Calamity at Harwood 1943
7 He'd rather be dead 1944
8 Death in the night watches 1944
9 Crime at the Halfpenny Bridge 1945
10 Case of the scared rabbits 1945
11 Death on the last train 1946
12 Outrage on Gallows Hill 1946
13 Case of the Seven Whistlers 1947
14 Case of the famished parson 1947
15 Case of the demented spiv 1948
16 Case of the headless Jesuit 1949
17 Dead march for Penelope Blow 1949
18 Death in dark glasses 1950
19 Crime in Leper's Hollow 1950
20 A knife for Harry Dodd 1951
21 Half mast for the Deemster 1952
22 Corpses in Enderby 1953
23 The cursing stones murder 1953
24 Death in room 5 1954
25 Death treads softly 1954
26 Death drops the pilot 1955
27 Death in High Provence 1956
28 Death sends for the doctor 1956
29 Corpse at the carnival 1957
30 Murder makes mistakes 1957
31 Bones in the wilderness 1958
32 Toll the bell for murder 1959
33 Death in the fearful night 1959
34 Death in despair 1960
35 Death of a tin god 1960
36 Body in the Dumb river 1961
37 Death before breakfast 1961
38 The tormentors 1962
39 Death in the wasteland 1963
40 Surfeit of suspects 1964
41 Death of a shadow 1965
42 Death spins the wheel 1965
43 Intruder in the dark 1966
44 Strangers among the dead 1966
45 Death in desolation 1967
46 Single ticket to death 1967
47 Fatal alibi 1968
48 Murder gone mad 1969
49 Tycoon's death bed 1970
50 The night they killed Joss Varron 1971
51 Murder adrift 1972

52 Pomeroy deceased 1972
53 Devious murder 1973
54 Fear round about 1975
55 Close all roads to Sospel 1977
56 An old man dies 1980
Littlejohn progresses in rank and becomes Chief-Superintendent from No. 46.

BELLAMANN, N. H.
1 King's Row
2 Parris Mitchell of King's Row
Completed by Katherine Bellamann

BELLE, P.
1 The moon in the water 1984
2 The chains of fate 1984
3 Alathea 1985 (pb) 1989 (hb)
4 The lodestar 1987
5 Falling star 1990
A family chronicle set at the time of the English Civil War and its aftermath.

WINTERCOMBE
1 Wintercombe 1988
2 Herald of joy 1989

BENFORD, G.
1 Great sky river 1987
2 Tides of light 1989
Science fiction

BENNETT, P.
CALLADINE FAMILY:
1 There is a season 1976
2 The beggar's virtue 1978
3 A rough music 1980

BENNETT, D.
ALLARDYCE:
1 Chaos makers 1968
2 Operation chaos 1970

BENNETT, W. R.
ADAM KANE:
1 Man from checkmate 1971
2 Dossier on a mantis 1972

BENNETTS, P.
CESARE BORGIA:
1 Borgia bull 1966
2 Borgia prince 1968
EDWARD, I:
1 A dragon for Edward 1975
2 The she-wolf 1975

BENNEY, M.
1 Low company 1934

2 Almost a gentleman 1966
N.F. Autobiography. The story of a reformed burglar

BENSON, B.
RALPH LINDSAY SERIES:
1 The girl in the cage 1954
2 The silver cobweb 1955
3 Broken shield 1955
4 The running man 1957
5 The end of violence 1959
6 Seven steps East 1959

BENSON, E. F.
LUCIA SERIES:
1 Queen Lucia 1920
2 Miss Mapp 1922
3 Lucia in London 1927
4 Mapp and Lucia 1935
5 Lucia's progress 1935 (Worshipful Lucia)
6 Trouble for Lucia 1939
The Lucia series were re-issued between 1984 and 1985. Miss Mapp' includes a new short story. 'The male impersonator'.
'Lucia in Wartime' (1985) and 'Lucia Triumphant' (1986), both by Tom Holt, are continuations.

BENTLEY, J.
1 Proud Riley's daughter 1988
2 Sing me a new song 1990

BENTLEY, P.
WEST RIDING SERIES:
1 Panorama 1952
2 Take courage 1940
3 Manhold 1941
4 The house of Moreys 1953
5 Inheritance 1932
6 Carr 1929
7 Life story 1952
8 The spinner of the years 1928
9 A modern tragedy 1934
10 Sleep in peace 1938
11 The rise of Henry Morcar 1946
12 Quorum 1950
13 Noble in reason 1955
14 Love and money 1957
15 Crescendo 1958
16 Kith and kin 1960
17 Tales of the West Riding 1965
18 A man of his times 1966
19 Ring in the new 1969
20 More tales of West Riding 1974
This is the author's own arrangement. Except for no's 5, 11, 18 & 19 which

are sequels, characters do not reappear, but the series gives a picture of West Riding life from the 17th century to the present day. 'The partnership' and 'Trio' are not part of the series, but serve to contribute background material to the West Riding pictures.

***

1 Environment 1922
2 Cat-in-the-manger 1923

BENTON, K.
PETER CRAIG SERIES:
1 Twenty-fourth level 1969
2 Sole agent 1970
3 Spy in Chancery 1972
4 Craig and the Jaguar 1973
5 Craig and the Tunisian tangle 1974

BENZONI, J.
CATHERINE SERIES:
1 One love is enough 1963
2 Catherine 1963
3 Belle Catherine 1966
4 Catherine and Arnaud 1967
5 Catherine and a time for love 1968
6 A snare for Catherine 1974
  Historical romances about France during the Hundred Years War

MARIANNE SERIES:
1 Marianne 1969
2 Marianne and the masked prince 1971
3 Marianne and the privateer 1972
4 Marianne and the rebels 1973
5 Marianne and the Lords of the East 1975
6 Marianne and the crown of fire 1976
  Romances about a young French girl during Napoleonic times

FALCON SERIES:
1 Lure of the falcon 1978
2 The devil's diamonds 1980

BERGER, J.
1 The foot of Clive 1963
2 Corker's freedom 1964

REINHART:
1 Reinhart in love 1963
2 Vital parts 1971
3 Crazy in Berlin 1976
4 Reinhart's women 1982

INTO THEIR LABOURS:
1 Pig earth 1979
2 Once in Europa 1987
3 Lilac and flag 1991

BERGMAN, A.
JACK LEVINE:
1 The Big kiss-off of 1944 1975
2 Hollywood & Le Vine 1976

BERKELEY, T.
1 We kept a pub 1955
2 I go on the films 1958
3 We cope with the kids 1960
  N.F. Autobiography

BERLIN, I.
1 I am Lazarus
2 The dark monarch
  N.F. Autobiography

BERRY, A.
1 Koyana's diamond 1984
2 Labyrinth of lies 1985
  Science fiction

BERSTL, J.
LIFE OF ST. PAUL:
1 The tentmaker 1951
2 The cross and the eagle

BEST, R.
THE YARROW SERIES:
1 The house called Yarrow 1961
2 The honest rogue 1962
3 High tide 1964
4 Idle rainbow 1955
5 Greenwood 1967

BICKERS, R. T.
DAEDALUS QUARTET:
1 The gifts of Jove 1983
2 A time for haste 1984
3 Too late the morrow 1984
4 The sure recompense 1985

BIDERMAN, B.
JOSEPH RUDKIN:
1 The Genesis files 1988
2 Judgement of death 1989

BIGGLE, L. J.
JAN DARZEK:
1 This darkening universe 1979
2 All the colours of darkness 1964
3 Watchers of the dark 1968
4 Silence is deadly 1980

BINGHAM, C.
1 Coronet among the weeds 1969

2 Coronet among the grass 1971
N.F. Autobiography
See also **'Upstairs downstairs'** *TV*
series.
See also **BRADY, T.**
1 Belgravia 1983
2 Country life 1985
3 At home 1986
Satires on upper-class life

BINGHAM, J.
SUPT. BROCK:
1 Brock 1981
2 Brock and the defector 1982

BIRDSALL, J.
1 The boys and the butterflies 1988
2 Moths in the memory 1990
N.F. Autobiography.

BIRMINGHAM, M.
KATE WEATHERLEY:
1 You can help me 1974
2 The heat of the sun 1976
3 Sleep in a ditch 1978
Detective stories about a Citizen's
Advice Bureau adviser.

BIRMINGHAM, S.
1 Our crowd 1968
2 The rest of us
N.F. Jewish immigrants in New York

BISHOP, M.
1 It's a dog's life
2 Love in the dog house

BISHOP, S. P.
TRACK:
1 Track
2 Partners in death
3 Apache gold
Paperback Westerns

BISSET, SIR J.
1 Sail ho! 1958
2 Tramps and ladies 1959
3 Commodore's farewell 1960
N.F. Autobiography

BJARNHOF, K.
1 The stars grow pale 1957
2 The good light 1959
The story of a blind boy growing up in
Copenhagen in the early 1900's.

BJORN, T. F.
1 Papa's wife 1953

2 Papa's daughter 1958
3 Mama'a way 1959
3 Dear papa 1963
Stories of a Swedish-American pastor
and his family

BLACK, G.
PAUL HARRIS SERIES:
1 Suddenly at Singapore 1959
2 Dead man calling 1961
3 A dragon for Christmas 1962
4 A wind of death 1967
5 The cold jungle 1969
6 A time for pirates 1970
7 The bitter tea 1973
8 The golden cocatrice 1974
9 A big wind for summer 1975
10 A moon for killers 1976
11 A path for serpents 1991

BLACK, L.
KATE THEOBALD:
1 The penny murders 1979
2 The eve of the wedding 1980
3 The Rumanian circle 1981

BLACK, LIONEL
EMMA GREAVES:
1 The Bait 1965
2 Two ladies in Verona 1967 (The lady is
a spy).

BLACK, M.
RICK VANESS SERIES:
1 Dead on course 1951
2 Sinister cargo 1952
3 Shadow of evil 1953
4 Steps in the dark 1954

BLACKBURN, J.
GENERAL KIRK:
1 The gaunt woman 1962
2 Colonel Bogus 1964 (Packed for
murder)
3 A ring of roses 1965
4 Nothing but the night 1968
5 The young man from Lima
6 Broken boy

BLACKBURN, M.
DELGADO SERIES:
1 Sultan's turret
2 Ruler of Shaihait
3 Market of the mountain man
4 Arabian nightmare 1968

BLACKER, I.
GENERAL LE GRANDE AND GENOPS SERIES:
1 Chain of command 1965
2 The valley of Hanoi 1966
3 To hell in a basket 1967

BLACKLOCK, J. P.
1 The elfin ship
2 The disappearing dwarf

BLAIR, A.
1 A tree in the West 1979
2 The rowan on the ridge 1980

BLAISDELL, A. (E. Linington)
SGT. IVOR MADDOX & WILCOX ST. PRECINCT:
1 Greenmask 1965
2 No evil angel 1966
3 Date with death 1967
4 Something wrong 1968
5 Policeman's lot 1969
6 Practice to deceive 1971
7 Crime by chance 1974
8 Perchance of death 1978
9 No villain need be 1979
10 Consequence of death 1981
11 Skeleton in the closet 1983
12 Felony report 1985
13 Strange felony 1986

BLAKE, K. see THE PROFESSIONALS

BLAKE, M. G.
AYESTHORPE SERIES:
1 The Peterloo weaver 1981
2 The Peterloo inheritance 1981
3 Bitter legacy 1982
The Lancashire cotton trade in the Industrial Revolution

BLAKE, NICKOLAS, *pseud.* (C. Day Lewis)
NIGEL STRANGEWAYS SERIES:
1 A question of proof 1935
2 Thou shell of death 1936
3 There's trouble brewing 1937
4 The beast must die 1938
5 The smiler with the knife 1939
6 Malice in wonderland 1940 (Summer camp mystery)
7 The case of the abominable snowman 1941
8 Minute for murder 1947
9 Head of a traveller 1949
10 The dreadful hollow 1953

11 This whisper in the gloom 1954
12 End of a chapter 1958
13 Widow's cruise 1959
14 The worm of death 1960
15 The morning after death 1966

BLAKE, V.
JENNY WINFIELD:
1 Gay gallant
2 Bride of chance

BLAKE'S SEVEN
1 Blake's Seven, by T. Nation 1980
2 Project Avalon, by T. Hoyle 1981
3 Scorpio attack, by T. Hoyle 1981
4 Afterlife 1984
Paperback science fiction, based on the TV series

BLAKER, R.
1 Here lies a most beautiful lady
2 But beauty vanishes

BLAKESTON, O.
1 And then screaming started 1968
2 For crying out loud

BLAMIRES, H.
TRILOGY OF HEAVEN AND HELL:
1 The devil's hunting ground 1954
2 Cold war in Hell 1955
3 Blessing unbounded 1956
***
1 Kirkbride conversations
2 Kirkbride and company

BLANC, S.
MIGUEL MERNANDES SERIES:
1 The green stone 1963
2 The yellow villa 1964
3 The rose window 1968

BLANDY, M.
1 Razor's edge 1969
2 Harvest from rotten apples 1971
N.F. Two connected books on youth clubs and help to young people.

BLATTY, W.
1 The exorcist 1971
2 The legion 1983

BLEASDALE, A.
SCULLY:
1 Scully 1975
2 Who's been sleeping in my bed? 1977

BLEECK, O.
PHILIP ST. IVES SERIES:
1 Brass go-between 1970
2 Protocol for a kidnapping 1971
3 The thief who painted sunlight 1973
4 The highbinders 1974
5 No questions asked 1976

BLIGH, E.
1 Tooting corner
2 Faintly smiling mouth
N.F. Autobiography

BLISH, J.
CITIES IN FLIGHT:
1 They shall have stars
2 A life for the stars
3 Earthman come home
4 A clash of cymbals
*Science fiction. Connected novels. Parts
of these have been published in
magazine form under other titles.*
'AFTER SUCH KNOWLEDGE':
1 Case of conscience 1959
2 Dr. Mirabilis
3 Black Easter 1969
4 The day after judgement 1972
*3 & 4 are direct sequels, but the author
considers this a series as a whole.*

BLISHEN, E.
1 Roaring boys 1964
2 This right soft lot 1969
3 A cack-handed war 1972
4 Uncommon entrance 1974
5 Sorry, Dad 1977
6 A nest of teachers 1980
7 Shaky relations 1981
8 Lizzie Pye 1982
9 Donkey work 1983
10 A second skin 1984
11 Outside contributor 1986
12 The disturbance fee 1988
13 The penny world 1990
*N.F. Autobiography. The author calls it
'Recycling my memories'.*

BLOCH, R.
1 Psycho 1960
2 Psycho 2 1986

BLOCK, L.
EVAN TANNER:
1 The thief who couldn't sleep
2 The cancelled Czech
3 Tanner's twelve swingers
4 Two for Tanner
5 Tanner's tiger

6 Here comes a hero
7 Me Tanner, you Jane
BERNIE RHODENBARR:
1 Burglars can't be choosers 1979
2 The burglar in the closet 1980
3 The burglar who liked to quote Kipling
1981
4 The burglar who studied Spinoza 1982
5 The burglar who painted like Mondrian
1984

LEO HAIG:
1 Five little rich girls 1984
2 The topless tulip caper 1984

MATTHEW SCUDDER:
1 Sins of the fathers 1978
2 Time to murder and create 1979
3 In the midst of death 1980
4 A stab in the dark 1982
5 Eight million ways to die 1983
6 When the sacred ginmill closes 1987

BLOOM, U.
1 Rosemary for Stratford on Avon 1966
2 Rosemary for Frinton 1970
3 Rosemary for Chelsea 1971
*N.F. Autobiographical account of
places the author has lived in.*

NO LADY SERIES:
1 Log on no lady 1940
2 No lady buys a cot 1943
3 No lady in bed 1944
4 No lady with a pen 1947
5 No lady meets a gentleman 1947
6 No lady in the cart 1949
7 Mum's girl was no lady 1950
8 No lady on the spree 1954
9 No lady has a dog's day 1956
N.F. Autobiography
***
1 Victorian vinaigrette 1956
2 The elegant Edwardian 1957
3 Youth at the gate 1959
4 Down to the sea in ships 1957
5 War isn't wonderful 1961
6 Life is no fairytale 1976
*N.F. Autobiography. Not published in
this order.*
***
1 Parson extraordinary 1963
2 Price above rubies 1965
N.F. Life of her father.
***
1 Now Barabbas was a robber 1977
2 Pilate's wife 1978
3 Song of Salome 1978
Trilogy set in the time of Christ.

BLUMENFELD, J.
1 Pin a rose on me
2 See me dance the polka 1962
N.F. Autobiography

BLUNT, B.
1 Treacherous moon
2 Deep ran the river 1986
3 Star sapphire 1988

BLUNT, W.
1 Married to a single life 1983
2 Slow on the feather 1986
N.F. Autobiography

BOGARDE, D.
1 A postillion struck by lightning 1977
2 Snakes and ladders 1978
3 An orderly man 1983
4 Backcloth 1986
5 A particular friendship 1989
N.F. Autobiography

BOGGIS, D.
1 Killer instinct 1980
2 A time to betray 1981

BOISSARD, J.
MOREAU FAMILY:
1 A matter of feeling 1979
2 Christmas lessons 1984
3 A time to choose 1986

BOLAND, J.
1 Counterpol 1963
2 Counterpol in Paris 1964
★★★
1 League of gentlemen 1960
2 The gentlemen reform 1961
3 The gentlemen at large 1962

BOLTON, M.
LAWSON OF SPECIAL BRANCH
1 The softener 1986
2 The testing 1987

BOND, M.
M. PAMPLEMOUSSE:
1 Monsieur Pamplemousse 1983
2 Monsieur Pamplemousse and the secret mission 1985
3 Monsieur Pamplemousse on the spot 1986
4 Monsieur Pamplemousse takes the cure 1987
5 Monsieur Pamplemousse aloft 1988
6 Monsieur Pamplemousse investigates 1990

7 Monsieur Pamplemouse rests his case 1991

BONE, E.
1 Thirty years hard 1964
2 Seven years solitary 1960
N.F. Autobiography
Orders of events, not publication.

BONETT. J. and E.
INSPECTOR BORGES SERIES:
1 Better dead 1964
2 The private face of murder 1965
3 This side murder 1967 (Murder on the Costa Brava)
4 The sound of murder 1970
5 No time to kill 1972

BONFIGLIOLI, K.
CHARLIE MORTDECAL:
1 Don't point that thing at me 1974
2 Something nasty in the woodshed 1977
3 After you with the pistol 1979

BONINGTON, C.
1 I chose to climb 1966
2 The next horizon 1973
N.F. Autobiography

BONNEY, F.
SIMON ROLFE:
1 Death by dynamite
2 No man's hand

BOONE, J. C.
REMINGTON:
1 Lawman's justice 1988
2 Showdown at Comanche Butte 1988
3 West of the Pecos 1989
4
5 Wyoming blood trail 1990

BOORE, W. H.
1 The valley and the shadow 1965
2 Cry on the wind 1967
Two novels about Bryncoed, a Welsh village but otherwise not connected.

BOOTHROYD, D.
1 Value for money 1955
2 Shoddy kingdom 1957
Novels about the woollen industry in the West Riding. Not otherwise sequels.

BORG, J.
HOGLEG BAILEY SERIES:
1 Hellbent trail

2 Sheriff of Clinton 1954
3 Cannon Kid 1955
4 Big Cheroke 1956
5 Sheriff's deputy 1956
6 Bushwack Canyon 1956
7 Bronco justice 1957
8 Gunsmoke feud 1957
9 Rawhide tenderfoot 1958
10 Cheroke trail 1958
11 Kansas trail 1958
12 Badlands fury 1959
13 Rustler's Range 1959
14 Range wolves 1960
15 Saddle tramp 1960
16 Horsethieves hang high 1961
17 Kid with a colt 1961
18 Guns of the lawless 1962
19 Cast a wide loop 1963
20 Texas wolves 1963
21 Gun feud at Sun Creek 1964
22 Rope for a rustler 1965
23 Stagecoach to Concho 1966
24 Owlhooter 1968
25 Dry Valley war 1968

BORGEN, J.
WILFRED SAGEN:
1 Lillelord 1955
2 The dark springs 1956
3 We've got him now 1957
A trilogy about a Norwegian adolscent and his awakening social conscience. Vol. 1 only in English.

BORGES, J. L.
1 Six problems for Don Isidro Parodi 1981
2 Chronicles of Bustos Domecq 1982
Short stories featuring the same characters.

BOSSE, M.
ASIAN SAGA:
1 The warlord 1984
2 Fire in Heaven 1986

BOTTOME, P.
1 Search for a soul 1947
2 Challenge 1952
N.F. Autobiography

BOURNE, L. R.
COPPERKNOB SERIES:
1 Copperknob Buckland
2 Copperknob second mate
3 Captain Copperknob
4 Copperknob: shipowner

BOURNE, P.
1 Black saga 1953
2 Ten thousand shall die 1954
Henry Stewart, the hero of 2 is the son of Duncan Stewart of 1.

BOVA, B.
KINSMAN SAGA:
1 Kinsman 1965
2 Millenium 1976
3 Colony 1979
ORION:
1 Orion 1984
2 Vengeance of Orion 1988
3 Orion in the dying time
VOYAGERS:
1 Voyagers 1986
2 The alien within 1987
3 Star brothers 1990
Science fiction

BOWDEN, J.
DAN MCCOY SERIES:
1 Return of the sheriff
2 Wayman's Ford
3 Two gun justice
4 Roaring Valley
5 Revenge in Red Springs
6 Black Water Canyon
7 Brazo feud
8 Guns along the Brazo
9 Gun loose

BOWIE, J.
1 Penny buff 1975
2 Penny boss 1976
3 Penny change 1977
N.F. Autobiography of a Clydeside teacher

① Gaslight.. PS

BOWLES, C.
MIKE HAZZARD:
1 Flying blind 1986 ② Civil from CL
2 Flying Hazzard 1987 ③ Bqacsteer C,
BOWLING, H

BOWRING, M.
1 The animals came first 1976
2 Animals before breakfast 1978
3 Animals round the clock 1981
N.F. Autobiography of a vet's wife

BOX, E., *pseud.* **(Gore Vidal)**
PETER CUTLER SERGEANT II SERIES:
1 Death in the fifth position 1954
2 Death before bedtime 1955
3 Death likes it hot 1955

BOYD, M.

THE LANGTONS:
1 The cardboard clown 1952
2 A difficult young man 1955
3 Outbreak of love 1957
4 Much in evidence 1957
A series of novels about a Anglo Australian family. Characters change in all the novels.

BOYD, N.

FATHER DUDDLESWELL:
1 Bless me, Father 1976
2 A Father before Christmas 1978
3 Father in a fix 1979
4 Father under fire 1980
5 Bless me again father 1981
Stories about a Catholic priest.

BOYER, E. H.

WORLD OF THE ALFAR:
1 The sword and the satchel
2 The elves and the otterskin
3 The thrall and the dragon's heart
4 The wizard and the warlord
5 The troll's grindstone
6 The curse of Slagfid
Paperback fantasy

BOYER, R.

DOC ADAMS:
1 Billingsgate shoal 1985
2 Penny Ferry 1985
3 Moscow metal 1988

BOYLE, D.

COMMANDER MORETON SHADE:
1 Strange corpse on Murder Mile 1960
2 Death at Devil-Fish Point 1961

BOYLE, J.

1 A sense of freedom 1977
2 The pain of confinement 1984
N.F. Prison diaries

BOYLE, T.

DET. FRANCIS DE SALES:
1 Only the dead know Brooklyn 1987
2 Post-mortem effects 1988

BRADDON, G.

MICHAEL GAUNT:
1 Death in the picture 1951
2 Death rings no bell 1951
3 Death doubles death 1952
4 Time off for death 1952

BRADDON, R.

1 The naked island 1951
2 End of a hate 1958
N.F. Autobiography

BRADFORD, B.T.

EMMA HARTE:
1 A woman of substance 1979
2 Hold the dream 1985
3 To be the best 1988

BRADLEY, H.

1 And Miss Carter wore pink 1971
2 Miss Carter came with us 1973
3 In the beginning, said Great Aunt Jane 1975
4 The Queen who came to tea 1978
N.F. Reminiscences of Lancashire in Edwardian days, told mainly in pictures.

BRADLEY, J.

BATTLESQUAD:
1 Alamein attack 1982
2 Slaughter in Sicily 1983
3 Killer winter 1983
4 Bloody bridgehead 1984

BRADLEY, M. Z.

DARKOVER SERIES:
1 Darkover landfall
2 The spell sword 1990
3 Star of danger
4 Shattered chain
5 The winds of Darkover
6 The bloody sun
7 Sword of Aldones
8 Heritage of Hastur
9 The planet savers
10 The world wreckers 1989
11 Hunters of the red moon
12 The forbidden tower
13 Stormqueen
14 Two to conquer
15 Sharra's exile
16 Thendara's house
17 City of sorcery 1990
18 The heirs of Hammerfell 1991
Fantasy. Dates given are for hardback editions.

BRADSHAW, G.

ARTHUR AND GAWAIN:
1 Hawk of May 1981
2 Kingdom of summer 1982
3 In Winter's shadow 1982

BRADY, J.
MATT MINOGUE:
1 A stone of the heart 1988
2 Unholy ground 1989
3 Kaddish in Dublin 1990

BRADY, T. and BINGHAM, C.
1 Victoria 1972
2 Victoria and Company 1974
Originally a TV series 'Take three girls'.
See also **'Upstairs, downstairs'** *TV*
series.

BRADY, W. S.
HAWK:
1 The sudden guns
2 Blood money
3 Death's bounty
4 Killing time
5 Fool's gold
6 Blood kin
7 The gates of death
8 Desperadoes
9 The widowmaker
10 Dead man's hand
11 Sierra gold
12 Death and Jack Shade
13 Killer's breed
14 Border war
Paperback Westerns
PEACEMAKER:
1 Comanche
2 Outlaws
3 Whiplash
4 Lynch law
5 Blood run
6 War party
7 $1000 death
8
9 Shootout
Paperback Westerns

BRAGG, M.
THE TALLENTIRE FAMILY:
1 The hired man 1968
2 A place in England 1970
3 Kingdom come 1980
A family history set in Cumberland.

BRAINE, J.
JOE LAMPTON:
1 Room at the top 1959
2 Life at the top 1962
XAVIER FLYNN:
1 The pious agent 1975
2 Finger of fire 1977
  ★★★

1 One and last love 1981
2 These golden days 1985
Novels based on incidents in the
author's life.
CLIVE AND ROBIN LENDRICK:
1 Stay with me till morning 1970
2 The two of us 1984
3 My one true love 1985

BRAITHWAITE, E. R.
1 To sir, with love 1959
2 Paid servant 1962
N.F. Autobiography

BRAITHWAITE, R.
A YORKSHIRE TRILOGY:
1 Martha 1983
2 Ben 1984
3 The house in Kingston Square 1985
The history of a Bridlington family.

BRAMBLE, F.
1 Regent Square 1978
2 The iron roads 1982
Set in 18th century England.

BRAND, C.
INSPECTOR COCKERILL SERIES:
1 Death in high heels 1939
2 Heads you lose 1944
3 Green for danger 1945
4 Suddenly at his residence 1947
5 Death of Jezebel 1948
6 Cat and mouse 1950
7 London particular 1954
8 Tour de force 1955

BRANDNER, G.
THE HOWLING:
1 The howling
2 The return
3 Echoes
Paperback horror stories

BRANDON, J. G.
INSPECTOR MCCARTHY SERIES:
1 The blue print murders
2 Candidate for a coffin
3 The crooked fire
4 The case of the withering hand
5 Death burns swiftly
6 Death in the quarry
7 Death in duplicate
8 Death on delivery
9 The dragnet
10 The espionage killings
11 The 50 marriage case
12 The frame up

13 Fingerprints never lie
14 The hand of Seeta
15 The mail van mystery
16 The mark of fang
17 Murder at the yard
18 Murder in Soho
19 Murder for a milliom
20 McCarthy, C.I.D.
21 The night club murder
22 The Regent St. raid
23 A scream in Soho
24 The transport murders 1955
25 Yellow gods 1956
26 Bonus for murder 1957
27 The corpse from the city 1958

A. S. PENNINGTON SERIES:
1 The Cork St. crime
2 Death in the ditch
3 Mr. Pennington goes nap
4 Mr. Pennington comes through
5 Mr. Pennington barges in
6 Mr. Pennington see red
7 The riverside mystery 1950
8 Murder in Mayfair
9 One-minute murder
10 The pawnshop murder
11 The 'snatch' game
12 The Bond St. murders
13 Death in D division
14 Death in Downing St.
15 Death in Jermyn St.
16 Death foils the gang
17 M is for murder
18 The call-girl murders 1954
19 The case of the would-be widow 1955
20 The coffin rode on 1955
21 Murderers stands 1956
22 Murder on the beam 1956
23 Death of a Greek 1957
24 Death of a socialite 1957
25 Death stalks in Soho 1958
26 Murder in Pimlico 1958
27 Murder comes smiling 1959
28 Death of a mermaid 1960

BRANSON, H. C.
JOHN BENT SERIES:
1 I'll eat you last
2 The pricking thimb
3 The case of the giant killer
4 The fearful passage
5 Last year's blood
6 The leaden bubble

BRASON, J.
1 Secret army 1978
2 Secret army dossier 1979

3 End of the line 1980
4 Kessler 1981
Novels about the Belgian Resistance in WW2. No. 4 is about their attempts to trace war criminals 30 years later.

BRASON, J.
HOWARD'S WAY:
1 Howard's way 1986
2 Howard's way 2 1987
3 Howard's way 3 1988
Based on the TV series

BRATA, S.
1 My god died young 1968
2 Confessions of an Indian womaneater 1971
3 A traitor to India 1976
N.F. Autobiography of an Indian Brahmin.

BRATBY, J.
PETER CARR:
1 Breakfast and elevenses 1960
2 Brake pedal down 1962

BRATHWAITE, E.
1 The flying fish 1963
2 The needle's eye 1965
3 The evil day 1967
A trilogy on the Maori wars in New Zealand.

BRAUN, L. J.
QWILLERAN AND KOKO SERIES:
1 The cat who could read backwards 1966
2 The cat who ate Danish modern 1967
3 The cat who turned on and off 1968
4 The cat who played Brahms
5 The cat who played Post Office 1987
6 The cat who knew Shakespeare 1989
7 The cat who sniffed glue
8 The cat who had 14 tales
Short stories

BRAUN, M.
LUKE STARBUCK:
1 Hangman's Creek
2 Jury of six
3 The spoilers
4 Tombstone
5 Manhunter
6 Deadwood
7 The Judas tree
Paperback Westerns

BRAY, D.
CAPTAIN DAVY:
1 Between two shores 1984
2 The captain's wife 1985
*Naval adventure stories in the 18th
century.*

BREAM, F.
REV. JABAL JARRETT:
1 The Vicar done it 1982
2 The Vicar investigates 1983
3 Sealed and despatched 1984
4 With murder in mind 1985
5 The problem at Piha 1986

BREEN, J.
JERRY BROGAN:
1 Vicar's roses 1984
2 The gathering place 1984
3 Triple crown 1985
4 Loose lips 1990

BREESE, A.
1 Setting out 1981
2 A loving imprint 1982

BREEZE, P.
1 While my guitar gently weeps 1979
2 Back street runner 1980

BREMOND D'ARS, Y. DE
1 In the heart of Paris 1959
2 An antique dealer's tale 1961
3 The chest with a secret 1964
*N.F. Anecdotes of antique dealing in
Paris*

BRENNAN, J. H.
DEMONSPAWN:
1 Firewolf
2 Crypts of terror
Paperback horror stories

BRENT, N
BARNEY HYDE SERIES:
1 The scarlet lily
2 Motive for murder
3 Blood in the bank
4 Dig the grave deep
5 Murder swings high
6 The leopard died too 1957
7 The golden angel 1959
8 Badger in the dusk 1960
9 No space for murder 1960
10 Spider in the web 1961

BRESLER, F.
1 Within the law 1956

2 Strictly legal
3 Strictly illegal

BRETT, M.
HUGO BARON SERIES:
1 Diecast 1964
2 A plague of dragons 1965
3 A cargo of spent evil 1966

BRETT, S.
CHARLES PARIS SERIES
1 Cast in order of disappearance 1975
2 So much blood 1976
3 Star trap 1977
4 An amateur corpse 1978
5 A comedian dies 1979
6 Dead side of the mike 1980
7 Situation tragedy 1981
8 Murder unprompted 1982
9 Murder in the title 1983
10 Not dead only resting 1984
11 Dead giveaway 1985
12 What bloody man is that? 1987
13 A series of murders 1989
MRS. PARGETER SERIES:
1 A nice class of corpse 1986
2 Mrs., presumed dead 1988
3 Mrs. Pargeter's package 1990

BRIDGE, A.
JULIA PROBYN SERIES:
1 The lighthearted quest 1956
2 The Portuguese quest 1956
3 The numbered account 1960
4 The dangerous islands 1964
5 Emergency in the Pyrenees 1965
(Miss Probyn becomes Julia Jamieson)
6 The episode at Toledo 1967
7 The malady in Madeira 1969
*Nos. 2 and 6 though part of the series,
mainly concern Hetta Atherley, and are
direct sequels in the sequence.*

BRIERLEY, D.
CODY:
1 Cold war 1979
2 Blood group O 1980
3 Skorpion's death 1985
4 Snowline 1986

BRIGGS, V.
THE WAY AHEAD
1 Sacred ground 1975
2 Reap the harvest 1976
3 Yours is the earth 1977
*A family saga set in Bristol and the
Cotswolds.*

BRIGHT, P.
1 Life in our hands 1955
2 Breakfast at night 1956
3 The day's end 1959
N.F. Autobiography

BRIN, D.
1 Startide rising
2 The uplift war
Paperback science fiction

BRINDLEY, L.
1 They must have seen me coming 1980
2 There's one born every minute 1982
3 Vicky and I 1984
Semi-autobiographical stories about the warden of an Old People's Home.
TANQUILLAN:
1 Tanquillan 1986
2 The tender leaves of hope 1987
3 Our summer faces 1988

BRINTON, H.
JOHN STRANG SERIES:
1 Death to windward 1952
2 One down and two to slay 1953
3 Now like to die 1955
4 Coppers and gold 1957
5 Drug on the market 1958
Nos. 4 and 5 mainly concern Sally Strang.

BRITTAIN, V.
1 Testament of youth 1933
2 Testament of experience 1957
N.F. Autobiography
1 Chronicle of youth 1984
2 Chronicle of friendship 1986
3 Wartime chronicle 1989
N.F. Diaries

BROCH, H.
THE SLEEPWALKERS:
1 The romantic 1888
2 The anarchist 1903
3 The realist 1918
Reprinted under the title of the series in 1986

BROCKWAY, F., LORD
1 Inside the left 1960
2 Outside the right 1962
N.F. Autobiography

BROD, D. C.
QUINT MCCAULEY:
1 Murder in store 1990
2 Error in Judgement 1991

BRODE, A.
1 Picture of a country vicarage 1952
2 To bed on Thursday 1958
N.F. Autobiography

BRODIE, G.
JOHN BORHAM SERIES:
1 Lady had a tiger 1967
2 Poison of poppies 1968
3 Who called diamonds? 1969

BROMIGE, I.
THE RAINWOOD FAMILY:
1 The quiet hills 1966
2 The stepdaughter 1967
3 An April girl 1969
4 The tangled wood 1969
5 A sheltering tree 1970
6 A magic place 1971
7 A bend in the river 1975
8 The distant song 1977
9 The happy fortress 1978

BROMLEY, G.
INSPECTOR SEVERN:
1 In the absence of the body 1972
2 Chance to poison 1973

BRONTE, C.
Jane Eyre
'The wild Sargasso sea', by J. Rhys, 1966, is the story of Rochester's first wife.
'The quiet stranger', by R. Kydd, 1991 is a pendant. The main characters are Richard Mason and his sister who becomes Rochester's mad wife.

BRONTE, E.
1 Wuthering Heights
'Heathcliff', by J. Caine, 1982, is the story of Heathcliff's wanderings.

BRONTE, LOUISA
GREYSTONE SERIES:
1 Greystone tavern
2 Gathering at Greystone
3 Freedom trail to Greystone
4 Cassino Greystone
5 Moonlight at Greystone
6 Greystone heritage
A family saga set in New England. Published in this country in Large Print format.

BROOKE, C.
THE MARSHALL FAMILY:
1 As other see us

2 The changing tide
3 Bitter summer
4 The way of life 1956

BROOKE, J.
ORCHID TRILOGY:
1 The military orchid
2 A mine of serpents
3 The goose cathedral
Autobiographical novels. Published in 1 vol., 1981.

BROOKE-ROSE, C.
JIB AND JAB:
1 Xorandor 1986
2 Verbivore 1990

BROOKES, E.
1 Proud waters 1954
2 The glass years
1 is a war novel. Of 2 the author says, 'I have tried to follow the story of a few of the characters in 'Proud waters'.'

BROOKS, J.
1 Jampot Smith 1962
2 Smith, as hero 1964
The diary of a young man, first in adolescence and then as a young naval officer in World War II.

BROOKS, T.
MAGIC KINGDOM OF LANDOVER:
1 Magic kingdom for sale/sold 1986
2 The black unicorn 1988
3 Wizard at large 1988
Fantasy
SHANNARA:
1 Sword of Shannara 1981
2 Elfstones of Shannara 1982
3 Wishsong of Snannara 1984
4 The scions of Shannara 1990
Fantasies, in the style of Tolkien.

BROOKS, V. W.
1 Scenes and portraits
2 Days of the phoenix
3 From the shadows of the mountain
N.F. Autobiography

BROSNAN, J.
SKY LORDS TRILOGY:
1 The sky lords 1988
2 War of the sky lords 1989
3 The fall of the sky lords 1991
Science fiction

THE BROTHERS
BOOKS 1-6:
Based on the TV series about a haulage firm.

BROUN, D.
HARRY EGYPT, MASTER CRIMINAL:
1 The subject of Harry Egypt 1963
2 Egypt's choice 1964

BROWN, CARTER
DANNY BOYD SERIES:
1 Nymph to the slaughter
2 Wayward wahine
3 Siren signs off 1958
4 Walk softly, witch 1959
5 The sometimes wife 1965
6 Catch me a phoenix 1965
7 Terror comes creeping 1967
RICK HELMAN SERIES:
1 Who killed Dr. Sex?
2 Blonde on a broomstick 1963
3 Murder is a package deal 1964
4 The white bikini 1965
5 The girl from outer space 1965
6 Nude - with a view 1965
7 No tears from the widow 1968
MAVIS SEIDLIZT SERIES:
1 None but the lethal heart 1959
2 Lament for a lousy lover 1968
AL WHEELER SERIES:
1 Girl in a shroud
2 The dame 1959
3 The passionate 1959
4 The temptress 1960
5 The velvet vixen 1964
6 A corpse for Christmas 1965
7 The corpse 1966
8 Target for their dark desire 1968
Al Wheeler also appears in 'Lament for a lousy lover'. All these series are in paperback only.

BROWN, CHRISTY
1 My left Foot
2 Down all the days 1970
1 is an autobiography, 2 is an autobiographical novel. They are not sequels but complementary.

BROWN, D.
MAJOR PAT MCLANAHAN
1 Flight of the old dog 1988
2 Day of the cheetah 1989
Aviation thrillers

BROWN, EDWARD
MAJOR TITTERTON:
1 A penny to spend 1966
2 Vandersley 1967

BROWN, F.
ED HUNTER SERIES:
1 The fabulous clipjoint 1947
2 The dead ringer 1948
3 Murder in moonlight 1950 (The bloody moonlight)
4 Death has many doors 1952
5 Compliments of a friend 1951
6 The late lamented 1957
7 Mrs. Murphy's underpants 1964

BROWN, FRANCES
ROMANY SERIES:
1 The haresfoot legacy 1990
2 Dancing on the rainbow 1991

BROWN, HOSANNA
FRANK LE ROUX:
1 I spy, you die 1984
2 Death upon a spear 1986

BROWN, R.
1 Then the woods became the trees 1965
2 A forest is a long time growing 1967
Two novels about Rhodesia

BROWN, W,
1 Duffers on the deep
2 No distress signals
3 Under six planets 1955
N.F. Autobiography

BROWNE, D. G.
MR. HARVEY TUKE SERIES:
1 What beckoning ghost 1947
2 Too many cousins 1953
3 Rustling end
4 Death is perpetuity 1956
5 Death in seven volumes 1958
6 Sergeant Death 1961

BRUCE, H. J.
1 Silken dalliance
2 Thirty dozen moons
N.F. Autobiography

BRUCE, J.
SECRET AGENT OSS17:
1 Deep freeze 1963
2 Short wave 1964
3 Double take 1964
4 Flash point 1965

5 Pole reaction 1965
6 Shock tactics 1965
7 Live wire 1966
8 Softsell 1966
9 Photo finish 1967
10 Hot line 1967
11 High treason 1968
12 Top secret 1968
13 Cold spell 1968
14 Dead silence 1969
15 Strip tease 1969

BRUCE, L.
CAROLUS DEENE SERIES:
1 Cold blood 1952
2 At death's door 1955
3 Death of cold 1956
4 Dead for a ducat 1956
5 Dead man's shoes 1958
6 A louse for the hangman 1959
7 Our jubilee is death 1959
8 Jack on the gallows tree 1960
9 Furious old women 1960
10 A bone and a hank of hair 1960
11 Die, all, die merrily 1961
12 Nothing like blood 1961
13 Crack of doom 1962 (Such is death)
14 Death in Albert Park 1963
15 Death at Hallows End 1963
16 Death in the Black Sands 1964
17 Death at St. Asprey's School 1967
18 Death of a commuter 1967
19 Death on Romney Marsh 1968
20 Death with blue ribbon 1969
21 Death on All-Hallowe'en 1970
22 Death by the lake 1971
23 Death in the middle watch 1974
24 Death of a bovver boy 1974

SERGEANT BEEF SERIES:
1 Case of three dectectives 1935
2 Case without a corpse 1937
3 Case with no conclusion 1939
4 Case with four clowns 1939
5 Case with ropes and rings 1939
6 Case of Sergeant Beef 1947

BRUNNER, J.
MAX CURFEW SERIES:
1 A plague on both your causes 1969
2 Good men do nothing 1970
3 Honky in the woodpile 1971
***
1 Stand at Zanzibar
2 The sheep look up 1974

BRUTON, E.
1 The laughing policeman 1963

2 The Finsbury mob 1964
3 The Smithfield slayer 1965
4 The wicked saint 1965
5 The firebug 1967
*Novels about the City of London
Police*

BRYAN, J.
RICHARD SARET SERIES:
1 The difference to me 1956
2 The contessa came too 1957
3 The man who came back 1958

BRYANT, SIR A.
1 The man in the making 1933
2 The years of peril 1935
3 The saviour of the navy 1938
N.F. Biography of Samuel Pepys.
***
1 The years of endurance (1793-1802) 1942
2 The years of victory (1802-1812) 1944
3 The age of elegance (1812-1822) 1950
N.F. A history of England in the struggle against Napoleon.
THE STORY OF ENGLAND:
1 Makers of the realm 1953
2 The age of chivalry 1963
N.F. History

BRYCE, I.
1 Canals are my home 1979
2 Canals are my life 1982
N.F. Autobiography

BUBB, L.
CHRISTIANSSON FAMILY TRILOGY:
1 April snow 1951
2 Land of strangers 1953
3 April harvest 1957

BUCHAN, S. C., VISCOUNTESS TWEEDSMUIR
VICTORIAN TRILOGY:
1 Cousin Harriet 1959
2 Dashbury Park 1960
3 A stone in a pool 1961

BUCK, P. S.
1 The good earth 1931
2 Sons 1932
3 A house divided 1935
***
1 Exile 1936
2 Fighting angel 1936

***
1 Dragon seed 1942
2 The promise 1943
***
1 The long love 1949
2 The townsman 1945
3 Voices in the house 1953
Facets of American life. Designed as a series, but characters do not recur
***
1 My several worlds 1955
2 A bridge for passing 1963
N.F. Autobiography

BUCKINGHAM, B.
DON PANCHO SERIES:
1 Three bad nights
2 Boiled alive 1957

BUCKLEY, E.
1 For benefits received
2 Fiorana 1961
***
1 Blue Danube
2 Family from Vienna
SANDOR RAIMANN SERIES:
1 They walk on earth 1966
2 The man on the rope 1966
3 Diamonds in the family 1967
4 The flaming sword 1969
Stories of a musician-healer.

BUCKLEY, H. B.
1 Grandmother and I
2 Grandfather and I 1962
N.F. Autobiography

BUCKLEY, W. F.
BLACKFORD OAKES:
1 Saving the Queen 1976
2 Stained glass 1978
3 Who's on first? 1980
4 The story of Henri Tod 1984
5 Marco polo if you can 1982
6 See you later, alligator 1986
7 High jinx 1987
8 Mongoose R.I.P. 1988

BUDD, M.
1 Dust to dust 1966
2 Prospect of love 1969
3 Fit for a duchess 1970
N.F. Family history

BUDE, J.
DET.-INSPECTOR MEREDITH SERIES:
1 The Cornish coast murder

2 The Cheltenham Square murder
3 Hand on the alibi
4 Loss of a head
5 Death on paper
6 Death of a cad
7 Death knows no calendar
8 Death deals a double
9 Slow vengeance
10 Death in ambush
11 Death in white pyjamas
12 Trouble brewing
13 Death makes a prophet
14 Dangerous sunlight
15 A glint of red herrings
16 Death steals the show
17 The constable and the lady
18 Death on the Riviera
19 When the case was opened
20 Twice dead
21 So much is dark 1954
22 Two ends to the town 1955
23 Shift of guilt 1957
24 Telegram from Le Touquet 1956
25 Another man's shadow 1957
INSPECTOR SHERWOOD SERIES:
1 Night the fog came down 1958
2 A twist of the rope 1958

BUECHNER, T. F.
LEO BEBB, EVANGELIST
1 Lion country 1971
2 Open heart 1972
3 The love feast 1975
4 Treasure hunt 1978

BUFFERY, J.
STAR LORD SAGA:
1 The Sheeg 1979
2 Saffron 1979
3 The iron clog 1979
4 Gringolweed 1980
Science fiction

BUHET, G.
1 The honey siege
2 The grand catch

BULL, P.
1 To sea in a sieve 1956
2 Bulls in the meadows 1957
3 I know the face but... 1959
4 I say, look here 1965
5 It isn't all Greek to me 1967
6 Life is a cucumber 1973
N.F. Autobiography

BULLETT, G.
1 The daughter of Mrs. Peacock 1956

2 The Peacock brides 1958
GEORGE LYDNEY SERIES:
1 One man's poison 1960
2 Odd woman out 1961
*First published under the name of
S. Fox.*

BULMER, K.
SEA WOLF:
1 Steel shark 1979
2 Shark north 1979
3 Shark pack 1980
4 Shark hunt 1980
5 Shark Africa 1980
6 Shark raid 1982
7 Shark America 1983
8 Shark trap 1983
*Originally in paperback, under
Krauss, B.*

BUNTING, J.
'BRITISH INTERNATIONAL AIRWAYS'
SERIES:
1 Devil mountain 1968
2 Flight of the lobster 1970
3 Vapour trail 1972

BURDEN, P.
1 Screaming bones 1989
2 Wreath of honesty 1990
3 Bury him kindly 1991

BURGESS, A.
ENDERBY:
1 Inside Mr. Enderby 1964
2 Enderby outside 1968
3 The clockwork testament, or Enderby's end 1974
4 Enderby's dark lady or No end to
Enderby 1984

BURGESS, E.
HARRY TONG SERIES:
1 A killing frost 1961
2 Deadly deceit 1963
3 Closely confined 1968

BURGESS, E. and FRIGGENS, A.
1 Mortorio 1973
2 Mortorio 2 1975
Science fiction

BURGH, A.
DAUGHTERS OF A GRANITE LAND:
1 The azure bowl 1989
2 The golden butterfly 1990
3 The stone mistress 1991
A family chronicle set in Cornwall

BURKE, B., and SKIPP, C.
1 With a feather on my nose
2 With powder on my nose
N.F. *Autobiography*

BURKE, J.
MIKE MERRIMAN:
1 Fear by instalments 1960
2 Deadly downbeat 1962
DR. CASPIAN:
1 The devil's footsteps 1976
2 Black charade 1977
3 Ladygrove 1978
Supernatural stories

BURKE, J. L.
DAVE ROBICHEAUX
1 The neon rain 1989
2 Heaven's prisoners 1990

BURKHOLZ, H.
1 The sensitives 1988
2 Strange bedfellows 1989

BURKHOLZ, H. & IRVING, C.
MANCUSO AND BORGNEFF:
1 The death freak 1983
2 The sleeping spy 1984

BURLAND, B.
JAMES BERKELEY:
1 A fall from aloft 1968
2 A few flowers for St. George 1969
*Two novels about a young man's
problems, loneliness and incapacity
to love or be loved.*

BURLEY, W. J.
DET. SUPT. WYCLIFFE
1 Three-toed pussy 1969
2 To kill a cat 1970
3 Guilt edged 1971
4 Death in a salubrious place 1972
5 Death in Stanley Street 1973
6 Wycliffe and the pea green boat
1975
7 Wycliffe and the schoolgirls 1976
8 Wycliffe and the scapegoat 1978
9 Wycliffe in Paul's court 1980
10 Wycliffe's wild goose chase 1982
11 Wycliffe and the Beales 1983
12 Wycliffe and the four Jacks 1985
13 Wycliffe and the quiet virgin 1986
14 Wycliffe and the Winsor Blue 1987
15 Wycliffe and the tangled web 1988
16 Wycliffe and the cycle of death 1990
17 Wycliffe and the dead flautist 1991

DR. PYM:
1 A taste of power 1966
2 Death in willow pattern 1969

BURNETT, W. R.
1 Adobe walls 1955
2 Pale moon 1957

BURNLEY, J
1 The wife 1977
2 Unrepentant woman 1982
3 The woman herself 1986

BURNS, P.
1 Stacey's flyer 1986
2 Kezzy 1988

BURNS, R.
GABE WAGER:
1 The Alvarez journal
2 The Farnsworth score
3 Speak for the dead
4 Angle of attack
5 The avenging angel
6 Strip search
7 Ground money

BURNS, TEX, *Pseud.,* see
MULFORD, C. E.

BURR, S.
LISA LONGLAND
1 Life with Lisa 1958
2 Leave it to Lisa 1959

BURRARD, G.
1 The tiger of Tibet
2 The mystery of Mekong

BURROUGHS, E. R.
MARTIAN SERIES:
1 A Princess of Mars
2 The gods of Mars
3 The warlord of Mars
4 Thuvia, maid of Mars
5 Chessmen of Mars
6 A fighting man of Mars
7 Master mind of Mars
8 Synthetic men of Mars
9 Swords of Mars
10 Llana of Gathol
11 John Carter of Mars
Available in paperback only.
TARZAN SERIES:
1 Tarzan of the apes 1914
2 The return of Tarzan 1915
3 The beasts of Tarzan 1916
4 The son of Tarzan 1917

5 Tarzan and the jewels of Opar 1918
6 Jungle tales of Tarzan 1919
7 Tarzan the untamed 1920
8 Tarzan the terrible 1921
9 Tarzan and the golden lion 1923
10 Tarzan and the Antmen 1924
11 Tarzan, Lord of the jungle 1928
12 Tarzan and the lost empire 1929
13 Tarzan at the Earth's core 1930
14 Tarzan the invincible 1931
15 Tarzan triumphant 1932
16 Tarzan and the city of gold 1933
17 Tarzan and the lion man 1934
18 Tarzan and the leopard men 1935
19 Tarzan's quest 1936
20 Tarzan and the forbidden city 1938
21 Tarzan the magnificent 1939
22 Tarzan and the Foreign Legion 1947
23 Tarzan and the madman 1965
24 Tarzan and the castaways 1965
25 Tarzan and the valley of gold 1965
26 Tarzan lives, by P. J. Farmer 1974
   Nos. 1 - 24 reprinted in paperback.
PELLUCIDAR SERIES:
1 At the earth's core
2 Pellucidar
3 Tarzan at the earth's core 1930
4 Tarzan of Pellucidar
5 Back to the stone-age
6 Land of terror
VENUS SERIES:
1 Pirates of Venus
2 Lost on Venus
3 Carson of Venus
4 Escape on Venus
5 Planet Venus
6 Wizard of Venus
   ★★★
1 The mucker
2 The man without a soul
1 Land that time forgot 1918
2 The people that time forgot 1918
3 Out of time's abyss 1918
   *First published as separate novels in
   magazine form. Republished in one
   volume 1924. Republished 1963*
   ★★★
1 War Chief
2 Apache devil 1973
   *The sequel is a 'rediscovered' Bur-
   roughs, presumably first published
   in magazine form.*
   ★★★
1 The moon maid 1923
2 The moon and men 1925
3 The Red Hawk 1925
   First published in magazine form.

*Republished in one vol. 1926.
Republished with 'Land that time
forgot', 1963. First published in
U.K. as 'Moonmaid', 1972.*

BURROUGHS, W.
1 Cities of red night 1981
2 The place of dead woods 1984
3 The western lands 1988

BURROWS, J.
SUPERINTENDENT BOWMAN &
SERGEANT PEART:
1 No need for violence 1970
2 Like an evening gone 1971

BURTON, A.
THE NAVIGATORS:
1 The master idol 1975
2 The navigators 1976
3 A place to stand 1977
   A trilogy about early canal building.

BURTON, B.
NUGENT FAMILY:
1 Jude 1986
2 Jaen 1986
3 Women of no account 1988
4 Hard loves, easy riches 1988

BURTON, M.
INSPECTOR ARNOLD AND DESMOND
MERRION SERIES:
1 The Hardway diamond mystery
   1930
2 The secret of High Eldersham 1930
3 The three crimes 1931
4 Menace on the downs 1931
5 Death of Mr. Gantley 1932
6 Murder at the moorings 1932
7 Fate at the fair 1933
8 Tragedy at the thirteenth hole 1933
9 Death at the crossroads 1933
10 The charabanc mystery 1934
11 To catch a thief 1934
12 The Devereaux Court mystery 1935
13 The milk churn murders 1935 (Clue
   of the silver brush)
14 Death in the tunnel 1936 (Dark is
   the tunnel)
15 Murder of a chemist 1936
16 Where is Barbara Prentice? 1936
   (The clue of the silver cellar)
17 Death at the club 1937 (Clue of the
   fourteen keys)
18 Murder in Crown passage 1937
   (Man with tattooed face)
19 Death at low tide 1938

20 The platinum cat 1938
21 Death leaves no card 1939
22 Mr. Babbacombe dies 1939
23 Murder in the coal hole 1940
(Written in dust)
24 Mr. Westerby missing 1940
25 Death takes a flat 1940
26 Death of two brothers 1941
27 Up the garden path 1941
28 This undesirable residence 1942
(Death at Ash House)
29 Dead stop 1943
30 Murder M.D. 1943 (Who killed the
doctor?)
31 Four ply yarn 1944 (The shadow on
the cliff)
32 The three corpse trick 1944
33 Not a leg to stand on 1945
34 Early morning murder 1945
(Accidents do happen)
35 The cat jumps 1946
36 Situation Vacant 1946
37 Heir of Lucifer 1947
38 A will in the way 1947
39 Death in shallow water 1948
40 Devil's reckoning 1948
41 Death takes the living (The disappearing parson)
42 Look alive 1949
43 Ground for suspicion 1950
44 A village afraid
45 Beware your neighbour 1951
46 Murder out of school 1951
47 Murder on duty 1952
48 Something to hide 1953
49 Heir to murder 1953
50 Murder in absence 1954
51 Unwanted corpse 1954
52 Murder unrecognised 1955
53 Found drowned 1956
54 A crime in turn 1956
55 Death in a duffle coat 1956
56 The Chinese puzzle 1957
57 The moth-watch murder 1957
58 Bones in the brickfield 1958
59 Death takes a detour 1958
60 Return from the dead 1959
61 A smell of smoke 1959
62 Death paints a picture 1960
63 Legacy of death 1961
*Inspector Arnold does not appear in
the first three.*

BUSBY, R.
DET.-SGT. LERIC SERIES:
1 Robbery blue 1969
2 The frighteners 1970
3 Deadlock 1971

4 A reasonable man 1972
5 Pattern of violence 1973
Promoted to Det-Inspector in no. 4.

BUSCH, N.
1 California Street 1959
2 The San Fransciscans 1962

BUSH, C.
LUDOVIC TRAVERS SERIES:
1 The perfect murder case
2 Dancing death
3 Dead man's music
4 Dead man twice
5 Murder at Fenwold
6 Cut-throat
7 Case of the green felt hat
8 Case of the unfortunate village
9 Case of the April fools
10 Case of the three strange faces
11 Case of the 100% alibis
12 Case of the dead shepherd
13 Case of the Chinese gong
14 Case of the Monday murders
15 Case of the bonfire body
16 Case of the missing minutes
17 Case of the hanging rope
18 Case of the Tudor Queen
19 Case of the leaning man
20 Case of the flying ass
21 Case of the fighting soldier
22 Case of the climbing rat
23 Case of the kidnapped colonel
24 Case of the murdered major
25 Case of the magic mirror
26 Case of the running mouse
27 Case of the platinum blonde
28 Case of the corporal's leave
29 Case of the missing men
30 Case of the second chance
31 Case of the curious client
32 Case of the Haven Hotel
33 Case of the housekeeper's hair
34 Case of the seven bells
35 Case of the purloined picture
36 Case of the happy warrior
37 Case of the corner cottage
38 Case of the fourth detective
39 Case of the happy medium
40 Case of the counterfeit colonel
41 Case of the burnt Bohemian
42 Case of the silken petticoat
43 Case of the red brunette
44 Case of the three lost letters
45 Case of the benevolent bookie
46 Case of the amateur actor 1955
47 Case of the extra man 1956
48 Case of the flowery corpse 1956

49 Case of the Russian cross 1957
50 Case of the treble twist
51 Case of the running man 1958
52 Case of the careless thieves 1959
53 Case of the sapphire brooch 1960
54 Case of the extra grave 1961
55 Case of the dead man gone 1961
56 Three ring puzzle 1962
57 Heavenly twins 1963
58 Case of the grand alliance 1964
59 Case of the jumbo sandwich 1965
60 Case of the good employer 1966
61 Case of the deadly diamonds 1966
62 Case of the prodigal daughter 1967

BUSHBY, J.
CAPT. JAMES ROLLO:
1 The Spanish General 1982
2 Mondego Bay 1983
*Sea stories set at the time of the
Napoleonic Wars.*

BUTLER, D.
1 We'll meet again 1982
2 The end of an era 1983
*Based on the TV series about the
USAAF in Britain during WW2.*

BUTLER, G.
INSPECTOR COFFIN SERIES:
1 The murdering kind 1958
2 The interloper 1959
3 Death lives next door 1960
4 Make me a murderer 1961
5 Coffin in Oxford 1962
6 Coffin on the water 1986
7 Coffin for baby 1963
8 Coffin waiting 1964
9 Coffin in Malta 1964
10 A nameless Coffin 1966
11 Coffin following 1968
12 Coffin's dark number 1969
13 A Coffin from the past 1970
14 A Coffin for the canary 1974
15 Coffin in fashion 1987
16 Coffin underground 1988
17 Coffin in the Black Museum 1989
18 Coffin and the paper man 1990
19 Coffin on Murder Street 1991
*Coffin first appears as a Sergeant in
'The Dull Dead' 1958.*

BUTLER, L.
HORTON AND JORDAN SERIES:
1 Night and the judgement
2 Recover or kill
3 Man who crawled away

BUTLER, MARGARET
HENRY II:
1 Lion of England 1974
2 The lion of Justice 1975
3 This turbulent priest 1977

BUTLER, O.
XENOGENESIS:
1 Dawn 1987
2 Adulthood rites 1988
3 Imago 1989

BUTLER, RAGAN
CAPTAIN NASH SERIES:
1 Capt. Nash and the wroth inheritance 1975
2 Capt. Nash and the honour of
England 1977

BUTLER, RICHARD
MAX FARNE SERIES:
1 Where all the girls are sweeter 1975
2 Italian assets 1976

BUTLER, W. V.
'OLD IRELAND YARD':
1 Scarepower 1968
2 The lie witnesses 1969
3 Clampdown 1971

BYAM, W.
1 The road to Harley St. 1963
2 Dr. Byam in Harley St. 1961
N.F. Autobiography

BYATT, A. S.
1 The virgin in the garden 1978
2 Still life 1985

BYRD, M.
MIKE HALLER:
1 California thriller 1984
2 Fly away Jill 1984
3 Finders weepers 1985

CADELL, E.
WAYNES OF WOOD MOUNT SERIES:
1 Lark shall sing 1952
2 Blue sky of spring 1956
3 Six impossible things 1961

CAGNEY, P.
MIKE STRANG:
1 No diamonds for a doll
2 Hear the stripper scream
3 A grave for Madam

CAIDIN, M.
STEVE AUSTIN:
1 Cyborg 1973
2 Operation Nuke 1974
3 High Crystal 1975
4 Cyborg IV 1976

CALDECOTT, M.
1 The tall stones 1976
2 The temple of the sun 1977
3 Shadow on the stones 1978
Fantasy

CALDERINI, P.
1 Mount Subasio 1985
2 Borderland 1987

CALDWELL, T.
1 Dynasty of death 1938
2 The eagles gather 1940
3 The final hour 1944

***

1 The man who listens 1961
2 No-one hears but him 1967
A sanctuary in a great city to comfort the dispairing

CALLISON, B.
BREVET CABLE:
1 A plague of sailors 1971
2 A frenzy of merchantmen 1977
CAPT. EDWARD TRAPP:
1 Trapp's war 1978
2 Trapp's peace 1979
3 Trapp and World War Three 1988

CALLOW, P.
COLIN PATON:
1 Going to the moon 1967
2 The Bliss body 1969
3 Flesh of morning 1971

CALLOWAY SISTERS
1 Mariah, by Sandra Canfield 1989
2 Jo, by Tracy Hughes 1989
3 Tess, by Katherine Burton 1990
4 Eden, by Penny Richards 1990

CALVINO, I
QFWFQ SERIES:
1 Cosmicomics 1969
2 Time and the Hunter 1970
Science fiction

CAMERON, D.
1 The field of sighing 1966
2 Sons of Eldorado 1968
N.F. Autobiography

CAMERON, D.K.
1 The ballad and the plough 1978
2 Willie Gavin, Crofterman 1980
3 The cornkister days 1984
N.F. Farming life in 19th C Scotland

CAMERON, I.
1 The doctor 1954
2 More about the doctor 1954
3 The doctor calls again 1954
4 The doctor and his friend 1954
5 More friends of the doctor 1954

***

1 The but and ben 1945
2 Tattered tartan 1950
3 Heather mixture 1952
4 Kirk of the Corrie 1956
Not strictly sequels, but characters reappear in all novels

CAMERON, J.
1 Point of departure 1967
2 An Indian Summer 1974
N.F. Autobiography

CAMPBELL, D.
HOPEWELL SAGA:
1 Broken promises
2 Silent dreams
3 Stolen Passions
4 Tomorrow's journey
Paperback

CAMPBELL, K.
MIKE BRETT SERIES:
1 Goodbye, gorgeous
2 Listen lovely
3 Born beautiful
4 Darling, don't
5 That was no lady
6 Pardon my gun

CAMPBELL, M.
1 Peter Perry 1956
2 Nothing doing 1970

CAMPBELL, R.
1 Broken record
2 Light on a dark horse 1951

CAMPBELL, ROBERT
WHISTLER:
1 In La-La land we trust 1987
2 Alice in La-La land 1988
3 Sweet La-La land 1990

CANDY, E. (A. NEVILLE)
BURNIVEL:
1 Which doctor 1953
2 Bones of contention 1954

CANETTI, E.
1 Earwitness 1979
2 The torch in my ear 1989
N.F. Autobiography

CANNELL, D.
ELLIE HASKELL:
1 The thin woman 1990
2 Mum's the word 1991

CANNING, V.
1 Mr. Finchley discovers his England
1934 (Mr. Finchley's holiday)
2 Mr. Finchley goes to Paris 1936
3 Mr. Finchley takes the road 1939

REX CARVER SERIES:
1 Whiphand 1965
2 Doubled in diamonds 1966
3 Python project 1967
4 Melting man 1968

'SMILER' MILES TRILOGY:
1 The runaways 1970
2 Flight of the grey goose 1973
3 The painted tent 1974

ARTHURIAN TRILOGY:
1 The crimson chalice 1976
2 Circle of the Gods 1977
3 The immortal wound 1978

BIRDCAGE:
1 Birdcage 1977
2 The satan sampler 1979
3 Vanishing point 1982

CAO, XUEGIN
THE STORY OF THE STONE:
1 Golden days
2 The crab-flower club
3 The warning voice
4 The debt of tears
5 The dreamer wakes

CAPON, P.
ANTIGEOS TRILOGY:
1 The other side of the sun
2 The other half of the planet
3 Down to earth
Science fiction

'TIGER' WRAGGE:
1 The host of Midian 1946
2 Dead man's chest 1947
3 Image of a murder 1949

CARD, O.S.
1 Ender's game 1985
2 Speakers for the dead 1987
Science fiction
TALES OF ALVIN MAKER:
1 Seventh son 1988
2 Red prophet 1989
3 Prentice Alvin 1989

CARDUS, N.
1 Autobiography 1947
2 Second innings 1950
3 Full score
4 Cardus on cricket
5 Cardus in the covers
N.F. Autobiography & Cricket

CAERNARVON, HENRY, Earl of
1 No regrets 1976
2 Ermine tales 1980
N.F. Autobiography

CAREY, E.G., *see* GILLBRETH, F.B. *and* CAREY, E.G.

CARLON, P.
JEFFERSON SHIELDS:
1 The Souvenir 1970
2 Death by demonstration 1970

CARMICHAEL, H.
PIPER AND QUINN SERIES:
1 Death leaves a diary 1952
2 The vanishing trick 1952
3 Deadly nightcap 1953
4 School for murder 1953
5 Why kill Johnnie? 1954
6 Death counts three 1954
7 Noose for a lady 1955
8 Justice enough 1956
9 Emergency exit 1957
10 Put out that star 1957
11 James Knowland dec. 1958
12 Or he be dead 1959
13 Stranghold 1959
14 The seeds of hate 1960
15 Requiem for Charles 1960
16 Alibi 1961
17 The link 1962
18 Of unsound mind 1962
19 Vendetta 1963
20 Flashback 1964
21 Post mortem 1965
22 Suicide clause 1966
23 The condemned 1967
24 Murder by proxy 1967
25 Remote control 1970
26 Death trap 1970

27 The quiet woman 1971
28 Most deadly hate 1971
29 Naked to the grave 1972
30 Too late for tears 1973
31 Candles for the dead 1973
32 The motive 1974
33 False evidence 1975
34 Grave for two 1977
35 Life cycle 1978
Quinn, a reporter, does not appear in earlier volumes. 'A slightly bitter taste', 1968, features Quinn alone.

CARNAC, C.
JULIAN RIVERS SERIES:
1 A double for detection 1945
2 The striped suitcase 1946
3 When the devil was sick 1946
4 Clue sinister 1947
5 Over the garden wall 1947
6 Copy for crime 1947
7 Upstairs downstairs 1950
8 Its her own funeral 1951
9 Crossed skis 1952
10 Murder among members 1957
11 Long shadows 1958
12 A policeman at the door 1959
INSPECTOR STRANG:
1 Double turn 1956
2 Death of a ladykiller 1958

CARNEGIE, S.
MAJOR GAIR MAINWEARING:
1 Noble purpose
2 Sunset in the East
THE DESTINY OF EAGLES SEQUENCE:
1 The banners of love 1967
2 The banners of war 1970
3 The banners of power 1972
4 The banners of courage 1976
5 The banners of revolt 1977
A series of novels on the history of Poland

CARNEY, D.
1 The wild geese 1977
2 The square circle 1983

CARR, G.
SIR ABERCROMBIE LEWKER SERIES:
1 Murder on the Matterhorn 1951
2 The youth hostel murders 1952
3 The corpse in the crevasse 1952
4 Death on Milestone buttress 1953
5 Death under Snowdon 1954
6 Death finds a foothold 1954
7 Holiday with murder 1955
8 A corpse at camp 2 1955

9 Murder of an owl 1956
10 The ice-axe murders 1958
11 Swing away climber 1959
12 Lewker in Norway 1963
13 Death of a weirdy 1965
14 Lewker in Tirol 1967
15 Fat man's agony 1969

CARR, J. B.
OCEOLA ARCHER SERIES:
1 Death whispers
2 The man with bated breath

CARR, J. D.
DR. FELL SERIES:
1 Hag's nook 1933
2 The mad hatter mystery 1933
3 The eight of swords 1934
4 The blind barber 1934
5 Death watch 1935
6 The hollow man 1935
7 To wake the dead 1937
8 The crooked hinge 1938
9 The man who could not shudder 1940
10 The black spectacles 1940 (The green capsule)
11 The problem of the wire cage 1940
12 The case of the constant suicides 1941 (Case of the ten teacups)
13 Till death do us part 1944
14 He who whispers 1946
15 Below suspicion 1950
16 The dead man's knock 1958
17 In spite of thunder 1960
18 The house at Satan's elbow 1965
19 Panic in Box C 1966
20 The dark of the moon 1968
'The men who explained miracles' (1964) has two Dr. Fell short stories and one about Sir Henry Merivale (originally published under the name of Carter Dickson).

BENCOLIN SERIES:
1 It walks by night 1930
2 Castle skull 1931
(not published in UK)
3 Lost gallows 1931
4 Four false weapons 1937
5 Waxworks murder 1952
***
1 Fire burn! 1957
2 Scandal at High Chimneys 1959
(The seat of the scornful)
3 The witch of the low-tide 1961
A trilogy of novels showing episodes in the history of the Metropolitan

Police. 1 is Georgian, 2 Mid-
Victorian, 3 Edwardian.
See also **DICKSON, C.**

CARR, P.
DAUGHTERS OF ENGLAND:
1 The miracle at St. Bruno's
2 The lion triumphant 1974
3 The witch from the sea 1975
4 Saraband for two sisters 1976
5 Lament for a lost lover 1977
6 The lovechild 1978
7 Song of the siren 1980
8 The drop of the dice 1981
9 The adulteress 1982
10 Zipporah's daughter
11 Voices in a haunted room 1984
12 The return of the gypsy 1985
13 Midsummer's eve 1986
14 The pool of St. Branok 1987
15 The changeling 1989
16 Black swan 1990
17 A time for silence 1991

CARREL, M.
ANDREW MCCALL SERIES:
1 The blood pit 1965
2 Shadow of a hawk 1966
3 Tears of blood 1967
4 A sword of silk 1968
5 The dark age of violence 1969

CARRIER, J. G.
1 My father's house 1974
2 Family 1977
3 A cage of bone 1979

CARRINGTON, C.
1 A subaltern's war 1929
2 Soldier from the wars returning
1965
N.F. Autobiography

CARSON, A.
1 The adventures of Mr. Quick 1965
2 The golden kiss 1967

CARSON, R.
1 Silent spring 1966 continued by
Frank Graham
2 Since silent spring 1970
Rachel Carson's famous book
sounded a warning against the use
of chemicals in agriculture. The
sequel looks at the progress, or lack
of it, in the following years.

CARSTAIRS, H.
LYDFORD LONG SERIES:
1 Harpinger's hunch 1943
2 Drifting death 1944
3 Black burying 1945
4 Secretary of State for death 1946
5 Cruel dart 1947
6 Blood m'lud 1948
7 Who lies bleeding?
8 Blackdrop Hall 1950
9 Lying down below 1951
10 Oh no you don't 1952
11 When three makes two
12 Death's duet 1954
13 Winton St. mystery 1955

CARSTAIRS, J. P.
GARWAY TRENTON SERIES:
1 Gardenias bruise easily 1959
2 No wooden overcoat 1959
3 The concrete kimono 1964
4 Touch of a French pom-pom 1965
5 Pardon my gun 1966
6 A smell of peardrops 1966
7 No thanks for the shroud 1967

***

1 Vinegar and brown paper
2 Sunshine and champagne 1955

CARTER, A.
BLACKOAKS:
1 Master of Blackoaks 1977
2 Sword of the golden stud 1978
3 Secrets of Blackoaks 1980
4 Heritage of Blackoaks 1982
5 A farewell to Blackoaks 1984
A series about plantation life, closely
linked to the 'Falconhurst' series,
which he also writes. See the entry
under Onstott, K.

CARTER, F.
JOSEY WALES:
1 The outlaw Josey Wales
2 The vengeance trail of Josey Wales
Paperback. Westerns

CARTER, J. see NEW AVENGERS

CARTER, L.
THONGOR SERIES:
1 Thongor of Lemmuria
2 Wizard of Lemmuria
3 Thongor fights the pirates of
Taracus
4 Thongor against the Gods
5 Thongor at the end of Time

6 Thongor in the city of the
  Magicians
  Fantasy

CARTER, N.

NICK CARTER SERIES:
1 The sea trap
2 Macao
3 The N3 conspiracy
4 The Arab plague
5 Operation snake
6 Assignment intercept
7 The ebony cross
8 The terrible ones
9 Cambodia
10 Rhodesia
11 The mark of Cosa Nostra
12 Code name Werewolf
13 The death strain
14 The death's head conspiracy
15 The defector
16 The executioners
17 The human time bomb
18 The Omega terror
19 The ultimate code
20 The Red Guard
21 Deadly doubles
22 Safari for spies
23 The man who sold death
24 Time clock of death
25 The cobra kill
26 The Jerusalem file
27 Trouble in Paradise
28 Thunderstrike in Syria
29 Hawaii
30 The Pamplona Affair
31 Race of Death
32 Reich 4
33 The Satan Trap
34 Tropical Deathpact
35 Under the Wall
  Paperback thrillers

CARTLAND, B.

1 The isthmus years, 1919-39 1943
2 The years of opportunity, 1939-45
  1947
3 I search for rainbows, 1945-66 1967
4 We danced all night 1970
  N.F. Autobiography
  No. 4 is about people met in the
  '20's

CARTWRIGHT, J. see NEW AVENGERS

CARVIC, H.

MISS SEETON SERIES:
1 Picture Miss Seeton 1968

2 Miss Seeton draws the line 1970
3 Miss Seeton bewitched 1971
4 Miss Seeton sings 1974
5 Odds on Miss Seeton 1976

CARY, J.

ART TRILOGY:
1 Herself surprised 1948
2 To be a pilgrim 1949
3 The horse's mouth 1950

THE LIFE OF CHESTER NIMMO:
1 Except the Lord 1953
2 Prisoner of grace 1952
3 Not honour more 1955
  1 and 2 published in reverse order.
  Cary's technique in these two
  trilogies is of triple representation,
  each aspect of the subject being told
  by a different person.

CASEY, M.

1 An Australian story 1964
2 Tides and eddies 1966
  N.F. Autobiography

CASSELLS, J.

LUDOVIC SAXON (PICAROON) SERIES:
1 Enter the Picaroon 1954
2 The avenging Picaroon 1956
3 Beware the Picaroon 1956
4 Meet the Picaroon 1957
5 The engaging Picaroon 1958
6 The enterprising Picaroon 1960
7 Salute the Picaroon 1960
8 The Picaroon goes west 1962
9 Prey for the Picaroon 1962
10 Challenge for the Picaroon 1965
11 The benevolent Picaroon 1965
12 Plunder for the Picaroon 1967
13 The audacious Picaroon 1967
14 The elusive Picaroon 1968
15 Night of the Picaroon 1969
16 Quest for the Picaroon 1970
17 The Picaroon collects 1970
18 Profit for the Picaroon 1972
19 The Picaroon laughs last 1973
20 Action for the Picaroon 1975
21 The Picaroon gets the runaround
   1976

CHIEF-INSPECTOR FLAGG SERIES:
1 Doctor deals with murder 1944
2 Murder comes to Rothesay 1949
3 Master in the dark 1949
4 The castle of sin 1949
5 League of nameless men 1951
6 Clue of the purple asters 1952
7 Waters of sadness 1952

8 Death comes to Lady's Step 1952
9 The circle of dust 1952
10 The grey ghost 1952
11 The second Mrs. Locke 1952
12 The rattler 1953
13 Salute Inspector Flagg 1953
14 Case for Inspector Flagg 1954
15 Inspector Flagg and the scarlett skeleton 1955
16 Again Inspector Flagg 1956
17 Presenting Supt. Flagg 1959
18 Case 29 1959
19 Enter Supt. Flagg 1960
20 Score for Supt. Flagg 1960
21 Problem for Supt. Flagg 1961
22 The brothers of benevolence 1962
23 The Council of the Rat 1963
24 Blue mask 1964
25 Grey face 1965
26 Black fingers 1966
27 The room in Quiver Court 1967
28 Call for Supt. Flagg 1968
29 The double crosser 1969
30 The grafter 1970
31 The hatchet man 1971
32 The enforcer 1973
33 Killer's rope 1974
34 Quest for Supt. Flagg 1975

CASSERLY, G.
1 The elephant god
2 The jungle girl
3 Ghost tiger

CASTANEDA, C.
1 The teachings of Don Juan
2 A Separate reality
3 Journey to Ixtlan 1973
4 Tales of power 1975
5 The second ring of power 1978
N.F. Best described as 'cult' books on sorcery and Mexican witchcraft with the aid of hallucinogenic plants

CATLING, P. S.
1 The experiment 1969
2 The surrogate 1972
Two novels about a sex research laboratory

CATO, N.
AUSTRALIAN TRILOGY:
1 All the rivers run
2 Time, flow softly
3 But still the stream 1962

CATTO, M.
LIMPIE:
1 Mister Midas 1976
2 The empty tiger 1976

CATTON, B.
1 The coming fury 1961
2 Terrible swift sword 1963
3 Never call retreat 1965
N.F. American Civil War
★★★
1 Mr. Lincoln's Army 1951
2 Glory Road 1952
3 A stillness at Appomattox 1953
N.F. History of the army of the Potamac in the American Civil War

CAUDWELL, S.
PROFESSOR TAMAR:
1 Thus was Adonis murdered 1981
2 The shortest way to Hades 1984
3 The sirens sang of murder 1989

CAUTE, D.
THE CONFRONTATION:
1 The demonstration 1970
2 The illusion 1971
3 The occupation 1971
A trilogy on the writer's problems of commitment. 1 is a play, 3 a novel and 2 is an essay attributed to the central character of 1 and 3.

CAVE, P. *see* **NEW AVENGERS**

CECIL, LORD DAVID
1 The young Melbourne 1939
2 'Lord M' 1954
N.F. Biography
Reprinted in one volume

CECIL, H.
ROGER THURSBY:
1 Brothers in law 1955
2 Friends at court 1956
3 Sober as a judge 1957
Three novels about law. There is a gap of 12 years between 1 and 2.

CELINE, L. F.
1 Journey to the end of the night 1932
2 Death on credit 1936

CHABER, M.E.
MILO MARCH SERIES:
1 No grave for March 1954
2 The man inside 1954

3 The splintered man 1955
4 A lonely walk 1957
5 The gallows garden 1958 (The lady came to kill)
6 A hearse of another colour 1959
7 So dead the rose 1960
8 Jade for a lady 1961
9 Softly in the night 1962
10 Hangman's harvest 1962
11 As old as Cain 1963
12 Uneasy lies the dead 1964
13 Six who ran 1964
14 Wanted: dead men 1966
15 The day it rained diamonds 1966
16 The flaming man 1970
17 Green grow the graves 1971
18 The loaded dead 1972

CHAKRABONGSE, PRINCE CHULA OF THAILAND
1 The twain have met
2 First class ticket
N.F. Autobiography

CHALKER, J.L.
DANCING GODS:
1 Demons of the Dancing Gods
2 Vengeance of the Dancing Gods
3 The river of the Dancing Gods
4 Songs of the Dancing Gods
CHANGEWINDS:
1 When the changewinds blow
2 Riders of the winds
3 War of the malestrom
FOUR LORDS OF THE DIAMOND:
1 Lilith
2 Cerberus
3 Charon
4 Medusa
GOD INC:
1 The labyrinth of dreams
2 The shadow dancers
3 The maze in the mirrors
Paperback fantasy
RINGS OF THE MASTER:
1 Lords of the middle dark
2 Pirates of the thunder
3 Warriors of the storm
4 Marks of the martyrs
Paperback fantasy
1 and 2 published in hardback 1989
THE WELLWORLD SAGA:
1 Midnight at the Well of Souls
2 Exiles at the Well of Souls
3 Quest for the Well of Souls
4 The return of Nathan Brazil
5 Twilight at the Well of Souls
Paperback fantasy

CHALLONER, R.
COMMANDER LORD CHARLES OAKSHOTT:
1 Run out the guns 1984
2 Give fire! 1986
3 Into battle! 1987
Naval stories set in the Napoleonic War period

CHAMBERS, D.
JIM STEELE SERIES:
1 Some day I'll kill you
2 She'll be dead by morning
3 Too like the lightning
4 The blonde died first
5 Darling this is death
6 The last secret
7 Rope for an ape
8 Case of Caroline Animus
9 Death against Venus

CHAMBERS, P.
MARK PRESTON SERIES:
1 This'll kill you 1963
2 Nobody lives forever 1964
3 You're better off dead 1966
4 Always take the big ones 1966
5 No gold where you go 1966
6 The bad die young 1967
7 Don't bother to knock 1968
8 The blonde wore black 1968
9 No peace for the wicked 1968
10 Speak ill of the dead 1968
11 They call it murder 1969
12 Somebody has to lose 1975
13 The deader they fall 1976
14 Lady, you're killing me 1977
15 The day of the big dollar 1978
16 The beautiful golden frame 1979
17 Nothing personal 1980
18 The deep blue cradle 1980
19 A long time dead 1980
20 The lady who never was 1981
21 Female - handle with care 1981
22 Murder is its own reward 1982
23 The highly explosive case 1982
24 A miniature murder mystery 1982
25 Jail bait 1983
26 Dragons can be dangerous 1983
27 Bomb scare - Flight 147 1984
28 The moving picture writes 1984
29 The vanishing holes murders 1985

CHAMBERS, R.
HANK MOODY:
1 Moth in a rag shop 1969
2 The lesser evil 1971

CHANCE, J. N.

MR. DE HAVILLAND SERIES:
1 Wheels in the forest 1935
2 Maiden possessed 1937
3 Death of an innocent 1938
4 The red knight 1945
5 Knight and the castle 1946
6 The black highway 1947
7 Coven gibbett 1948
8 The brandy pole 1949
9 Night of the full moon 1950
10 Alarm at Black Brake 1960
11 The forest affair 1962
12 Stormlight 1965
JASON SERIES:
1 The Jason affair 1954
2 Jason and the sleep game 1954
3 The Jason murders 1954
4 Jason goes west 1955
CHANCE SERIES:
1 Screaming fog 1944 (Death stalks the cobbled square)
2 The eye in darkness 1946
3 The man in my shoes 1952
JONATHAN BLAKE SERIES:
1 The affair at Dead End 1966
2 The double death 1966
3 The mask of pursuit 1966
4 The death women 1967
5 The hurricane drift 1967
6 Dead men's shoes 1968
7 Man trap 1968
8 Death of the wild bird 1968
9 Fate of the lying jade 1968
10 The rogue aunt 1968
11 The Hallowe'en murders 1968
12 Involvement in Austria
13 The Abel coincidence 1967
14 The killer reaction 1969
15 The killing experiment 1969
16 The ice maidens 1969
17 The mists of treason 1970
18 The mirror train 1970
19 A ring of liars 1970
20 A wreath of bones 1971
21 The cat watchers 1971
22 The faces of a bad girl 1971
23 The man with two heads 1972
24 Last train to Limbo 1972
25 The dead take tellers 1972
26 A bad dream of death 1973
27 The farm villains 1973
28 The grab operation 1973
29 The starfish affair 1974
30 Girl in the crime belt 1974
31 The shadows of the killer 1975
32 Hill fog 1975
33 The monstrous regiment 1975

34 The devil's edge 1975
35 The murder makers 1976
36 Return to Death Alley 1976
37 A fall out of thieves 1976
38 House of dead ones 1977
39 The frightened fisherman 1977
40 Mists of treason 1977
41 The Ducrow folly 1978
42 A drop of hot gold 1978
43 The guilty witnesses 1979
44 The death watch ladies 1980
45 Mayhem Madchen 1980
46 The reluctant agent 1988
JOHN MARSH AND LOHM SERIES:
1 Case of the death computer 1967
2 Case of the fear makers 1968
3 Thug executive 1969
4 The three masks of death 1970

CHANDLER, B.

RIM RUNNERS
1 The rim of space 1981
2 When the dream dies 1981
3 Bring back yesterday 1982
4 Beyond the galactic rim 1982

CHANDLER, R.

PHILIP MARLOWE SERIES:
1 The big sleep 1939
2 Farewell my lovely 1940
3 The high window 1942
4 Lady in the lake 1944
5 Little sister 1949
6 Simple art of murder 1950
Short stories, some of which feature Philip Marlowe
7 The long good-bye 1953
8 Playback 1958
9 Marlow takes on the syndicate
This is an abbreviated version published by the 'Daily Mail' of a 12,000 word story originally called 'The Pencil'. This story also appeared in the magazine 'Manhunt' under the title 'Wrong pigeon', and in Ellery Queen's Mystery Magazine as 'Philip Marlowe's last case'. It now appears in 'The smell of fear' 1965, again as 'The Pencil'. This volume also contains Marlowe stories from 'The simple art of murder'.
10 Poodle springs by Robert B. Parker 1990
A completion of Chandler's unfinished M.S. 'Perchance to dream' by Parker, Robert B. (1991) is a sequel to 'The big sleep'.

CHANDOS, D.
1 Village in the sun 1948
2 House in the sun 1950
N.F. Travel in Mexico

***

1 Abbie 1951
2 Abbie and Arthur 1961

CHAPMAN, E.
1 The Eddie Chapman story *told by*
Frank Owen
2 Free agent 1956
N.F. Autobiography

CHAPMAN, J.
1 The long weekend 1984
2 Regretting it 1987

CHAPMAN, R.
REX BANNER SERIES:
1 One jump ahead 1951
2 Crime on my hands 1952
3 Winter wears a shroud 1953
4 Murder for a million 1953
5 Behind the headlines 1955
6 Frozen stiff 1956

CHAPPELL, M.
1 A valley of lilacs 1971
2 Cressey 1973

CHARDONNE, J.
HOUSE OF BARNERY SERIES:
1 Wife of Jean Barnery 1955
2 Pauline 1956
3 Porcelain de Limoges
*3 has not yet been translated.
Originally in French, 'Destinees
sentimentales'.*

CHARLES, R.
SIMON LARREN SERIES:
1 Nothing to lose
2 One must survive
3 Dark vendetta
4 Mission of murder 1965
5 Arctic assignment 1966
6 The fourth shadow 1968
7 Assassins for peace 1968
8 Stamboul intrigue 1969
9 The big fish 1969
10 Strikefast 1969

CHARLIE'S ANGELS
1 Charlie's Angels
2 The killing kind
3 Angels on a string

4 Angels in chains
5 Angels on ice

CHARNOS, S. M.
ALLDERA:
1 Walk to the end of the world
2 Motherlines 1980
Science fiction

CHARQUES, D.
1 Time's harvest 1953
2 The returning heart
3 Between the twilights

CHARRIERE, H.
1 Papillon 1968
2 Banco 1973
*N.F. Autobiography. There has been
some controversy as to its
authenticity*

CHARTERIS, L.
1 X esquire
2 The white rider
SAINT SERIES:
1 Meet the tiger (The Saint meets the
tiger) 1928
2 Enter the Saint 1936
3 The last hero (The Saint closes the
case) 1936
4 Knight Templar (The avenging
Saint) 1936
5 Featuring the Saint 1936
6 Alias the Saint 1936
7 She was a lady (The Saint meets his
match) 1936
8 The holy terror (The Saint versus
Scotland Yard) 1936
9 Getaway (The Saint's getaway) 1936
10 Once more the Saint (The Saint and
Mr. Teal) 1936
11 The brighter buccaneer 1936
12 Misfortunes of Mr. Teal (The Saint
in London) 1936
13 Boodle (The Saint intervenes) 1936
14 The Saint goes on 1936
15 The Saint in New York 1936
16 Saint overboard 1936
17 The ace of knaves 1937
18 Thieves' picnic (The Saint bids
diamonds) 1937
19 Prelude for war (The Saint plays
with fire) 1938
20 Follow the Saint 1938
21 The happy highwayman 1939
22 The Saint in Miami 1941
23 The Saint goes west 1942
24 The Saint steps in 1944

25 The Saint on guard 1945
26 The Saint sees it through 1946
27 Call for the Saint 1948
28 Saint errant (Saint to the rescue) 1948
29 The Saint in Europe 1954
30 The Saint in the Spanish Main 1955
31 Saint around the world 1959
32 Thanks to the Saint 1961
33 Senor Saint 1961
34 Trust the Saint 1962
35 The Saint in the sun 1963
36 Vendetta for the Saint 1964
37 The Saint on TV 1968
38 The Saint returns 1969
39 The Saint and the fiction makers 1969
40 The Saint abroad 1969
41 The Saint in pursuit 1971
42 The Saint and the people importers 1971
From No. 36, the stories are adaptations of TV series revised by the author, but not originally written by him. Each contains two stories.
43 Saints alive 1974
Short stories previously appearing in magazines
44 Catch the Saint 1975
45 The Saint and the Habsburg necklace 1977
46 Send for the Saint 1978
47 The Saint in trouble 1978
48 The Saint and the Templar treasure 1979
49 Count on the Saint 1980
50 The fantastic Saint 1981

CHARYN, J.
ISAAC SIDEL
1 Marilyn the wild 1991
2 Blue eyes
3 The education of Patrick Silver
4 Secret Isaac
5 The good policeman 1991
2 to 4 are not yet published in the UK

CHASE, I.
1 Past imperfect
2 Free admission
3 The Carthaginian rose 1961
N.F. Autobiography. 3 is mainly travel over a number of years.

CHASE, J. H.
MARK GIRLAND:

1 This is for real 1965
2 You have yourself a deal 1960
3 Have this one on me 1967
4 The whiff of money 1969
MADDOX, INSURANCE INVESTIGATOR:
1 Shock treatment
2 The double shuffle
3 Tell it to the birds 1963
AL BARNEY:
1 An ear to the ground
2 You're dead without money
CORRIDON:
1 Mallory 1950
2 Why pick on me 1951
HELGA ROLFE:
1 An ace up my sleeve 1971
2 The joker in the pack 1975
3 I hold the four aces 1977

CHAUDHURI, N. C.
1 The autobiography of an unknown Indian 1951
2 A passage to England 1963
3 Thy hand, great Anarch 1987
N.F. Autobiography

CHEEK, M.
1 Pause between acts 1988
2 Parlour games 1989

CHEESEMAN, E.
1 Things worthwhile
2 Time well spent
N.F. Autobiography

CHEEVER, J.
1 The Wapshott chronicle 1962
2 The Wapshott scandal 1964
Two novels about an eccentric New England family

CHERRYH, C.J.
1 The dreamstone
2 The tree of swords and jewels
Paperback fantasy
CHANUR
1 Pride of Chanur
2 Chanur's venture
3 Chanur's homecoming
Paperback fantasy
MERCHANTER
1 Downbelow station
2 Cyteen
3 Merchanter's luck
4 Rim runners
5 Heavy time
Paperback fantasy

MORGAINE CHRONICLES:
1 Gate of Ivrel 1981
2 Well of Shuian
3 The fires of Azeroth
Paperback fantasy

CHESBRO, G. C.
MONGO MYSTERIES:
1 City of whispering stone 1979
2 An affair of sorcerers 1980
3 Shadow of a broken man 1981

CHESNEY, M.
A HOUSE FOR THE SEASON:
1 The miser of Mayfair 1987
2 Plain Jane 1987
3 The wicked godmother 1988
4 Rakes progress 1988
5 The adventuress 1989
6 Rainbird's revenge 1989
SCHOOL FOR MANNERS:
1 Refining Felicity 1989
2 Perfecting Fiona 1990
3 Enlightened Delilah 1990
4 Finessing Clarissa 1991
SIX SISTERS
1 Minerva 1983
2 The taming of Annabelle 1983
3 Deirdre and desire 1984
4 Daphne 1984
5 Diana the huntress 1985
6 Frederica in fashion 1986

CHESSMAN, C.
1 Cell 2455 death row 1956
2 Trial by ordeal
3 The face of justice
N.F. Autobiography

CHETWYND-HAYES, R.
CLAVERING GRANGE:
1 Tales of darkness 1981
2 Tales of the other side 1983
3 Ghosts from the mists of time 1985
4 The King's ghost 1985
5 Tales from the haunted house 1987
6 Tales from the hidden world 1988
*Supernatural stories, centred around
an old house*

CHEVALLIER, G.
1 Clochemerle 1950
2 Clochemerle-Babylon 1959
3 Clochemerle-les Bains 1964
*Trilogy of humorous novels on a small
French provincial town*

CHEYNEY, P.
LEMMY CAUTION SERIES:
1 This man is dangerous
2 Poison Ivy
3 Dames don't care
4 Can ladies kill
5 Don't get me wrong
6 You'd be surprised
7 Mister Caution - Mr. Callaghan
8 Your deal, my lovely
9 Never a dull moment
10 You can always duck
11 I'll say she does
12 G2 man at the yard
SLIM CALLAGHAN SERIES:
1 The urgent hangman
2 Dangerous curves
3 You can't keep the change
4 Mister Caution - Mister Callaghan
5 It couldn't matter less
6 Sorry you've been troubled
7 They never say when
8 Uneasy terms
SECRET SERVICE SERIES: (KELLS IS A
MAIN CHARACTER)
1 Dark duet
2 The stars are dark
3 The dark street
4 Sinister errand
5 Dark hero
6 Dark interlude
7 Dark Wanton
8 But ladies won't wait
JOHNY VALLON:
1 You can call it a day
2 Dark bahama

CHISHOLM, M.
MCALLISTER SERIES:
1 McAllister
2 McAllister rides
3 McAllister makes war
4 Kill McAllister
5 McAllister's fury
6 McAllister fights
7 McAllister strikes
8 McAllister runs wild
9 McAllister: the hard man
10 Death at noon
11 McAllister justice
12 The hangman rides tall
13 Hell for McAllister
14 McAllister: tough to kill
BLADE:
1 The Indian incident
2 The Tucson conspiracy
3 The Lareda assignment
4 The Pecos manhunt

5 The Colorado virgins
6 The Mexican proposition
7 The Arizona climax
8 The Nevada mustang
9 The Montana deadlock
10 The Cheyenne trap
11 The Navajo trail
Paperback westerns
MCALLISTER:
1 On the Comanche crossing
2 McAllister and the Spanish gold
3 McAllister never surrenders
4 McAllister and the Cheyenne death
5 McAllister: quarry
6 Diehard
7 Wolfbait
8 Firebrand
A new series in paperback

CHOTZINOFF, S.
1 A lost paradise
2 Days at the Mona

CHRISTIAN, F. H.
FRANK ANGEL:
1 Kill Angel 1973
2 Send Angel 1973
3 Find Angel 1975
4 Trap Angel 1975
5 Hang Angel 1975

See also **STRANGE, O.**

CHRISTIAN, J.
RICHARD DEUTSCH:
1 Five gates to Armageddon 1971
2 The Persian death trap 1976

CHRISTIE, A.
POIROT SERIES:
1 The mysterious affair at Styles 1920
2 The murder on the links 1923
3 Poirot investigates 1924
Short stories
4 The murder of Roger Ackroyd 1926
5 The big four 1927
6 The mystery of the blue train 1928
7 Peril at End House 1932
8 Lord Edgeware dies 1933 (Thirteen at dinner)
9 Murder on the Orient Express 1934 (Murder on the Calais coach)
10 ABC murders 1935
11 Three act tragedy 1935 (Murder in three acts)
12 Death in the clouds 1935 (Death in the air)
13 Murder in Mesopotamia 1936

14 Cards on the table 1936
15 Dumb witness 1937 (Poirot loses a client *or* Murder at Littlegreen House)
16 Death on the Nile 1937
17 Appointment with death 1938 (Deadman's mirror)
18 Murder in the mews 1938
Short stories
19 Hercule Poirot's Christmas 1939 (Murder for Christmas *or* Holiday for Murder)
20 Sad Cypress 1940
21 One two buckle my shoe 1940 (The patriotic murders)
22 Evil under the sun 1941
23 Five little pigs 1943
24 The hollow 1946 (Murder after hours)
25 Labours of Hercules 1947
Short stories
26 Taken at the flood 1948 (There is a tide)
27 Mrs. McGinty's dead 1952 (Blood will tell)
28 After the funeral 1953 (Funerals are fatal) *paperback title* Murder at the gallop
29 Hickory dickory dock 1955
30 Dead man's folly 1956
31 Cat among the pigeons 1959
32 The adventure of the Christmas pudding 1959
Short stories. Contains one Miss Marple story
33 The clocks 1963
34 Third girl 1966
35 Hallowe'en party 1969
36 Elephants can remember 1972
37 Poirot's early cases 1974
Short stories not previously collected
38 Curtain: Poirot's last case 1976
Short story collections published in U.S.A., only: 'Double sin' 1961, 'Regatta mystery' 1939, 'Three blind men' 1950, 'Underdog' 1952. These contain Poirot and Miss Marple stories, some not published in U.K.
MISS MARPLE SERIES:
1 Murder at the vicarage 1930
2 Body in the library 1942
3 The thirteen problems 1942 (The Tuesday club murders)
4 The moving finger 1943
5 A murder is announced 1950
6 They do it with mirrors 1952 (Murder with mirrors)
7 A pocket full of rye 1953

8 The 4.50 from Paddington 1957
(Murder she said *or* What Mrs.
Gillicuddy saw)
9 The mirror crack'd from side to side
1962
10 A Caribbean mystery 1964
11 At Bertram's hotel 1965
12 Nemesis 1971
This is a direct sequel to no. 10.
13 Sleeping murder 1976
14 Miss Marple's final cases 1979
*Short stories previously published in
U.S.A.*
TOMMY AND TUPPENCE SERIES:
1 The secret adversary 1922
2 Partners in crime 1929
Short stories
3 N or M 1941
4 By the pricking of my thumbs 1968
5 Postern of fate 1973
SUPT. BATTLE:
1 The secret of Chimneys 1925
2 Murder is easy 1939
3 Towards zero 1944 (Come and be
hanged)
*'The Seven Dials Mystery' is a
sequel to 'The Secret of Chimneys'.*
COL. RACE:
1 The man in the brown suit 1924
2 Sparkling cyanide 1945
*Mrs. Ariadne Oliver, detective
novelist, appears in several of the
novels, and is the detective in 'Pale
Horse', 1961.*
*There is a complete list, to 1967, of
all Christie novels and short stories
in 'Agatha Christie, mistress of
mystery', by G. C. Ramsey, 1968.*
MISS MARPLE SERIES:
*'The life and times of Miss Jane
Marple', by Anne Hart, is a fictional
biography (1986).*
POIROT:
Life and times of Hercule Poirot, by
A. Hart 1990

CHRISTIE, ANNE
1 First act 1983
2 My secret gorilla 1981
3 A time to weep 1987

CHRISTIE, K.
1 Smith 1954
2 Harold in London 1956

CHRISTIE, R.S.
THE BOOK OF SARAH:
1 Young experience

2 Gay application

CHUN CHAN YEH
QUIET ARE THE MOUNTAINS:
1 The mountain village 1988
2 The open fields 1988

CHURCH, R.
JOHN QUICKSHOTT SERIES:
1 The porch 1955
2 The stronghold 1959
3 The room within 1961
***
1 Over the bridge
2 The golden sovereign
3 The voyage home 1964
N.F. Autobiography

CHURCHILL, P.
1 Of their own choice 1952
2 Duel of wits 1953
3 The spirit in the cage 1954
N.F. War memoirs

CHURCHWARD, J.
1 Lost continent of Mu
2 The children of Mu 1959
N.F. Archaeology

CIRNI, J.
FRANK FONTANA:
1 The kiss off 1988
2 The come on 1989

CITRINE, W.M., 1ST BARON
1 Men and work 1965
2 Two careers 1967
N.F. Autobiography

CLANCY, TOM.
JACK RYAN:
1 The hunt for red October 1985
2 Patriot games 1987
3 The Cardinal of the Kremlin 1988
4 The sum of all fears 1991

CLAPTON, P.
TOY:
1 Toy 1968
2 Truffles for Toy 1971

CLARK, D.
CHIEF INSPECTOR MASTERS:
1 Nobody's perfect 1969
2 Death after evensong 1969
3 Deadly pattern 1970
4 Sweet poison 1970

5 Sick to death 1971
6 The miracle makers 1971
7 Premedicated murder 1975
8 Dread and water 1976
9 Table d'hote 1977
10 The gimmel flask 1977
11 The Libertines 1978
12 Heberden's seat 1979
13 Poacher's bag 1979
14 Golden rain 1980
15 Roast eggs 1981
16 The longest pleasure 1981
17 Shelf life 1981
18 Doone walk 1982
19 Vicious circle 1983
20 The Monday theory 1983
21 Bouquet garni 1984
22 Dead letter 1984
23 Performance 1985
24 Jewelled eye 1985
25 Storm centre 1986
26 The big grouse 1986
27 Plain sailing 1987

CLARK, W.
1 No. 10 1966
2 Special relationship 1968
*Political novels, the main characters
being a Prime Minister, Patrick Pyrton
and his Foreign Secretary, Holden
Britwell.*

CLARKE, A.
1 Twice round the black church 1965
2 A penny in the clouds 1967
N.F. Autobiography

CLARKE, A.C.
1 2001: a space odyssey 1968
2 2010: odyssey 2 1982
3 2061: odyssey 3 1988
RAMA:
1 Rendezvous with Rama 1973
2 Rama II (with Lee Gentry) 1989
THE FALL OF NIGHT:
1 Against the fall of night 1953
2 Beyond the fall of night, by G. Benford
1991

CLARKE, R.
SUMMER WINE CHRONICLES:
1 Gala week 1986
2 The moonbather 1987
Based on the TV series

CLAVELL, J.
ASIAN SAGA:
1 Sho-gun 1975

2 Tai-pan 1966
3 King Rat 1962
4 Noble House 1981
*Not direct sequels but linked by subject
and location*

CLAYTON, C.G.
THE BLAKENEY PAPERS:
1 Daughter of the Revolution 1984
2 Such mighty rage 1985
3 Bordeaux red 1986
*A series following Baroness Orczy,
about Lady Blakeney, wife of the
Scarlet Pimpernel*

CLERY, D.
THEODORE J. CASH:
1 Shameful 1970
2 The rattler 1972

CLEARY, D. and MAHER, F.
BREAKENRIDGE SERIES:
1 The hook 1980
2 Sahara strike 1981
3 Break-out 1981

CLEARY, J.
SCOBIE MALONE SERIES:
1 The High Commissioner 1970
2 Helga's web 1971
3 Ransom 1972
4 Dragons at the party 1987
5 Now and then, Amen 1988
6 Babylon south 1989
7 Murder song 1990
8 Pride's harvest 1991

CLEEVE, B.
SEAN RYAN:
1 Dark blood dark terror 1966
2 Judas goat 1966

CLEEVES, A.
GEORGE PALMER-JONES:
1 A bird in the hand 1986
2 Come death and high water 1987
3 Murder in paradise 1988
4 A prey to murder 1989
*Detective stories with a background of
birdwatching*
INSPECTOR RAMSAY:
1 A lesson in dying 1990
2 Murder in my back yard 1991

CLEMENT, D. and LA FRENAIS, I.
PORRIDGE:
1 Porridge 1976
2 Another stretch of porridge 1977

3 A further stir of porridge 1977
4 Going straight 1978
(Based on the TV series)
THE LIKELY LADS:
1 The likely lads 1974
2 Whatever happened to the likely lads 1975

CLEMENTS, E.A.
1 Let him die
2 Bright intervals

CLEMENTS, E.H.
ALISTER WOODHEAD SERIES:
1 The other island 1956
2 Back in daylight 1956
3 Uncommon cold 1958
4 High tension 1959
5 Honey for the marshall 1960
6 A note of enchantments 1961

CLEIFE, P.
MARTYN FINCH:
1 The pinchbeck masterpiece 1971
2 The slick and the dead 1972

CLEVELEY, H.
1 The gang-smasher
2 Gang-smasher again
★★★
1 Justin Kelly 1961
2 Garland of valour 1963
The Justin of 2 is the grandson of Justin Kelly.

CLEWES, D.
GRANT FAMILY:
1 Missing from home 1975
2 Testing year 1977

CLEWS, R.
1 Young Jethro 1975
2 King's bounty 1976
3 The drums of war 1978

CLIFFORD, J.L.
1 Young Samuel Johnson 1955
2 Dictionary Johnson 1979
N.F. Biography

CLIFFORD, R.
1 Just here doctor 1976
2 Not there, doctor 1978
3 What next, doctor? 1979
4 Oh dear, doctor 1980
5 Look out, doctor 1983
6 Surely not, doctor 1985

7 There you are, doctor 1986
8 On holiday again, doctor? 1987
N.F. Humorous autobiography

CLINTON-BADDELEY, V.C.
DR. DAVIE SERIES:
1 Death's bright dart 1966
2 My foe outstretch'd beneath the tree 1967
3 Only a matter of time 1968
4 No case for the police 1970
5 To study a long silence 1972

CLIVE, W.
RIFLEMAN JOSEPH DANDO SERIES:
1 Dando on Delhi Ridge 1971
2 Dando and the Summer Palace 1972
3 The tunes that they play 1973
4 Dando and the mad Emperor 1974
5 Blood of an Englishman 1975
Novels about the Victorian army

CLOETE, S.
THE VANDER BERG FAMILY:
1 The turning wheels 1937
2 Watch for the dawn 1939
3 The hill of doves 1941
4 The mask 1958
A series of novels on the early Boer settlements
★★★
1 A Victorian son (1897-1922) 1972
2 The gambler (1920-1939) 1973
N.F. Autobiography
1 The Thousand and one nights of Jean Macaque 1967
2 More nights of Jean Macaque 1975

CLOSS, H.
THE ABLIGENSIAN CRUSADE:
1 High are the mountains 1959
2 And sombre the valleys 1960
3 The silent tarn 1963

COATES, J. *see* AUSTEN, J.

COBB, B.
CHEVIOT BURMANN SERIES:
1 No alibi 1936
2 The poisoner's mistake 1937
3 Fatal dose 1938
4 Quickly dead 1938
5 Like a guilty thing 1938
6 The fatal holiday 1938
7 Inspector Burmann's busiest day 1939
8 Death defies the doctor 1939
9 Inspector Burmann's blackout 1941

COFFMAN, V.
1 Veronique 1978
2 Marsanne 1979
Two parts of a trilogy set in Napoleonic Europe

***

1 The Gaynor women 1981
2 Dinah Faire 1982
A family saga set in Virginia
LOMBARD FAMILY:
1 Pacific cavalcade 1986
2 The Lombard cavalcade 1986
3 The Lombard heiress 1986
Publication dates are for UK editions

COGGIN,J.
DUBLIN TRILOGY:
1 McIlhenney 1989
2 Leaving 1989
3 Northside 1990

COHEN, A.
THE GALLANTS:
1 Solal of the Solals
2 The Nailcruncher

COHEN, ANTHEA
NURSE CARMICHAEL:
1 Angel without mercy 1981
2 Angel of vengeance 1982
3 Angel of death 1983
4 Fallen angel 1984
5 Guardian angel 1985
6 Hell's angel 1986
7 Ministering angel 1987
8 Destroying angel 1988
9 Angel dust 1990
10 Recording angel 1991
Thrillers with a hospital setting

COLE, A.
OMARAN SAGA:
1 A place among the fallen 1986
2 Throne of fools 1987
3 The King of light and shadows 1988
4 The gods in anger 1988
STAR REQUIEM:
1 Mother of storms 1989
2 Thief of dreams 1989
3 Warlord of heaven 1990
4 Labyrinth of worlds 1990
Paperback fantasy

COLE, H.
SIR JOHN HAWKWOOD SERIES:
1 Hawkwood 1967
2 Hawkwood in Paris 1969

3 Hawkwood and the towers of Pisa 1973
Novels about an English mercenary captain during and after the battles of Crecy and Poitiers

COLE, HARRY
1 Policeman's prelude
2 Policeman's patch
3 Policeman's lot
4 Policeman's progress
5 Policeman's patrol
6 Policeman's story
7 Policeman's gazette 1987
N.F. Autobiography of a Police Constable. Paperback though some titles have been published in hardback and large print format in 1987-8

COLE, J. A.
1 Just back from Germany 1938
2 My host, Michael 1955
N.F. Travel. Although 20 years apart, these views of Germany are to be considered as a sequence.

COLEGATE, I.
ORLANDO KING SERIES:
1 Orlando King 1969
2 Orlando at the brazen threshold 1971
3 Agatha 1973
In no. 3 Orlando is dead and his daughter is the central character.

COLEMAN, L.
BEULAH LAND:
1 Beulah land 1973
2 Look away, Beulah Land 1977
3 The legacy of Beulah Land 1980
A trilogy set in the American Deep South

COLES, M.
HAMBLEDON SERIES:
1 Drink to yesterday
2 Pray silence (Toast to tomorrow)
3 They tell no tales
4 Without lawful authority
5 Green hazard
6 Fifth man
7 Brother for Hugh (With intent to deceive)
8 Among those absent
9 Not negotiable
10 Let the tiger die
11 Diamonds to Amsterdam
12 Dangerous by nature
13 Now or never
14 Night train to Paris

15 Alias Uncle Hugo
16 Knife for a juggler
17 Not for export
18 Man in the green hat 1955
19 Basle Express 1956
20 The three beans 1957
21 Death of an ambassador 1958
22 No entry 1958
23 Crime in concrete 1960
24 Search for a sultan 1961
25 The house at Pluck's gutter 1962
1 and 2 are direct sequels

COLES, P. J. C.
CHAMPION
1 Champion's folly 1984
2 Champion's chariot 1985
3 Champion's calamity 1987
Humorous novels

COLLENETTE, E. J.
1 90 feet to the sun 1984
2 The Gemini plot 1985
3 The secret of the Kara Sea 1986
4 The Monday mutiny 1987
5 A capful of glory 1988
6 Sea wolf hunter 1989
Sea stories about submarines

COLLINS, J.
1 Chances 1981
2 Lucky 1985
3 Lady boss 1990

COLLINS, M.
DAN FORTUNE SERIES:
1 Act of fear 1969
2 The brass rainbow 1970
3 Night of the toads 1971
4 Walk a black wind 1973
5 Shadow of a tiger 1974
6 The silent scream 1975
7 Blue death 1975
8 Blood red dream 1976
9 The slasher 1981

COLLINS, M. A.
MALLORY:
1 The baby-blue ripoff 1984
2 Cure for death 1985
NATHAN HELLER:
1 True detective
2 True crime
3 The million-dollar wound 1989
4 Neon mirage 1989

COLLINS, W.
1 Challenge 1990

56

2 New world 1991

COLSON, J.
1 The Goose and I 1963
2 The Goose up the creek 1964
3 Goose at sea 1965

COMMON, J.
1 Kiddar's luck 1951
2 The ampersand 1954

CONAN, see HOWARD, R. E.

CONDON, R.
PRIZZI:
1 Prizzi's honour 1984
2 Prizzi's family 1986
3 Prizzi's glory 1988

CONEY, M.
1 The celestial steam locomotive 1984
2 Gods of the greataway 1986
Science fiction

CONLON, K.
1 A forgotten season 1980
2 Consequences 1981

CONNELL, E.
1 Mrs. Bridge 1967
2 Mr. Bridge 1969

CONQUEST, J.
1 Desert love
2 The Hawk of Egypt

CONRAN, S.
1 Lace 1982
2 Lace II 1985

CONSTANDUROS, M. and D.
1 Here comes the Huggetts 1947
2 Vote for Huggett 1949
3 The Huggetts abroad 1952

CONSTANTINE, K. C.
MARIO BALZIC:
1 The Rocksburg railroad murders
2 The man who liked to look at himself 1986
3 The blank page
4 A fix like this
5 The man who liked to grow tomatoes 1984
6 Always a body to trade 1985
7 Upon some midnight's clear 1986
8 Joey's case 1988
9 Sunshine enemies 1990

CONSTANTINE, S.
WRAETHTHU:
1 The enchantments of flesh and spirit 1987
2 The bewitchments of love and hate 1988
3 The fulfilments of fate and desire 1989
Fantasies

CONWAY, A. *and* F.
1 Enchanted islands
2 Return to the island
N.F. Travel

CONWAY, P.
INSPECTOR NEWTON:
1 Victims of circumstance 1977
2 30 days to live 1979
3 Nut case 1980
4 Needle track 1981
5 Dead drunk 1982
6 Cryptic clue 1984

COOK, BOB
MICHAEL WYMAN:
1 Disorderly elements 1986
2 Questions of identity 1987

COOK, D.
1 Walter 1978
2 Winter doves 1979
Two novels about a mentally handicapped boy

COOK, H.
CHRONICLES OF AN AGE OF DARKNESS:
1 The wizards and the warriors 1987
2 The wordsmiths and the warguild 1987
3 The women and the warlords 1988
4 The walrus and the warwolf 1988
5 The wicked and the witless 1989
6 The wishstone and the wonderworkers 1990
7 The Wazir and the witch 1990
Fantasies

COOK, T. H.
1 Sacrificial ground 1988
2 Flesh and blood 1989
3 Streets of fire 1990
4 Night secrets 1991

COOKE, C.
1 The winged assassin
2 Realm of the gods
Paperback fantasy

COOKE, D. C.
PETER ROURKE:
1 c/o American Embassy 1969
2 The 14th agent 1969
3 Sleep with nightmares 1969

COOKE, G. W.
PETER MITCHELL SERIES:
1 Death can wait 1957
2 Death takes a dive 1962
3 Death is the end 1965

COOKSON, C.
BILL BAILEY:
1 Bill Bailey 1986
2 Bill Bailey's lot 1987
3 Bill Bailey's daughter 1988
HAMILTON:
1 Hamilton 1983
2 Goodbye Hamilton 1984
3 Harold 1985
MARY ANN SHAUGHNESSY:
1 A grand man 1954
2 The Lord and Mary Ann 1956
3 The devil and Mary Ann 1958
4 Love and Mary Ann 1961
5 Life and Mary Ann 1962
6 Marriage and Mary Ann 1964
7 Mary Ann's angels 1965
8 Mary Ann and Bill 1967
   'Fanny McBride', 1959, is not in series but re-introduces some minor characters.
THE MALLEN FAMILY TRILOGY:
1 The Mallen streak 1973
2 The Mallen girl 1973
3 The Mallen litter 1974
TILLY TROTTER:
1 Tilly Trotter 1980
2 Tilly Trotter wed 1981
3 Tilly Trotter widowed 1982

COONEY, M.
THE QUEEN'S INVESTIGATOR:
1 Doomsday England 1967
2 Ten days to oblivion 1968

COONTS, S.
JAKE GRAFTON:
1 Flight of the intruder 1987
2 Final flight 1989
3 The minotaur 1990
4 Under seige 1990
Aviation thrillers

COOPER, C.
MATT SAVAGE SERIES:
1 Blackmail is murder 1966

2 Dame in distress 1967
3 What's funny about murder? 1968
4 You'll die laughing 1968
5 Catch and squeeze 1969
6 Who killed Honey Bee? 1970

COOPER, LADY D.
1 The rainbow comes and goes 1957
2 The light of common day 1959
3 Trumpets from the steep 1960
N.F. Autobiography. Reprinted in one volume 1979

COOPER, DIANA
1 Animal hotel 1979
2 Up to scratch 1981
3 Mere folly 1982
N.F. Adventures with animals

COOPER, E.
1 The Expendables 1975
2 The Rings of Tantalus 1977
Science fiction

COOPER, L.
DET. CHIEF INSPECTOR CORBY:
1 Tea on Sunday 1973
2 Unusual behaviour 1986

COOPER, LOUISE
INDIGO:
1 Nemesis
2 Inferno
3 Infanta
4 Nocturne
5 Troika
6 Avatar
Paperback fantasy
TIME MASTER TRILOGY:
1 The initiate 1986
2 The outcast 1986
3 The master 1987
Paperback fantasies

COOPER, N.
WILLOW KING:
1 Festering lilies 1990
2 Poison flowers 1991
Detective stories featuring a Civil Servant. The author also writes under her real name, Daphne Wright.

COOPER, W.
1 Scenes from provincial life 1950
2 Scenes from married life 1961
3 Scenes from metropolitan life 1982
4 Scenes from later life 1983

COPPER, B.
MIKE FARADAY:
1 The dark mirror 1965
2 Night frost 1966
3 No flowers for the general 1967
4 Scratch on the dark 1967
5 Die now, live later 1967
6 Don't bleed on me 1968
7 The marble orchard 1969
8 Dead file 1970
9 No letters from the grave 1971
10 Big chill 1972
11 Strong-arm 1972
12 A great year for dying 1973
13 Shockwave 1973
14 The breaking point 1974
15 A voice from the dead 1974
16 Feedback 1974
17 Ricochet 1974
18 The high wall 1975
19 Impact 1975
20 A good place to die 1976
21 The lonely place 1976
22 Crack in the sidewalk 1976
23 Tight corner 1976
24 The year of the dragon 1977
25 Death squad 1977
26 Murder one 1977
27 A quiet room in Hell 1978
28 The big ripoff 1978
29 The Caligari complex 1979
30 Flip-side 1980
31 The long rest 1981
32 The empty silence 1981
33 Dark entry 1981
34 Hang loose 1982
35 Shoot-out 1982
36 The far horizon 1982
37 Trigger-man 1983
38 Pressure point 1983
39 The narrow corner 1983
40 Hard contract 1984
41 The hook 1984
42 You only die once 1984
43 Tuxedo Park 1985
44 The far side of fear 1985
45 Snow job 1985
46 Jet-lag 1986
47 Blood on the moon 1986
48 Heavy iron 1987
49 Turn down an empty glass 1987
50 Bad scene 1987
51 House-dick 1988
52 Print-out 1988
SOLAR PONS:
1 The dossier of Solar Pons
2 The further adventures of Solar Pons
3 The Secret files of Solar Pons

4 The exploits of Solar Pons
5 Some uncollected cases of Solar Pons
6 The recollections of Solar Pons
7 The further recollections of Solar Pons

CORDELL, A.
1 This proud and savage land 1988
2 Rape of the fair country 1966
3 The hosts of Rebecca 1968
4 Song of the earth 1969
5 The fire people 1972
6 This sweet and bitter earth 1977
7 Land of my fathers 1983
Two separate trilogies, covering the years of Industrial Revolution in Wales, 1826-1913 No. 1 is a prequel to the series

CORDER, E.
1 Slave ship 1969
2 Slave 1971

COREY, P.
1 Three miles square
2 The road returns
3 County seat

CORK, B.
INSPECTOR ANGUS STRAUN:
1 Dead ball 1988
2 Unnatural hazard 1989
3 Laid dead 1990
4 Winter rules 1991
Detective stories set around the golf course

CORNWELL, B.
RICHARD SHARPE:
1 Sharpe's rifles (Galicia 1809) 1988
2 Sharpe's eagle (Talavera 1809) 1980
3 Sharpe's gold (Almeida 1810) 1981
4 Sharpe's company (Badajoz 1812) 1982
5 Sharpe's sword (Salamanca 1812) 1983
6 Sharpe's enemy (Defence of Portugal 1812) 1984
7 Sharpe's honour (Vitoria 1813) 1985
8 Sharpe's regiment (1813) 1986
9 Sharpe's siege (1814) 1987
10 Sharpe's revenge (1814) 1989
11 Sharpe's Waterloo (1815) 1990
Novels about the British Army in the Peninsular War

CORRIGAN, M.
CORRIGAN AND TUCKER SERIES:
1 Bullets and brown eyes 1948
2 Sinner takes all 1949
3 Lovely lady 1949

4 Wayward blonde 1950
5 Golden angel 1950
6 Shanghai Jezebel 1951
7 Madam Sly 1951
8 Baby face 1952
9 Lady of China St. 1952
10 All brides are beautiful 1952
11 Sweet and deadly 1953
12 The naked lady 1954
13 Madam and Eve 1955
14 The big squeeze 1955
15 Big boys don't cry
16 Sydney for sin 1956
17 The cruel lady 1957
18 Dumb as they come 1957
19 Menace in Siam 1958
20 Honolulu Snatch 1958
21 Singapore downbeat 1959
22 Sin of Hong Kong 1960
23 Lady from Tokyo 1960
24 Girl from Moscow 1961
25 Danger's green eyes 1961
26 Riddle of double island 1962
27 Why do women 1963
28 Riddle of the Spanish circus 1964

CORY, D.
LINDA GRAY SERIES:
1 Begin, murderer 1951
2 This is Jezebel 1952
3 Lady lost 1953

JOHNNY FEDORA SERIES:
1 Secret ministry 1951
2 This traitor death 1952
3 Dead man falling 1953
4 Intrigue 1954
5 Height of day 1955
6 High requiem 1955
7 Johnny goes north 1956
8 Johnny goes east 1959
9 Johnny goes west 1959
10 Johnny goes south 1959
11 The head 1960
12 Undertow 1961 (Johnny goes under)
13 Hammerhead 1962
(*re-issued as* Shockwave)
14 Feramontov 1966
15 Timelock 1967
16 Sunburst 1971
The last five titles form 'The Feramontov quintet'.

M. PILGRIM:
1 Pilgrim at the gate 1958
2 Pilgrim on the island 1961
DEE:
1 Stranglehold 1962
2 The name of the game 1964

COSGRAVE, P.
COLONEL CHEYNEY
1 Cheyney's law 1977
2 The three Colonels 1979
3 Adventure of state 1984

COST, M.
1 The hour awaits
2 Invitation from Minerva

COURTENAY, B.
1 The power of one 1989
2 Tandia 1991

COURTNEY, E.
KIT HEMSWORTHY:
1 The price of loving 1987
2 Over the bridge 1988

COUSINS, E. G.
STORY OF LARRY GRAIL:
1 Untimely frost 1953
2 To comfort the Signora 1950
3 Moab is my washpot 1952
Not published in this order. Minor characters recur in many of this author's novels. Captain Mofatt appears in 2 and in 'Come like a storm', Brigadier Worriall in 2 and in 'Any kind of danger'.

COWARD, N.
1 Present indicative 1937
2 Future indefinite 1954
N.F. Autobiography

COWPER, R.
BIRD OF KINSHIP SAGA:
1 Piper at the gates of dawn 1976
2 The road to Corlay 1978
3 A dream of Kinship 1981
4 A tapestry of time 1982
Fantasy

COX, J.
1 Her father's sins 1987
2 Let loose the tigers 1988

1 Outcast 1990
2 Alley urchin 1991

COXE, G. H.
KENT MURDOCH SERIES:
1 The camera clue 1937
2 The frightened woman 1939 (Four frightened women)
3 The lady is afraid 1940
4 Murder is for the asking 1940

5 The Jade Venus 1946
6 The fifth key 1950
7 The hollow needle 1951
8 Eye witness 1953
9 The widow had a gun 1954
10 Lady killer 1955
11 The crimson clue 1955
12 Focus on murder 1956
13 Murder on their minds 1958
14 The big gamble 1960
15 The last commandment 1961
16 The hidden key 1964
17 The reluctant heiress 1965
18 With intent to kill 1966
19 The ring of truth 1967
20 An easy way to go 1968

CRADDOCK, M.
1 A north country maid 1965
2 Return to Rainton 1968
N.F. Autobiography

CRADOCK, F.
THE LORMES OF CASTLE RISING:
1 The Lormes of Castle Rising 1975
2 Shadows over Castle Rising 1977
3 War comes to Castle Rising 1977
4 Wind of change over Castle Rising 1978
5 Uneasy peace at Castle Rising 1979
6 Thunder over Castle Rising 1980
7 Gathering clouds at Castle Rising 1982
8 Fateful years at Castle Rising 1982
9 The defence of Castle Rising 1984
10 The loneliness of Castle Rising 1986

CRADOCK, P.
1 Gateway to remembrance
2 The eternal echo

CRAGOE, E.
1 Buttercups and Daisy 1974
2 Cowslips and clover 1978
3 Yorkshire relish 1979
4 Sweet nothings 1980
5 The untidy gardener 1982
N.F. The first three are about the author's country childhood, the last two about the creation of a Welsh garden.

CRAIG, D.
ROY RICKMAN TRILOGY:
1 The alias man 1969
2 Message ends 1969
3 Contact lost 1970
A trilogy of thrillers, about the immediate future, following the withdrawal of the U.S.A. from Europe.

SHEILA ROATH:
1 Young men may die 1970
2 A walk by night 1971
PETER GALE:
1 The Albion case 1975
2 Faith hope and death 1976

CRAIS, R.
ELVIS COLE:
1 The monkey's raincoat 1988
2 Stalking the angel 1990

CRANE, F.
PAT ABBOTT SERIES:
1 The turquoise shop 1943
2 The golden box 1944
3 The yellow violet 1944
4 The pink umbrella 1944
5 The applegreen cat 1945
6 The amethyst spectacles 1946
7 The indigo necklace 1946
8 The shocking pink hat 1948
9 The cinnamon murder 1949
10 Murder on the purple water 1949
11 Black cypress 1950
12 Flying red horse 1951
13 The daffodil blonde 1951
14 The polkadot murder 1952
15 Death in the blue hour 1952
16 13 white tulips 1953
17 Murder in bright red 1954
18 The coral princess murders 1955
19 Death in lilac time 1955
20 Horror on the Ruby X 1956
21 The ultra-violet window 1957
22 The grey stranger 1958
23 The buttercup case 1958
24 Death-wish green 1960
25 Amber eyes 1962
26 Body beneath a mandarin tree 1965

CRANE, T.
1 Tomorrow, Jerusalem 1989
2 Green and pleasant land 1991

CRAWFORD, R.
SALISBURY AND SHEARER SERIES:
1 Cockleburr 1969
2 Kiss the boss goodbye 1970
3 The Badger's daughter 1971

CRAWLEY, A.
SULEIMAN THE MAGNIFICENT:
1 The bride of Suleiman 1981
2 The shadow of God 1982
3 The house of war 1984

CREASEY, J., (Ashe, G., Deane, N.,

Halliday, M., Marric, J. J., Morton, A., York, J., pseuds.)
   This author, as well as writing under his own name, has written many books under the above pseudonyms. Since these are now disclosed as being by John Creasey on title pages they are collected here under the real name.
THE TOFF SERIES:
1 Introducing the Toff 1938
2 The Toff steps out 1939
3 The Toff goes on 1939
4 The Toff breaks in 1940
5 Here comes the Toff 1940
6 Salute the Toff 1941
7 The Toff proceeds 1941
8 The Toff is back 1942
9 The Toff goes to market 1942
10 Accuse the Toff 1943
11 The Toff among the millions 1943
12 The Toff and the great illusion 1944
13 The Toff and the curate 1944
14 Feathers for the Toff 1945
15 The Toff and the lady 1946
16 Hammer the Toff 1947
17 The Toff on ice (Poison for the Toff)
18 The Toff in town 1948
19 The Toff takes a share 1948
20 The Toff and old Harry 1949
21 The Toff on board 1949
22 Kill the Toff 1950
23 Fool the Toff 1950
24 The Toff goes gay 1951 (A mask for the Toff)
25 Knife for the Toff 1951
26 Hunt the Toff 1952
27 Call the Toff 1953
28 The Toff down under 1953
29 The Toff at Butlins 1954
30 The Toff at the fair 1954
31 A six for the Toff 1955
32 The Toff and the deep blue sea 1955
33 Make up for the Toff 1956
34 The Toff in New York 1956
35 The Toff on fire 1956
36 Model for the Toff 1957
37 The Toff and the stolen tresses 1957
38 The Toff on the farm 1958
39 The Toff and the runaway bride 1958
40 Double for the Toff 1959
41 The Toff and the kidnapped child 1959
42 A rocket for the Toff 1960
43 Follow the Toff 1961
44 The Toff and the Teds 1961 (The Toff and the toughs)
45 Leave it to the Toff 1962
46 A doll for the Toff 1964
47 The Toff and the spider 1965

25 Death of a racehorse 1959
26 The case of the innocent victims 1959
27 Murder on the line 1960
28 The scene of the crime 1960
29 Death in cold print 1961
30 Policeman's dread 1962
31 Hang the little man 1963
32 Look three ways at murder 1964
33 Murder, London-Australia 1965
34 Murder, London-South Africa 1966
35 The Executioners 1967
36 So young to burn 1968
37 Murder, London-Miami 1969
38 A part for a policeman 1970
39 Alibi? 1971
40 Splinter of glass 1972
41 The theft of Magna Carta 1973
42 The extortioners 1974
43 A sharp rise in crime 1978

As **G. ASHE,** *pseud.*
PATRICK DAWLISH SERIES:
1 Speaker 1939
2 Death on demand 1939
3 Terror by day 1940
4 Secret murder 1940
5 'Ware danger 1941
6 Murder most foul 1941
7 There goes death 1941
8 Death in high places 1941
9 Death in flames 1943
10 Two men missing 1943
11 Rogues rampant 1944
12 Death on the move 1945
13 Invitation to adventure 1946
14 Here is danger 1946
15 Give me murder 1947
16 Murder too late 1947
17 Engagement with death 1947
18 Dark mystery 1948
19 A puzzle in pearls 1949
20 Kill or be killed 1949
21 The dark circle 1951
22 Murder with mushrooms 1950
23 Death in diamonds 1952
24 Missing or dead 1952
25 Death in a hurry 1952
26 Sleepy death 1953
27 The long search 1953
28 Death in the trees 1954
29 Double for death 1954
30 The kidnapped child 1955
31 Day of fear 1956
32 Wait for death 1957
33 Come home to death 1958
34 Elope to death 1959
35 Don't let him kill 1960
36 The crime haters 1961

37 Rogue's ransom 1961
38 Death from below 1963
39 The big call 1964
40 A promise of diamonds 1965
41 A taste of treasure 1965
42 A clutch of coppers 1967
43 A shadow of death 1968
44 A scream of murder 1969
45 A nest of traitors 1970
46 A rabble of rebels 1971
47 A life for a death 1973
48 A herald of doom 1974
49 A blast of trumpets 1975
50 A plague of demons 1976
   *From no. 36 this series is called 'The
   crime haters', though Patrick Dawlish
   is still the leader.*

As **N. DEANE,** *pseud.*
BRUCE MURDOCH SERIES:
1 Secret errand 1939
2 Dangerous journey 1939
3 Unknown mission 1940
4 The withered man 1940
5 I am the withered man 1941
6 Where is the withered man? 1942
   4, 5 and 6 are sequels within the series.

LIBERATOR SERIES:
1 Return to adventure 1943
2 Gateway to escape 1944
3 Come home to crime 1945

As **M. HALLIDAY,** *pseud.*
FANE BROTHERS SERIES:
1 Take the body 1952
2 Lame dog murder 1952
3 Murder in the stars 1953
4 Man on the run 1953

DR. CELLINI SERIES:
1 Cunning as a fox 1965
2 Wicked as the devil 1966
3 Sly as a serpent 1967
4 Cruel as a cat 1968
5 Too good to be true 1969
6 A period of evil 1970
7 As lonely as the damned 1971
8 As empty as hate 1972
9 As merry as hell 1973
10 This man did I kill 1974
11 The man who was not himself 1976
   *The M. Halliday pseudonym was not
   used in the U.S.A., where the Halliday
   books were published under the name
   of J. York, K. Hunt or P. Manton. The
   J. York pseudonym has also been used
   for British reprint.*

As **J. J. MARRIC,** *pseud.*

GIDEON SERIES:
1 Gideon's day 1955
2 Gideon's week 1956
3 Gideon's night 1957
4 Gideon's month 1958
5 Gideon's staff 1959
6 Gideon's risk 1960
7 Gideon's fire 1961
8 Gideon's march 1962
9 Gideon's ride 1963
10 Gideon's vote 1964
11 Gideon's lot 1965
12 Gideon's badge 1966
13 Gideon's wrath 1967
14 Gideon's river 1968
15 Gideon's power 1969
16 Gideon's sport 1970
17 Gideon's art 1971
18 Gideon's men 1972
19 Gideon's press 1973
20 Gideon's fog 1974
21 Gideon's drive 1976
22 Gideon's law 1981 *by* W. V. Butler
23 Gideon's raid 1986 *by* W. V. Butler

As **A. MORTON,** *pseud.*

THE BARON SERIES:
1 Meet the Baron 1937
2 The Baron returns 1937
3 The Baron at bay 1938
4 The Baron again 1938
5 The Baron at large 1939
6 Alias the Baron 1939
7 Versus the Baron 1939
8 Call for the Baron 1940
9 The Baron comes back 1943
10 A case for the Baron 1945
11 Reward for the Baron 1945
12 Career for the Baron 1946
13 The Baron and the beggar 1947
14 A rope for the Baron 1948
15 Blame the Baron 1949
16 Books for the Baron 1949
17 Cry for the Baron 1950
18 Trap the Baron 1950
19 Shadow the Baron 1951
20 Attack the Baron 1951
21 Warn the Baron 1952
22 The Baron goes east 1953
23 Danger for the Baron 1953
24 The Baron in France 1953
25 The Baron goes fast 1954
26 Nest egg for the Baron 1954 (Deaf,
   dumb and blonde)
27 Help from the Baron 1955
28 Hide the Baron 1956
29 Frame the Baron 1957

30 Red eye for the Baron 1958 (Blood red)
31 Black for the Baron 1959 (If anything
   happened to Hester)
32 Salute to the Baron 1960
33 A branch for the Baron 1961
34 Bad for the Baron 1962 (The Baron and
   the stolen legacy)
35 A sword for the Baron 1963 (The Baron
   and the Mogul Sword)
36 The Baron on board 1964
37 The Baron and the Chinese puzzle 1965
38 Sport for the Baron 1966
39 Affair for the Baron 1967
40 The Baron and the missing Old Masters
   1968
41 The Baron and the unfinished portrait
   1969
42 Last laugh for the Baron 1970
43 The Baron goes a-buying 1971
44 The Baron and the arrogant artist 1972
45 Burgle the Baron 1973
46 The Baron - King maker 1975
47 Love for the Baron 1979
   *Earlier American editions used 'Blue
   Mask' instead of 'The Baron'. The
   Baron himself becomes better known as
   John Mannering, antique dealer, in
   later volumes in the series.*

As **J. YORK,** *pseud.*

SUPERINTENDENT FOLLY SERIES:
1 Foul play suspected 1942
2 Crime with many voices 1945
3 No crime more cruel 1945
4 Mystery motive 1947
5 First a murder 1947
   *These were originally under the
   Halliday pseud., and did not contain
   the character Supt. Folly. They have
   been revised and republished as by J.
   York after 1970.*
1 Find the body 1946
2 Runaway to murder 1947
3 Close the door on murder 1947
4 Let's kill Uncle Lionel 1949
5 The gallows are waiting 1949
   *This was the original Folly series,
   published as by J. York both in the
   U.K. and U.S.A.*

CREATON, D.
1 The beasts of my field 1976
2 Beasts and babies 1978
3 The beasts go West 1979
   N.F. Autobiography of a farmer

CREMER, J.
1 I, Jan Cremer 1965

2 Jan Cremer 1967

CRISP, J. H.
SOE SERIES:
1 Dragon's spoor 1979
2 Final act 1979

CRISP, N. J.
INSPECTOR KENYON SERIES:
1 The Gotland deal
2 The odd job man
3 The London deal

CRISP, W.
WESTFALL:
1 Spytrap 1984
2 Vengeance is thine 1986

CRISPIN, E.
GERVASE FEN:
1 The case of the gilded fly 1944
2 Holy disorders 1945
3 The moving toyshop 1946
4 Swan song 1947
5 Love lies bleeding 1948
6 Buried for pleasure 1949
7 Frequent hearses 1950
8 The long divorce 1951
9 Beware of the trains 1953
10 Glimpses of the moon 1977
11 Fen country 1979

CROFTE-COOKE, R.
THE SENSUAL LIFE:
1 The gardens of Camelot 1957
2 The altar in the loft 1959
3 The drums of morning 1960
4 The glittering pastures 1962
5 The numbers came 1963
6 The last of spring 1964
7 The purple streak 1966
8 The wild hills 1967
9 The happy highways 1967
10 The sound of revelry 1969
11 The moon in my pocket
12 The licentious soldiery
13 The blood red island
14 The gorgeous East
15 The dogs of peace
16 The life for me
17 The verdict of you all
18 The tangerine house
19 The quest for Quixote
20 The wintry sea
21 The ghost of June 1968
22 The caves of Hercules 1974
23 The long way home 1975
24 The green, green grass 1977

SUPPLEMENTARY:
25 The world is young
26 The man in Europe street
27 The circus has no home
N.F. Autobiography
This is the author's own preferred
arrangement, but the volumes were not
published in this order.

CROFTS, F. W.
INSPECTOR FRENCH SERIES:
1 Inspector French's greatest case 1924
2 Inspector French and the Cheyne mystery 1926
3 Inspector French and the Starvel tragedy 1927
4 The sea mystery 1928
5 The box office murders 1929
6 Sir John Magill's last journey 1930
7 Mystery in the Channel 1931
8 Sudden death 1932
9 Death on the way 1932
10 The Hog's Back mystery 1933
11 12.30 from Croydon 1934
12 Crime at Guildford 1935 (Crime at Noxnes)
13 Mystery on Southampton water 1935
14 The loss of the *Jane Vosper* 1936
15 Man overboard 1936
16 Found floating 1937
17 The end of Andrew Harrison 1938 (Futile alibi)
18 Antidote to venom 1938
19 Fatal venture 1939
20 Golden ashes 1940
21 James Tarrant adventurer 1941
22 The losing game 1941
23 Fear comes to Chalfont 1942
24 The affair at little Wokeham 1943 (Double tragedy)
25 Enemy unseen 1945
26 Death of a train 1946
27 Murderers make mistakes 1947
28 Silence for the murderer 1948
29 French strikes oil 1952
30 Many a slip 1955
31 The mystery of the sleeping car express 1956
32 Anything to declare? 1957

CRONIN, A. J.
1 The green years 1944
2 Shannon's way 1948
LAWRENCE CARROLL:
1 A song of sixpence 1967
2 A pocketful of rye 1969
The story of a young doctor

CRONIN, M.

MR. PILGRIM SERIES:
1 Paid in full 1956
2 Sweet water 1958
3 Begin with a gun 1959
4 Curtain call 1960

JAMES HELLIER SERIES:
1 Man alive 1968
2 Dead loss 1970
3 Emergency exit 1970
4 The long memory 1971
5 Escape at sunrise 1972
6 Nobody needs a corpse 1972
7 The big C 1973

SAM HARRIS SERIES:
1 A proper carve up 1970
2 A black leather case 1971
3 The con game 1972
4 The big tickle 1974
5 Strictly private business 1975
6 The final instalment 1976
7 A pair of knaves 1977
8 Unfinished business 1978
9 Epitaph for a lady 1980

CROSBY, J.

HORATIO CASSIDY:
1 An affair of strangers 1975
2 The company of friends 1977
3 Party of the year 1980
4 Men at arms 1984
5 Take no prisoners 1986

CROSS, A.

KATE FANSLER:
1 In the last analysis 1966
2 The James Joyce murder 1967
3 Poetic justice 1970
4 The Theban mysteries 1972
5 The question of Max 1976
6 A death in the faculty 1981
7 Sweet death, kind death 1984
8 No word from Winifred 1987
9 A trap for fools 1990

CROSS, M.

DAPHNE WRAY SERIES:
1 The shadow of the four
2 The grip of the four
3 The hand of the four
4 The way of the four
5 The mark of the four
6 The four strike home
7 Surprise for the four
8 The four make holiday
9 The four get going
10 Challenge to the four
11 The four at bay

12 It couldn't be murder
13 Find the professor
14 Murder in the pool
15 How was it done?
16 The mystery of Gruden's Gap
17 The green circle
18 Murder as arranged
19 Murder in the air
20 Murder in black
21 The mystery of Joan Marryat
22 Secret of the Grange
23 Strange affair at Greylands
24 Other than natural causes
25 Missing from his home
26 On the night of the 14th
27 Who killed Henry Wickenston?
28 Jaws of Darkness
29 The black spider
30 The circle of freedom
31 Murder will speak
32 The strange case of Pamela Wilson
33 In the dead of night
34 The best laid schemes
35 When thieves fall out 1956
36 The mystery of the corded box 1956
37 Desperate steps 1957
38 When danger threatens 1957
39 Over thin ice 1958
40 Foul deeds will rise 1958
41 Not long to live 1959
42 Third time unlucky 1959
43 Wanted for questioning 1960
44 Once too often 1960
45 Once upon a time 1961
46 Perilous hazard 1961

CROW, D.

1 The first summer 1967
2 The crimson petal 1969
Projected as a quartet of novels tracing the life of Simon Ire

CROWLEY, E.

O'HARA FAMILY:
1 Dreams of other days 1984
2 Waves upon the shore 1989

CROZIER, B.

1 The warrior 1973
2 The statesmen 1974
N.F. Biography of Charles de Gaulle

CRUISE, T. E.

WINGS OF GOLD
1 Wings of gold 1989
2 Skies of gold 1990
3 Pilots of gold 1991
Aviation stories

CUDDON, J. A.
GOTOBED TRILOGY:
1 Gotobed dawn
2 Gotobedlam 1963
3 John Gotobed alone 1963
Novels about a young English painter

CULLEN, S.
1 A noose of light
2 The Sultan's turret
Paperback fantasy

CULPAN, M.
INSPECTOR HOUGHTON SERIES:
1 A nice place to die 1965
2 The Minister of Injustice 1966
3 In a deadly vein 1967
4 The Vasiliko affair 1968
5 Bloody success 1969

CUMBERLAND, M.
SATURNIN DAX SERIES:
1 Someone must die
2 Questionable shape
3 Quislings over Paris
4 The knife will fall
5 Steps in the dark
6 Not expected to live
7 A lovely corpse
8 Hearsed in death
9 And worms have eaten them (Hate finds a way)
10 And then came fear
11 Policeman's nightmare
12 On a danger list
13 Confetti can be red
14 Man who covered mirrors
15 One foot in the grave
16 Booked for death
17 Fade out the stars
18 Which of us is safe
19 Etched in violence
20 The frightened brides
21 Unto death utterly
22 The charge is murder 1956
23 Lying at death's door 1956
24 Far better dead 1957
25 Hate for sale 1958
26 Out of this world 1958
27 Murmurs in the Rue Morgue
28 Remains to be seen 1960
29 There must be victims 1961
30 Attention! Saturnin Dax! 1962
31 Postscript to a death 1963
32 The dice were loaded 1965
33 No sentiment in murder 1966

CUNNINGHAM, E. V.
MASAO MASUTO:
1 The case of the one-penny orange 1978
2 The case of the Russian diplomat 1979
3 The case of the poisoned eclairs 1980
4 The case of the sliding pool 1982
5 The case of the kidnapped angel 1983
6 The case of the murdered Mackenzie 1985

CURRY, G.
SADDLER
1 A dirty way to die
2 Colorado crossing
3 Hot as a pistol
4 Wild wild women
Paperback Westerns

CURWOOD, J. O.
1 Kazan, the wolf-dog 1953
2 The son of Kazan
3 The courage of Marge O'Doon
★★★
1 Wolf hunters
2 Gold hunters
★★★
1 The black hunter
2 The pains of Abraham

CURZON, C.
DET. SUPT. MIKE YEADINGS
1 I give you five days 1983
2 Masks and faces 1984
3 The Trojan hearse 1985
4 Cat's cradle 1991

CUSSLER, C.
DIRK PITT:
1 Pacific vortex 1983
2 Raise the Titanic 1980
3 Night probe 1981
4 Deep six 1984
5 Cyclops 1986
6 Treasure 1988
7 Dragon 1990

DACRE, R.
SAM HOSKINS:
1 The blood runs hot 1987
2 Scream blue murder 1988
3 Money with menaces 1989

DAHL, R.
1 Boy 1984
2 Going solo 1986
N.F. Autobiography

DAICHES, D.
1 Two worlds 1965
2 A third world 1971
N.F. Autobiography

DAILEY, J.
CALDERS:
1 This Calder range 1983
2 The Calder sky 1982
3 Stands a Calder man 1983
4 Calder born, Calder bred 1984

DAISH, E.
1 The shop on Coppins Bridge 1985
2 The family on Coppins Bridge 1986
3 Ebbtide at Coppins Bridge 1988
*Emma'a War, 1989, contains some of
the characters.*

DALEY, B.
ALACRITY FITZHUGH AND HOBART
FLOYT
1 Requiem for a ruler of worlds
2 Jinx on a terran inheritance
3 Fall of the white ship Avatar
CORAMONDE:
1 The doomfarers of Coramonde
2 The starfollowers of Coramonde
Paperback fantasies

DALTON, H., 1st BARON
1 Call back yesterday 1953
2 The fateful years 1957
3 High tide and after 1962
N.F. Autobiography

DALY, E.
HENRY GAMADGE SERIES:
1 Unexpected night 1940
2 Murders in vol. 2 1941
3 House without the door 1942
4 Nothing can rescue me 1945
5 Evidence of things seen 1946
6 Arrow pointing nowhere 1946
7 Book of the dead 1946
8 Deadly nightshade 1948
9 Any shape or form 1949
10 Somewhere in the house 1949
11 Wrong way down 1950
12 Night walk 1950
13 The book of the lion 1951
14 And dangerous to know 1952
15 Death and letters 1953
16 The book of the crime 1954

DANE, E.
SCHROEDER FAMILY:
1 Shadows in the fire 1976
2 A lion by the mane 1977

3 The Vaaldorp diamond 1978
Set in the Transvaal

DANIEL, G. (DILWYN REES, *pseud.*)
SIR RICHARD CHERRINGTON
1 The Cambridge murders 1948
2 Welcome death 1954

DANIEL, J.
DESERT TRILOGY:
1 The siege 1979
2 Dispatch rider 1980

DANIELS, N., see **BRAND, M.**

DANIELSON, P.
1 Children of the lion 1985
2 The shepherd kings 1985
3 Vengeance of the lion 1985
4 The lion in Egypt 1985

DANIKEN, E. VON
1 Chariots of the Gods 1969
2 Return to the stars 1971
3 The gold of the Gods 1973
4 The search of Ancient Gods 1974
5 Miracles of Gods 1975
6 Signs of the Gods 1980
*N.F. A theory that Earth was once
visited by beings from another planet,
and traces can be found, in mythology
and archaeology.*

DANINOS, P.
MAJOR THOMPSON:
1 Major Thompson lives in Paris
(The notebooks of Major Thompson
1955)
2 Major Thompson and I 1957
*Later issued in one volume under the
title of 'Major Thompson'.*

DANISCHENSKY, M.
1 White Russian - red face 1970
2 Out of my mind 1972
N.F. Autobiography

DANKS, D.
GEORGINA POWERS:
1 The pizza house crash 1990
2 Better off dead 1991

DARBY, C.
FALCON SERIES;
1 Falcon for a witch 1975
2 Game for a Falcon 1976
3 Falcon's claw 1986
4 Falcon to the lure 1981

5 Fortune for a Falcon 1976
6 Season of the Falcon 1976
7 A pride of Falcons 1977
8 The Falcon tree 1977
9 The Falcon and the moon 1977
10 Falcon rising 1978
11 Falcon sunset 1978
12 Seed of the Falcons 1981
ROWAN SERIES:
1 Rowan Garth 1982
2 Rowan for a Queen 1983
3 A scent of Rowan 1983
4 A circle of Rowan 1983
5 The Rowan maid 1984
6 Song of the Rowan 1984
SABRE:
1 Sabre 1984
2 Sabres child 1985
3 The silken sabre 1985
4 House of Sabre 1986
5 A breed of Sabres 1987
6 Morning of a Sabre 1987
7 Fruit of the Sabre 1988
8 Gentle Sabre 1988
BOSTOCKS:
1 Cobweb across the moon 1980
2 Sing me a moon 1980
3 Moon in Pisces 1980
4 Whisper down the moon 1978
5 Frost on the moon 1979
6 Flaunting moon 1979

DARBY, L.
EYE OF TIME TRILOGY;
1 Crystal and steel 1988
2 Bloodshed 1988
3 Phoenixfire
Paperback fantasy

DARBYSHIRE, S.
MELBURY TRILOGY:
1 Journey to Melbury 1950
2 The years at Melbury 1952
3 High Noon at Melbury 1954

DARK, E.
THE MANNION FAMILY:
1 The timeless land 1941
2 Storm of time 1948
3 No barrier 1953
Novels on the history of Australia

DARKE, J.
THE WITCHES:
1 The prisoner
2 The trials
3 The torture
4 No escape

5 The meeting
6 The killing
Paperback horror stories

DARRELL, E.
SHERIDAN FAMILY:
1 At the going down of the sun 1984
2 And in the morning 1988
About a family in World War II

DAVENAT, C.
1 Deborah: the springtime of love 1973
2 Deborah: the many faces of love 1974
3 Deborah: the siege of Paris 1975
Historical romances of the Elizabethan period.

DAVEY, J.
ABROSE USHER SERIES:
1 The undoubted deed 1956
2 The naked villany 1958
3 A touch of stage fright 1960
4 A killing in hats 1965

DAVEY, N.
1 The pilgrim of a smile
2 The penultimate adventure

DAVID, J.
1 A square of sky 1965
2 A touch of earth 1966
3 A part of the main 1969
A semi-autobiographical trilogy

DAVIES, A.
1 A very peculiar practice 1987
2 The new frontier 1988

DAVIES, F.
1 Death of a hitman 1982
2 Snow in Venice 1983

DAVIES, R.
CORNISH TRILOGY:
1 Rebel angels 1981
2 What's bred in the bone 1985
3 The lyre of Orpheus 1988
EISENGRIN TRILOGY:
1 The fifth business 1971
2 The Manticore 1973
3 World of wonders 1977
Published as one volume called 'The Deptford Trilogy' in 1983
SALTERTON TRILOGY:
1 Tempest-tost
2 Leaven of malice
3 Mixture of frailties

DAVIES, T.
1 One winter of the Holy Spirit NYP
2 Fire in the bay 1989
3 The dragon's war NYP
4 Black sunlight 1987
A chronicle of 20th C. Wales

DAVIS, D. S.
JIMMIE JARVIS SERIES:
1 Death of an old sinner 1958
2 A gentleman called 1959
3 Old sinners never die 1960
JULIE HAYES SERIES
1 A death in the life 1980
2 Scarlet night 1981
3 Lullaby of murder 1984

DAVIS, G.
ROAG'S CRIME SYNDICATE SERIES:
1 Roag's syndicate 1960
2 Toledano 1962
3 Friday before bank holiday 1964
4 Crime in Threadneedle St. 1968
5 The killer grew tired 1971
6 Death of a fire-raiser 1973
THE SERGEANT:
1 Death train
2 Hell harbour
3 Bloody bush
4 The liberation of Paris
5 Doom river
6 Slaughter city
7 Bullet bridge
8 Bloody Bastogne
9 Hammerhead
Paperback war stories

DAVIS, J.
THE MACLEOD'S OF VIRGINA:
1 Cloud on the land 1954
2 Bridle the wind 1955
3 Eagle on the sun 1957
Novels about the development of the Missouri country and the Shenandoah valley in the 1920's.

DAVIS, J. G.
1 Hold my hand, I'm dying 1980
2 Sieze the reckless wind 1984

DAVIS, L.
FALCO:
1 The silver pigs 1989
2 Shadows in bronze 1990
3 Venus in copper 1991
Detective stories set in Ancient Rome.

DAVIS, M.T.
GLASGOW TRILOGY:
1 The breadmakers 1971
2 A baby might be crying 1973
3 A sort of peace
***
1 The prince and the tobacco lords 1975
2 The roots of bondage 1976
3 Scorpion in the fire 1977
Set in 18th century Scotland.
***
1 Rag woman, rich woman 1987
2 Daughters and mothers 1988
3 Wounds of war 1989

DAVIS. O. H.
ARDENCESTER SERIES:
1 Soft goods 1923
2 Smite the rock 1924
3 Home brewed 1932
4 This great city 1976
A series of novels about Birmingham.

DAVISON, G.
STEPHEN FLETCHER SERIES:
1 The spy who swopped shoes 1966
2 Nest of spies 1968
3 The chessboard spies 1969

DAWES, F. V.
COLE FAMILY:
1 A family album 1982
2 Inheritance 1984

DAWSON, D.
1 Vet in the vale
2 Vet in the paddock
N.F. Autobiography of a vet.

DAYUS, K.
1 Her people 1982
2 Where there's life 1985
3 All my days 1988
N.F. Working class life in Birmingham in the early 1990's

DEAL, P.
1 Nurse! nurse! nurse!
2 Forward staff nurse
3 Nurse at Butlins
4 Surgery nurse
5 Village nurse 1960
6 Factory nurse 1962
N.F. Autobiography

DEAN, S.
DON CADEE SERIES:

1 Merchant of murder 1954
2 The frightened fingers 1955
3 The scent of fear 1956
4 Marked down for murder 1958
5 Murder on delivery 1958
6 Dishonour among thieves 1959

DEAN, S. F. X.
NEIL KELLY:
1 By frequent anguish 1982
2 Such pretty toys 1983
3 It can't be my grave 1983
4 Ceremony of innocence 1985
5 Death and the mad heroine 1986

DEANE, N., *pseud., see* CREASEY, J.

DE BANKE, C.
1 Hand over hand
2 Bright weft
3 American plaid
N.F. Autobiography

DE BOISSIERE, R.
1 Crown jewel 1982
2 Rum and coca-cola 1984
Novels set in contemporary Trinidad

DE BORN, E.
THE DE KAILERN FAMILY:
1 Schloss Fielding (Fielding Castle)
2 The house in Vienna
3 The flat in Paris
4 A question of age
JIMMY CHESTER TRILOGY:
1 The disintegrator 1969
2 The fight for Pelignano 1970
3 The end of the struggle 1972
The young son of an American film star, and his effect on people around him.

DE CHAIR, S.
1 The golden carpet 1945
2 Buried pleasures 1986
N.F. Autobiography of a soldier/diplomat.

DE SILVA, C.
1 Winds of Sinhala 1982
2 Founts of Sinhala 1984
3 The fires of Sinhala 1986
4 The last Sinhala lions 1987

DEFOE, D.
1 Robinson Crusoe
2 The return of Robinson Crusoe 1958 by Henry Treece

FOE by J. M. Coetzee (1987) same character and theme.

DEFORGES, R.
THE BLUE BICYCLE:
1 The blue bicycle 1985
2 101 Avenue Henri-Martin 1986
3 The devil is still laughing 1987

DE HAAN, T.
BRYCHMACHRYE:
1 A mirror for princes 1988
2 The child of good fortune 1989

DEIGHTON, B.
FELICITY TRAVERS:
1 A little learning 1987
2 Good intentions 1988
Thrillers about a polytechnic lecturer.

DEIGHTON, L.
1 The Ipcress file 1962
2 Horse under water 1963
3 Funeral in Berlin 1964
4 Billion dollar brain 1966
5 An expensive place to die 1969
BERNARD SAMSON:
1 Berlin game 1983
2 Mexico set 1984
3 London match 1985
Published in one volume in 1987 as 'Game, set and Match'. 'Winter: a Berlin family' (1987) is a pendant to the first trilogy, with some of the same characters.
4 Spy hook 1988
5 Spy line 1989
6 Spy sinker 1990
4-6 comprise a second trilogy, 'Hook, line and sinker'.

DELACORTA
GORODISH AND ALBA:
1 Nana 1984
2 Diva 1984
3 Luna 1985
4 Lola, 1986
5 Vida 1986

DELAFIELD, E. M.
1 Diary of a provincial lady 1930
2 A provincial lady goes further 1932
3 A provincial lady in America 1934
4 Provincial lady in war-time 1940
Reprinted in 1 vol. 1985

DELANEY, J.
1 No starch in my coat 1970

2 Smile at me doctor 1972
3 Pass the happy pills 1978
4 It's my nerves, Doctor 1980
N.F. A doctor's life in a mental hospital.

DELANY, S. R.
1 Fall of the towers 1971
2 Out of the dead city 1966
3 The towers of Toron
NEVERYON:
1 Tales of Neveryon
2 Neveryone
3 Flight from Neveryon
4 Return to Neveryon

DE LA ROCHE, M.
WHITEOAKS SERIES:
1 The building of Jalna 1944
2 Morning in Jalna 1960
3 Mary Wakefield 1949
4 Young Renny 1935
5 Whiteoak heritage 1940
6 Whiteoak brothers 1953
7 Jalna 1927
8 Whiteoaks 1929
9 Finch's fortune 1931
10 Master of Jalna 1933
11 Whiteoak harvest 1936
12 Wakefield's course 1941
13 Return to Jalna 1946
14 Renny's daughter 1937
15 Variable winds at Jalna 1954
16 Centenary at Jalna 1958
This is the correct order of reading, not of publication.
***
1 Beside a Norman tower
2 The very house

DELDERFIELD, R. F.
1 The dreaming suburb
2 The avenue goes to war
Republished 1964, in one volume as 'The avenue story'.
***
1 There was a fair maid dwelling 1960
2 The unjust skies 1962
The story of an adolscent love affair and a later reunion.
***
1 Napoleon in love 1964
2 The march of the 26 1966
3 The retreat from Moscow 1967
4 Imperial sunset 1969
N.F. Episodes in the life of Napoleon I.

THE CRADDOCKS OF SHALLOWFORD:
1 The horseman riding by 1966
2 The green gauntlet 1968
Paperback edition is in three volumes - 'Long summer's day', 'Post of honour', 'Green gauntlet'.
THE SWANN SAGA:
1 God is an Englishman (1857-1866) 1970
2 Theirs was the kingdom (1878-1897) 1971
3 Give us this day (1900-1914) 1973
***
1 For my own amusement 1968
2 Overture for beginners 1971
N.F. Autobiography

DELISLE, F.
1 Francoise: in love with love 1963
2 Friendship's Odyssey: in love with life 1946 *(rev. ed. 1962)*
N.F. Autobiography. 2 is mainly the story of her life with Havelock Ellis and complementary to Ellis's 'My Life'.

DELMAN, D.
JACOB & HELEN HOROWITZ:
1 Sudden death 1973
2 One man's murder 1975
3 The nice murderers 1977
4 Death of a nymph 1986
5 Dead faces laughing 1987
6 The liar's league 1989
7 Last gambit 1990

DELVING, M.
EDISON AND CANNON SERIES:
1 Smiling, the boy fell dead 1969
2 The devil finds work 1970
3 Die like a man 1970
4 A shadow of himself 1972
5 A wave of fatalities 1976
6 No sign of life 1978
7 The China expert 1979
The two main characters - New York booksellers - do not both appear in all the series.

DE MANIO, J.
1 To auntie, with love 1968
2 Life begins too early 1970
N.F. Autobiography

DE MILLE, A.
1 Dance to the piper 1952
2 And promenade home 1958
N.F. Autobiography

DEMING, R.
MANNY MOON:
1 The gallows in my garden 1953
2 Tweak the devil's nose 1953
3 Whistle past the graveyard 1954

DENHAM, B.
DEREK THYRDE:
1 The man who lost his shadow 1985
2 Two Thyrdes 1986
3 Foxhunt 1988

DENIS, C.
1 King's wench 1977
2 King's bastard 1977
About the mistresses of Charles II.

DENISON, M.
1 Overture and beginners 1973
2 Double act 1985
N.F. Autobiography of the actor and his wife.

DENNIS, I.
THE PRINCE OF STARS IN THE CAVERN OF TIME
1 Baghdad
2 The Prince of Stars
Paperback science fiction.

DENNIS, P.
AUNTIE MAME:
1 Auntie Mame
2 Around the world with Auntie Mame

DENNIS, R.C.
READERS, PSYCHIC DETECTIVE:
1 Sweat of fear 1973
2 Conversations with a corpse 1974

DENTINGER, J.
JOCELYN O'ROURKE:
1 Murder on cue 1985
2 First hit of the season 1986
3 Death mask 1988

DENVER, L.
CHEYENNE JONES:
1 The gun code of Cheyenne Jones 1969
2 Cheyenne swings a wide loop 1970
3 Three slugs for Cheyenne 1971
4 Cheyenne pays in lead 1972
5 Lone trail for Cheyenne 1973
6 Cheyenne Jones maverick marshall 1977
7 Cheyenne's sixgun justice 1980
8 Cheyenne's trial to perdition 1982
9 Cheyenne's two-gun shootout 1983

10 Cheyenne at Dull Knife Pass 1984

DE POLNAY, P.
1 Death and tomorrow 1942
2 Fools of choice 1955
3 A door ajar 1959
4 Rough childhood 1960
N.F. Autobiography

1 Out of the square 1950
2 Mario 1961
Mario and Giovanna are minor characters in 1, but principal in 2.

DERLETH, A. W.
SOLAR PONS SERIES:
1 A Praed St. dossier
2 Mr. Fairlie's final journey
3 The adventure of the unique Dickensians
4 The adventures of Solar Pons
5 The reminiscences of Solar Pons
6 The casebook of Solar Pons
7 The chronicles of Solar Pons
Many of the Derleth books have been issued in limited editions. None have been published in U.K., except the Solar Pons series.
See also **COPPER, B.**

DERWENT, L.
1 A breath of Border air 1975
2 Another breath of Border air 1977
3 A Border bairn 1979
4 God bless the borders 1981
5 Lady of the manse 1983
6 A mouse in the Manse 1985
N.F. Autobiography set in the Scottish Borders.

DE SELINCOURT, H.
CONSTANCE HOWARD SERIES:
1 A daughter of the morning
2 Realms of day
3 Evening light
GAUVINER SERIES:
1 The cricket match 1924
2 Game of the season 1952
3 Gauviner takes to bowls

DESMOND, H.
ALAN FRASER:
1 Death walks in scarlet
2 Suicide pact

DESSAU, J.
ELIZABETH I;
1 The red-haired brat 1978

2 Absolute Elizabeth 1978
3 Fantastical, marvellous Queen 1979

DEUTSCH, D.
THE EQUALISER:
1 The equaliser
2 To even the odds
3 Blood and wine
Paperbacks, based on the TV series.

DEUTSCHER, I.
1 The prophet armed 1879-1921
2 The prophet unarmed 1921-1929
3 The prophet outcast 1929-1940
N.F. Biography of Leon Trotsky.

DEVERAUX, J.
CHANDLER TWINS:
1 Twin of ice
2 Twin of fire
Paperback
JAMES RIVER TRILOGY:
1 Counterfeit lady
2 Lost lady
3 River lady
Paperback
MONTGOMERY FAMILY:
1 The velvet promise
2 Highland velvet
3 Velvet angel
4 Velvet song
5 The temptress
6 The princess
7 The raider 1988
Paperback. 7 is in hardback.

DIVINE, R.
FLESHTRADERS:
1 Master of the Black River
2 Black River affair
3 Black River breed
Paperback slave saga

DEWES, S.
1 A Suffolk childhood
2 Essex schooldays
3 When all the world was young
N.F. Autobiography

DEWEY, T. B.
SINGER BATTS SERIES:
1 Every bets a sure thing
2 Mourning after
3 Handle with fear
PRIVATE EYE 'MAC' SERIES:
1 The mean street 1955
2 Prey for me 1955
3 The brave bad girls 1957

4 The chased and the unchaste 1960
5 You've got him cold 1960
6 The girls who wasn't there 1960
7 How hard to kill 1963
8 A sad song for singing 1964
9 Don't cry for long 1964
10 Portrait of a dead heiress 1965
11 Every bet's a sure thing 1965
12 Deadline 1966
13 Death and taxes 1967
14 Death turns right 1969
15 The Taurus trip 1972
PETE SCHOFIELD SERIES:
1 Go to sleep, Jeannie 1960
2 I.O.U. murder 1961
3 Mexican slay-ride 1961
4 Go, Honeylou! 1962
5 Too hot for Hawaii 1963
6 The girl with the sweet plump knees 1963
7 Only on Tuesdays 1963
8 The girl in the punchbowl 1965
9 Nude in Nevada 1966

DEWHURST, E.
HELEN JOHNSON:
1 Whoever I am 1981
2 Playing safe 1985
NEIL CARTER:
1 Trio in three flats 1982
2 There was a little girl 1984
3 Nice little business 1990

DEXTER, C.
DET. CHIEF INSPECTOR MORSE:
1 Last bus to Woodstock 1975
2 Last seen wearing 1976
3 The silent world of Nicholas Quinn 1977
4 Service of all the dead 1979
5 The dead of Jericho 1981
6 The riddle of the third mile 1983
7 The secret of Annexe 3 1986
8 The wench is dead 1989
9 The jewel that was ours 1991

DEXTER, S.
THE WINTER KING'S WAR:
1 The ring of Allaire 1987
2 The sword of Calandra 1987
3 The mountains of Channadran 1987
Fantasy

DEXTER, T. and MAKINS, C.
JACK STENTON SERIES:
1 Test kill 1978
2 Deadly putter 1979

DIBBA, E.
1 Chaff in the wind 1984
2 Fafa 1989

DICK, K.
ROBERT STAIREY SERIES:
1 By the lake
2 Young man
3 Told on a summer night

DICKASON, C
1 The dragon riders 1988
2 The years of the tiger 1989

DICKENS, C.
1 Great expectations
   'Magwitch' by M. Noonan covers the adventures of Magwitch in Australia. 1982
   'Estalla: her expectations', by S. Roe is based on the character of Miss Havisham. 1982
   'Estella', by Alanna Knight (1986) follows 'Great Expectations'.
   'God bless us every one' by A. A. Dalrymple is a sequel to 'A Christmas Carol'.
1 Pickwick papers
2 Pickwick abroad *by G. W. M. Reynolds*
3 Mr. Pickwick's second time on earth, *by C. G. Harper.*
   'The mystery of Edwin Drood'. This unfinished story has been 'completed' by several authors. There is quite a literature on Edwin Drood.
   The disappearance of Edwin Drood, by P. Rowland (1991) also concerns Sherlock Holmes.
   'The Gay Dombeys', and 'The Veneerings', by Sir H. Johnston, are sequels to 'Dombey and Son', and 'Our mutual friend' respectively.

DICKENS, M.
1 One pair of hands 1939
2 One pair of feet 1942
3 My turn to make the tea 1951
   N.F. Autobiography.

DICKINSON, M.
ABBEYFORD TRILOGY:
1 Sarah 1981
2 Adeline 1981
3 Carrie 1982

DICKINSON, P.
DETECTIVE SUPERINTENDENT PIBBLE SERIES:

1 Skin deep 1968
2 A pride of heroes 1969
3 The seals 1970
4 Sleep and his brother 1971
5 The lizard in the cup 1972
6 One foot in the grave 1979
ALTERNATIVE ROYAL FAMILY:
1 King and joker 1976
2 Skeleton-in-waiting 1989

DICKSON, C., *pseud.* (JOHN DICKSON CARR)
SIR HENRY MERIVALE SERIES:
1 The bowstring murders 1933
2 The Plague Court murders 1935
3 The White Priory Murders 1935
4 The Red widow murders 1935
5 The unicorn murders 1936
6 The magic lantern murders 1936
7 The ten teacups 1937
8 The Judas window 1938
9 Death in five boxes 1938
10 The reader is warned 1939
11 Murder in the submarine zone 1940 (Nine and death makes ten)
12 The department of queer complaints 1940
13 And so to murder 1941
14 Seeing is believing 1942
15 The glided man 1942
16 She died a lady 1943
17 He wouldn't kill patience 1944
18 Lord of the scorcerers 1946
19 My late wives 1947
20 Skeleton in the clock 1949
21 Graveyard to let 1950
22 Night at the mocking window 1951
23 Tangier 1952 (Behind the crimson blind)
24 Cavelier's cup 1954
   See also under **CARR, J. D.**

DICKSON, G.
SUPERINTENDENT MARLOW:
1 Knight's gambit
2 The seven screens
DORSAI:
1 Tactics of mistake
2 Dorsai
3 Soldier, ask not
4 The spirit of Dorsai
5 Lost Dorsai
   Paperback science fiction.

DICKSON, G. R.
SEA PEOPLE:
1 Home from the shore

2 The Space swimmers
Paperback science fiction.

DICKSON, L.
1 The ante-room
2 The house of words
N.F. Autobiography

DIDELOT, F.
COMMANDER BIGNON:
1 The tenth leper 1961
2 Death on the Champs Elysees 1965

DILLON, A.
1 Seasons 1990
2 Another time, another season 1991

DILLON, E.
PROFESSOR DALY:
1 Death at Crane's Court
2 Death in the quadrangle
***
1 Across the bitter sea 1974
2 Blood relation 1978
A family saga set in Ireland in the early part of the century.
***
1 Wild geese 1981
2 Citizen Burke 1984
Novels set in present-day Ireland

DIMENT, A.
PHILIP MACALPINE SERIES:
1 The dolly dolly spy 1966
2 The great spy race 1967
3 The bang bang birds 1968

DINES, M.
JOHNNY MANNING:
1 Operation - deadline 1961
2 Operation - to kill a man 1968
3 Operation - kill or be killed 1969

DISCH, T. M. *editor*
1 The ruins of Earth 1973
2 Bad moon rising 1974
3 The new improved sun 1976
Science fiction

DIXON, R.
1 The Messiah 1974
2 Christ on trial 1972
Novels on the life of Jesus. This is order of reading, not of publication.

DJEBAR, A.
ALGERIAN QUARTET:

1 Fantasia, 1989
2 A sister to Scheherezade 1989

DOBLIN, A.
NOVEMBER 1918: A GERMAN REVOLUTION:
1 A people betrayed 1986
2 The troops return 1986
3 Karl and Rosa 1986
Originally published 1948-50.

DOBYNS, S.
CHARLIE BRADSHAW:
1 Saratoga swimmer
2 Saratoga headhunter
3 Saratoga longshot 1988
4 Saratoga snapper 1988
5 Saratoga bestiary 1989
6 Saratoga hexameter 1990

DODGE, D.
AT COLBY SERIES:
1 The long escape
2 Plunder of the sun
3 The red tassel
JAMES WHITNEY SERIES:
1 A drug on the market
2 Shear the black sheep 1949
3 Bullets for the bridegroom 1950
4 Death and taxes
***
1 How lost was my weekend
2 How green was my father 1951
3 High life in the Andes
N.F. Autobiography
JOHN ABRAHAM LINCOLN:
1 Hatchet man 1970
2 Troubleshooter 1972

DOELL, E. W.
1 Doctor against witch doctor
2 Hospital in the bush
3 Mission doctor sees the wind of change 1960
N.F. Autobiography

DOHERTY, L.
1 The good lion 1958
2 The good husband 1959

DOHERTY, P. C.
1 The prince of Drakulya 1986
2 The Lord Count Drakulya 1986

DOMINIC, R. B. (E. LATHEN)
CONGRESSMAN BEN SAFFORD:
1 Murder in high places 1970
2 Murder out of court 1971

3 Epitaph for a lobbyist 1974
4 Murder out of commission 1976
5 Attending physician 1980
6 A flaw in the system 1983

DONALDSON, S. R.
MORDANT'S NEED:
1 A mirror for her dreams 1986
2 A man rides through 1988
THE CHRONICLES OF THOMAS
COVENANT, UNBELIEVER
1 Lord Foul's bare 1980
2 The Illearth war 1980
3 The power that preserves 1980
4 The wounded land 1980
5 The one tree 1982
6 White gold wielder 1983
*'Gildfire', 1983, links with 2, 4-6, were
subtitled 'The second chronicles'.*

DONALDSON, W.
1 Both the ladies and the gentlemen 1975
2 The balloons in the black bag 1975
3 The English way of doing things 1984
*2 was reissued in 1985 as 'Nicknames
only'.*

DONLEAVY, J. P.
1 The destinies of Darcy Dancer,
gentleman 1978
2 Leila 1983
3 That Darcy, that Dancer, that
gentleman 1990
SCHULTZ:
1 Schultz
2 Are you listening, Rabbi Low? 1987

DOUGLAS, A.
JOHNATHAN GRAYTHORNE:
1 The goods 1985
2 Last rights 1986
3 A very wrong number 1987
4 A worm turns 1987

DOUGLAS of KIRTLESIDE, W. S. D., 1st BARON
1 Years of combat 1963
2 Years of command 1966
N.F. Autobiography

DOUGLAS, C. N.
SWORD AND CIRCLET:
1 Keepers of Edenvant
2 Heir of Rengarth
3 Seven of swords

DOUGLAS, COLIN
1 The Houseman's tale 1975

2 The greatest breakthrough since
lunchtime 1977
3 Bleeders come first 1979
4 Wellies from the Queen 1981
5 A cure from living 1983
6 For services to medicine 1985
7 Ethics made easy 1986
8 Hazards of the profession 1987
*A series of novels about young doctors
in a Scottish hospital.*

DOUGLAS, E.
1 Family's affairs 1962
2 Black cloud, white cloud 1964

DOUGLAS, F.
FAYE BOSWELL:
1 Within these walls
2 The Governor
*Based on the TV series set in a
women's prison.*

DOUGLAS, GAVIN
CAPTAIN SAMSON:
1 Obstinate Captain Samson
2 Captain Samson, A.B.

DOUGLAS, GEORGE
DET. SUP. HALLAM AND SERGEANT
SPRATT SERIES:
1 Odd woman out 1965
2 Unwanted witness 1963
3 Death went hunting 1966
4 Death unheralded 1967
5 Death in duplicate 1968
6 Gunman at large 1968
7 Devil to pay 1969
8 Dead reckoning 1970
9 Murder unmourned 1971
10 Crime most foul 1971
11 Time to die 1971
12 One to jump 1972
13 Death in darkness 1973
14 Death on the doorstep 1973
15 Dead on the dot 1974
16 Crime without reason 1975
17 Final score 1975
18 Death in retreat 1976
19 Dead on delivery 1976
20 Luckless lady 1976
21 Double cross 1977
22 End of the line 1979
23 Death of a big shot 1981
*With no. 5 the series becomes 'North
Central Region crime squad' and other
characters are introduced.*

DOUGLAS, P.
1 Down the village street 1979
2 About this village 1980
N.F. Country stories set in Norfolk

DOUGLAS, D. McN.
BOLIVAR MANCHENIL SERIES:
1 Rebacca's pride
2 Many brave hearts 1959
3 Saba's treasure 1963

DOWNE, P.
1 Dear doctor 1958
2 The doctor calls again 1959
3 Come, in doctor 1960
N.F. Autobiography

DOYLE, A. C.
SHERLOCK HOLMES SERIES:
1 A study in scarlet 1888
2 The sign of four 1980
3 Adventures of Sherlock Holmes 1892
4 The memoirs of Sherlock Holmes 1894
  (Last adventure of Sherlock Holmes)
5 The hounds of the Baskervilles 1902
6 The return of Sherlock Holmes 1905
7 The valley of fear 1915
8 His last bow 1917
9 The case-book of Sherlock Holmes
  1927
  *'The exploits of Sherlock Holmes', by
  Adrian Conan Doyle and J. D. Carr, is
  based on unrecorded exploits
  mentioned by Dr. Watson.*
  *'Misadventures of Sherlock Holmes',
  edited by Ellery Queen, is a collection
  of parodies of the Holmes stories by
  various writers, including Maurice Le
  Blanc, S. Leacock, Sir James Barrie,
  Agatha Chrisitie and others. Hall, T. H.
  and Harrison, M. have written studies
  in the Holmes series.*
Meyer, N. Seven percent solution 1975
Meyer, N. West End Horror 1976
Boyer, R. L. Giant rat of Sumatra 1977
Hall, R. L. Exit Sherlock Holmes 1977
Davies, D. S. Tangled skein 1978
Dibdin, M. The last Sherlock Holmes
story 1978
Estleman, L. D. Sherlock Holmes
versus Dracula 1978
Hardwick, M. Prisoner of the devil
1979
Jeffers, H. P. Adventures of the stalwart
companions 1979
Kurland, M. Infernal device 1979
Newman, R. Puzzle for Sherlock
Holmes 1979

Collins, R. Case of the philosopher's
ring 1980
D'Agreau, M. Curse of the Nibelurgen
1981
Haining, P. Final adventures of
Sherlock Holmes 1983
Walsh, R. The Mycroft memoranda
1984
Hardwick, M. Sherlock Holmes 1984
Van Ash, C. Ten years beyond Baker
Street 1985
Shaw, S. Sherlock Holmes at the 1902
5th Test 1985
Hardwick, M. Private life of Doctor
Watson 1985
Trow, M. J. Adventures of Inspector
Lestrade 1985
Shaw, S. Sherlock Holmes meets Annie
Oakley 1986
Symmons, J. The Kentish Manor
murders 1988
Trow, M. J. Brigade 1986
Trow, M. J. Lestrade and the hallowed
house 1986
Trow, M. J. Lestrade and the Leviathan
1987
Trow, M. J. Lestrade and the brother of
death 1987
Trow, M. J. Lestrade and the Ripper
1988
Hardwick, M. Revenge of the hound
1988
Piercy, R. My dearest Holmes 1988
Andrews, V. Sherlock Holmes and the
eminent Thespian 1988
Dibdin, M. The last Sherlock Holmes
story 1988
Pearsall, R. Sherlock Holmes
investigates the murder in Euston
Square 1989
Andrews, V. Sherlock Holmes and the
Brighton Pavilion mystery 1990
Brooks, C. Sherlock Holmes revisited
1990
Thomson, J. Secret files of Sherlock
Holmes 1990
Trow, M. J. Lestrade and the deadly
game 1990
Rowland, P. The disappearance of
Edwin Drood 1991
Davies, D. S. Sherlock Holmes and the
Hentzau affair 1991

DRABBLE, M.
1 The radiant way 1988
2 A natural curiosity 1989

DRABBLE, P.
1 Country scene 1975
2 Country seasons 1976
3 Badgers at my window 1976
4 A weasel in my meatsafe 1977
5 No badgers in my wood 1979
*N.F. Describes the author's work with
wild animals.*

DRAGONLANCE
DRAGONLANCE PRELUDES:
1 Darkness and light, *by* P. B. Thompson
2 Kendermore, *by* M. Kirchoff
3 Brothers Majere, *by* K. Stein
DRAGONLANCE PRELUDES II:
1 Riverwind the plains, *by* P. B.
Thompson
2 Flint the king *by* M. Kirchoff
DRAGONLANCE SAGA HEROES:
1 The legend of Huma, *by* R. A. Kraak
2
3 Weasel's luck, *by* M. Williams
DRAGONLANCE SAGA HEROES II:
1 Kaz the monster, *by* R. A. Kraak
2 The gates of Thorbarden, *by* D.
Parkinson
THE DRAGONLANCE CHRONICLES:
1 Dragons of autumn twilight
2 Dragons of winter night
3 Dragons of spring dawning
Written by M. Weis and T. Hickman
THE DRAGONLANCE LEGENDS:
1 Time of the twins
2 War of the twins
3 Test of the twins
THE DRAGONLANCE TALES:
1 The magic of Krynn
2 Kenders, Gully Dwarfs and Gnomes
3 Love and war
*Dragonlance is a cult series based on
the Dungeons and Dragons games,
with pendants in the form of maps,
guides, etc. The series is confusing
because of the number of authors
involved, hence its entry under series
rather than authors.*

DRAPER, A.
CRISPIN PATON, R.N.:
1 Grey seal 1982
2 The restless waves 1983
3 The raging deep 1985
4 Storm over Singapore 1986
5 The great avenging day 1988

DRAPER, H.
1 Wiggery pockery
2 Wigged and gowned 1958

DRUMMOND, C.
SERGEANT REED SERIES:
1 Death at the furlong post 1967
2 Death and the leaping ladies 1968
3 Odds on death 1969
4 Stab in the back 1970
5 Death at the bar 1972

DRUMMOND, I.
LADY JENNIFER, SANDRO, AND COLLY
SERIES:
1 The man with the tiny head 1969
2 The priest of the abomination 1970
3 The frog in the moonflower 1972
4 The jaws of the watchdog 1973
5 The power of the bug 1974
6 The tank of sacred eels 1976
7 The necklace of skulls 1977
8 A stench of poppies 1978
9 The diamonds of Loreta 1980

DRUON, M.
THE ACCURSED KINGS SERIES:
1 The iron king 1956
2 The strangled queen 1956
3 The poisoned crown 1957
4 The royal succession 1958
THE ACCURSED KING SERIES II:
5 She-wolf of France 1960
6 The lily and the lion 1961
*A series of novels about the long
tragedy of France under the weak
Captetan and Valois kings of the 14th
century.
The curse is the one supposed to been
uttered on the scaffold by the master of
the Templars when executed by Philip
the Fair.
The scene changes from France to Italy
and England, and the story is
immensely detailed with a huge cast of
characters, but always following the
main theme.*
THE CURTAIN FALLS:
1 The mangnates 1948
2 Feet of clay 1949
3 Rendezvous in hell 1951
*Republished in one volume under title
'The curtain falls' 1959. French title,
'Les grandes familles'. Prix Goncourt.*

DRURY, A.
1 Advise and consent 1962
2 A shade of difference 1964
3 Capable of honor 1966
4 Preserve and protect 1968
5 Come Nineveh, come Tyre 1974
6 Promise of joy 1975

7 Anna Hastings 1978
American political life. Not strictly sequels, but characters reappear.
***
1 A god against Gods 1976
2 Return to Thebes 1977
Novels about the 18th dynasty in Ancient Egypt.
1 The hill of summer 1983
2 The roads of earth 1985

DRYSDALE, A.
1 Faint heart never kissed a pig 1982
2 Sows ears and silk purses 1984
3 Pearls before swine 1985
N.F. Autobiography of a hill farmer.

DRYSDALE, MARGAET
ROBERT DUDLEY, EARL OF LEICESTER:
1 Quest for a crown 1982
2 Heir for the Earl 1983
3

DU BARRY, M.
THE LOVES OF ANGELA CARLYLE:
1 Into passion's dawn
2 Across captive seas
3 Towards love's horizon
Paperback bodice rippers.

DUBUS, E. N.
1 Where love rules 1986
2 To love and to dream 1987
A family saga set in America's Deep South.

DUDLEY, E.
DR. MORRELL'S SERIES:
1 Meet Dr. Morelle 1944
2 Dr. Morelle again 1947
3 Menace for Dr. Morelle 1947
4 Dr. Morelle and the drummer girl 1950
5 Dr. Morelle takes a bow 1957
6 Callers for Dr. Morelle 1957
7 The mind of Dr. Morelle 1958
8 Dr. Morelle and destiny 1958
9 Confess to Dr. Morelle 1958
10 Dr. Morelle at midnight 1959
11 Alibi for Dr. Morelle 1959
12 Nightmare for Dr. Morelle 1960
13 Dr. Morelle and the doll 1960

DUFFY, M.
PATRICK & INGRID LANGLEY:
1 A murder of crows 1987
2 Death of a raven 1988
3 Brass eagle 1988

4 Who killed Cock Robin? 1990
5 Rook-shoot 1991

DUGGAN, A.
SAXON TRILOGY:
1 Conscience of the king 1948
2 Cunning of the dove 1950
3 The king of Athelney 1961

DUKE, M.
THE SUNDMANS: A TRIPTYCH:
1 A city built to music 1960
2 Ride the brooding wind 1961
3 The Sovereign Lords 1963
A trilogy of novels dealing with world events from the 1840's to World War II
***
1 Sobaka 1968
2 The lethal innocents 1970
3 Because of fear in the night 1973
A trilogy of novels about modern youth.
DR. NORAH NORTH:
1 Death at the wedding 1975
2 Death of a holy murderer 1976
3 Death of a Dandie Dinmont 1978

DU MAURIER, A.
1 It's only the sister 1951
2 Old maids remember 1966
N.F. Autobiography

DUMITRIU, P.
THE BOYARS TRILOGY:
1 Family jewels 1960
2 The prodigals 1962
Novels of modern Romania not completed.

DUNCAN, A.
1 It's a vet's life
2 The vet has nine lives
3 Vets in the belfry 1963
4 A vet exposed 1977
5 Vets in congress 1978
6 Vets in the manger 1979
7 Vet among the pigeons 1979
8 Vet in a state 1980
9 Vet on vacation 1980
COUNTRY DOCTOR:
1 To be a country doctor 1980
2 God and the doctor 1981
3 Diary of a country doctor 1982
4 The doctor's affairs all told 1983

DUNCAN, F.
M. E. TREMAINE SERIES:

1 Murderer's bluff
2 They'll never find out
3 So pretty a problem
4 In at the death
5 Behold a fair woman 1955
PETER JUSTICE SERIES:
1 Hand of justice
2 Sword of justice
3 The league of justice
4 Justice returns
5 Justice limited

DUNCAN, J.
REACHFAR SERIES:
1 My friends the Miss Boyds 1958
2 My friend Muriel 1959
3 My friend Monica 1960
4 My friend Annie 1960
5 My friend Sandy 1961
6 My friend Martha's aunt 1961
7 My friend Flora 1962
8 My friend Madame Zora 1963
9 My friend Rose 1964
10 My friend Emmie 1964
11 My friends the Mrs. Millers 1965
12 My friend from Cairnton 1966
13 My friend my father 1966
14 My friends the Macleans 1967
15 My friends the hungry generation 1968
16 My friend the swallow 1969
17 My friend Sachie 1970
18 My friends the Misses Kindness 1974
19 My friends George and Tom 1976
   (*Letter from Reachfar', 1975 is an
   autobiography*).
   See also **J. SANDISON**, *pseud.*

DUNCAN, R.
1 All men are islands 1964
2 How to make enemies 1968
3 Obsessed 1977
N.F. Autobiography

DUNCAN, W. M.
SUPERINTENDENT DONALD REAMER
SERIES:
1 Meet the Dreamer 1963
2 Again the Dreamer 1964
3 Presenting the Dreamer 1966
4 Case for the Dreamer 1966
5 Problem for the Dreamer 1967
6 The Dreamer intervenes 1968
7 Salute the Dreamer 1968
8 Challenge for the Dreamer 1969
9 The Dreamer deals with murder 1970
10 Detail for the Dreamer 1971
11 The Dreamer at large 1972
12 Prey for the Dreamer 1974

13 Laurels for the Dreamer 1975
GREENSLEEVES SERIES:
1 Mystery on the Clyde
2 Straight ahead for danger
3 Cult of queer people
SUPERINTENDENT LESLIE:
1 The Council of comforters 1968
2 The green triangle 1969

DUNDAS, L.
SALMOND SERIES:
1 He liked them murderous 1964
2 The strange smell of murder 1965

DUNN, M.
1 Lady Addle at home
2 Lady Addle remembers
3 The memoirs of Mipsie
Paperback humour

DUNNE, C.
JOE HUSSEY:
1 Retrieval 1984
2 Ratcatcher 1985
3 Hooligan 1987

DUNNETT, D.
FRANCIS CRAWFORD OF LYMOND:
1 The game of kings 1965
2 Queen's play 1966
3 The disorderly knights 1968
4 Pawn in Frankincense 1969
5 The ringed castle 1971
6 Checkmate 1975
   *Historical novels on Scotland and
   Europe in the 16th century.*
THE HOUSE OF NICCOLO:
1 Niccolo rising 1986
2 The spring of the ram 1987
3 Race of scorpions 1989
JOHNSON JOHNSON
1 Tropical issue 1983
2 Rum affair 1968
3 Ibiza surprise 1970
4 Operation Nassau 1971
5 Roman nights 1973
6 Split code 1977
7 Moroccan traffic 1991
   *Formerly published under the name of
   Dorothy Halliday, with different titles.
   All reprinted in paperback in 1991. For
   the original titles, see under*
   HALLIDAY, D.

DURACK, M.
1 Kings in grass castles 1959
2 Sons in the saddles 1983
   N.F. Australian pioneering history.

DURBRIDGE, F.

PAUL TEMPLE:
1 Send for Paul Temple
2 Paul Temple and the front page men
3 Paul Temple intervenes
4 News of Paul Temple
5 Send for Paul Temple again 1948
6 Paul Temple and the Kelby affair 1970
7 Paul Temple and the Harkdale robbery 1970
8 The Geneva mystery 1972
9 The Curzon case 1972
10 Paul Temple and the Margo mystery 1986
11 Paul Temple and the Madison case 1988
★★★
1 World of Tim Frazer 1961
2 Tim Frazer again 1964
3 Tim Frazer gets the message 1979

DURRANT, D.
1 With my littel eye 1975
2 Trunch 1978
3 Addle 1980

DURRELL, G.
1 My family and other animals 1956
2 Birds beasts and relatives 1969
3 The garden of the Gods 1978
N.F. Autobiography

DURRELL, L.
THE ALEXANDRIA QUARTET:
1 Justine 1957
2 Balthazar 1958
3 Mountolive 1958
4 Clea 1960
Now published in one volume 1962
★★★
1 Prospero's cell 1945
2 Reflections on a marine Venus 1953
3 Bitter lemons of Cyprus 1957
Three connected travel books on Mediterranean islands - Rhodes, Capri and Cyprus.
ANTROBUS SERIES:
1 Esprit de corps 1957
2 Stiff upper lip 1958
3 Sauve qui peut 1966
Selection published as *The best of Antrobus* 1974
Antrobus complete 1985
★★★
1 Tunc 1967
2 Nunquam 1970
Republished in one volume, 1974 as 'The revolt of Aphrodite'.

AVIGNON QUINTET:
1 Monsieur 1974
2 Livia or Buried alive 1978
3 Constance 1982
4 Sebastien 1983
5 Quinx 1985

DURST, P.
MICHAEL CARMICHAEL:
1 Backlash 1967
2 Badge of infamy 1968

DUTTON, G.
1 A long way south 1953
2 Africa in black and white 1956
N.F. Autobiography

DWYER-JOYCE, A.
DR. ROSS SERIES:
1 Dr. Ross of Harton 1966
2 The story of Dr. Esmond Ross 1967
3 Verdict of Dr. Esmond Ross 1968
4 Dial emergency for Dr. Ross 1969

DYMOKE, J.
TRILOGY ON HENRY I:
1 The ring of Earls 1970
2 Henry of the high rock 1971
3 The lion's legacy 1972
THE PLANTAGENETS:
1 A pride of Kings 1978
2 The Royal griffin 1978
3 The lion of Mortimer 1979
4 Lady of the Garter 1978
5 The Lord of Greenwich 1980
6 The sun in splendour 1980
FRENCH REVOLUTION SERIES:
1 The white cockade 1979
2 The Queen's diamond 1983
3 The march to Corunna 1985
4 Two flags for France 1986

DYSON, E.
REVILL-GORDON;
1 With swords in their lips 1956
2 Proud suitor 1959

EASTON, N.
BILL BANING SERIES:
1 Always the wolf 1956
2 One good turn 1957
3 Bill for damages 1958
4 Mistake me not 1959
5 A book for Banning 1959
6 Right for trouble 1960
7 Quick tempo 1960
8 Moment on ice 1960

EASTWOOD, J.
ANNA ZORDAN:
1 The Chinese visitor 1965
2 Little dragon from Peking 1967
3 Come die with me 1969

EATON, E.
1 Every month was May
2 North star is nearer
N.F. Autobiography

EBDON, J.
1 Ebdon's Odyssey 1979
2 Ebdon's Iliad 1983
3 Ebdon's England 1985
N.F. Autobiography of a broadcaster

EBEL, S.
SIR ROBERT WARING:
1 A name in lights 1967
2 A most auspicious star 1969
3 To seek a star 1973
Novels about life in the theatre today

EBERHART, M. G.
SARAH KEATE SERIES:
1 The patient in room 18
2 While the patient slept
3 The mystery of Huntings End
4 From this dark stairway
5 Murder of my patient
6 Wolf in Man's clothing
7 Man missing

EBERSOHN, W.
YUDEL GORDON:
1 A lonely place to die 1979
2 Divide the night 1980
3 Closed circle 1990

EBERT, A.
TIERNAN FAMILY:
1 Traditions 1982
2 The long way home 1985

ECCLES, M.
INSPECTOR GIL MAYO:
1 Death of a good woman 1989
2 Requiem for a dove 1990
3 More deaths than one 1991

ECKERT, A. W.
1 The great auk 1963
2 The silent sky: the incredible extinction
of the passenger pigeon 1969
*Two companion documentary novels
about the callous extermination of an
animal species by man*

ECKHARDT, K.
SS DIVISION VATERLAND:
1 Heroes without honour 1980
2 Stalingrad heroes 1981
3 Heroes of Cassino 1982
4 Achtung Normandy 1982

EDDINGS, D.
THE BELGARIAD:
1 The pawn of prophecy 1982
2 Queen of sorcery 1982
3 Magician's gambit 1983
4 Castle of Wizardry 1984
5 Enchanter's endgame 1985
Fantasy
THE MALLOREON:
1 Guardians of the West 1987
2 King of the Murgos 1988
3 Demon Lord of Karanda 1988
4 Sorceress of Darshiva 1989
5 Seeress of Kell 1991
ELENIUM:
1 The diamond throne 1989
2 The ruby knight 1990

EDEL, L.
1 The untried years 1959
2 The conquest of London 1961
3 The middle years 1884-1894 1963
4 The treacherous years 1895-1901 1969
N.F. Biography of Henry James

EDELMAN, M.
1 The minister 1963
2 The Prime Minister's daughter 1964
DISRAELI:
1 Disraeli in love
2 Disraeli rising 1975

EDEN, M.
MARC SAVAGE:
1 Countdown to crisis 1968
2 Dangerous exchange 1969
3 Flight of hawks 1969
4 The man who fell 1970

EDEN, R. A., 1st EARL of AVON
1 Facing the dictators 1962
2 The reckoning 1965
3 Full circle 1960
N.F. Autobiography

EDGAR, J.
1 Duchess 1976
2 Countess 1978
***
1 Margaret Normanby 1983
2 A dark and alien rose 1991

EDMONDS, H.
1 The clockmaker of Heidelberg
2 The rockets - operation Manhattan
3 The orphans of Brandenburg 1953

EDMONDS, J.
LINUS RINTOUL:
1 Dog's body 1988
2 Dead spit 1989
3 Judge and be damned 1990
Thrillers set in the world of dog showing

EDMUNDS, B.
PETE MARVIN SERIES:
1 A gun in my back
2 Ride a dark horse
3 Beware the crimson cord 1956
4 Spiders in the night 1956

EDSON, J. T.
OLD DEVIL HARDIN SERIES:
1 Young Ole Devil
2 Old Devil and the Caplocks
3 Ole Devil and the mule train
4 Old Devil at San Jacinto
5 Get Urrea
THE CIVIL WAR SERIES:
1 Commanche
2 You're in command now, Mr. Fog
3 The big gun
4 Under the stars and bars
5 The fastest gun in Texas
6 Killy Dusty Fog!
7 The devil gun
8 The colt and the sabre
9 The rebel spy
10 The bloody border
11 Back to the bloody border
THE FLOATING OUTFIT SERIES:
1 The Ysabel Kid
2 .44 calibre man
3 A horse called Mogollan
4 Goodnight's dream
5 From hide and horn
6 Set Texas back on her feet
7 The hide and tallow men
8 The hooded riders
9 Quiet town
10 Trail boss
11 Wagons to Backsight
12 Troubled range
13 Sidewinder
14 Rangeland hercules
15 McGraw's inheritance
16 The half breed
17 The wildcats
18 The bad bunch

19 The fast gun
20 Chuchilo
21 A town called Yellowdog
22 Trigger fast
23 The making of a lawman
24 The trouble busters
25 Set a-foot
26 The law of the gun
27 The peacemakers
28 To arms! To arms! in Dixie!
29 Hell in the Palo Duro
30 Go back to hell
31 The south will rise again
32 The quest for Bowie's blade
33 Beguinage
34 Beguinage is dead!
35 The Rushers
36 The fortune hunters
37 Rio guns
38 Gun wizard
39 The Texan
40 The Rio Hondo Kid
41 Waco's debt
42 The hard riders
43 The floating outfit
44 Apache rampage
45 The Rio Hondo war
46 The man from Texas
47 Gunsmoke thunder
48 The small Texan
49 The town tamers
50 Return to Backsight
51 Terror valley
52 Guns in the night
WACO SERIES:
1 Sagebrush sleuth
2 Arizona ranger
3 Waco rides in
4 The drifter
5 Doc Leroy. M.D.
6 Hound dog man
CALAMITY JANE SERIES:
1 Cold deck, hot lead
2 The bull whip breed
3 Trouble trail
4 The cow thieves
5 Calamity spells trouble
6 White stallion, red mare
7 The remittance kid
8 The whip and the war lance
9 The big hunt
ALVIN DUSTINE 'CAP' FOG SERIES:
1 You're a Texas Ranger, Alvin Fog
2 Rapido Clint
3 The instice of Company K
4 'Cap' Fog, Texas Ranger, meet Mr. J. G. Reeder
5 Decision for Dusty Fog 1987

THE ROCKABY COUNTY SERIES:
1 The sixteen dollar shooter
2 The professional killers
3 The ¼ second draw
4 The deputies
5 Point of contact
6 The owlhoot
7 Run for the border
8 Bad hombre
BUNDUKI SERIES:
1 Bunduki
2 Bunduki and dawn
3 Sacrifice for the Quagga god
4 Fearless master of the jungle

EDWARDS, H.
1 Under your flags
2 Their lawful occasions
N.F. Autobiography

EDWARDS, R.
RICHARD III:
1 Fortune's wheel 1978
2 Some touch of pity 1976

EDWARDS, R. D.
ROBERT AMISS:
1 Corridors of death 1981
2 The St. Valentine's Day murders 1984
3 The School of English murder 1990

EGAN, L.
GLENDALE POLICE DEPT.:
1 A case for appeal 1962
2 Scenes of crime 1976
3 A dream apart 1978
4 Random death 1982
5 Crime for Christmas 1984
6 Chain of violence 1985
*These stories involve the whole police
force, including Falkenstein and Varallo*
VIC VARALLO:
1 The borrowed alibi 1962
2 Run to evil 1963
3 Detective's due 1965
4 The nameless ones 1967
5 The wine of violence 1970
6 Malicious mischief 1972
7 The hunters and the hunted 1980
8 A choice of crimes 1981
JESSE FALKENSTEIN:
1 Against the evidence 1963
2 My name is death 1965
3 Some avenger, rise! 1967
4 A serious investigation 1969
5 In the death of a man 1970
6 Paper chase 1973
7 The blind search 1977

8 Look back on death 1979
9 Motive in shadow 1980
10 The miser 1982
11 Little boy lost 1984
12 The wine of life 1986

EGLETON, C.
1 A piece of resistance 1968
2 Last post for a partisan 1970
3 The Judas mandate 1972
*A trilogy of novels on the events during
a Russian occupation of Britain*
CHARLES WINTER:
1 The winter touch 1981
2 The Russian enigma 1983

EHLE, J.
THE WRIGHT FAMILY:
1 The land breakers 1964
2 The road 1967
3 Time of drums 1970
A pioneer family in N. Carolina

EHRENBURG, I.
1 The thaw 1955
2 the spring
***
1 The storm 1949
2 The ninth wave 1952
MEN, YEARS AND LIFE:
1 Childhood and youth (1891-1917) 1961
2 First years of revolution (1918-1921)
1963
3 Truce (1921-1933) 1963
4 Eve of war (1933-1941) 1963
5 The war (1914-1945) 1963
6 The post-war years (1945-1954) 1964
N.F. Autobiography

EICHER, A.
MARTIN AMES:
1 Death at the mike 1954
2 Death of an artist 1955

ELAND, C.
MARK RANDALL SERIES:
1 Dossier closed 1970
2 The desperate search 1971
3 The gold hijack 1973

ELDER, M.
THE BARCLAYS:
1 Nowhere on earth 1972
2 The perfumed planet 1973
3 Down to earth 1975
4 The seeds of frenzy 1976
Science fiction

PHILIP STEVENSON:
1 Mindslip 1976
2 Mindquest 1977

ELGIN, S. H.
NATIVE TONGUE:
1 Native tongue
2 The Judas rose
Paperback science fiction

ELIAS, E.
1 On Sunday we wore white 1978
2 Straw hats and serge bloomers 1979
N.F. Autobiography

ELKINS, A.
GIDEON OLIVER:
1 Murder in the Queen's Armes 1990
2 Icy clutches 1991

**ELLIOT, J., see HOYLE, F. and
ELLIOT, J.**

ELLIOTT, JANICE
WILSON FAMILY TRILOGY:
1 A state of peace 1970
2 Private life 1972
3 Heaven on earth 1974
*Political and private problems in a
working-class family*

ELLIS, A. T.
1 The clothes in the wardrobe 1987
2 The skeleton in the cupboard 1988
3 The fly in the ointment 1989
*Not true sequels. The same story is told
from the viewpoint of different
characters*

ELLIS, H. F.
1 A. J. Wentworth, BA 1980
2 The Swansong of A. J. Wentworth 1982
*1 was originally published by Penguin
Books as 'The world of A. J.
Wentworth'*

ELLIS, W. D.
THE OHIO FRONTIER:
1 The Bounty lands 1952
2 Jonathan Blair 1954
3 The Brooks legend 1958
*Although characters re-appear, the real
connection is the story of the settlement
of Ohio.*

ELMAN, R. M.
THE YAGODAH FAMILY TRILOGY:
1 The 28th day of Elul 1967

2 Lilo's diary 1968
3 The reckoning 1969
*The story of a Jewish family in
Hungary before and during World War
II. Not published in U.K.*

ELSNA, H.
1 A house called Pleasance 1962
2 Too well beloved 1964
3 The undying past 1964
*Novels on the history of a country
house, from Tudor times to Victorian*

EMECHETA, B.
1 Second class citizen 1974
2 In the ditch 1979
*Novels about a Nigerian woman in
Britain
Publ. as one volume "Adah's story"
1986*

EMERSON, D.
1 Pride of Parson Carnaby 1953
2 The trouble at Shaplinck 1959
***
1 The surgeon of Sedbridge 1955
2 The warden of Greys 1957

EMERSON, R.
THE TALE OF NEDAO:
1 To the haunted mountains
2 In the caves of exile
3 On the seas of destiny
Paperback fantasy

EMERSON, S.
1 Second sight 1980
2 The listeners 1983

EMPIRES TRILOGY:
1 Horselords, by David Cook
2 Dragonwell, by Troy Denning
3 Crusade, by James Lowden
Paperback fantasy

ENEFER, D.
DALE SHAND SERIES:
1 The painted death 1966
2 The long hot night 1967
3 The girl chase 1968
4 Girl in arms 1968
5 The gilded kiss 1969
6 The deadline dolly 1970
7 The screaming orchid 1971
8 Pacific Northwest 1975
9 Seven nights at the resort 1976
10 Ice in the sun 1977

11 The goodbye blonde 1978
SAM BAWTRY:
1 Pierhead 627 1968
2 13 steps to Lime Street 1969
3 Riverside 90 1970
4 Girl in a million 1972
5 A long way to Pitt Street 1972
6 Girl on the M6 1973
7 Lakeside zero 1973
8 The jade green judy 1974
9 Last train to Rock Ferry 1975
10 The sixth raid 1979
11 The deadly streak 1982
12 The last leap 1983

ENGEL, H.
BENNY COOPERMAN:
1 The ransom game 1982
2 Murder on location 1983
3 The suicide murders 1984
4 murder sees the light 1985
5 A city called July 1987
6 A victim must be found 1988

ENRIGHT, D. J.
1 Academic year 1955
2 Heaven knows where 1956
*Adventures of a schoolmaster in foreign
countries. Not sequels but main
character is the same*

ERDMAN, L. G.
PIERCE FAMILY SERIES:
1 The wind blows free
2 The wide horizon
3 The good land 1960
Novels about pioneer farming in Texas

ERDRICH, L.
1 love medicine 1984
2 The beet queen 1987
3 Tracks 1988
*Related novels about present-day
American indians*

ERSKINE, M.
SEPTIMUS FINCH SERIES:
1 Give up the ghost 1948
2 I knew Macbean 1949
3 Whispering house 1950
4 Dead by now 1951
5 And being dead 1953
6 The disappearing bridegroom 1954
7 Fatal relations 1955
8 The voice of murder 1956
9 Death of our dear one 1957
10 Sleep no more 1958
11 The house of enchantress 1959

12 The women at Belguardo 1961
13 The house of Belmont Square 1963
14 Take a dark journey 1965
15 Case with three husbands 1966
16 The ewe lamb 1968
17 The case of Mary Fielding 1970
18 The brood of folly 1971
19 Besides the wench is dead 1973
20 Harriet, farewell 1975

ERSKINE, R.
1 The passion-flower hotel 1962
2 Passion flowers in Italy 1963
3 Passion flowers in business 1965

ESMONDE, J. and LARBEY, B.
1 the good life 1976
2 More of the good life 1977
Based on the TV series

ESTES, R.
GREYHAWK ADVENTURES:
1 Master Wolf
2 The price of power
3 The demon hand
Paperback fantasy

ESTLEMAN, L. D.
AMOS WALKER:
1 Motor City blues 1981
2 Angel eyes 1982
3 The midnight man 1983
4 The glass highway 1984
5 Sugartown 1986
6 Every brilliant eye 1986
7 Lady yesterday 1987
8 Downriver 1988
9 General murders 1989
10 Silent thunder 1989
11 Sweet women lie 1990

ETTINGER, E.
1 Kindergarten 1988
2 Quicksand 1989

EVANS, A.
CRAGG AND FRAYNE:
1 The end of the running 1965
2 Mantrap 1967
COMMANDER SMITH:
1 Thunder at dawn 1979
2 Ship of force 1979
3 Dauntless 1980
4 Seek out and destroy 1982

EVANS, C.
1 Love from Belinda 1961
2 Lalage in love 1962

EVANS, G. E.
1 Ask the fellows who cut the hay 1962
2 The horse in the furrow 1963
3 The pattern under the plough 1966
N.F. Connected books on farm life before the mechanical revolution

EVANS, J.
HABBAKUK PARTON:
1 The Portobello virgin 1986
2 The Mexico novice 1987
3 The Alamo design 1989

EVANS, M.
1 Autobiograph
2 Ray of darkness
N.F. Autobiography

EVANS, S.
WINDMILL HILL:
1 Centres of ritual 1978
2 Occupational debris 1979
3 Temporary hearths 1982
4 Houses on the site 1984
5 Seasonal tribal feasts 1987

EVANS, T.
LONGARM:
1 Longarm
2 Longarm on the border
3 Longarm and the avenging angels
4 Longarm and the Wendigo
5 Longarm in the Indian Nation
6 Longarm and the logger
7 Longarm and the high graders
8 Longarm and the nesters
9 Longarm and the hatchetmen
10 Longarm and the Molly Maguires
11 Longarm and the Texas Rangers
12 Longarm in Lincoln County
Paperback Westerns

EXLEY, F.
1 A fan's notes
2 Last notes from home 1990

EYRE, D. C.
CAPTAIN O'DONNELL:
1 Foxes have holes
2 Drum beat

FAIR, A. A., *pseud.* (E. S. GARDNER)
BERTHA COOL-DONALD LAM SERIES:
1 Lam to the slaughter
2 Turn on the heat
3 Gold comes in bricks

4 Spill the jackpot
5 Axe to grind
6 Crows can't count
7 Owl's don't blink
8 Cats prowl at night
9 Bats fly at dusk
10 Double or quits
11 Fools die on Friday 1955
12 Bedrooms have windows 1956
13 top of the heap 1957
14 Some women won't wait 1957
15 beware of the curves 1958
16 You can die laughing 1958
17 Some slips don't show 1959
18 The count of nine 1959
19 Pass the gravy 1959
20 Kept women can't quit 1960
21 Bachelors get lonely 1961
22 Stop at the red 1962
23 Try anything once 1963
24 Fish or cut bait 1963
25 up for grabs 1965
26 Cut thin to win 1966
27 Widows wear weeds 1966
28 Traps need fresh bait 1968
29 All grass isn't green 1969

FAIRBROTHER, N.
1 Children in the house
2 The cheerful day
N.F. Autobiography

FAIRLIE, G.
MR. MALCOLM SERIES:
1 A shot in the dark 1950
2 Mr. Malcolm presents
3 Men for counters
CARYLL SERIES:
1 Scissors cut paper
2 Man who laughed
3 Stone blunts scissors
JOHN MACALL SERIES:
1 Winner take all 1954
2 No sleep for Macall 1955
3 Deadline for Macall 1956
4 Double for bluff 1957
5 Macall gets curious 1959
6 Murder most discreet 1960
7 Please kill my cousin 1961
see also **SAPPER** *pseud.*

FALKIRK, R.
1 Blackstone 1972
2 Blackstone's fancy 1973
3 Beau Blackstone 1973
4 Blackstone and the scourge of Europe 1974
5 Blackstone underground 1976

6 Blackstone on Broadway 1977
*Historical detective stories about a Bow
St. runner*

FALLA, R.
1 Life in Emergency Ward 10 1959
2 Love in Emergency Ward 10 1969
3 The sisters of Emergency Ward 10 1961
4 Case for Emergency Ward 10 1962
5 The boy in Emergency Ward 10 1963

FALLON, M.
PAUL CHAVASSE SERIES:
1 Testament of Caspar Schultz 1963
2 The year of the tiger 1964
3 The keys of hell 1965
4 Midnight never comes 1966
5 Dark side of the street 1967
6 A fine night for dying 1969
*Later reprinted under the name of Jack
Higgins*

FAMILY AT WAR SERIES
1 A family at war *by* K. Baker 1970
2 To the turn of the tide *by* J. Powell 1971
3 Towards victory *by* R. Russell 1972
*Adapted from the famous TV series.
Paperback only*

FANTE, J.
ARTURO BANDINI:
1 Wait until Spring, Bandini 1938
2 Ask the dust 1939
3 Dreams from Bunker Hill 1982

FANTONI, M.
MIKE DIME:
1 Mike Dime 1981
2 Stickman 1982

FARAH, N.
VARIATIONS ON THE THEME OF AFRICAN
DICTATORSHIP:
1 Sweet and sour milk 1979
2 Sardines 1981
3 Close Sesame 1983

FARALLA, D.
1 The magnificent barb 1947
2 Black renegade 1954
*Horse breeding and plantation life in
Georgia at the turn of the 19th century*

FARELY, A.
1 Crown of splendour 1966
2 Devil's royal 1968
3 The lion and the wolf 1968
4 The last roar of the lion 1970

5 Leopard from Anjou 1974
6 King Wolf 1974
7 Kingdom under tyranny 1975
8 Last howl of the wolf 1975
*Historical novels on the Plantagenet
dynasty*

FAREWELL, N.
1 The unfair sex 1953
2 Someone to love 1958

FARMER, B. J.
SERGEANT WIGAN SERIES:
1 Death at the cascades 1955
2 Death of a bookseller 1956
3 Once and then the funeral 1957
4 Murder next year 1959

FARMER, P. J.
AN EXORCISM:
1 Blown
2 The image of the beast
DAYWORLD:
1 Dayworld 1987
2 Dayworld rebel 1988
DOC CALIBAN:
1 Lord of the trees 1981
2 Keepers of secrets 1985
OPAR SERIES:
1 Hadon of Ancient Opar
2 Flight to Opar
RIVERWORLD SAGA:
1 To your scattered bodies go
2 The fabulous riverboat
3 Dark design 1987
4 The magic labyrinth
5 Gods of Riverworld 1987
*Fantasy, mainly paperback. Dates are
for hardback.*
WORLD OF THE TIERS:
1 Makers of Universes
2 Private Cosmos
3 The gates of Creation
4 Behind the walls of Terra
5 The green odyssey
Paperback science fiction

FARRAN, R.
1 Winged dagger 1955
2 Operation Tombola 1960
*N.F. Wartime experiences with Special
Air Service*

FARRAR, S.
1 The snake on 99 1962
2 Zero in the gate 1963
3 Death in the wrong bed 1964

FARRE, R.
1 Seal morning 1957
2 A time from the world 1962
3 The beckoning land 1969
N.F. Autobiography

FARRELL, J. G.
1 The seige of Krishnapur 1974
2 The hill station 1981
   *2 is unfinished, but the central
   character appears in 1*

FARRER, K.
DET.-INSP. RINGWOOD SERIES:
1 The missing link 1952
2 The Cretan counterfeit 1954
3 Gownsman's gallows 1957

FARRIMOND, J.
1 Dust in my throat 1963
2 Dust is forever 1969
   Two novels about coalmining

FARRINGTON, R.
HENRY MORANE:
1 The killing of Richard the Third 1972
2 Tudor agent 1974
3 The traitors of Bosworth 1978

FARSON, N.
1 Way of a transgressor 1935
2 A mirror for Narcissus 1956
   N.F. Autobiography

FAST, H.
LAVETTE FAMILY:
1 The immigrants 1977
2 Second generation 1979
3 The establishment 1980
4 The legacy 1981
5 The immigrant's daughter 1985
   *A family saga about Jewish immigrants
   in America*

FAULCON, R.
NIGHT HUNTER:
1 The stalking
2 The talisman
3 The ghost dance
4 The shrine
5 The labyrinth
6 The hexing
   Paperback horror stories

FAULKNER, W.
1 Sartoris 1929
2 The sound and the fury 1929
3 As I lay dying 1930

4 Sanctuary 1932
5 Light in August 1932
6 Absalom, Absalom! 1936
7 The hamlet
8 Requiem for a nun 1951
9 The town 1957
10 The mansion 1959
   *Of these, 4 and 8 are direct sequels, and
   other minor characters re-appear. Gavin
   Stephens appears in 8 and also in
   'Knight's gambit', and 'Intruder in the
   dust'. 7, 9 and 10 form a trilogy on the
   Snopes family, but they are also part of
   the series. The main body of Mr.
   Faulkner's work is in the nature of a
   continuous 'Roman Fleuve', each
   volume of which is complete in itself,
   although the novels exist in the mind of
   the author as interdependent and
   inseparable one from the other. Thus
   Narcissa in 'Sanctuary' is a main figure
   in 'Sartoris' and the Quentin who
   commits suicide in 'The sound and the
   fury' reappears as the Listener in
   'Absalom'. These additions and
   developments never appear to have been
   looked on as afterthoughts, but seem to
   have been held in reserve until the time
   was ripe for telling.*

FAULKNOR, C.
1 The white calf 1966
2 The white peril 1968

FAY, G.
1 Passenger to London 1962
2 Fay's third book 1964

FEARON, D.
MISS ARABELLA FRANT:
1 Death before breakfast 1959
2 Murder-on-Thames 1960

FECHER, C.
RALEGH FAMILY SERIES:
1 Queen's delight 1964
2 Traitor's son 1967
3 King's legacy 1968
4 Player queen 1968

FEIST, R. E.
RIFTWAR:
1 Magician 1983
2 Silverthorn 1985
3 A darkness at Sethanon 1986
4 Prince of the blood 1989

FEIST, R. E. *and* **WURTS, J.**
EMPIRE:
1 Daughter of the Empire 1989
2 Servant of the Empire 1990
Fantasy

FELICITY, SISTER
1 Barefoot journey 1961
2 Spring comes barefoot 1965
N.F. Autobiography

FEN, E.
1 A Russian childhood 1961
2 A girl grew up in Russia 1970
3 Remember Russia 1973
N.F. Autobiography

FENNELLY, T.
MATTY SINCLAIR:
1 The glory hole murders 1986
2 The closet hanging 1987

FENTON, S.
1 All the beasts in the field 1984
2 Creature comforts 1985
N.F. Rural life

FERGUSSON, B.
1 Beyond the Chindwin 1951
2 The wild green earth 1952
N.F. Account of the Burma campaign

FERGUSSON, H.
FOLLOWERS OF THE SUN: A TRILOGY OF
THE SOUTH-WEST:
1 Wolf song
2 In those days 1954
3 Blood of the conquerors

FERMOR, P. L.
1 Mani 1963
2 Roumeli 1965
N.F. Travel in Greece
1 Between the woods and the water 1986
2 A time of gifts 1977
N.F. Autobiography

FERRARI, I.
RYEMINSTER HOSPITAL SERIES:
1 Doctor at Ryeminster 1964
2 Nurse at Ryeminster 1964
3 Sister at Ryeminster 1965
4 Almoner at Ryeminster 1965

FERRARS, E.
ANDREW BASNETT:
1 Something wicked 1983
2 Root of all evil 1984

3 The crime and the crystal 1985
4 The other devil's name 1986
5 A murder too many 1988
6 Smoke without fire 1990

FELIX FREER:
1 Last will and testament 1979
2 Frog in the throat 1980
3 Thinner than water 1981
4 Death of a minor character 1983
5 I met murder 1985
6 Woman slaughter 1989
7 Sleep of the unjust 1990

FERRIS, C.
1 The darkness is light enough 1986
2 Out of the darkness 1988
4 The badgers of Ashcroft woods 1990
*N.F. An account of the author's study
of badgers, and her efforts to protect
them from poachers*

FIELD, P.
POWDER VALLEY SERIES:
1 Law man of Powder Valley
2 Trail south from Powder Valley
3 Fight for Powder Valley
4 Death rides the night
5 Smoking iron
6 Guns from Powder Valley
7 Powder Valley vengeance
8 Canyon hideout
9 Road to Laramie
10 End of the trail
11 Powder Valley showdown
12 Ravaged Range
13 Sheriff wanted
14 Gamblers gold
15 Trail from Needle rock
16 Outlaw valley
17 Sheriff on the spot
18 Return to Powder Valley
19 Blacksnake trail
20 Powder Valley ambush
21 Back trail to danger 1951
22 Three guns from Colorado
23 Guns in the saddle 1952
24 Powder Valley holdup
25 Mustang mesa 1952
26 Outlaw of Eagle's Nest 1952
27 Riders of the outlaw trail
28 Powder Valley stampede
29 Powder Valley deadlock 1954
30 War in the painted buttes 1954
31 Outlaw of Cattle Canyon 1955
32 Breakneck Pass 1955
33 Rawhide rider 1955

FIELDING, G.

JOHN BLAYDON:
1 Brotherly love 1947
2 In the time of the greenbloom 1956
3 Pretty doll houses 1979
4 The women of Guinea Lane 1986

FIELDING, H.

1 Tom Jones
'The later adventures of Tom Jones,' by
B. Coleman (1986) is a sequel.

FINCH, J.

1 The spoils of war
2 The promised land
Paperback novels based on the TV
series

FINCH, M.

1 Dentist in the chair 1955
2 Teething troubles 1956
3 The beauty bazaar 1965
DICK LANGHAM SERIES:
1 Five are the symbols 1964
2 Jones is a rainbow 1965
3 The succubus 1967

FINCH, S.

1 The Golden voyager 1978
2 Pagan voyager 1979
3 Voyager in bondage 1981
Novels about a galley slave in Ancient
Rome

FINDLEY, D.

JOHNNY MALONE:
1 My old man's badge
2 Remember that face

FINLAY, D. G.

BAYLESS FAMILY:
1 Watchman 1984
2 The grey regard 1985
3 Deadly relations 1986
4 Graven image 1987

FINN, R. L.

1 Time remembered 1963
2 Spring in Aldgate 1968
N. F. A Jewish boyhood in London's
East End. 2 was reprinted as 'Grief
Forgotten' in 1985

FINN, T.

1 Knapworth at war 1982
2 Knapworth fights on 1989

FINNEGAN, R.

DAN BANION SERIES:
1 The lying ladies
2 The bandaged nude 1954
3 Many a monster

FINNEY, P.

. LUGH THE HARPER:
1 Shadow of gulls 1977
2 The crow goddess 1978
Irish mythology

FIRBANK, T.

1 I bought a mountain 1940
2 From mountain so rocky
3 I bought a star 1949
4 Country of memorable honour
5 Log hut 1954
6 I am a traveller
N.F. Autobiography

FISH, R. L.

CAPTAIN JOSE DA SILVA SERIES:
1 The fugitive 1962
2 Isle of the snakes 1963
3 The shrunken head 1964
4 The diamond bubble 1965
5 Brazilian sleigh ride 1966
6 Always kiss a stranger
7 The bridge that went nowhere
8 The Xavier affair
9 The green hell treasure
10 Trouble in Paradise
MURDER LEAGUE SERIES:
1 The murder league
2 Tricks of the trade
3 Rub a dub dub
4 A gross carriage of justice
SCHLOCK HOMES SERIES:
1 The incredible Schlock Homes
2 The memoirs of Schlock Homes

FISHER, D. E.

1 The man you sleep with 1982
2 Variation on a theme 1982
Linked novels, giving two views of a
murder

FISHER, E.

1 Shakespeare and son 1963
2 Love's labour won 1965
3 The best house in Stratford 1966
A trilogy on the life of Shakespeare

FISHER, J. A., 1st BARON

FEAR GOD AND DREAD NOUGHT:
1 The making of an admiral (1854-1904)
1952

2 Years of power (1904-1914) 1956
3 Restoration, abdication and last years
(1914-1920) 1958
N.F. Autobiography

FISHER, N.
NIGEL MORRISON SERIES:
1 Walk at a steady pace 1970
2 Rise at dawn 1971
3 The last assignment 1972

FITT, M.
SUPERINTENDENT MALLETT SERIES:
1 Expected death
2 Sky rocket 1938
3 Death at dancing stones 1939
4 Murder of a mouse 1939
5 Death starts a rumour
6 Death and Mary Dazill
7 Death on Heron's mere
8 Requiem for Robert
9 Death and the pleasant voices
10 Clues re Christabel
11 Death and the bright day
12 The banquet ceases
13 Death and the shortest day 1952
14 An ill wind
15 The man who shot birds
16 Love from Elizabeth
17 Mizmaze 1959

FITZGERALD, J. D.
1 Papa married a Mormon 1956
2 Mamma's boarding house
3 Uncle Will and the Fitzgerald curse
N.F. Autobiography

FITZGERALD, JULIA
1 Desert queen 1986
2 Taboo 1985

FITZGERALD, N.
SUPERINTENDENT DUFFY SERIES:
1 Midsummer malice 1952
2 The rosy pastor 1953
3 The house is falling 1955
4 Imagine a man 1956
5 Candles are all out 1957
6 The student body 1958
7 This won't hurt 1958
8 Suffer a witch 1958
9 Ghost in the making 1960
10 Black welcome 1961
11 Day of the adder 1963
12 Affairs of death 1967

FITZGERALD, P.
1 Bella Donna

2 Jenny Bell
3 Seventy-five Brooke Street

FITZGIBBON, T.
1 With love 1982
2 Love lies at a loss 1982
N.F. Autobiography

FITZROY, R.
MALLAMSHIRE SERIES:
1 The Manor of Braye 1979
2 The widow's might 1980
3 The American Duchess 1980
4 Ill fares the land 1987
5 Barnaby's Charity 1988
6 The Rockport rubies 1989

FITZWILLIAM, J.
1 Anyway, this particular Sunday 1976
2 How many years was it now? 1978
A Scottish adolescence in the 1930's

FLANDERS, P.
1 Doctor, doctor 1986
2 Mercenary doctor 1987
N.F. Autobiography

FLEETWOOD, F.
1 Concordia 1971
2 Concordia errant 1973
*1 is the story of Paolo and Francesca,
seen through the eyes of Concordia, her
daughter*

FLEISCHER, L.
1 Saturday night fever 1980
2 Staying alive 1983
*Novels based on the films of the same
name*

FLEMING, G. H.
1 Rossetti and the Pre-Raphaelite
Brotherhood 1968
2 That ne'er shall meet again 1971
*N.F. The Brotherhood and the careers
of the three principal members after its
dissolution*

FLEMING, I.
JAMES BOND:
1 Casino Royale 1953
2 Live and let die 1954
3 Moonraker 1955
4 Diamonds are forever 1956
5 From Russia with love 1957
6 Dr. No 1958
7 Goldfinger 1959
8 For your eyes only 1960

9 Thunderball 1961
10 The spy who loved me 1961
11 On Her Majesty's Secret Service 1963
12 You only live twice 1964
13 The man with the golden gun 1965
14 Octopussy and The Living Daylights 1966
15 Dr. Sun, by R. Markham, i.e. K. Amis 1975
16 Licence renewed, by J. Gardner 1981
17 For special services, by J. Gardner 1982
18 Icebreaker, by J. Gardner 1983
19 Role of honour, by J. Gardner 1984
20 Nobody lives forever, by J. Gardner 1986
21 No deals, Mr Bond, by J. Gardner 1987
22 Scorpius, by J. Gardner 1988
23 Win lose or die, by J. Gardner 1990
24 Brokenclaw, by J. Gardner 1990
25 The man from Barbarossa, by J. Gardner 1991
3 and 10 were revised and rewritten for the films by Christopher Wood in 1979 and 1973. J. N. Chance has also written about a character called James Bond, but these do not carry on in the Fleming tradition, as do those by John Gardner.

FLEMING, J.
NURI BEY SERIES:
1 When I grow rich 1964
2 Nothing is the number when you die 1965

FLETCHER, D.
RAINBOW:
1 Rainbow in hell 1983
2 Rainbows end in tears 1984
ROBERT LUMAN:
1 The accident of Robert Luman 1988
2 A wagon-load of monkeys 1988

FLETCHER, G. N.
1 In my father's house
2 Preacher's kids
N.F. Autobiography

FLETCHER, I.
HISTORY OF VIRGINIA SERIES:
1 Roanoke hundred (Elizabethan) 1948
2 Bennett's welcome (Cromwellian) 1950
3 Men of Albemarle (1710-1712) 1945
4 Cormorant's brood (1712-1718) 1959
5 Lusty wind for Carolina (1718-1725) 1944
6 Raleigh's Eden (1765-1782) 1940
7 The wind in the forest (1771) 1957

8 Toil of the brave (1779-1780) 1946
9 Queen's gift (1788) 1952
This is the suggested order of reading, not order of publication. Although this is regarded as a series, nos. 3, 5 and 6 were originally a trilogy about North Carolina, with 8 as a pendant with the same characters.

FLINT, E.
1 Hot bread and chips 1963
2 Kipper stew 1964
N.F. Autobiography

FLINT, K. C.
THE SIDHE LEGENDS:
1 The hound of Culain
2 Riders of the Sidhe
3 Champions of the Sidhe
4 Master of the Sidhe
5 The challenge of the Clans
6 Storm shield
7 The dark druid
Paperback fantasy

FLOWER, P.
INSPECTOR SWINTON SERIES:
1 Goodby Sweet William
2 Wax flowers for Gloria
3 A wreath of water lilies 1959
4 One rose less 1960
5 Hell for Heather 1963

FLYNN, B.
ANTHONY BATHURST SERIES:
1 The billiard room mystery 1928
2 The case of the black twenty-two 1928
3 Mystery of the peacock's eye 1928
4 The murders near Mapleton 1928
5 Invisible death 1929
6 The five red fingers 1929
7 The creeping Jenny mystery 1930
8 Murder en route 1930
9 The orange axe 1931
10 The triple bit 1931
11 The padded door 1932
12 The edge of terror 1932
13 The spiked lion 1933
14 The League of Matthias 1934
15 The horn 1934
16 The case of the purple calf 1934
17 The Sussex cuckoo 1935
18 The Fortescue candle 1936
19 Fear and trembling 1936
20 Cold evil 1938
21 Tread softly 1937
22 The ebony stag 1938
23 Black edged 1939

24 The case of the faithful heart 1939
25 The case of the painted ladies 1940
26 They never came back 1940
27 Such bright disguises 1941
28 Glittering prizes 1942
29 Reverse the charge 1943
30 The grim maiden 1944
31 The case of Elymas the sorcerer 1945
32 Conspiracy at Angel 1946
33 The sharp quillet 1947
34 Exit Sir John 1948
35 The swinging death 1948
36 Men for pieces 1949
37 Black agent 1950
38 Where there was smoke 1951
39 And cauldron bubble 1951
40 The ring of Innocent 1952
41 The seventh sign 1952
42 The running nun 1952
43 Out of the dusk 1953
44 The feet of death 1954
45 The doll's done dancing 1954
46 The shaking spear 1955
47 Conspiracy at Angel 1955
48 The dice are dark 1955
49 The toy lamb 1956
50 The murder collection 1956
51 The wife who disappeared 1956
52 The hands of justice 1956
53 The nine cuts 1957
54 The saints are sinister 1958

FOLEY, R.
HIRAM POTTER SERIES:
1 Dangerous to me 1960
2 The deadly noose 1963
3 It's murder, Mr. Potter 1963
4 Back door to death 1964
5 Fatal lady 1964
6 Call it accident 1966
7 A calculated risk 1968

FOLEY, W.
1 Child in the forest 1974
2 Return to the forest 1981
N.F. Autobiography

FOLLETT, K.
PIERS ROPER SERIES:
1 The shake out 1975
2 The bear raid 1976

FORBES, C.
TWEED & NEWMAN:
1 Terminal 1984
2 Cover story 1985
3 The Janus man 1987
4 Deadlock 1987

5 The Greek key 1988
6 Shockwave 1989
7 Whirlpool 1990

FORD, D.
GWYNETH SERIES:
1 The following seasons
2 The catch of time 1960
3 No further elegy 1961

FORD, E.
THE TYLDENS:
1 Meeting in spring
2 One fine day
MAPLECHESTER SERIES:
1 The empty heart 1960
2 The cottage at Tumble 1961
3 Heron's nest 1962
4 A week by the sea 1963
5 A holiday engagement 1963
6 No room for Joanna 1964

FORD, H.
1 Felix walking 1968
2 Felix running 1969

FORD, J. A.
1 The brave white flag 1961
2 Season of escape 1964

FORD, L.
COLONEL PRIMROSE SERIES:
1 The strangled witness
2 Ill met by moonlight 1939
3 The simple way of poison 1939
4 Mr. Cromwell is dead (Reno
  rendezvous) 1939
5 Snow-white murder (False to any man) 1939
6 Old lover's ghost
7 A capital crime (The murder of the fifth
  columnist)
8 Priority murder (Murder in the O.P.M.)
9 Siren in the night
10 Crack of dawn (All for the love of a
  lady)
11 The Philadelphia murder story
12 Honolulu murder story
13 Woman in black
14 The Devil's stronghold
15 Shot in the dark
16 Murder is the payoff
17 The lying jade (Washington whispers
  murder)
18 Road to folly
19 Three bright pebbles 1939
20 The town cried murder
21 Date with death
22 Bahamas murder case 1954

23 Invitation to murder
24 Murder comes to Eden 1956

FORD, R.
FARADAWN:
1 Quest for Faradawn 1982
2 Melvaig's vision 1984
3 Children of Ashgaroth 1986
Fantasy

FORDE, NICHOLAS
MARK URGENT SERIES:
1 Urgent enquiry 1973
2 Urgent action 1974
3 Urgent delivery 1975
4 Urgent trip 1977
5 Urgent wedding 1979
6 Urgent honeymoon 1981

FOREMAN, R.
1 Long pig 1959
2 Sandlewood Island 1961

FORES, J.
1 Forgotten place 1955
2 The springboard 1956
Novels about London airport

FORESTER, C. S.
HORNBLOWER SERIES:
1 Mr. Midshipman Hornblower 1950
2 Lieutenant Hornblower 1952
3 Hornblower and the Atropos 1956
4 Hornblower and the Hotspur 1962
5 The happy return 1937 (Beat to quarters)
6 Ship of the line 1937
7 Flying colours 1938
8 The Commodore 1945
9 Lord Hornblower 1946
10 Hornblower in the West Indies 1958
11 Hornblower and the crisis 1967
This novel was unfinished.
Chronologically, it comes after 4, but also included are two short stories, 'Hornblower and the widow McCool' which comes at 2 and 'The last encounter', which is the final event in Hornblower's career.
Nos. 4, 5 and 6 published in one volume 'Captain Hornblower , R. N.'.
Nos 7, 8 and 9 published as 'The young Hornblower'. 'Hornblower's triumph', and 'Hornblower in captivity' are abridgements of 8 and 9 and 6 and 7 for junior reading. 'The Hornblower companion', 1964, is Forester's own

description of the background of the series.

★★★

1 The voyage of the Annie Marble
2 The Annie Marble in Germany
N.F. Travel

FORREST, A.
CAPTAIN JUSTICE:
1 Captain Justice 1981
2 The Pandora secret 1982
3 A balance of dangers 1984

FORREST, K. V.
KATE DEELAFIELD:
1 Amateur city
2 At the Nightwood Bar
3 Beverly Malibu 1990
Feminist "Private Eye" stories

FORREST, R.
LYON WENTWORTH:
1 Death through the looking glass 1978
2 The wizard of death 1979
3 A child's garland of death 1979
4 Death in the Willows 1980
5 Death at Yew Corner 1981

FORRESTER, H.
1 Twopence to cross the Mersey 1974
2 Minerva's step-child 1979
3 By the waters of Liverpool 1981
4 Lime street at two 1985
N.F. Autobiography of a Liverpool childhood

FORSTER, P.
ALEX SMITH AND TONY BROWN:
1 Play the ball 1967
2 Play the man 1970
3 The disinherited 1973
A trilogy on World War II and its effects on a generation of Englishmen who were schoolboys when it started

FORSYTE, C.
DETECTIVE INSPECTOR LEFT:
1 Diplomatic death 1961
2 Diving death 1962
3 Double death 1964

FORTESCUE, LADY WINIFRED
1 Perfume from Provence 1950
2 Sunset house 1949
3 There's Rosemary, there's rue 1950
4 Trampled lilies 1949
5 Mountain madness 1951

6 Beauty for ashes 1948
7 Laughter in Provence 1951
N.F. Autobiography

FORTUNE, D.
VIVIEN LE FAY MORGAN:
1 The sea priestess
2 Moon magic

FORWARD, R.
THE OWL:
1 The owl
2 Scarlet serenade
Paperback horror stories

FOSTER, A. D.
FLINX AND PIP:
1 The Tar Aiym Krang 1972
2 Nor crystal tears 1983
3 Flix in flux 1989
4 The end of the matter 1991
Fantasy
ICERIGGER TRILOGY:
1 Ice rigger 1978
2 Mission to Moulokin 1979
3 The deluge drivers 1990
SPELLSINGER:
1 Spellsinger 1986
2 The hour of the gate 1986
3 The day of the dissonance
4 The moment of the magician
5 The paths of the Perambulator 1986
6 The time of the transference 1988

1 Aliens 1979
2 Aliens 1986
Based on the films

FOUNTAINE, M.
1 Love among the butterflies 1980
2 Butterflies and late loves 1986
N.F. Biography

FOWLES, A.
RICHARD POWELL:
1 Dupe negative 1970
2 Double feature 1971

FOX, A.
1 Slightly foxed 1986
2 Completely foxed 1989
N.F. Autobiography of the theatrical family

FOXALL, P. A.
DET. SGT. SCAMP:
1 Vultures in the smoke 1972
2 The big time 1973

3 Confessions of a convict 1974
4 Scamp's law 1975
5 No life for a loser 1977
6 Taming the furies 1978
7 Hostage of the damned 1979
INSPECTOR DERBEN:
1 The murder machine 1976
2 Inspector Derben's war 1976
3 Inspector Derben and the widow maker 1977
4 The Hell's Angel Kidnapping 1978
CATFORD POLICE STATION:
1 A dishonest way to die 1977
2 Act of terror 1979
3 Sequel to yesterday's crime 1979
4 To kill a call girl 1980
5 The silent informer 1981

FOXALL, R.
1 The devil's smile 1963
2 The devil's spawn 1965
Historical Novels of the Stuart period. Not strictly sequels, but characters recur

FOXALL, RAYMOND
HARRY ADKINS SERIES:
1 The little ferret 1970
2 Brandy for the parson 1971
3 The dark forest 1972
4 The silver goblet 1974
5 The last Jacobite 1980
Detective stories set in the early 19th century

FOXELL, N.
EMMA HAMILTON:
1 Loving Emma 1986
2 Emma expects 1987

FOYLE, K.
AUGHERIM SERIES:
1 The doctor's lady
2 Whither thou goest
3 Other people's shoes 1954

FRALEY, O.
1 The 'untouchables' 1967
2 Four against the mob 1968
3 The last of the 'untouchables'

FRAME, J.
1 To the Is-land 1983
2 An angel at my table 1984
3 The envoy from Mirror City 1985
N.F. Autobiography of a New Zealand author

FRANCIS, C.
1 Come wind or weather 1977
2 Come hell or high water 1978
*N.F. The author's accounts of her
single-handed voyages*

FRANCIS, D.
KIT FIELDING:
1 Break-in 1985
2 Bolt 1986
SID HALLEY:
1 Odds against 1965
2 Whip hand 1980

FRANKAU, P.
CLOTHES FOR A KING'S SON:
1 Sing for your supper 1963
2 Slaves of the lamp 1965
3 Over the mountains 1966
*A trilogy about an English family, the
Westons*

FRANKEN, R.
1 Claudia 1939
2 Claudia and David 1940
3 Another Claudia 1943
4 Young Claudia 1945
5 The marriage of Claudia 1947
6 From Claudia to David 1950
7 The fragile years 1953
8 Return of Claudia 1955
*Later published in one volume as 'The
Book of Claudia'. Again republished in
separate volumes, 1972*

FRANKLIN, C.
ANNABEL:
1 Adventures of Annabel
2 Face the music
GRANT GARFIELD SERIES:
1 Exit without permit 1946
2 Cocktails with a stranger 1947
3 Rope of sand 1948
4 Storm in an inkpot 1949
5 The mask of Kane 1949
6 She'll love you dead 1950
7 One night to kill 1950
8 Maid for murder 1951
9 Escape to death 1951
10 No other victim 1952
11 Gallows for a fool 1952
12 The stranger came back 1953
13 Stop that man 1954
14 Girl in shadow 1955
15 Out of time 1956
16 Death on my shoulder 1958
17 Gently you must be 1959
18 Breathe no more 1959

19 Handful of sinners 1959
20 Fear runs softly 1961
JIM BURGESS SERIES:
1 Guilt for innocence 1960
2 Kill me and live 1961
3 The bath of acid
4 Murder before dinner 1963
MRS. MAXINE DANGERFIELD:
1 The dangerous ones 1964
2 On the day of the shooting 1965
3 Death in the East 1966
4 Escape 1967

FRANKLIN, M.
STARSKY AND HUTCH:
1 Starsky and Hutch
2 Death ride
3 Kill Huggy Bear
4 The bounty hunter
5 The psychic
6 Watcher on the docks
7 The set up
8 Murder on Playboy Island
Paperbacks

FRASER, ANTHEA
CHIEF INSPECTOR WEBB:
1 A shroud for Delilah 1984
2 A necessary end 1985
3 Pretty maids all in a row 1986
4 Death speaks softly 1987
5 The nine bright shiners 1987
6 Six proud walkers 1988
7 The April rainers 1989
8 Symbols at your door 1990
9 The lily white-boys 1991

FRASER, ANTONIA
JEMIMA SHORE:
1 Quiet as a nun 1977
2 The wild island 1978
3 A splash of red 1981
4 Cool repentance 1982
5 Oxford blood 1985
6 Jemima Shore's first case and other
stories 1986
7 Your Royal Hostage 1987
8 The Cavalier case 1990
9 Jemima Shore at the sunny grave 1991
*Jemima also appears in a short story,
'The Parr children'
9 contains four Jemima Shore short
stories, with several others.*

FRASER, A. S.
1 The hills of home 1973
2 In memory long 1977

3 Roses in December 1979
N.F. Autobiography

FRASER, C. M.
1 Blue above the chimneys 1980
2 Roses round the door 1986
3 Green are my mountains 1990
N.F. Autobiography of the author of
'Rhanna'
RHANNA:
1 Rhanna 1978
2 Rhanna at war 1979
3 Children of Rhanna 1984
4 Return to Rhanna 1984
5 A song of Rhanna 1985
6 Storm over Rhanna 1988
Novels about a Hebridean island
THE GRANTS OF ROTHIEDRUM:
1 King's Croft 1986
2 King's Acre 1987
3 King's Exile 1989
4 King's Close 1991

FRASER, D.
TREASON IN ARMS:
1 A kiss for the enemy 1985
2 The killing times 1986
3 The dragon's teeth 1987
4 The seizure 1987
5 A candle for Judas 1989

FRASER, G. M.
FLASHMAN:
1 Flashman (1839-42) 1969
2 Royal Flash (1842-3) 1970
3 Flash for freedom (1848-9) 1971
4 Flashman at the charge (1854-5) 1972
5 Flashman in the great game (1836-8)
  1975
6 Flashman's lady (1842-5) 1977
7 Flashman and the Redskins (1849 &
  1875/6) 1982
8 Flashman and the dragon (1860) 1985
9 Flashman and the mountain of light
  1990
The later adventures of the bully in
'Tom Brown's Schooldays'. The order
is that of publication

★ ★ ★

1 The General danced at dawn 1973
2 McAuslan in the rough 1974
3 The Sheikh and the dustbin 1988
McAuslan is a character in one of the
stories in 1.

FRASER, J.
DET.-INSPECTOR BILL AVEYARD:

1 The evergreen death 1968
2 A cockpit of roses 1969
3 Deadly nightshade 1970
4 Death in a pheasant's eye 1971
5 Blood on a widow's cross 1972
6 The five leaved clover 1974
7 A wreath of lords and ladies 1974
8 Who steals my name 1976
9 Hearts ease in death 1977
Superintendent Aveyard from No. 4

FRASER, M.
THE VILLAGE:
1 The first summer 1979
2 The long winter 1980
3 Time of charge 1981

FRASER, R.
1 A visit to Venus 1957
2 Jupiter in the chair 1958
3 Trout's testament 1959
4 City of the sun 1961

FRASER, S. (R. CLEWS)
TILDY CRAWFORD:
1 Tildy 1985
2 Poorhouse woman 1986
3 Nursing woman 1987
4 Pointing woman 1988
5 Radical woman 1989
6 Gang woman 1989
7 Widow woman 1991
GRAINNE MCDERMOT:
1 The bitter dawning 1989
2 The harsh noontide 1990

FRAZER, R. C.
MARK KILBY SERIES:
1 Secret syndicate 1963
2 The Hollywood hoax 1964
3 The Miami mob *and* Mark Kilby
  stands alone 1965

FREDMAN, J.
CHARLES DEXTER:
1 The fourth agency 1968
2 The false Joanna 1970

FREDMAN, M.
WILLIE HALLIDAY SERIES:
1 You can always blame the rain 1977
2 Kisses leave no fingerprints 1979

FREE, C.
POLLITT FAMILY:
1 Vinegar hill
2 Bay of shadows
3 Brannan 1981

FREELING, N.
VAN DER VALK SERIES:
1 Love in Amsterdam 1962
2 Because of the cats 1963
3 Gun before butter 1963
4 Double-barrel 1964
5 Criminal conversations 1965
6 The king of the rainy country 1966
7 The Dresden green 1966
8 Strike out where not applicable 1967
9 Tsing-boum 1969
10 Over the high side 1971
11 A long silence 1972
ARLETTE VAN DER VALK:
1 The widow 1979
2 One damn thing after another 1981
3 Sand castle 1989
Novels about Van der Valk's widow
HENRI CASTANG:
1 Dressing of diamond 1974
2 What are the bugles blowing for 1975
3 Lake Isle 1976
4 Night lords 1978
5 Castang's city 1980
6 Wolfnight 1982
7 Back of the north wind 1983
8 No part in your death 1984
9 Cold iron 1986
10 Lady Macbeth 1988
11 Not as far as Velma 1989
12 Those in peril 1990
Arlette Van der Valk appears in 10.

FREEMANTLE, B.
CHARLIE MUFFIN:
1 Charlie Muffin 1977
2 Clap hands here comes Charlie 1978
3 The inscrutable Charlie Muffin 1979
4 Charlie Muffin's Uncle Sam 1980
5 Madrigal for Charlie Muffin 1981
6 Charlie Muffin and Russian Rose 1985
7 Charlie Muffin San 1987
8 The run around 1988
9 Comrade Charlie 1989

FRENCH, F.
GENERAL OGLE-OXLEY:
1 Smouldering fuse 1970
2 Invitation to die 1970

FRENCH, H.
1 I swore I never would 1970
2 I thought I never could 1973
N.F. Autobiography

FRERE, R.
1 Maxwell's ghost 1976

2 Beyond the Highland line 1984
N.F. Autobiography of a climber

FREUND, P.
THE VOLCANO GOD TRILOGY:
1 Saturnalia and the nomads 1956
2 Eurasia and the rooftops
3 How the world began

FRIEDMAN, M.
GEORGINA LEE MAXWELL:
1 Deadly reflections 1989
2 Temporary ghost 1990

FRIEDMAN, R.
1 A loving mistress 1983
2 A second wife 1985
SHELTON FAMILY:
1 Proofs of affection 1982
2 Rose of Jericho 1984
3 To live in peace 1988

FRIESNER, E.
1 Here be demons
2 Demon blues

FROST, G. R.
1 Recon
2 Recon strike
Paperback war stories

FRYE, P.
LIFE OF LORD NELSON:
1 Game for empires 1953
2 Sleeping sword

FULLER, E.
THE TROUBLESHOOTERS:
1 The troubleshooters
2 The savage west
3 Violence in the Black Hills
4 The big killing 1970
All paperback only

FULLER, K.
RIVERVIEW:
1 Bitter legacy 1988
2 The lion's share 1988
3 Pride of place 1989

FULLER, R., *see* METALIOUS, G.

FULLER, R.
1 Souvenirs 1981
2 Vamp until ready 1982
3 Home and dry 1984
N.F. Autobiography

FULLERTON, A.
NICK EVERARD:
1 Sixty minutes for St. George 1975
2 The blooding of the guns 1976
3 Patrol to the Golden Horn 1978
4 Storm force to Narvik 1979
5 Last lift from Crete 1980
6 All the drowning seas 1981
7 A share of honour 1982
8 The torch bearers 1983
9 The gate-crashers 1984
SBS
1 Special deliverance 1986
2 Special dynamic 1987
3 Special deception 1988
Adventure stories about the Special Boat Service

FURNELL, J.
1 Dark portal
2 God on the mountain

FURST, R.
ROGER LEVIN:
1 The Paris drop 1982
2 The Caribbean account 1983

FUSSEY, J.
1 Milk my ewes and weep 1974
2 Cows in the corn 1978
3 Calf love 1984
4 Cats in the coffee 1986
N.F. Family life on a remote Yorkshire farm

FYSH, H.
1 Quantas rising 1966
2 Quantas at war 1968
N.F. History of the Australian national airline

GAAN, M.
OPIUM WAR TRILOGY:
1 Red barbarian 1984
2 White poppy 1986
3 Blue mountain 1987

GAGE, N.
1 Eleni 1983
2 A place for us 1990
N.F. Autobiography

GAGNON, M.
DIEDRE O'HARA:
1 The inner ring 1985
2 A dark night offshore 1986
3 Doubtful motives 1987

GAINHAM, S.
VIENNESE TRILOGY:
1 Night falls on the city 1967
2 A place in the country 1969
3 Private worlds 1971
From the Hitler take-over to the creation of a post-war, neutral Austria. The main character is Julia Homburg, a famous actress, but 2 is told by an English officer during the occupation.

GAIR, M.
MARK RAEBURN SERIES:
1 Sapphires on Wednesday
2 A long hard look 1958
3 The burning of Troy

GAITE, F.
JAMES AND CHARLES LATIMER (DIED 1870):
1 Brief candles
2 A family matter
3 Come and go 1958
Adventures of two ghosts.

GALLAGHER, T.
BILL THOMPSON:
1 Apprentice 1983
2 Journeyman 1984
3 Survivor 1985

GALLAGHER, J.
THE ARCHERS:
1 To the victors the spoils 1987
2 Return to Ambridge 1987
3 Borchester echoes 1987
A trilogy based on the radio series.

GALLAGHER, P.
1 Castles in the air
2 No greater love
Paperback

GALLICO, P.
1 Adventures of Hiram Holliday
2 The secret front
MRS. HARRIS SERIES:
1 Flowers for Mrs. Harris 1958
2 Mrs. Harris goes to New York 1960
3 Mrs. Harris goes to Paris 1958
4 Mrs. Harris, M.P. 1965
5 Mrs. Harris goes to Moscow 1974
ALEXANDER HERO:
1 Too many ghosts 1961
2 The hand of Mary Constable 1964
Two novels about physical research.
POSEIDON:
1 The Poseidon adventure 1969

2 Beyond the Poseidon 1978

GALLISON, K.
1 Unbalanced accounts 1986
2 The death tape 1987

GALWAY, R. C.
JAMES PACKARD SERIES:
1 Assignment New York 1961
2 Assignment London 1963
3 Assignment Andalusia 1964
4 Assignment gaolbreak 1966
5 Assignment Argentina 1967
6 Assignment Fenland 1969
7 Assignment seabed 1969
8 Assignment Sydney 1970
9 Assignment deathsquad 1970

GANN, E. K.
1 The triumph 1986
2 The antagonists 1971

GARDNER, A.
DAVIS TROY SERIES:
1 The escalator 1963
2 Assignment Tahiti 1964
3 Six day week 1965
4 Man who was too much 1967

GARDNER, C. S.
1 A difficulty with dwarves
2 A disagreement with death
3 An excess of enchantments
4 A malady of magicks
5 A multitude of monsters
6 A night in the Netherhells
Paperback fantasy

GARDNER, E. S.
PERRY MASON SERIES:
1 The case of the velvet claw 1933
2 The case of the sulky girl 1933
3 The case of the lucky legs 1934
4 The case of the howling dog 1934
5 The case of the curious bride 1934
6 The case of the counterfeit eye 1935
7 The case of the caretaker's cat 1935
8 The case of the sleepwalker's niece 1938
9 The case of the dangerous dowager 1939
10 The case of the lame canary 1939
11 The case of the substitute face 1939
12 The case of the perjured parrot 1939
13 The case of the silent partner 1940
14 The case of the empty tin 1940
15 The case of the stuttering bishop 1940
16 The case of the rolling bones 1940

17 The case of the shoplifter's shoe 1941
18 The case of the baited hook 1941
19 The case of the haunted husband 1942
20 The case of the turning tide 1942
21 The case of the drowning duck 1944
22 The case of the careless kitten 1945
23 The case of the smoking chimney 1945
24 The case of the goldigger's purse 1945
25 The case of the half-awakened wife 1945
26 The case of the buried clock 1946
27 The case of the drowsy mosquito 1946
28 The case of the crooked candle 1947
29 The case of the black eyes blonde 1948
30 The case of the borrowed brunette 1951
31 The case of the fan-dancer's horse 1952
32 The case of the vagabond virgin 1953
33 The case of the lonely heiress 1953
34 The case of the lazy lover 1954
35 The case of the dubious bridegroom 1954
36 The case of the backward mule 1955
37 The case of the cautious coquette 1955
38 The case of the negligent nymph 1956
39 The case of the one-eyed witness 1956
40 The case of the musical cow 1956
41 The case of the angry mourner 1957
42 The case of the fiery fingers 1957
43 The case of the grinning gorilla 1958
44 The case of the moth-eaten mink 1958
45 The case of the green-eyed sister 1959
46 The case of the hesitant hostess 1959
47 The case of the fugitive nurse 1959
48 The case of the runaway corpse 1960
49 The case of the restless redhead 1960
50 The case of the glamorous ghost 1960
51 The case of the sunbather's diary 1961
52 The case of the nervous accomplice 1961
53 The case of the terrified typist 1961
54 The case of the gilded lily 1962
55 The case of the demure defendent 1962 (The case of the missing poison)
56 The case of the lucky loser 1962
57 The case of the screaming woman 1963
58 The case of the daring decoy 1963
59 The case of the long-legged models 1963 (The case of the dead-man's daughter)
60 The case of the footloose doll 1964
61 The case of the calendar girl 1964
62 The case of the deadly toy 1964 (The case of the greedy grandpa)
63 The case of the mythical monkeys 1965
64 The case of the singing skirt 1965
65 The case of the waylaid wolf 1965
66 The case of the duplicate daughter 1966
67 The case of the shapely shadow 1966

68 The case of the spurious spinster 1966
69 The case of the bigamous spouse 1967
70 The case of the reluctant model 1967
71 The case of the blonde bonanza 1967
72 The case of the ice-cold hands 1968
73 The case of the mischievous doll 1968
74 The case of the stepdaughter's secret 1968
75 The case of the amorous aunt 1969
76 The case of the daring divorcee 1969
77 The case of the phantom fortune 1970
78 The case of the horrified heirs 1971
79 The case of the troubled trustee 1971
80 The case of the beautiful beggar 1972
81 The case of the worried waitress 1972
82 The case of the careless Cupid 1973
83 The case of the queenly contestant 1973
84 The case of the fabulous fake 1974
85 The case of the crying swallow 1974
86 The case of the crimson kiss 1975
87 The case of the irate witness 1975
88 The case of the fenced-in woman 1976
89 The case of the postponed murder 1977
DISTRICT ATTORNEY SERIES::
1 The District Attorney calls it murder 1977
2 The District Attorney holds a candle 1941
3 The District Attorney draws a circle 1940
4 The District Attorney goes to trial 1941
5 District Attorney calls a turn 1947
6 District Attorney cooks a goose 1943
7 District Attorney breaks a seal 1950
8 District Attorney takes a chance 1956
9 The District Attorney breaks an egg 1957
See also **A. A. Fair,** *pseud.*

GARDNER, JEROME
DIPSPRING SERIES:
1 Gunman
2 Dilemma at Dipspring 1976
3 The underhand mail 1976
4 The old timers 1979
5 Confession at Dipspring 1982
6 The Jayhawk legacy 1983

GARDNER, JOHN
1 The secret generations 1987
2 The secret houses 1988
3 The secret families 1989
BOYSIE L. OAKES SERIES:
1 The liquidator 1964
2 The understrike 1965
3 Amber nine 1967
4 Madrigal 1967
5 Founder member 1969

6 Traitor's exit 1970
7 The airline pirates 1970
8 The champagne communist 1971
9 A killer for a song 1974
DEREK TORRY SERIES:
1 A complete state of death 1969
2 The Corner men 1974
MORIARTY:
1 Return of Moriarty 1974
2 Revenge of Moriarty 1975
Based on A. C. Doyle's character
HERBIE KRUGER:
1 The Nostrodamus traitor 1978
2 The garden of weapons 1980
3 The quiet dogs 1982

GARFIELD, B.
PAUL BENJAMIN SERIES:
1 Death wish 1974
2 Death sentence 1975
3 Recoil 1977

GARLOCK, D.
WABASH RIVER TRILOGY:
1 Dream River 1990
2 Lonesome River 1990
3 River of tomorrow 1991

GARNER, W.
MIKE JAGGER SERIES:
1 Overkill 1966
2 The deep, deep freeze 1967
3 The us or then war 1968
4 A big enough wreath 1974
JOHN MORPURGO:
1 Think big, think dirty 1983
2 Rats alley 1984

GARNETT, D.
1 Golden echo 1953
2 Flowers of the forest 1955
3 The familiar faces 1962
N.F. Autobiography

GARNETT, W.
1 Farmer Gribbins and Farmer Green
2 Wrangledale Chase 1989

GARRETT, C. G.
GUNSLINGER:
1 The massacre trail
2 The golden gun
3 White Apache
4 Fifty calibre kill
5 Arizona bloodline
6 Rebel vengeance
7 Death canyon
8 Peace maker!

9 The Russian lode

GARRETT, R.
ALAN BRETT:
1 Run down: the world of Alan Brett
1970
2 Spiral 1971

GASH, J.
LOVEJOY:
1 The Judas pair 1978
2 Gold from Gemini 1979
3 The Grail tree 1979
4 The spend game 1980
5 The Vatican rip 1981
6 The firefly gadroon 1982
7 The sleepers of Erin 1983
8 The gondola scam 1984
9 Pearlhanger 1985
10 The Tartan ringers 1986
11 Moonspender 1986
12 Jade woman 1988
13 The very last gambado 1989
14 The great California game 1990

GASH, N.
1 Mr. Secretary Peel 1961
2 Sir Robert Peel 1972
N.F. Biography

GASK, A.
GILBERT LAROSE SERIES:
1 Dark highway 1928
2 Lonely house 1929
3 Shadow of Larose 1931
4 House on the island
5 Secret of the Sandhills 1932
6 Gentlemen of crime 1932
7 Judgement of Larose 1934
8 The hidden door 1934
9 Poisoned goblet 1935
10 Hangman's knot, 1936
11 Cloud the smiter 1936
12 The jest of life 1937
13 Master spy 1937
14 Night of the storm 1938
15 Grave digger of Monk's Arden 1939
16 Fall of a dictator 1939
17 Vengeance of Laros 1939
18 House of the fens 1940
19 Tragedy of the silver moon 1940
20 Beachy head murder 1941
21 His prey was a man 1943
22 Mystery of Fell Castle 1944
23 Man of death 1946
24 The dark mill stream 1948
25 The unfolding years 1950
26 Vaults of Blackarden Castle 1952

27 Silent dead 1953
28 Storm breaks 1953
29 House with high walls 1951
30 Marauders by night 1953
31 Night and fog 1953
32 Crime upon crime 1954

GASKELL, E.
CRANFORD:
1 Cranford revisited, by J. R. Townsend
1989

GASKELL, J.
1 The serpent 1963
2 Atlan 1965
3 The city 1966
4 Some summer lands 1977
Novels about an imaginery semi-
primitive world

GASTON, B.
LT. JASON WINTER:
1 Winter and the 'Wild Cat' 1980
2 Winter and the 'White Witch' 1981
3 Winter and the 'Wild Rover' 1982
4 Winter and the widowmakers 1984
5 Winter and the 'Wanderer' 1986
Novels about a Customs Revenue cutter
in the 18thC

GATES, T.
1 Scipio 1969
2 Ancora Scipio 1970

GAULLE, C. de
1 The call to honour (1940-1942) 1955
2 Unity (1942-1944) 1959
3 Salvation (1944-1946) 1960
4 Memoirs of hope 1971
Renewal, 1958-62; Endeavours 1962-
N.F. Autobiography. No. 4 was
published in France in two parts.

GAUNT, R.
BORGIA SERIES:
1 Blood for Borgia 1965
2 Vendetta 1968
3 Lucrezi Borgia's lover 1971
ENGLISH CIVIL WAR SERIES:
1 Brother enemy 1969
2 The iron girdle 1969

GAVIN, C.
1 A light woman 1986
2 The glory road 1987
***
1 Clyde valley
2 The hostile shore

SECOND EMPIRE QUARTET:
1 The Fortress (Finland, 1855) 1950
2 The moon into blood (Italy, 1859) 1952
3 The cactus and the crown (Mexico, 1866) 1954
4 Madeleine (France 1870) 1957 (rev. ed 1971)
Novels about 19th century Europe. Although characters do not recur, the series is seen by the author as a unity.
***
1 The devil in the harbour 1968
2 The house of war 1970
3 Give me the daggers 1972
4 The snow mountain 1973
A series of novels about World War I and its aftermath. There is a connection between no. 3 and no. 1 in the 2nd Empire quartet, but they are not sequels.
***
RESISTANCE TRILOGY:
1 Traitor's Gate 1976
2 None dare call it treason 1979
3 How sleep the brave 1980
France under De Gaulle in WW2

GAYE, C.
1 Jane Scott 1963
2 Jane Scott again 1964
3 Jane Scott meets the doctor 1965
4 Jane Scott married 1965
5 Jane Scott meets the Pops 1966
6 Jane Scott, crime reporter 1967

GAYE, P. F.
THE VANDERWOOD TRILOGY:
1 The French prisoner
2 Louisa Vanderwood
3 On a darkling plain

GEDDES, P.
VENNIKER:
1 The high game 1968
2 A November wind 1970
3 The Ottawa allegation 1973
4 A state of corruption 1985

GEE, M.
1 Plumb 1979
2 Meg 1981
3 Sole survivor 1983

GELLIS, R.
ROSELYNDE CHRONICLES:
1 Roselynde 1978
2 Alinor 1979

3 Joanna 1979
4 Gilliane 1980
5 Rhiannon 1984
6 Sybelle 1984

GEMMEL, D.
1 Lion of Macedon 1991
2 Dark Prince 1991
THE DRENAI SAGA:
1 Legend 1984
2 The King beyond the gate 1985
3 Waylander 1986
4 Quest for lost heroes 1990
SIPSTRASSI TALES:
1 Wolf in shadow 1987
2 Ghost king 1988
3 Last sword of power 1988
4 The last guardian 1989
Fantasy

GEMS, P.
MRS. FRAMPTON:
1 Mrs. Frampton 1988
2 Bon Voyage, Mrs. Frampton 1990

GENTLE, M.
1 Golden witchbreed 1983
2 Ancient light 1987
Fantasy

GEORGE, E.
DET. CHIEF INSPECTOR LYNLEY:
1 A suitable vengeance 1991
2 A great deliverance 1989
3 Payment in blood 1989
4 Well-schooled in murder 1990

GEORGESON, V.
SHADOW OF THE ELEPHANT:
1 Seeds of love 1986
2 Whispering roots 1987
3 The haunted tree 1989

GERROLD, D.
WAR AGAINST THE CHTORR:
1 A matter for men
2 A day for damnation
Paperback science fiction

GERSON, J.
INSPECTOR LOHMANN:
1 Deaths head Berlin 1987
2 Death squad London 1989

GETHIN, D.
HALLORAN:
1 Jack Lane's Browning 1985
2 Dane's testament 1986

WYATT:
1 Wyatt 1982
2 Wyatt and the Moresby legacy 1983
3 Wyatt's orphan 1985

GHOSE, S. N.
1 And gazelles leaping
2 Cradle of the clouds
***
1 The vermilion boat
2 The flame of the forest 1955
N.F. Autobiography

GHOSE, Z.
1 The incredible Brazilion
2 The beautiful Empire 1975
3 A different world 1978
A trilogy about Brazil

GIBB, L.
1 The Joneses: how to keep up with them 1959
2 The higher Jones 1960
N.F. Humour

GIBBINGS, R.
1 Sweet Thames run softly 1940
2 Till I end my song 1957
N.F. Travel

GIBBON, L. G., *pseud* (I. L. MITCHELL)
A SCOTS QUAIR:
1 Sunset song 1950
2 Cloud Howe
3 Grey granite

GIBBONS, S.
1 Cold Comfort Farm 1932
2 Christmas at Cold Farm 1940
3 Conference at Cold Comfort Farm 1949

GIBBS, H.
THE PRIOR REPORT:
1 Not to the swift
2 Blue days and fair
3 Withered garland
A trilogy of modern marriage
SOUTH AFRICAN HISTORY SERIES:
1 The splendour and the dust 1955
2 The winds of time 1956
3 Thunder at dawn 1957
4 The tumult and the shouting 1959

GIBBS, L.
1 Kitty Villiers
2 The good beauties
Complementary. 2 concerns the life of

Kitty's maid, Elizabeth Spencer.

GIBSON, M.
1 One man's medicine 1983
2 Doctor in the west 1984
N.F. Autobiography

GIBSON, W.
CYBERSPACE:
1 Neuromancer 1984
2 Count Zero 1986
3 Mona Lisa overdrive 1988
Science fiction

GIDE, A.
1 Fruits of the earth 1949
2 Later fruits of the earth
***
1 Journals 1947-51
2 So be it, or the chips are down 1960
N.F. Autobiography

GIELGUD, V.
PELLEW AND CLYMPING SERIES:
1 The goggle-box affair 1965
2 Prinvest-London 1966
3 Conduct of a member 1967
4 A necessary end 1969
5 The candle holders 1970
6 The Black Sambo affair 1972
7 In such a night 1974
After no. 1. the series is referred to as 'Prinvest'.

GILBERT, A.
SCOTT EGERTON SERIES:
1 The tragedy at Freyne
2 The murder of Mrs. Davenport
3 Death at Four corners
4 Mystery of the open window
5 The night of the fog
6 The body on the beam
7 The long shadow
8 The musical comedy crime
9 An old lady dies
10 The man who was too clever
M. DUPUY SERIES:
1 The man in button boots
2 Courtier to death
ARTHUR CROOK SERIES:
1 Murder by experts
2 The man who wasn't there
3 Murder has no tongue
4 Treason in my breast
5 The clock in the hat-box
6 The bell of death
7 Dear dead woman
8 The vanishing corpse

9 The woman in red
10 Something nasty in the woodshed
11 The case of the tea-cosy's aunt
12 The mouse who wouldn't play ball
13 He came by night
14 The scarlet button
15 Don't open the door
16 The black stage 1956
17 The spinster's secret
18 Death in the wrong room
19 Spy for Mr. Crook
20 Die in the dark
21 Lift up the lid
22 Death knocks three times
23 Murder comes home
24 A nice cup of tea
25 Lady killer
26 Miss Pinnegar disappears
27 Footsteps behind me
28 Snake in the grass
29 Give death a name 1957
30 Death against the clock 1959
31 Third time lucky 1959
32 Death takes a wife 1959
33 Out for the kill 1960
34 She shall die 1961
35 Uncertain death 1962
36 Ring for a noose 1963
37 Knock knock who's there? 1964
38 Passenger to nowhere 1965
39 Fingerprint 1966
40 Looking glass murder 1966
41 The visitor 1967
42 Night encounter 1968
43 Missing from her home 1969
44 Death wears a mask 1970
45 Tenant for the tomb 1971
46 Murder's a waiting game 1972
47 A nice little killing 1974

GILBERT, M.
CHIEF INSPECTOR HAZELRIGG SERIES:
1 Close quarters 1947
2 They never looked inside 1948
3 The doors open 1949
4 Smallbone deceased 1950
5 Death has deep roots 1951
6 Fear to tread 1953
Although Hazelrigg appears in all the above, he is not always the leading character. MacCann, Noel Rumbold, and Henry Bohun also appear, and often play the principal parts. They also appear in 'Stay of Execution', 1971.

CALDER AND BEHRENS:
1 Game without rules 1965
2 Mr. Calder and Mr. Behrens 1982

GILBRETH, F. B. *and* CAREY, E. G.
1 Cheaper by the dozen
2 Belles on their toes
3 Inside Nantucket 1955
N.F. Autobiography of a family.

GILCHRIST, R.
DRAGONARD SERIES:
1 Dragonard 1975
2 Master of Dragonard Hill 1976
3 Dragonard blood 1977
4 Dragonard rising 1978
5 The siege of Dragonard Hill 1979
6 Guns of Dragonard 1980
SLAVES WITHOUT MASTERS:
1 The house at 3 o'clock 1982
2 A girl called Friday Night 1983
3 The wrong side of town 1985

GILES, J. H.
THE FOWLER FAMILY:
1 Hannah Fowler 1956
2 The believers 1957
3 Johnny Osage 1960
4 Voyage to Sante Fe 1962
5 Savanna 1961
6 The great adventure 1966
7 Shadygrove 1968
8 Six horse hitch 1969
Novels of frontier life in the U.S.A. 3 and 4, and 6 and 8 are direct sequels about the same characters. Others are on other members of the family:
KENTUCKY SERIES:
1 Enduring hills 1950
2 Miss Willie 1951
3 Tara's healing

GILES, K.
INSPECTOR JAMES AND SGT. HONEYBODY:
1 Some beasts no more 1964
2 The big greed 1965
3 A provenance of death 1966
4 Death in diamonds 1966
5 Death and Mr. Prettyman 1967
6 Death among the stars 1968
7 Death cracks a bottle 1969
8 A death in the church 1970
9 Murder pluperfect 1971
10 A file on death 1973

GILES, R.
SABREHILL:
1 Sabrehill 1987
2 Slaves of Sabrehill 1988
3 Rebels of Sabrehill
4 Storm over Sabrehill

5 Hell cat of Sabrehill
Paperback plantation novels.

GILL, B.

CHIEF INSPECTOR McGARR:
1 McGarr and the Siamese conspiracy 1978
2 McGarr and the politician's wife 1979
3 McGarr on the Cliffs of Moher 1980
4 McGarr at the Dublin Horse Show 1981
5 McGarr and the Prime Minister of Belgrave Square 1983
6 McGarr and the method of Descartes 1985
7 McGarr and the legacy of a woman scorned 1987
8 The death of a Joyce scholar 1989

GILL, B. N.

DET. CHIEF INSPECTOR MAYBRIDGE:
1 Seminar for murder 1985
2 The fifth Rapunzel 1991

GILL, E.

BENVENUTO BROWN SERIES:
1 Strange holiday
2 What dread hand
3 Crime de luxe

GILLESPIE, S.

LONGDEN-LORRISTONE FAMILY SERIES:
1 The martyr 1955
2 The grandson 1957
3 The visitors 1959
4 The neighbour 1960
5 The summer at home 1961
6 The green blade 1963

GILLULY, S.

1 Greenbriar Queen 1989
2 The crystal keep 1989
3 Ritmyin's daughter 1989
Fantasy

GILMAN, D.

MRS. POLLIFAX:
1 The unexpected Mrs. Pollifax 1966
2 The amazing Mrs. Pollifax 1970
3 The elusive Mrs. Pollifax 1973
4 A palm for Mrs. Pollifax 1974
5 Mrs. Pollifax on the China Station 1985
6 Mrs. Pollifax and the Hong Kong Buddah 1986
7 Mrs. Pollifax and the golden triangle 1989

GILMAN, G. G.

ADAM STEELE:
1 The violent peace
2 Bounty hunter
3 Hell's junction
4 Valley of blood
5 Gun run
6 The killing art
7 Crossfire
8 Comanche carnage
9 Badge in the dust
10 The losers
11 Lynch town
12 Death trail
13 Bloody border
14 Delta duel
15 River of death
16 Nightmare at noon
17 Satan's daughter
18 The hard way
19 The tarnished star
20 Wanted for murder
21 Wagons East
22 The big game
23 Fort Despair
24 Manhunt
25 Steele's war: the woman
26 Steele's war: the preacher
27 Steele's war: the storekeeper
28 Steele's war: the stranger
29 The big prize
30 The killer mountains
31 The cheaters
32 The wrong man
33 The valley of the shadow
34 The runaways
35 Stranger in a strange town
36 The hellraisers
37 Kanyon of death
38 High stakes
39 Rough justice
40 The sunset ride
41 The killing train
42 The big gunfire
43 The hunted
44 Code of the West
45 The outcasts
EDGE MEETS STEELE:
1 Two of a kind
2 Matching pair
3 Double action
EDGE THE LONER:
1 The loner
2 $10,000 American
3 Apache death
4 Killer's breed
5 Blood on silver
6 The blue, the grey and the red

7 California killing
8 Seven out of hell
9 Bloody summer
10 Vengeance is black
11 Sioux uprising
12 The biggest bounty
13 A town called hate
14 The big gold
15 Blood run
16 The final shot
17 Vengeance valley
18 Ten tombstones to Texas
19 Ashes to dust
20 Sullivan's law
21 Rhapsody in red
22 Slaughter road
23 Echoes of war
24 The day democracy died
25 Violence trail
26 Savage dawn
27 Death drive
28 Eve of evil
29 The living, the dying and the dead
30 Waiting for a train
31 The guilty ones
32 The frightened gun
33 The hated
34 A ride in the sun
35 Death deal
36 Town on trial
37 Vengeance at Ventura
38 Massacre mission
39 The prisoners
40 Montana melodrama
41 The killing claim
42 Bloody sunrise
43 Arapaho revenge
44 The blind side
45 House on the range
46 The godforsaken
47 The moving cage
48 School for slaughter
49 Revenge ride
50 Shadow of the gallows
51 A time for killing
52 Brutal border
53 Hitting paydirt
54 Backshot
55 Uneasy riders
56 Doom town
57 Dying is forever
58 The desperadoes
59 Terror town
60 The breed woman
THE UNDERTAKER:
1 Black as death
2 Destined to die
3 Funeral by the sea

4 Three graves to a showdown
5 Back from the dead
6 Death in the desert
Paperback Westerns

GILRUTH, S.
INSPECTOR HUGH GORDON:
1 Dawn her remembrance 1961
2 The snake is living yet 1963

GIOVENE, A.
1 The book of Giuliam Sanservero 1970
2 The dilemma of love 1973
3 The dice of war
A continuous story of life in a remote Calabrian village.

GIRTIN, T.
1 Come landlord!
2 Not entirely serious
N.F. Autobiography.

GITTINGS, R.
1 Young Thomas Hardy 1975
2 The older Hardy 1975
N.F. Biography.

GLANFIELD, J.
1 Hotel Quadriga 1987
2 Viktoria 1989
Novels set in Vienna at the turn of the century.

GLASKIN, G. M.
1 Windows of the mind
2 Worlds within
3 A door to eternity
N.F. A trilogy about Christos mind travel.

GLASSER, R.
1 Growing up in the Gorbals 1986
2 Gorbals boy at Oxford 1988
3 Gorbals voices, siren songs 1990
N.F. Autobiography.

GLAZEBROOK, P.
1 Captain Vinegar's commission 1988
2 The gate at the end of the world 1989

GLEMSER, B.
ROBERT CRANE SERIES:
1 High noon
2 Strangers in Florida
3 The dove on his shoulder

GLOAG, J.
1 Caesar of the narrow seas 1970

2 The eagles depart 1973
3 Artorius Rex 1977
*The last years of the Roman Empire in
Britain.*

GLOVER, J.
FLYNN FAMILY:
1 The stallion man 1982
2 Sisters and brothers 1984
3 To everything a season 1986
4 Birds in a gilded cage 1987

GLUBB, SIR J.
1 A soldier with the Arabs 1957
2 War in the desert 1960
N.F. Autobiography
HISTORY OF ARABIA:
1 The great Arab conquests, A.D.
630-680 1961
2 The empire of the Arabs, A.D. 680-860
1963
3 The curse of the empire, A.D. 860-1150
1964

GLUYAS, C.
1 Savage Eden
2 Rogue's mistress
3 Flame of the South
*Novels about the American Deep
South.*

GLYN, C.
1 Don't knock the corners off 1964
2 Love and joy in the Mabillon 1985
THE STORY OF FULLIE:
1 The unicorn girl 1965
2 Heights and depths 1967
3 The tree 1969

GOBINEAU, M.
STEPHANIE:
1 Stephanie; the passions of spring 1974
2 Stephanie; the snows of Sebastopol
1975
3 Stephanie, The emperor's agent 1976
4 Stephanie; all for my love 1976
5 Stephanie; the savage land 1976
6 Stephanie; the price of freedom 1977
Set in 19th century France

GODDEN, R.
1 A time to dance, a time to weep 1987
2 A house with four rooms 1989
N.F. Autobiography of the novelist.

GODFREY, W.
1 Malleson at Melbourne

2 The friendly game 1957
Stories about cricket.

GODWIN, E.
CAPTAIN JOHN HUNTER:
1 Mission to Samarkand 1964
2 The towers of pain 1965

GOLD, H.
1 Fathers 1970
2 My last two thousand years 1973
*An autobiographical novel of a Jewish
family emigrating to U.S.A. and then to
Israel.*

GOLDING, W.
EDMUND TALBOT:
1 Rites of passage 1980
2 Close quarters 1987
3 Fire down below 1989

GOLDMAN, W.
1 Marathon man 1974
2 Brothers 1986

GOLDREICH, G.
LEAH:
1 Leah's journey 1983
2 Leah's children 1985

GOLDRING, D.
LOVE AMONG THE ARTISTS TRILOGY:
1 Nobody knows
2 The cuckoo
3 The facade

GOLDSBOROUGH, R.
NERO WOLFE:
1 Murder in E minor 1986
2 Death on deadline 1989
3 The bloodied ivy 1989
4 The last coincidence 1991
*A continuation of the series by Rex
Stout.*

GOLDTHORPE, J.
1 The same scourge
2 No crown of glory
3 The hidden splendour

GOLLANCZ, V.
1 My dear Timothy
2 More for Timothy
3 The last words for Timothy
N.F. Autobiographical letters.

GOLLIN, J.
1 The Verona Passamezzo 1987

2 Eliza's galiardo 1988
Thrillers with a musical background.

GOLON, A. *and* GOLON, S.
('SERGEANNE GOLON')
1 Angelique 1958
2 Angelique and the king 1960
3 Angelique and the Sultan 1961
4 Angelique in revolt 1962
5 Angelique in love 1963
6 The Countess Angelique 1965
7 The temptation of Angelique 1969
8 Angelique and the demon 1973
9 Angelique and the ghosts 1977

GOODCHILD, G.
1 Colorado Jim
2 Jim goes north
MACLEAN SERIES:
1 Maclean of Scotland Yard
2 Maclean investigates
3 Maclean at the Golden Owl
4 How now, Maclean
5 Chief Inspector Maclean
6 The triumph of Maclean
7 Yes, Inspector Maclean
8 Death on the centre court
9 Lead on, Maclean
10 Maclean remembers
11 Maclean finds a way
12 Maclean takes charge
13 Call Maclean
14 Maclean plays a hand
15 Maclean prevails
16 Maclean knows best
17 Maclean sees it through
18 Again Maclean
19 Up Maclean
20 Maclean intervenes
21 Maclean excels
22 Having no hearts
23 Maclean incomparable
24 Maclean deduces
25 Maclean the magnificent
26 Maclean non-stop
27 Maclean keeps going
28 Maclean takes a holiday
29 Uncle Oscar's niece
30 Hail Maclean
31 Companion to Sirius
32 Inspector Maclean's casebook
33 The Efford triangle
34 Maclean carries one
35 Maclean predominant
36 Maclean to the dark tower came
37 Maclean steps in
38 The last redoubt
39 Well caught Maclean

40 Double acrostic
41 Trust Maclean
42 Find the lady
43 Watch Maclean 1955
44 Maclean solves it 1956
45 Next of kin 1957
46 Forever Maclean 1957
47 Maclean disposes 1958
48 Tiger tiger 1959
49 Maclean scores again 1959
50 Follow Maclean 1960
51 Savage encounter 1962
52 Maclean invincible 1962
53 Laurels for Maclean 1963
54 Maclean takes over 1964
55 Maclean knows the answers 1967
★★★
NIGEL RISE SERIES:
1 Quest of Nigel Rise
2 Knock and come in
★★★
1 Q33
2 Q33 Spycatcher

GOODMAN, P.
EMPIRE CITY:
1 The state of nature 1946
2 The dead of spring 1950
3 The holy terror 1959
4 Grand piano 1942

GOODWIN, R.
1 Hongkong escape
2 Passport to eternity
N.F. Autobiography.

GOODWIN, S.
1 Winter spring 1978
2 Winter sisters 1980

GOOLDEN, B.
CONSETT TRILOGY:
1 Goodbye to yesterday 1975
2 In the melting pot 1976
3 Unborn tomorrow 1977

GORDON, D.
1 Blackbocks baby doctor 1956
2 Doctor down under 1957
N.F. Autobiography

GORDON, G.
1 Better to arrive 1968
2 The old warriors 1970
N.F. Autobiography

GORDON, GILES
1 About a marriage 1972
2 100 scenes from married life 1976

GORDON, K.
1 Emerald peacock 1978
2 Peacock in flight 1979
3 In the shadow of the peacock 1980
4 The peacock ring 1981
5 Peacock in jeopardy 1982
   A family chronicle set mainly in late 19th century India.

GORDON, R.
1 Doctor in the house 1952
2 Doctor at sea 1954
3 Doctor at large 1955
4 Doctor in love 1957
5 Doctor and son 1958
6 Doctor in clover 1960
7 Doctor on toast 1961
8 Doctor in the swim 1962
9 The summer of Sir Lancelot 1963
10 Love and Sir Lancelot 1965
11 Doctor on the boil 1970
12 Doctor on the brain 1972
13 Doctor in the nude 1973
14 Doctor on the job 1976
15 Doctor in the nest 1979
16 Doctor on the ball 1985
17 Doctor in the soup 1986
   ***
1 The facemaker 1967
2 Surgeon at arms 1968
   The story of a plastic surgeon, founded on fact.

GORDON, S.
1 One eye 1974
2 Two eyes 1975
3 Three eyes 1976
   Science fiction.
THE WATCHERS:
1 The watchers
2 The hidden world
3 The mask
   Paperback fantasy.

GORDON, THE, *pseud.* (M. GORDON and G. GORDON)
1 Undercover cat 1965
2 Undercover cat prowls again 1967
3 Cat napped 1973
FRANK AND GAIL MITCHELL SERIES:
1 Night before the wedding 1978
2 Night after the wedding 1980

GORES, J.
THE DKA FILE:
1 Dead skip 1973
2 Final notice 1974

GORSKY, B.
1 Moana
2 Moana returns
   N.F. Autobiography.

GOSLING, P.
LT. JACK STRYKER:
1 Monkey puzzle 1988
2 Backlash 1989
LUKE ABBOTT:
1 The Wychford murders 1986
2 Death penalties 1991

GOUDGE, E.
1 City of bells 1936
2 The sister of the angels
3 Blue hills
THE ELIOT FAMILY:
1 Bird in the tree 1940
2 The herb of grace (Pilgrim's Inn) 1948
3 Heart of the family 1953
   Later published in one volume as 'The Eliots of Damerosehay' 1957

GOUGH, L.
WILLOWS & PARKER:
1 The goldfish bowl 1987
2 Death on a No. 8 hook 1988
3 Hot shots 1989
4 Serious crimes 1990

GOULD, J.
1 The Texas years 1989
2 Lovemakers 1985

GOWER, I.
1 The copper cloud 1976
2 Return to Tip Row 1977
   Novels about copper smelting in South Wales. They are the fore-runners of her series about Swansea. Published in an omnibus edition in 1987 as 'The Loves of Catrin'.
SWEYNESEYE:
1 Copper kingdom 1983
2 Proud Mary 1984
3 Spinner's Wharf 1985
4 Morgan's woman 1986
5 Fiddler's ferry 1987
6 Black gold 1988
   A series of novels about Swansea from the late 19thC to the Second World

War. The same characters appear, with varying degrees of importance.

GRAFF, P.
JOSE DUST:
1 Dust and the curious boy 1958
2 Daughter fair 1958
3 The Sapphire conference 1959

GRADY, J.
1 Six days of the Condor 1975
2 Shadow of the Condor 1976
Spy stories

GRAEME, B.
1 Blackshirt 1925
2 The return of Blackshirt 1977
3 Blackshirt again 1929
4 Alias Blackshirt 1932
5 Blackshirt the audacious 1936
6 Blackshirt the adventurer 1936
7 Blackshirt takes a hand 1937
8 Blackshirt counter-spy 1938
9 Blackshirt interferes 1939
10 Blackshirt strikes back 1940
11 Son of Blackshirt 1942
12 Lord Blackshirt 1942
Continued by R. Graeme
13 Calling Lord Blackshirt 1944
14 Concerning Blackshirt 1947
15 Blackshirt wins the trick 1948
16 Blackshirt passes by 1950
17 Salute to Blackshirt 1952
18 Amazing, Mr. Blackshirt 1955
19 Blackshirt meets the lady 1956
20 Paging Blackshirt 1957
21 Blackshirt helps himself 1957
22 Double for Blackshirt 1958
23 Blackshirt sets the pace 1959
24 Blackshirt sees it through 1959
25 Blackshirt finds trouble
26 Blackshirt takes the trial 1962
27 Calls for Blackshirt 1962
28 Blackshirt on the spot 1963
29 Blackshirt saves the day 1964
30 Danger for Blackshirt 1965
31 Blackshirt at large 1966
32 Blackshirt in peril 1967
33 Blackshirt stirs things up 1968
THEODORE I. TERHUNE SERIES:
1 Seven clues in search of a crime 1941
2 House with crooked walls 1942
3 A case of Solomon 1943
4 Work for the hangman 1944
5 Ten trails to Tyburn 1944
6 A case of books 1946
7 And a bottle of rum 1948
8 Dead pigs at hungry farm

INSPECTOR ALLAIN SERIES:
1 Murder of some importance 1931
2 Epilogue 1933
3 Imperfect crime 1932
4 International affair 1934
5 Satan's mistress 1935
6 Not proven 1935
7 Mystery of the Queen Mary 1937
8 The man from Michigan 1938
9 Body unknown 1939
10 Poisoned sleep 1939
11 The corporal died in bed 1940
12 Encore Allain 1941
13 News travels by night 1943
AUGUSTE JANTRY SERIES:
1 Cherchez la femme 1951
2 Lady in black 1952

GRAEME, BRUCE
HENRY MAXWELL SERIES:
1 Blind date for a private eye 1969
2 The D notice (also featuring Det. Sgt. Mather) 1974
DET. SGT. MATHER SERIES:
1 The quiet ones 1970
2 Two and two make five 1973
3 The D notice 1974
4 The snatch 1976
5 Two faced 1977
6 Double trouble 1978
7 Mather again 1979
8 Invitation to Mather 1980
9 Mather investigates 1980

GRAFTON, S.
KINSEY MILLHONE:
1 A is for alibi 1985
2 B is for burglar 1986
3 C is for corpse 1987
4 D is for deadbeat 1987
5 E is for evidence 1988
6 F is for fugitive 1989
7 G is for gunshoe 1990
8 H is for homicide 1991

GRAHAM, B.
MICHAEL EVANS:
1 The spy trap 1971
2 Spy or die 1972

GRAHAM, C.
INSPECTOR TOM BARNABY:
1 The killings at Badger's Drift 1987
2 Death of a hollow man 1989

GRAHAM, F. see CARSON, R.

GRAHAM, N.
SUPERINTENDENT SANDYMAN SERIES:
1 Passport to murder
2 Murder walks on tiptoe
3 The quest of Mr. Sandyman
4 Again Mr. Sandyman
5 Amazing Mr. Sandyman
6 Salute Mr. Sandyman
SOLO MALCOLM SERIES:
1 Murder makes a date 1955
2 Play it solo 1956
3 Say it with murder 1957
4 You can't call it murder 1957
5 Hit me hard 1958
6 Salute to murder 1958
7 Murder rings the bell 1959
8 Killers are on velvet 1960
9 Murder is my weakness 1961
10 Murder on the Duchess 1962
11 Make mine murder 1962
12 Murder makes it certain 1962
13 Graft town 1963
14 Label it murder 1963
15 Murder made easy 1964
16 Murder of a black cat 1964
17 Murder on my hands 1965
18 Murderers always final 1965
19 Money for murder 1966
20 Murder on demand 1966
21 Murder makes the news 1967
22 Murder has been done 1967
23 Pay off 1968
24 Candidate for a coffin 1968
25 Death of a canary 1969
26 Murder lies in waiting 1969
27 Blood on the pavement 1970
28 One of the book 1970
29 A matter of murder 1971
30 Murder double murder 1971
31 Frame-up 1972
32 Cop in a tight frame 1973
33 Murder in a dark room 1973
34 Assignment murder 1974
35 Murder on the list 1975
36 Search for a missing lady 1976

GRAHAM, WINIFRED
1 That reminds me
2 Observations
3 I introduce
N.F. Autobiography

GRAHAM, WINSTON
POLDARK:
1 Ross Poldark (1783-87) 1945
2 Demelza (1788-90) 1946
3 Jeremy Poldark (1790-91) 1950
4 Warleggan (1792-93) 1953

5 The black moon (1794-95) 1973
6 The four swans (1795-97) 1976
7 The angry tide (1798-99) 1977
8 The stranger from the sea (1810-11) 1981
9 The miller's dance (1812-13) 1982
10 The loving cup (1813-15) 1984
11 Twisted sword 1990
A family saga set in Cornwall

GRAHAME, I.
1 Flying feathers 1976
2 Ruffled feathers 1978
N.F. An account of the author's centre for rare birds at Daws Hill

GRANGE, P.
THE L'EREE FAMILY:
1 King Creole 1967
2 Devil's emissary 1968
3 Tumult at the gate 1970
4 The golden goddess 1973

GRANGER, B.
1 Shattered eye 1984
2 The November man 1980
3 Schism 1982
4 The Zurich numbers 1985

GRANT, JAMES
MACE:
1 Mace 1984
2 Mace's luck 1985

GRANT-ADAMSON, L.
RAIN MORGAN:
1 Patterns in the dust 1984
2 Faces of death 1985
3 Guilty knowledge 1987
4 Wild justice 1987
5 Curse the darkness 1990

GRANT, JANE
1 Come hither, nurse
2 Come again, nurse
3 Sister under their skins 1966
4 Round-the-clock nurse 1968
N.F. Autobiography

GRANT, JOAN
1 Eyes of Horus
2 Lord of the horizon

GRASS, G.
THE DANZIG TRILOGY:
1 The tin drum 1959
2 Cat and mouse 1966
3 Dog years 1965

Published as one volume in 1987. The books are linked by background and period rather than characters

GRAVE, S.

MIAMI VICE:
1 China white
2 Hellhole
3 Probing by fire
4 The razor's edge
Paperbacks, based on the TV series

GRAVES, C.

1 The thin blue line
2 The avengers
3 Seven pilots
Semi-fictional account of the R.A.F.

GRAY, B.

NORMAN CONQUEST SERIES:
1 Mr. Mortimer gets the jitters
2 Vultures, Ltd.
3 Miss Dynamite
4 Conquest marches on
5 Leave it to Conquest
6 Conquest takes all
7 Meet the Don
8 Six to kill
9 Convict 1066
10 Thank you Mr. Conquest
11 Six feet of dynamite
12 Blonde for danger
13 The gay desperado
14 Cavalier Conquest
15 Alias Norman Conquest
16 Mr. Ball of fire
17 Killer Conquest
18 The Conquest touch
19 The spot marked X
20 Duel murder
21 Dare devil Conquest
22 Operation Conquest
23 Seven dawns to death
24 Conquest in Scotland
25 The lady is poison
26 The half-open door
27 Target for Conquest
28 Follow the lady
29 Conquest goes west
30 Turn left for danger
31 House of the lost 1956
32 Conquest at midnight 1957
33 Conquest goes home 1957
34 Conquest in command 1958
35 Conquest in California 1958
36 Death on the Hit-Parade 1958
37 The big brain 1959
38 Conquest on the run 1960

39 Get ready to die 1960
40 Call Conquest for danger 1961
41 Conquest in the underworld 1962
42 Count down for Conquest 1963
43 Conquest overboard 1964
44 Calamity Conquest 1965
45 Conquest likes it hot 1965
46 Curtains for Conquest 1966
47 Conquest calls the tune 1969
48 Conquest in Ireland 1969

GRAY, E.

1 No survivors 1975
2 Action Atlantic 1976
3 Tokyo torpedo 1977
Novels about German U-boats

GRAY, H.

1 Gold for gay masters
2 Bride of doom
3 The flame and the forest

GRAYLAND, V. M.

HOANI MATA SERIES:
1 Night of the reaper 1963
2 The grave-digger's apprentice 1964

GRAY, S.

1 Unnatural pursuit 1985
2 How's that for telling 'em, fat lady? 1988
N.F. Autobiography of the playwright

GRAYSON, RICHARD

1 Guncotton
2 Guncotton goes to Russia
3 Guncotton in Hollywood
4 Guncotton murder at the bank
5 Guncotton outside the law
6 Guncotton secret airman
7 Guncotton in Mexico
8 Guncotton ace high
9 Guncotton adventure nine
10 Guncotton at blind man's hood
11 Escape with Guncotton
12 Guncotton - adventurer
13 Guncotton - secret agent
INSPECTOR GAUTIER:
1 The murders at the Impasse Louvain 1979
2 The Monterant affair 1980
3 The death of Abbe Didier 1981
4 The Montmartre murders 1982
5 Crime without passion 1983
6 Death en voyage 1986
7 Death on the cards 1988
8 Death off stage 1991
Set in Paris at the turn of the century

GRAYSON, RUPERT
1 Voyage not completed 1969
2 Standfast the Holy Ghost 1973
N.F. Autobiography

GREATOREX, W.
AIRLINE:
1 Take-off 1981
2 Ruskin's Berlin 1982

GREAVES, J.
JACKIE GROVES:
1 The final 1979
2 The ball game 1980
About a professional footballer
STEVE WALKER:
1 The boss 1980
2 The second half 1981
About a football club manager

GREELEY, A. M.
FATHER 'BLACKIE' RYAN:
1 Happy are the meek 1986
2 Happy are the clean of heart 1987
3 Rite of spring 1988
4 Happy are those who thirst for justice
  1988
5 Love song 1990
6 St. Valentine's night 1990
THE PASSOVER TRILOGY:
1 Thy brother's wife 1982
2 Ascent into Hell 1983
3 Lord of the dance 1988
TIME BETWEEN THE STARS:
1 Virgin and martyr 1985
2 Angels of September 1986
3 Patience of a Saint 1988

GREEN, C.
INSPECTOR WIELD SERIES:
1 Beauty a snare
2 Devil spider
3 Poison sheath

GREEN, E.
1 Adam's empire 1990
2 Kalinda 1991
Historical novels set in Australia

GREEN, H.
TRIPLE AGENTS:
1 A woman called Omega 1984
2 The Fidelio affair 1985

GREEN, M.
1 The boy who shot down an airship 1988
2 Nobody lost in small earthquake 1990
N.F. Autobiography

GREEN, R.
1 Prophet without honour
2 Wilderness blossoms

GREEN, S.
1 The warrior within
2 The warrior enchained
Paperback fantasy

GREENE, B.
1 Summer of the German soldier 1974
2 Morning is a long time coming 1978

GREENLEAF, S.
JOHN TANNER, P.I.:
1 Grave error 1981
2 Death bed 1982
3 State's evidence 1984
4 Fatal obsession 1985
5 Beyong blame 1987

GREENWELL, D.
1 Two friends
2 Colloquia Crucis

GREENWOOD, J.
DET. INSPECTOR MOSLEY:
1 Murder, Mr. Mosley 1983
2 Mosely by moonlight 1984
3 Mosely went to mow 1985
4 Mists over Mosley 1986
5 The mind of Mr. Mosley 1987
6 What, me, Mr. Mosley? 1987
*Detective stories set in Yorkshire Dales.
See also entries under the author's real
name, J. B. Hilton*

GREENWOOD, R.
1 Mr. Bunting 1940
2 Mr. Bunting at war 1941
3 Mr. Bunting in the promised land 1949
STORY OF ROSIE DAWES:
1 Good angel slept 1952
2 O mistress mine 1955

GREENWOOD, W.
TRELOOE SERIES:
1 So brief the spring 1952
2 What everybody wants 1953
3 Down by the sea 1956
*Not sequels, but setting is the same for
all books and some characters recur.*

GREGG, C. F.
INSPECTOR HIGGINS SERIES:
1 The murdered manservant
2 The three daggers
3 The murder on the bus
4 The brazen confession

5 The Rutland mystery
6 The double solution
7 Inspector Higgins hurries
8 The body behind the bar
9 The duke's last trick
10 Inspector Higgins sees it through
11 The execution of Diamond Deutsch
12 The ten black pearls
13 Danger at Cliff House
14 Tragedy at Wembley
15 The wrong house
16 Mystery at Moor St.
17 Who dialled 999?
18 Danger in the dark
19 The fatal error
20 Justice!
21 The Vandor mystery
22 Two died at three
23 Melander's millions
24 The old manor
25 Exit Harlequin
26 Murder at midnight
27 Man with the monocle
28 The ugly customer
29 From information received
30 Inspector Higgins goes fishing
31 Accidental murder
32 Sufficient rope
33 Night flight to Zurich
34 The chief constable
35 Dead on time 1955
36 The obvious solution 1958
37 Professional jealousy 1959
HENRY PRINCE SERIES:
1 Henry Prince in action
2 The return of Henry Prince

GREGOIRE, J. A.
1 24 hours at Le Mans
2 The money masters

GREGORIAN, J. B.
THE TREDANA TRILOGY:
1 The broken citadel
2 Castle-down
3 The great wheel
Paperback fantasy

GREGORY, P.
1 Wideacre 1987
2 The favoured child 1989
3 Meridon 1990

GREGSON, J. M.
SUPT. JOHN LAMBERT:
1 Murder on the 19th 1989
2 For sale, with corpse 1990
3 Bring forth your dead 1991

GREIG, D.
1 Daisy 1978
2 Daisy reminisces 1979
N.F. Autobiography

GRENFELL, J.
1 Joyce Grenfell request the pleasure 1977
2 In pleasant places 1979
N.F. Autobiography

GREX, L.
PAUL IRVING SERIES:
1 The tragedy at Draythorp
2 The Madison murder
3 The Lonely Inn mystery
4 Stolen death
5 The Carlant Manor crime

GREY, ROMER ZANE
BUCK DUANE:
1 Rider of the distant trails 1969
2 High valley river 1970
3 King of the range 1970
4 Rustlers of the cattle range 1970
5 Three deaths for Buck Duane 1971
6 Track the man down 1971
LARAMIE NELSON:
1 Last stand at Indigo Flats 1970
2 The other side of the river 1990
*This character first appeared in
'Spanish Peaks', by Zane Grey, R. Z.
Grey wrote 2 more sequels to his
father's books 'Heritage of the Legions'
follows 'The Border Legion', and 'Siege
at Forlorn River' follows 'Desert Gold'.*

GRIBBIN, J. and CHOWN, M.
1 Double Planet 1988
2 Reunion 1991

GRIBBLE, L. R.
ANTHONY SLADE:
1 Gillespie suicide murder 1929
2 The Grand Modena murder 1930
3 The stolen Home Secretary 1932
4 Is this revenge? 1931
5 The secret of Tangles 1933
6 The riddle of the ravens 1934
7 Riley of the Special Branch 1936
8 The case of the Malverne diamonds
1936
9 The casebook of Anthony Slade 1937
10 Tragedy in E flat 1938
11 The Arsenal Stadium mystery 1939
12 Atomic murder 1947
13 Hangman's moon
14 They kidnapped Stanley Matthews
1950

8 The silver tombstone 1945
9 The honest dealer 1947
10 The whispering master 1947
11 The scarlet feather 1948
12 The leather duke 1949
13 The limping goose 1954
SIMON LASH SERIES:
1 Simon Lash, detective 1941
2 The buffalo box 1942
3 Murder '97 1944
OTIS BEAGLE SERIES:
1 The silver jackass 1941
2 The beaglescented murder 1952
3 The lonesome badger 1952
*Some of the above are not published in
the U.K.*

GUARESCHI, G.
1 Little world of Don Camillo
2 Don Camillo and the prodigal son
  (Don Camillo and his flock)
3 Don Camillo's dilemma
4 Don Camillo and the devil 1959
5 Comrade Don Camillo 1960
6 Don Camillo meets Hell's angels 1970
  *The last story was found in MS some
  time after the author's death.*

GUILD, N.
1 The Assyrian 1988
2 The blood star 1989

GULBRANNSSEN, T.
1 Beyond sing the woods
2 The wind in the mountains
  Chronicle of a Norwegian family.

GUNN, N. M.
1 Young Art and old Hector
2 The green Isle of the great deep

GUNN, V.
CHIEF INSPECTOR BILL CROMWELL
SERIES:
1 Footsteps of death
2 Ironsides of the Yard
3 Ironsides smashes through
4 Ironsides' lone hand
5 Death's doorway
6 Mad Hatter's rock
7 Ironsides sees red
8 The dead man laughs
9 Nice day for a murder
10 Ironsides smells blood
11 Death in shivering sand
12 Three dates with death
13 Ironsides on the spot 1948
14 Road to murder 1949

15 Dead man's morning 1949
16 Alias the hangman 1950
17 Murder on ice 1951
18 The Borgia head mystery 1951
19 The body vanishes 1952
20 Death comes laughing 1952
21 The whistling key 1953
22 The crooked staircase 1953
23 The crippled canary 1954
24 Laughing grave 1954
25 Castle dangerous 1955
26 The 64 thousand murder 1956
27 The painted dog 1956
28 Dead men's bells 1957
29 The treble chance murder 1958
30 Dead in a ditch 1959
31 Death on Bodmin Moor 1960
32 Devil in the maze 1960
33 Death at traitor's gate 1960
34 Sweet smelling death 1961
35 All change for murder 1962
36 The body in the boot 1962
37 Murder with a kiss 1963
38 The black cap murder 1965
39 Murder on Whispering Sands 1965
40 The Petticoat Lane murders 1966

GUNNARSON, G.
1 Ships in the sky
2 The night and the dream

GUTHRIE, A. B.
1 The big sky 1947
2 The way west 1956
3 These thousand hills 1957
4 Arfive 1972
  *Planned as a series on the development
  of the American West. 1 is the story of
  Daniel Boone.*

GUTTERIDGE, L.
MATHEW DILKE:
1 Cold war in a country garden 1971
2 Killer pine 1973
3 Fratricide is a gas 1975
  *Science fiction thrillers about a
  miniaturised detective.*

GUY, R.
1 The friends 1974
2 Edith Jackson 1979
3 Ruby 1981

HAAS, B.
THE CHANDLER FAMILY:
1 The Chandler heritage 1972
2 Daisy Canfield 1973

HABE, B.
1 Aftermath
2 Walk in darkness

HACKFORTH-JONES, G.
EARL OF MILLINGTON:
1 Submarine flotilla
2 Rough passage
3 The price was high
4 The questing hound
5 Sixteen bells
JOE GARTON SERIES:
1 Danger below 1962
2 I am the captain 1963
PAUL DEXTER SERIES:
1 Chinese poison 1968
2 All stations Malta 1970
3 An explosive situation 1973
4 Shadow of the rock 1973
5 Second-in-command 1974
6 The redoubtable Dexter 1975
7 Dexter at war 1976
Humorous novels about the Royal Navy

HACKNEY, A.
1 Private's progress 1955
2 Private life 1957
★★★
1 I'm all right Jack 1960
2 Whatever turns you on, Jack? 1972

HAEDRICH, M.
1 Belle, de Paris 1970
2 Belle in diamonds 1971

HAGAN, P.
COLTRANE FAMILY:
1 Love and war 1990
2 Raging hearts 1990

HAGGARD, L. R.
1 Norfolk life
2 A Norfolk notebook
3 A country scrapbook
N.F. Country life

HAGGARD, W.
COL. CHARLES RUSSELL:
1 Slow burner 1958
2 Venetian blind 1959
3 The arena 1961
4 The unquiet sleep 1962
5 The high wire 1963
6 The antagonists 1964
7 The powder barrel 1965
8 The hard sell 1965
9 The power house 1966

10 The conspirators 1967
11 A cool day for killing 1968
12 The doubtful disciples 1969
13 The hardliners 1970
14 The bitter harvest 1971
15 The old masters 1973
16 Scorpion's tail 1976
17 The poison people 1977
18 Visa to limbo 1978
19 The median line 1978
20 The money men 1981
21 The mischief maker 1982
22 The heirloom 1983
23 The need to know 1984
24 The meritocrats 1985
25 The vendettists 1990
PAUL MARTINY:
1 The protectors 1972
2 The kinsmen 1974

HAIG, A.
ALEC HAIG SERIES:
1 Sign on for Tokyo
2 Flight from Montego Bay 1972
3 Peruvian printout 1973

HALDEMAN, C.
1 The sun's attendant 1963
2 The snowman 1965
A small American town during World War II

HALDEMAN, J.
1 Worlds
2 Worlds apart
Science fiction

HALL, A. (E. TREVOR)
QUILLER:
1 The Berlin memorandum 1965
2 The ninth directive 1966
3 The striker portfolio 1969
4 The Warsaw document 1971
5 The Tango briefing 1973
6 The Mandarin cipher 1975
7 The Kobra manifesto 1976
8 The Sinkiang executive 1978
9 The scorpion signal 1980
10 The Peking target 1981
11 Northlight 1985
12 Quiller's run 1988
13 Quiller KGB 1989
14 Quiller Barracuda 1991

HALL, P.
1 The India man 1968
2 Sun and grey shadow 1974
A trilogy of novels in progress

HALL, T. H.
1 Sherlock Holmes: ten literary studies 1969
2 The late Mr. Holmes 1971
N.F. 'Pseudo' research into the Sherlock Holmes series

HALLIDAY, B.
MICHAEL SHAYNE SERIES:
1 Divided on death
2 Private practice of Michael Shayne
3 The uncomplaining corpses
4 Tickets for death
5 Michael Shayne investigates
6 Michael Shayne takes a hand
7 Michael Shayne's long chance
8 Murder is my business
9 Murder and the married virgin
10 Marked for murder
11 Blood on Biscayne Bay
12 Counterfeit wife
13 Murder is a habit
14 Call for Michael Shayne
15 A taste for violence
16 This is it Michael Shayne
17 Framed in blood
18 When Dorinda dances
19 What really happened
20 Lady came by night
21 She woke to darkness 1955
22 Death has three lives
23 Stranger in town 1956
24 Blonde cried murder 1956
25 Weep for a blonde 1956
26 Shot the works 1957
27 Murder of the wanton bride 1957
28 Death of a stranger 1957
29 Missing from home 1958
30 Fit to kill 1959
31 Date with a dead man 1960
32 Target: Mike Shayne 1960
33 Die like a dog 1961

HALLIDAY, D.
JOHNSON AND 'DOLLY':
1 'Dolly' and the singing bird 1968
2 'Dolly' and the cookie bird 1970
3 'Dolly' and the doctor bird 1971
4 'Dolly' and the starry bird 1973
5 'Dolly' and the nanny bird 1977
6 'Dolly' and the bird of paradise 1983
(see **DUNNETT, D.**)

HALLIDAY, M., *pseud. see* **CREASEY, J.**

HAMBLEDON, P.
DETECTIVE-INSPECTOR 'TUBBY' MARTINS:
1 Lucinder 1953
2 Keys for the criminal 1958

HAMBLY, B.
DARWATH TRILOGY:
1 The time of the dark
2 The walls of air
3 The armies of daylight
Paperback fantasy
SUN WOLF:
1 The ladies of Mandrigyu 1984
2 The witches of Wenshar 1987
3 Dark hand of magic 1990

HAMILTON, A.
NEFERTITI:
1 The beautiful one 1978
2 Lady of grace 1979
3 The devious being 1980

HAMILTON, D.
MATT HELM SERIES:
1 The removers
2 Murderer's row
3 The ambushers
4 The shadowers
5 The ravagers
6 The devastators
7 The silencers
8 Wrecking crew
9 Death of a citizen
10 The betrayers 1968
11 The menacers 1969
1-9 apparently only published in paperback

HAMILTON, E.
1 The river full of stars 1954
2 An Irish childhood 1963
N.F. Autobiography

HAMILTON, H.
JOHN AND SALLY HELDAR SERIES:
1 The two hundred ghost 1956
2 Death at one blow 1957
3 At night to die 1958
4 Answer in the negative 1959

HAMILTON, I.
PETE HEYSEN:
1 The persecutor 1965
2 Man with the brown paper face 1967
(The creeping vicar)
3 The thrill machine 1968

HAMILTON, J.
HABSBURG SERIES:
1 Changeling Queen 1977

2 The Emperor's daughter 1977
3 Pearl of the Habsburgs 1978
4 The Snow Queen 1979
5 The Habsburg inheritance 1980

HAMILTON, M.
MONTY:
1 Monty: the making of a general, 1887-1942 1981
2 Monty: master of the battlefield, 1942-44 1983
3 Monty the Field Marshall, 1944-46 1986
N.F. Biography of Field-Marshal Montgomery of Alamein

HAMILTON, MARY
1 Green and gold
2 Silver road
N.F. Autobiography

HAMMOND, G.
BEAU PEPYS SERIES:
1 Fred in situ 1965
2 The loose screw 1966
3 Mud in his eye 1967
KEITH CALDER:
1 Dead game 1979
2 The reward game 1980
3 The revenge game 1981
4 Fair game 1982
5 The game 1982
6 Sauce for the pigeon 1984
7 Cousin once removed 1984
8 Pursuit of arms 1985
9 Silver city scandal 1986
10 The executor 1986
11 The worried widow 1987
12 Adverse report 1987
13 Stray shot 1988
14 A brace of skeet 1989
15 Let us prey 1990
16 Home to roost 1990
Thrillers set in the Scottish Borders, whose hero is a gunsmith. From 14, Deborah, Keith Calder's daughter, plays a leading role.
JOHN CUNNINGHAM:
1 Dog in the dark 1989
2 Doghouse 1989
3 Whose dog are you? 1990
Thrillers about a breeder and trainer of gun dogs

HAMNER, E.
1 Spencer's mountain 1966
2 The homecoming 1970

HAMNETT, N.
1 Laughing torso
2 Is she a lady?
N.F. Autobiography

HANCOCK, N.
CIRCLE OF LIGHT:
1 Greyfax Grimwald
2 Faragon Fairingay
3 Calix stay
4 Squaring the circle
Paperback fantasies
THE WILDERNESS OF FOUR:
1 Across the far mountain
2 The plains of sea
3 On the boundaries of darkness
4 The road to the Middle Islands
Paperback fantasies

HANDKE, P.
1 The long way around 1979
2 The lesson of Monte-Sainte-Victoire 1980
3 Child's Story 1981
Publ. in 1 Vol. 'Slow Home Coming' 1986.

HANDL, I.
1 The Sioux 1970
2 The gold tipped Pfitzer 1973
Chronicles of a wealthy international family

HANFF, H.
1 84 Charing Cross Rd. 1973
2 The duchess of Bloomsbury St. 1974
3 Q's legacy 1985
N.F. Autobiography

HANLEY, J.
THE FURIES CHRONICLE:
1 The furies 1935
2 The secret journey 1936
3 Our time is gone 1938
4 Winter song 1939
5 An end and a beginning 1958

HANNUM, A.
1 Spin a silver coin
2 A shop in the desert
3 Paint the wind
N.F. Description of an Indian trading post in S. West U.S.A.

HANRAHAN, B.
1 The scent of eucalyptus 1973
2 Kewpie doll 1984

HANSEN, J.
DAVE BRANDSTETTER:
1 Fadeout 1972
2 Death claims 1973
3 The troublemaker 1975
4 The man everybody was afraid of 1978
5 Skinflick 1980
6 Gravedigger 1982
7 A smile in a lifetime 1983
8 Nightwork 1984

HANSON, V. J.
AMOS:
1 Amos lives! 1990
2 Shroud for Amos 1990
3 Legend of Amos 1991
Westerns

'HAN SUYIN'
1 The crippled tree 1964
2 A mortal flower 1966
3 Birdless summer 1968
4 My house has two doors 1975

HARBINSON, R.
1 No surrender
2 Song of Erne
3 Up spake the cabin boy
4 The protege
N.F. Autobiography of an Ulsterman

HARDCASTLE, M.
1 Soccer is also a game 1966
2 Shoot on sight 1967

HARDING, I.
ASSAULT TROOP:
1 Blood beach 1983
2 Death in the forest 1983
3 Clash on the Rhine 1984
4 End run 1984

HARDWICK, MICHAEL
THE CEDAR TREE:
1 The Cedar tree 1976
2 Autumn of an age 1977
3 The bough breaks 1978
RACKSTRAW:
1 Regency rake 1979
2 Regency revenge 1980
3 Regency revels 1982

HARDWICK, MOLLIE
DORAN FAIRWEATHER CHELMARSH:
1 Malice domestic 1986
2 Parson's pleasure 1987
3 Uneaseful death 1988
4 The bandersnatch 1989

5 Perish in July 1989
6 The dreaming Damozel 1990
THE DUCHESS OF DUKE STREET:
1 The way up 1976
2 The golden years 1976
3 The world keeps turning 1977
THE ATKINSON FAMILY:
1 The Atkinson inheritance 1978
2 Sisters in love 1979
3 The Atkinson century 1980
JULIET BRAVO:
1 New arrivals 1981
2 Calling Juliet Bravo 1981
See also **Upstairs, downstairs series**

HARDY, A.
GEORGE ABERCOMBE FOX:
1 The Press Gang 1973
2 Prize money 1973
3 Siege 1974
4 Treasure 1974
First published in paperback.
Republished in double volumes, 'Fox doubles', nos. 1 and 2.

HARDY, ADAM
STRIKEFORCE FALKLANDS:
1 Operation Exocet 1983
2 Raiders dawn 1984
3 Red alert
4 Recce patrol
5 Covert op
6 Ware mines!
4-6 are only in paperback

HARE, C.
SUPT. MALLETT AND M. PETTIGREW:
1 Tenant for death 1937
2 Death is no sportsman 1938
3 Tragedy at law 1942
4 With a bare bodkin 1946
5 When the wind blows 1949
6 The Yew tree's shade 1954
7 He should have died hereafter 1958
   (Untimely death)

HARGREAVES, E.A.I. STEWART-
1 Cotswold cider
2 The Hargreaves story
3 Man on the run
N.F. Autobiography

HARKNETT, T.
STEPHEN WAYNE SERIES:
1 The benevolent blackmailer 1962
2 Scratch on the surface 1962
3 Invitation to a funeral 1962
4 Dead little rich girl 1963

5 Evil money 1964
6 Man who did not die 1964
7 Death of an aunt 1966
8 Two way frame 1967
9 The softcover kill 1971

HARLOW, R.
1 Royal Murdoch 1963
2 A gift of echoes 1966
Not sequels, but some characters recur and the background is the same

HARRELL, A.
SAM SHANK:
1 The twin bridges murder 1982
2 Trailersnatch 1983
3 Rivermist 1983
4 Kickback 1984
5 A touch of jade 1985

HARRER, H.
1 Seven years in Tibet
2 Tibet is my country 1960
3 Return to Tibet 1984
N.F. Travel

HARRINGTON, J.
FRANK X KERRIGAN SERIES:
1 Last known address 1966
2 Blind spot 1967
3 Last doorbell 1968

HARRIS, D. T.
THE MAGES OF GARILLON:
1 The burning stone
2 The gauntlet of malice
Paperback fantasy

HARRIS, E.
LARGE LEE:
1 Largely luck 1984
2 Largely trouble 1986

HARRIS, J.
IRA PENALUNA:
1 The mustering of the hawks 1971
2 The mercenaries 1968
3 The Courtney entry 1970
A trilogy of the history of flight. This is a chronological, not published order.

HARRIS, M.
1 A kind of magic 1969
2 Another kind of magic 1972
N.F. Country life

HARRIS, MARION
1 Soldiers' wives 1987

2 Officers' ladies 1987
HEART OF THE DRAGON:
1 Nesta 1988
2 Amelda 1990

HARRIS, R. E.
PURCELL SISTERS:
1 The silent shore 1986
2 The beckoning hills 1987

HARRIS, W.
THE GUIANA QUARTET:
1 The palace of the peacock 1960
2 The far journey of Oudin 1961
3 The whole armour 1962
4 The secret ladder 1962
Novels of the Caribbean

1 Carnival 1985
2 Infinite rehearsal
3 Four banks of the river of space 1990

HARRISON, C.
1 Arctic rose 1985
2 Wild flower 1986

HARRISON, E.
ST. MARK'S HOSPITAL:
1 Emergency call 1969
2 Accident call 1971
3 Ambulance call
4 Surgeon's call
5 Hospital call
6 Dangerous call
***
1 The Ravelston affair 1967
2 Corridors of healing 1969

HARRISON, H.
STAINLESS STEEL RAT:
1 The stainless steel rat is born 1985
2 The stainless steel rat 1961
3 The stainless steel rat's revenge 1971
4 The stainless steel rat saves the world 1973
5 The stainless steel rat wants you 1975
6 The stainless steel rat for President 1983
7 The stainless steel rat gets drafted 1987
Science fiction detective stories
TO THE STARS:
1 Wheelworld
2 Epic to the stars
3 Starworld 1988
4 Homeworld
Paperback science fiction
WEST OF EDEN:
1 West of Eden 1986

2 Winter in Eden 1987
3 Return to Eden 1988
BILL THE GALACTIC HERO:
1 Bill... on the planet of robot slaves 1989
2 Bill... on the planet of bottled brains 1990
3 Bill... on the planet of tasteless pleasure 1991

HARRISON, M.
1 All the trees were green
2 Vernal equinox

HARRISON, MICHAEL
1 In the footsteps of Sherlock Holmes 1970
2 The London of Sherlock Holmes 1971
3 The world of Sherlock Holmes 1973
N.F. 'Pseudo' research into the Sherlock Holmes series

HARRISON, M. J.
1 In Viriconium 1981
2 Viriconium nights 1985
Science fiction

HARRISON, RAY
SGT. BRAGG & P.C. MORTON:
1 French ordinary murder 1983
2 Death of an Honourable member 1984
3 Death watch 1985
4 Death of a dancing lady 1985
5 Counterfeit of murder 1987
6 A season for death 1987
7 Tincture of death 1989
8 Sphere of death 1990
9 Patently murder 1991
Detective stories set in Victorian London

HARRISON, ROSINA
1 Rose: my life in service 1975
2 Gentlemen's gentlemen: my friends in service 1976
N.F. Reminiscences of life in private service

HARRISON, S.
1 Hot breath 1988
2 Cold feet 1989

HARROD-EAGLES, C.
MORLAND DYNASTY:
1 The foundling 1980
2 Dark rose 1981
3 The princeling 1981
4 The oak apple 1982

5 The black pearl 1982
6 The long shadow 1983
7 The Chevalier 1984
8 The maiden 1985
9 The flood-tide 1986
10 The tangled thread 1987
11 The Emperor 1988
12 The victory 1989
13 The Regency 1990
14 Campaigners 1991
A family saga set in Yorkshire from the 15th C to WW2
KIROV SAGA:
1 Anna 1990
2 Fleur 1991

HART, J.
CARL PEDERSON:
1 Some die young 1990
2 A decent killer 1991

HART, R.
DET. SUPT. ROPER:
1 Seascape with dead figures 1987
2 A pretty place for a murder 1987
3 A fox in the night 1988
4 Remains to be seen 1989
5 Robbed blind 1990
6 Breach of promise 1990

HART, SUSANNE
1 Too short a day 1967
2 Life with Daktari 1969
3 Listen to the wild 1972
N.F. Autobiographical account of work with wild life in Africa

HARTLAND, M.
DAVID NAIRN:
1 Down among the dead men 1983
2 The third betrayal 1986

HARTLEY, L. P.
THE LIFE OF EUSTACE CHERRINGTON:
1 The shrimp and the anemone (The west window) 1944
2 The sixth heaven 1946
3 Eustace and Hilda 1947
'The white wand' contains a Eustace and Hilda story, 'Hilda's letter'. Later published in one volume under the title, 'Eustace and Hilda' 1958
★★★
1 The brickfield 1964
2 The betrayal 1966

HARTMAN, D.
DIRTY HARRY:
1 Duel for cannons
2 Death on the docks
3 The long death
4 The Mexico kill
Paperback thrillers

HARTOG, J. DE
1 Stella 1952
2 Distant shore
THE PEACEABLE KINGDOM:
1 The children of the light
2 The holy experiment
*The story of the Quaker persecution
and the settlement in America. Not
published in library ed. in U.K.*

HARVESTER, S.
DORIAN SILK:
1 Unsung road
2 Silk road 1962
3 Red road 1963
4 Assassin's road 1965
5 Treacherous road 1956
6 Battle road 1967
7 Zion road 1968
8 Nameless road 1969
9 Moscow road 1970
10 Sahara road 1972
11 Forgotten road 1974
12 Siberian road 1975
M. MALCOLM KENTON:
1 The bamboo screen 1955
2 Dragon road 1955
BLUNDEN SERIES:
1 A breastplate for Aaron
2 Sheep may safely graze
3 Obols for Charon
HERON MARMORIN:
1 The Chinese hammer
2 Troika 1962

HARVEY, A.
1 Burning houses
2 The web 1987

HARVEY, J. B.
HART THE REGULATOR:
1 Cherokee outlet
2 Blood trail
3 Tago
4 The silver lie
5 Blood on the border
6 Ride the wide country
7 Arkansas breakout
8 John Wesley Hardin
9 California bloodlines

10 The skinning place
Paperback Westerns. 6 also in hardback

HARVEY, JOHN
DET. INSPECTOR CHARLIE RESNICK:
1 Lonely hearts 1989
2 Rough treatment 1990
3 Cutting edge 1991

HARVEY, M.
1 The dark horseman 1978
2 The proud hunter 1980
3 Foxgate 1982

HASEK, J.
1 The good soldier Schweik
2 Adventures of good comrade Schweik,
by H. Putz 1969
3 The red commissar 1981

HASTINGS, M.
MONTAGUE CORK SERIES:
1 Cork on the water 1953
2 Cork in bottle 1954
3 Cork and the serpent 1955
4 Cork in the doghouse 1957
5 Cork on the telly 1966 (Cork on
location)

HASTINGS, P.
LONDON QUARTET:
1 The candles of night 1977
2 Feast of the peacock 1978

HATCH, R. W.
THE BRADFORDS:
1 Into the wind
2 Leave the salt earth

HATTERSLEY, R.
1 The maker's mark 1990
2 In that quiet earth 1991
*Novels based on the author's family
history*

HAWKES, J.
1 The blood oranges 1971
2 Death, sleep and the traveller 1975
3 Travesty 1976

HAWKE, S.
TIME WARS:
1 The Ivanhoe gambit
2 The time-keeper conspiracy
3 The Pimpernel plot
4 The Zenda vendetta
5 The Nautilus sanction
6 The Khyber connection

7 The argonaut affair
8 The dracula caper
Paperback fantasy

HAWKESWORTH, J., *see* **UPSTAIRS, DOWNSTAIRS SERIES**

HAWKEY, R.
PRESIDENTIAL TRILOGY:
1 Wild card 1974
2 Side effect 1979
3 End stage 1983

HAWKINS, J.
CHOPPER:
1 Blood trails
2 Tunnel warriors
3 Jungle sweep
4
5 Renegade MIAs
Paperback war stories

HAWORTH, E.
HOWTON SERIES:
1 Mistress of Howton 1978
2 The Farrers of Howton 1979
3 The Howton inheritance 1980
Family life in Victorian Lancashire

HAY, HEATHER
THE MONTFORD SAGA:
1 Heritage 1990
2 Honour 1990
3 Heroes 1991

HAYES, D.
THE HISTORY OF A SELFISH MAN:
1 The father in his dizzerbell 1968
2 The shy young men 1969
3 The war of '39 1970
4 Tomorrow the apricots 1971
5 A player's hide 1972
6 Quite a good address 1973
The story of a young actor in the 'thirties, through the war, and into the 'fifties. The sequence is not yet complete.

HAYMON, S. T.
1 Opposite the Cross Keys 1989
2 The quivering tree 1990
N.F. Autobiography
DET. INSPECTOR BEN JURNET:
1 Death of a pregnant virgin 1980
2 Ritual murder 1982
3 Stately homicide 1985
4 Death of a god 1987
5 A very particular murder 1989

HAYNES, C.
PROFESSOR HARRY BISHOP:
1 Bishop's gambit, declined 1990
2 Perpetual check
3 Sacrifice play 1990

HAYTER, A.
1 Sheila in the wind
2 The second step

HAYTHORNE, J.
OLIVER MANDRAKE:
1 The Streslan dimension 1981
2 Mandrake in Granada 1984
3 Mandrake in the monastery 1985

HAYWOOD, G. A.
AARON GUNNER:
1 Fear of the dark 1988
2 Not long for this world 1991

HAZEL, P.
FINNBRANCH SAGA:
1 Yearwood
2 Undersea
3 Winterking
Paperback fantasy. Also published in one vol.

HEALD, T.
SIMON BOGNOR:
1 Unbecoming habits 1973
2 Blue blood will out 1974
3 Deadline 1975
4 Let sleeping dogs lie 1976
5 Just desserts 1977
6 Murder at Moose Jaw 1981
7 Masterstroke 1982
8 Red herrings 1985
9 Brought to book 1988
10 Business unusual 1989

HEALEY, B.
PAUL HEDLEY SERIES:
1 Waiting for a tiger 1966
2 Millstone men 1967
3 Death in three masks 1967
4 Murder without crime 1968
5 Trouble with Penelope 1972
6 Last ferry from the Lido 1980
HAVOC SERIES:
1 Havoc 1978
2 Havoc in the Indies 1979

HEALY, J.
J. F. CUDDY:
1 Blunt darts 1986
2 The tethered goat 1986

3 So like sleep 1987
4 Swan dive 1988
5 Yesterday's news 1989

HEATH, R.
1 From the heat of the day 1978
2 One generation 1980
3 Genetha 1981
Family life in Georgetown, Guyana

HEATH-MILLER, M.
THE RAYNES OF RAYLEIGH SERIES:
1 Never go back 1968
2 No exit 1969
3 Give me tomorrow 1970
4 The bitter herb 1973
5 The narrow stair 1974
Novels about a family running a seaside hotel
HARDWICK FAMILY:
1 The wrong side of the Park 1975
2 Storm above the Park 1976
3 A time for silence 1977
4 The day before yesterday 1978
Set in Edwardian London

HEAVEN, C.
AYLSHAM FAMILY:
1 Lord of Ravensley 1980
2 The Ravensley touch 1982
3 The raging fire 1987
4 The fire still burns 1989

1 House of Kuragin 1972
2 The Astrov inheritance 1973
3 Heir to Kuragin 1978

HEBDEN, MARK
COL. MOSTYN SERIES:
1 Mask of violence 1971
2 A pride of dolphins 1974
INSPECTOR PEL:
1 Death set to music 1978
2 Pel and the faceless corpse 1979
3 Pel under pressure 1980
4 Pel is puzzled 1981
5 Pel and the staghound 1982
6 Pel and the bombers 1983
7 Pel and the predators 1984
8 Pel and the pirates 1984
9 Pel and the prowler 1985
10 Pel and the Paris mob 1986
11 Pel among the pueblos 1987
12 Pel and the touch of pitch 1987
13 Pel and the picture of innocence 1988
14 Pel and the party spirit 1989
15 Pel and the missing persons 1990
16 Pel and the promised land 1991

HEENAN, J. C. CARDINAL
1 Not the whole truth 1971
2 A crown of thorns 1974
N.F. Autobiography

HEIMLER, E.
1 Night of the mist 1959
2 A link in the chain 1962
N.F. Autobiography

HEINLEIN, R.
FUTURE HISTORY:
1 Universe
2 Common sense
3 Methusaleh's children 1941
4 The man who sold the moon 1950
5 The green hills of Earth 1951
6 Revolt in 2100 1953
7 Time enough for love 1973
8 Number of the beast 1979
9 The cat who walks through walls 1985
10 To sail beyond the sunset
A loosely linked series, much of which is in the form of short stories. 1 & 2 were published together as 'Orphans of the Sky' in 1963. Many of the stories were collected together in 'The Past Through Tomorrow' 1967

HELLER, K.
GEORGE MAN:
1 Man's illegal life 1984
2 Man's storm 1985
3 Man's loving family 1986
Detective stories about the 18th C Parish Watch

HELLMAN, L.
1 An unfinished life 1969
2 Pentimento 1974
3 Scoundrel time 1978
N.F. Autobiography

HELM, E.
VIETNAM GROUND ZERO:
1 Strike
2 The raid
3 Incident at Plei Soi
4 Tet
5 Red dust
Paperback war stories

HENDERSON, C.
LONE RIDER SERIES:
1 Lone rider
2 Lone rider's guns
3 Lone rider's justice 1955
4 Lone rider's trail 1955

5 Lone rider's range 1957
6 Lone rider's quest 1957
7 Lone rider's war 1958

HENDERSON, Z.
1 Pilgrimage 1965
2 The people: no different flesh 1966
Science fiction

HENNEKER, P.
SUSAN CAMPBELL AND PAUL ROSS:
1 And one must die 1965
2 Don't be afraid of the dark 1967
3 Too late for tears 1969

HENNESSEY, M., *pseud.*, (JOHN HARRIS)
KELLY MAGUIRE SERIES:
1 The lion at sea 1977
2 The dangerous years 1978
3 Back to battle 1979
Sea stories
1 The bright blue sky 1982
2 The challenging heights 1983
3 Once more the hawks 1984
A trilogy about the RFC in WW1
CAVALRY TRILOGY:
1 Soldier of the Queen 1980
2 Regimental lance 1981
3 The iron stallions 1982

HENREY, MRS. R.
1 The little Madeleine 1951
2 An exile in Soho 1952
3 Julia 1971
4 A girl at twenty 1974
5 Madeleine grown up 1952
6 Madeleine young wife 1960
7 London under fire, 1940-45 1969
8 Her April days 1963
9 Wednesday at four 1964
10 Green leaves 1976
11 She who pays 1969
N.F. Autobiography. This is the chronological sequence, and read in this order they form one consecutive narrative.

***

1 Paloma 1951
2 Madeleine's journal 1953
3 A month in Paris 1954
4 Mistress of myself 1959
5 Bloomsbury Fair
6 Milou's daughter 1955
7 London 1949
8 The virgin of Aldermanbury 1958
9 Spring in a Soho Street 1962

10 Winter wild 1966
N.F. Reportage. These are 'fringe' books to the main sequence of autobiography. This is the author's own classification and arrangements of her books. The following volumes, 'The farm in Normandy', 'Return to the farm', 'A village in Piccadilly', 'The incredible city', 'The seige of London', were originally published as an experiment under the male pseudonym 'Robert Henrey', and were incorporated later by the authoress into her main autobiographical sequence. The original editions, all published in London during World War II, are now only of academic interest and will not be republished.

HENRY, M.
BOB AND HILARY DEAN:
1 Unlucky dip 1963
2 The householders 1964
The story of a young married couple in Australia

HEPPENSTALL, R.
1 The connecting door 1962
2 The woodshed 1962

HERBERT, SIR A. P.
1 Trials of Topsy 1928
2 Topsy, M.P.
3 Topsy turvy 1947
Later collected in 'The Topsy omnibus'
MISLEADING CASES:
1 Misleading cases
2 More misleading cases 1933
3 Still more misleading cases 1933
4 Codd's last case 1952
'Uncommon law' is an omnibus volume of 1, 2 and 3.
ADMIRAL OF THE FLEET, EARL OF CARAWAY:
1 Number nine 1951
2 Made from man 1958

HERBERT, F.
DUNE:
1 Dune 1976
2 Dune Messiah 1971
3 Children of Dune 1976
4 God Emperor of Dune 1981
5 Heretics of Dune 1984
6 Chapterhouse Dune 1985
'The road to Dune', a short story is in 'Eye' 1986

JORJ AND MCKIE:
1 Whipping star 1979
2 The Dosadi experiment 1978
*The characters also appear in 'Eye'
1986.*

HERBERT, F. & RANSON, B.
1 The Jesus incident 1982
2 The Lazarus effect 1983

HERBERT, J.
1 The rats 1977
2 Lair 1979
3 Domain 1984
Horror stories

HERBERT, K.
1 Queen of the lightning 1984
2 Ghost in the sunlight 1986
3 Bride of the spear 1988
*Historical novels set in England in the
Dark Ages*

HERLEY, R.
THE PAGANS:
1 The stone arrow 1979
2 The flint lord 1981
3 The earth goddess 1984

HERMAN, R.
1 Warbirds 1989
2 Force of eagles 1990

HERON, J.
JASON TRASK:
1 Trask the avenger 1982
2 Trask and the fighting Irishman 1983

HERRING, C.
1 The Waterloo legacy 1979
2 Waterloo's ward 1980

HERRIOT, J.
1 If only they could talk 1964
2 It shoudn't happen to a vet 1971
3 Let sleeping vets lie 1973
4 Vet in harness 1974
5 Vets might fly 1976
6 Vet in a spin 1977
7 The Lord God made them all 1981
N.F. Autobiography

HERRON, S.
1 Miro 1970
2 The Miro papers 1972
3 Through the dark and hairy wood 1973
*1 and 2 are spy stories. 3 is a novel
about contemporary politics in Ulster.*

The main character is the same.

HERVEY, E.
MISS UNWIN:
1 The governess 1984
2 The man of gold 1985
3 Into the valley of death 1986
*Detective stories set in Victorian
London.
A pseudonym of H.R.F. Keating,
author of the Inspector Ghote series.*

HESKY, O.
SHIMONI AND BARZILAI SERIES:
1 The serpent's smile 1966
2 Time for treason 1967
3 The sequin syndicate 1968
4 The different night 1970
*Political 'thrillers' about two Israeli
agents*

HEWITT, A.
1 Piccolo 1961
2 Piccolo and Maria 1962

HIGGINS, A.
1 Killochter meadow *in* Felo de se
2 Langrishe go down 1966
2 is an extension of 1, a short story.

HIGGINS, G. V.
1 Kennedy for the defense 1980
2 Penance for Jerry Kennedy 1985

HIGGINS, J.
LIAM DEVLIN:
1 The eagle has landed 1975
2 Touch the devil 1983
3 Confessional 1985
4 The eagle has flown 1991

HIGHSMITH, DOMINI
1 Frankie 1990
2 Mammy's boy 1991

HIGHSMITH, P.
1 The talented Mr. Ripley 1968
2 Ripley underground 1970
3 Ripley's game 1973
4 The boy who followed Ripley 1980
5 Ripley under water 1991

HILL, C., LORD
1 Both sides of the hill 1964
2 Behind the screen 1974
N.F. Autobiography

HILL, D.
1 This is the house 1977

2 The house of Kingsley Merrick 1979

HILL, P.
DET. SUPT. WYNDSOR SERIES:
1 The hunters 1976
2 The liars 1977
3 The enthusiast 1978
4 The savages 1980
COMMANDER DICE:
1 The fanatics 1978
2 The washermen 1979

HILL, PAMELA
1 Fenfallow 1987
2 The Sutburys 1988

HILL, PORTER
CAPT. ADAM HORNE:
1 The Bombay Marines 1985
2 The war chest 1986
3 China flyer 1987
Naval adventure in the 19th century

HILL, R.
DALZIEL AND PASCOE:
1 A clubbable woman 1971
2 Fell of dark 1971
3 An advancement of learning 1971
4 A fairly dangerous thing 1972
5 Ruling passion 1974
6 An April shroud 1976
7 A pinch of snuff 1978
8 Pascoe's ghost and other stories 1979
9 A killing kindness 1980
10 Deadheads 1983
11 Exit lines 1984
12 Child's play 1986
13 Under world 1988
14 Bones and silence 1990
15 One small step 1990
15 is a novella, in which Dalziel solves a murder committed in space

HILLARY, L.
1 A yak for Xmas 1971
2 High time 1973
N.F. Travel in Nepal

HILLERMAN, T.
JIM CHEE:
1 People of darkness 1982
2 The dark wind 1983
3 The ghostway 1985
4 Skinwalkers 1988
Detective stories set among American Indians.
Sgt. Chee is a Navajo.

LIEUT. JOE LEAPHORN:
1 The blessing way 1970
2 The fly on the wall 1971
3 Dance hall of the dead 1973
4 Listening women 1979
5 Skinwalkers 1988
Jim Chee also appears in 5
LEAPHORN AND CHEE:
1 A thief of time 1989
2 Talking God 1990
3 Coyote waits 1991

HILLIARD, N.
1 Maori girl 1960
2 Power of joy 1965
3 Maori woman 1974
4 Glory and the dream 1975

HILTON, J. B.
SGT. BRUNT:
1 The quiet stranger 1985
2 Gamekeeper's gallows 1973
3 Rescue from the Rose 1975
4 Dead nettle 1977
5 Mr. Fred 1983
6 Slickensides 1987
SUPT. SIMON KENWORTHY:
1 Death of an Alderman 1968
2 Death in midwinter 1969
3 Hangman's tide 1972
4 No birds sang 1975
5 Some run crooked 1977
6 The anathema stone 1979
7 Playground of death 1980
8 Surrender value 1981
9 The green frontier 1982
10 The sunset law 1982
11 The asking price 1983
12 Corridors of guilt 1984
13 The Hobbema prospect 1984
14 Passion in the Peak 1985
15 Moondrop to murder 1986
16 The innocents at home 1986
17 Displaced person 1987

HIMES, C.
GRAVE DIGGER JONES AND COFFIN ED
JOHNSON SERIES:
1 Cotton comes to Harlem 1965
2 The heat's on 1966
3 Run man run 1967
4 Blind man with a pistol 1968 (The crazy kill)
5 All shot up 1969
6 The real cool killers 1970

HIMMEL, R.
JOHNNY MAGUIRE SERIES:

1 The Chinese keyhole
2 I have Gloria Kirby
3 The cry of the flesh 1958
4 The rich and the damned 1958
5 The name's Maguire 1963
6 It's murder Maguire 1963
7 Two deaths must die 1964
*2 and 3 only published in paperback in
U.S.A. 1 was first published in
paperback in U.S.A., in U.K. hardback
1968*

HINXMAN, M.
DET. INSPECTOR RALPH BRAND:
1 One way cemetery 1977
2 Death of a good woman 1981
3 The telephone never tells 1983
4 The sound of murder 1986

HIRSCHFIELD, B.
FIRE ISLAND:
1 Fire island
2 Fire in the embers
3 Cindy on Fire
4 Return to Fire Island
Paperback
DALLAS:
1 The Ewings of Dallas 1980
2 The women of Dallas 1981
3 The men of Dallas 1982

HISCOCK, E. C.
1 Cruising under sail
2 Around the world in *Wanderer III*
3 Voyaging under sail
N.F. Autobiography

HISLOP, J.
1 Far from a gentleman 1963
2 Anything but a soldier 1965

HOBSON, H.
BRAD FORD SERIES:
1 The gallant affair
2 Death makes a claim 1958
3 The big twist 1959
4 Mission house murder 1959
5 Beyond tolerance 1960

HOBSON, R. B.
1 Grass beyond the mountains
2 Nothing too good for a cowboy
3 The rancher takes a wife
N.F. Autobiography

HOCKEN, S.
1 Emma and I 1977
2 Emma VIP 1980

3 Emma and Co. 1983
4 After Emma 1988
N.F. About the author's guide dog

HOCKING, A.
DET. CHIEF SUPT. WILLIAM AUSTEN:
1 Poison in paradise 1955
2 Murder at midday 1956
3 Relative murder 1957
4 Epitaph for a nurse 1958
5 To cease upon the midnight 1959
6 Poisoned chalice 1959
7 The thin-spun life 1960
8 Candidate for murder 1961
9 He had to die 1962
10 Spies have no friends 1962
11 Murder cries out 1963

HOCKING, M.
1 A time of war
2 The hopeful travellers 1970
*Stories of a group of W.A.A.Fs and
their post-war experiences*
FAIRLEYS:
1 Good daughters 1984
2 Indifferent heroes 1985
3 Welcome strangers 1986

HODGE, J. A.
PURCHIS FAMILY:
1 Judas flowering 1979
2 Wide is the water 1981
3 Savannah Purchase 1971
4 Runaway bride 1977
   LISTENBURG:
1 Last act 1979
2 First night 1989
3 Leading lady 1990

HODGES, A.
THE BLAKE FAMILY:
1 The man of substance
2 The glittering hour

HODGINS, E.
1 Mr. Blandings builds his dream house
1946
2 Blandings way 1950
N.F. Humour

HOGAN, J. P.
GIANTS TRILOGY:
1 Inherit the stars
2 The gentle giants of Garymede
3 Giants' Star

HOLBROOK, D.
1 Flesh wounds 1966

2 A play of passion 1978
3 Nothing larger than life 1987
4 A little Athens 1990

HOLDEN, M.
SQUADRON:
1 Sons of the morning 1978
2 The sun climbs slowly 1978
3 Scramble Dieppe 1979
4 Desert Spitfire 1980
5 Whirlwind at Arromanches 1981
6 Massacre at Falaise 1981

HOLDEN, U.
1 Tin toys 1986
2 The unicorn sisters 1988

HOLDSTOCK, R.
1 Mythago Wood 1985
2 Lavondyss 1988
3 The bore forest 1991 (Novella)
  Fantasy

HOLGATE, J.
1 Make a cow laugh
2 On a pig's back
3 A sheep's eye view
  N.F. Autobiography of a farmer

HOLLAND, I.
ST. ANSELM'S:
1 Death at St. Anselm's 1985
2 Bump in the night 1989
3 Thief 1989
4 A fatal Advent 1991
5 The long search 1991
  Detective stories set in an urban parish

HOLLAND, V.
1 Son of Oscar Wilde 1954
2 Time remembered after Pere Lachaise
  1966
  N.F. Autobiography

HOLME, T.
INSPECTOR ACHILLE PERONI:
1 The Neopolitan streak 1980
2 A funeral of gondolas 1981
3 The devil and the dolce vita 1982
4 The Assissi murders 1985
5 At the lake of sudden death 1987

HOLT, H.
SHEILA MALLORY:
1 Gone away 1989
2 The cruellest month 1991

HOLT, T.
THE WALLED ORCHARD:
1 Goatsong 1989
2 The walled orchard 1990

HOLT, W.
1 I haven't unpacked
2 I haven't unpacked yet
3 I still haven't unpacked
  N.F. Autobiography

HOLTON, L.
FATHER BREDDER SERIES:
1 The saint maker 1960
2 The pact with Satan 1961

HOLZER, H.
AMITYVILLE:
1 Murder in Amityville 1980
2 The Amityville curse 1981
3 The secret of Amityville 1985

HOME, M.
1 The place of little birds
2 House of shade
3 City of the soul
BRECKLAND SERIES:
1 God and the rabbit
2 In this valley
3 This string first
4 The questing man
5 The harvest is past
6 July at Fritham
7 No snow in Latching
8 Grain of the wood
9 The soundless years
10 Brackenford story
  Not strict series, but connected
JOHN BENHAM SERIES:
1 The strange prisoner
2 The Auber file

HOMER
1 The Iliad
2 The Odyssey
  *'The Odyssey': a modern sequel, 1959,
  by Nikos Kazantas, has been called 'a
  work of art in its own right'. Eyvind
  Johnson's (Nobel prize, 1974)
  'Strandermas Svall', 1946 is a modern
  version of the Odyssey. Trs. 1952 as
  'Return to Ithaca'.
  'The last voyage of Odysseus' by K. L.
  Carey. (1984) reconstructs the now lost
  final epic derived from classical sources.
  'The ladies from the Sea' by A. D.
  Hope recounts Odysseus rule after his
  return to Ithaca.*

HOOD, E.
1 A stranger in the town 1985
2 Silver bells, white linen 1988
Novels set in Paisley in the 18th century

HOOKE, N. W.
1 Striplings
2 Close of play
3 Own wilderness

HOOKER, R.
1 M*A*S*H
2 M*A*S*H goes to Maine 1973
3 M*A*S*H goes to Hollywood
4 M*A*S*H goes to New Orleans
5 M*A*S*H goes to Vienna
6 M*A*S*H goes to Paris
7 M*A*S*H goes to Texas
8 M*A*S*H goes to San Fransisco
9 M*A*S*H goes to Miami
10 M*A*S*H goes to Morocco
11 M*A*S*H goes to Montreal
12 M*A*S*H goes to Moscow
13 M*A*S*H mania
Stories of a U.S. Army mobile army surgical hospital. Paperback

HOOVER, H.
1 The gift of the deer
2 A place in woods
3 The years of the forest 1973
N.F. Autobiography

HOPE, J.
1 Don't do it!
2 All this and Burnham too
3 One term at Utopia
4 The Inspector suggests
N.F. Humours of teaching
***
1 Call me Florence
2 Leave it to Florence
Humorous sketches of the nursing profession

HOPKINS, K.
DR. BLOW-PROFESSOR MANCIPLE SERIES:
1 She died because 1958
2 Dead against my principles 1959
3 Body blow 1961
GERRY LEE SERIES:
1 The girl who dies
2 The forty-first passenger
3 Pierce with a pin
4 Camper's corpse

HORGAN, P.
1 Maine line west
2 A lamp on the plain
RICHARD SERIES:
1 Things as they are 1965
2 Everything to live for 1969
3 The thin mountain air 1978

HORNER, L., see ONSTOTT, K.
Later novels in the Falconhurst series are by Horner, but the sequence has been retained under the original author.

HORNIG, D.
LOREN SWIFT:
1 Hardball 1986
2 The dark side 1987

HORNUNG, E. W.
1 Raffles, the amateur cracksman 1901
2 A thief in night 1905
3 Mr. Justice Raffles 1909
1 was originally published as two separate collections of short stories, 'The amateur cracksman', and 'The black mask'. See note on bibliography of this work T.L.S. 18 8 50 Continued by Barry Perowne
4 Raffles after dark (Return of Raffles)
5 Raffles in pursuit 1934
6 Raffles under sentence 1936
7 She married Raffles 1936
8 Raffles and the key man 1940
No. 8 only published in U.S.A.
9 Raffles revisited 1977
10 Raffles of the Albany 1978
11 Raffles of the M.C.C. 1979
12 The Return of Raffles, by P. Tremayne 1990

HORST, K.
1 Sink the Ark Royal 1981
2 Caribbean pirate 1982
Novels about the German Navy in WW2

HORWOOD, W.
DUNCTON CHRONICLES:
1 Duncton Wood 1980
2 Duncton quest 1988
3 Duncton found 1989
4 Duncton tales 1991

HOSSENT, H.
MAX HEALD SERIES:
1 Spies die at dawn 1960
2 No end to fear 1961
3 Memory of treason 1962

4 Spies have no friends 1963
5 Run for your death 1965
6 The fear business 1966

HOUGH, R.
1 Angel's one-five 1978
2 Fight of the few 1979
3 Fight to the finish 1980
   About an R.A.F. Squadron in World War II
BULLER:
1 Buller's guns 1981
2 Buller's dreadnought 1982
3 Buller's victory 1984

HOUGH, S. B.
INSPECTOR BRENTFORD:
1 Dear daughter dead 1966
2 Sweet sister seduced 1968

HOUGRON, J.
M. LASTIN SERIES:
1 Blaze of the sun 1957
2 Reap the whirlwind 1958
   Last years of French rule in Indo-China

HOULT, N.
MONTY MALLORY SERIES:
1 Father and daughter 1957
2 Husband and wife 1959

   ***

1 Holy Ireland 1935
2 Coming from the fair 1937

   ***

1 Smilin' on the vine 1941
2 Augusta steps out 1942

HOUSEHOLD, G.
ROGER TAINE SERIES:
1 Rough shoot 1951
2 Time to kill 1952

   ***

1 Rogue male 1939
2 Rogue justice 1982

HOUSEMAN, J.
1 Run-through 1973
2 Front and centre 1979
3 Final dress 1983
   N.F. Autobiography of the film director. Published in one vol. as 'Unfinished Business' in 1986

HOWARD, A.
CHAPMAN FAMILY:
1 The mallow years 1990
2 Shining threads 1991

HOWARD, H.
GLENN BOWMAN SERIES:
1 Last appointment
2 Last deception
3 Last vanity
4 Death of Cecilia
5 The other side of the door
6 Bowman strikes again
7 Bowman on Broadway
8 Bowman at a venture
9 No target for Bowman
10 Sleep for the wicked 1955
11 A hearse for Cinderella 1956
12 The Bowman touch 1956
13 Key to the morgue 1957
14 Sleep my pretty one 1957
15 The long night 1957
16 The big snatch 1958
17 The Armitage secret 1958
18 Deadline 1959
19 Extortion 1960
20 Time bomb 1960
21 Fall guy 1960
22 I'm no hero 1961
23 Count-down 1962
24 Out of the fire 1965
25 Portrait of a beautiful harlot 1966
26 Routine investigation 1967
27 The secret of Simon Cornell 1969
28 Cry on my shoulder 1970
29 Room 37 1970
30 Million dollar snapshot 1971
31 Murder one 1971
32 Epitaph for Joanna 1972
33 Nice day for a funeral 1972
34 Highway to murder 1973
35 Dead drunk 1974
36 Treble cross 1975
37 Pay off 1977
38 One-way ticket 1978
39 The sealed envelope 1979
PHILIP SCOTT-DEPARTMENT K:
1 Department K 1966
2 The eye of the hurricane 1968

HOWARD, L.
FYTTON OF GAWSWORTH:
1 Elizabeth Fytton of Gawsworth Hall 1985
2 The master of Littlecote Manor 1986
3 The squire of Holdenby 1986
4 Isabel the girl 1989
5 Isabel the woman 1990

HOWARD, R. E.
CONAN:
1 Conan 1974
2 Conan the usurper, by L. Sprague de

Camp 1974
3 Conan the wanderer, by L. Sprague de
 Camp 1974
4 Conan the conqueror
5 Conan the adventurer 1973
6 Conan the avenger 1974
7 Conan of the Isles, by L. Sprague de
 Camp
8 Conan the Warrior 1967
9 Conan the buccaneer, by L. Sprague de
 Camp
10 Conan of Cimmeria, by L. Sprague de
 Camp 1974
11 Conan the freebooter 1974
12 Conan of Aquilonia, by L. Sprague de
 Camp
13 Conan the swordsman, by L. Sprague
 de Camp 1978
14 Conan the liberator, by A. J. Offut 1980
15 Conan the mercenary, by A. J. Offut
16 The sword of Skelos, by A. J. Offut
17 The road of kings, by K. E. Wagner
 1983
18 Conan and the spider god, by L.
 Sprague de Camp
19 Conan the rebel, by P. Anderson 1984
20 Conan the invincible, by R. Jordan
21 Conan the defender, by R. Jordan
22 Conan the unconquered, by R. Jordan
23 Conan the triumphant, by R. Jordan
24 Conan the barbarian, by R. Jordan
25 Conan the magnificent, by R. Jordan
26 Conan the victorious, by R. Jordan
27 Conan the valorous, by J. M. Roberts
28 Conan the champion, by J. M. Roberts
29 Conan the fearless, by S. Perry
 Science fiction, mainly in paperback

HOWATCH, S.
1 The rich are different 1978
2 Sins of the fathers 1980

1 Glittering images 1987
2 Glamorous powers 1988
3 Ultimate prizes 1989
4 Scandalous risks 1990

HOWE, B.
1 A galaxy of governesses
2 Child in Chile 1957
 N.F. Autobiography

HOWELL, W.
1 The voyage of *Wanderer II* 1957
2 Wanderer III 1956
 N.F. Travel

HOYLE, F., and ELLIOT, J.
1 A for Andromeda 1963
2 Andromeda breakthrough 1964

HOYT, R.
JOHN DENSON:
1 Decoy
2 30 for a Harry 1982
3 Fish story 1987

HUBBARD, L. R.
MISSION EARTH:
1 The invaders plan 1986
2 Black genesis 1986
3 The enemy within 1987
4 An alien affair 1987
5 Fortune of fear 1987
6 Death quest 1987
7 Voyage of vengeance 1988
8 Disaster 1988
9 Villainy victorious 1988
10 The doomed planet 1988
 Science fiction

HUGHART, B.
MASTER LI:
1 Bridge of birds 1989
2 The story of the stone 1989
3 Eight skilled gentlemen 1991

HUGHES, G.
GEORGE WILLIS:
1 Split on red 1980
2 Cover zero 1981
3 The French deal 1982

HUGHES, GLYN
1 The hawthorn goddess 1986
2 The rape of the rose 1987

HUGHES, L.
1 Simple speaks his mind 1950
2 Simple takes a wife
3 Simple stakes a claim 1957
 *Stories and anecdotes by, and about, a
 Harlem negro*

HUGHES, M. V.
A LONDON FAMILY, 1870-1900;
1 London child of the seventies 1978
2 London girl of the eighties 1979
3 London home in the nineties 1980
 N.F. Autobiography

HUGHES, P. C. ('Spike')
1 Opening bars
2 Second movement
 N.F. Autobiography

HUGHES, R. D.
PELMAN THE POWERSHAPER:
1 The prophet of Lamath
2 The wizard in waiting
Paperback fantasy

HUGHES, RICHARD
THE HUMAN PREDICAMENT:
1 The fox in the attic 1961
2 The wooden shepherdess 1973
*The first two volumes of what is
projected as a chronicle of our times
since World War I*

HULKE, M.
CROSSROADS MOTEL:
1 Crossroads - a new beginning 1974
2 Crossroads - a warm breeze 1975
3 Crossroads - something old, something
new 1976

HULME, A.
1 The flying man 1988
2 Whisper in the wind 1989

HUMPHREYS, E.
1 Flesh and blood 1974
2 The best of friends 1978
3 Salt of the earth 1985
4 An absolute hero 1986
5 Open secrets 1988
6 Bonds of attachment 1991
*Follows the lives and careers of two girls
in Wales in the 1920s and 30s*

HUNA, L.
BORGIA TRILOGY:
1 The Borgian bull (The bulls of Rome)
2 The star of the Orsini
3 The maid of the Nettuno

HUNT, D. BONAVIA-, see AUSTEN, J.

HUNT, J., LORD
1 Ascent of Everest 1953
2 Our Everest adventure 1954
N.F. Mountaineering

HUNT, R.
DET. CHIEF INSPECTOR SYDNEY WALSH:
1 Death in ruins 1991
2 Death sounds grand 1991

HUNTER, A.
SUPT. GEORGE GENTLY:
1 Gently does it 1955
2 Gently by the shore 1956
3 Gently down the stream 1957

4 Landed Gently 1958
5 Gently through the mill 1958
6 Gently in the sun 1959
7 Gently with the painters 1960
8 Gently to the summit 1960
9 Gently go man 1961
10 Gently where the roads go 1962
11 Gently floating 1963
12 Gently Sahib 1964
13 Gently with the ladies 1965
14 Gently northwest 1966
15 Gently continental 1968
16 Gently coloured 1969
17 Gently with the innocents 1970
18 Gently at a gallop 1971
19 Vivienne: Gently where she lay 1972
20 Gently French 1973
21 Gently in trees 1974
22 Gently with love 1975
23 Gently where the birds are 1976
24 Gently instrumental 1977
25 Gently to a sleep 1978
26 The Honfleur decision 1980
27 Gabrielle's way 1981
28 Fields of heather 1981
29 Gently between the tides 1982
30 Amorous Leander 1983
31 The unhung man 1983
32 Once a prostitute... 1984
33 The Chelsea ghost 1985
34 Goodnight, sweet prince 1986
35 Strangling man 1987
36 Traitor's end 1988
37 Gently with the millions 1989
38 Gently scandalous 1990

HUNTER, C.
1 Island of stone 1982
2 Fiercely the tempest 1984
Novels set in Portland, Dorset

HUNTER, EVAN
1 Last summer 1971
2 Come winter 1973
*The story of three delinquent
adolescents. There is a five year interval
between 1 and 2.*

HUNTER, J.
RUPERT OF THE RHINE:
1 Rupert the devil 1975
2 Cavalier 1977

HUNTER, J. D.
BRUNO STACHEL:
1 The blue Max 1965
2 Blood order 1980
3 The tin cravat 1981

HUNTER, N.
BODIE THE STALKER:
1 Trackdown
2 Bloody bounty
3 High hell
4 The killing trail
5 Hangtown
6 Day of the savage
Paperback Westerns

HUNTER, R.
SIMON QUARRY:
1 The fourth angel 1986
2 Quarry's contract 1987

HURD, D., and OSMOND, A.
1 Send him victorious 1967
2 The smile on the face of the tiger 1969
3 Scotch on the rocks 1971
A trilogy of political novels set in the near future. Each in a different setting but Harvey, the Prime Minister, and his colleagues appear in all

HURT, F. M.
INSPECTOR BROOM:
1 The body at Bowman's hollow
2 Death by request
3 Sweet death 1961
4 Acquainted with murder 1962

HUTCHINGS, M. M.
1 Chronicles of Church Farm
2 Romany Cottage, Silverlake
3 Rural reflections
4 Hundredfold
N.F. Rural life

HUTSON, S.
1 Slugs 1984
2 Breeding ground 1985
Horror stories
SGT. ROLF KESSLER:
1 Sledgehammer 1981
2 Kessler's raid 1982
3 Convoy of steel 1982
4 Slaughterhouse 1983
5 Men of blood 1984
6 No survivors 1985
7 Taken by force 1987

HUXLEY, E.
1 The flame trees of Thika 1959
2 The mottled lizard 1962
3 Love among the daughters 1968
4 Out in the midday sun 1985
N.F. Autobiography and travel in Kenya

HYLAND, S.
1 Who goes hang? 1968
2 Top bloody secret 1969
Two political thrillers in which characters reappear

IBARGUENGOITIA, J.
1 Two dead girls 1983
2 Two crimes 1984
Set in Mexico

IDELL, A. E.
ROGERS FAMILY:
1 Rogers' folly 1957
2 Centennial summer 1943
3 Bridge to Brooklyn 1944
4 Great blizzard 1948
1 was last written, but concerns a period 40 years earlier than the others

INCHBALD, P.
INSPECTOR FRANCO CORTI:
1 Tondo for short 1981
2 The sweet short grass 1982
3 Short break in Venice 1983
4 Or the bambino dies 1985

INCHBALD, R.
COL. PATERNOSTER SERIES:
1 Col. Paternoster 1953
2 The five inns 1954
3 September story 1955

INCHFAWN, F.
1 Those remembered days 1962
2 Something more to say 1965
3 Not the final word 1969
N.F. Autobiography

INFANTE, A.
MICKY DOUGLAS:
1 Death on a hot summer night 1989
2 Death among the dunes 1990
3 Deathwater 1991
Thrillers set in Australia

INGATE, M.
1 Sound of the weir 1974
2 This water laps gently 1977

INGRAM, S.
1 I found adventure
2 Land of mudcastles
N.F. Autobiography

INNES, B.
1 The Red Baron lives 1982

2 The red Red Baron 1983

INNES, M.
SIR JOHN APPLEBY:
1 Death at the President's lodging 1936
2 Hamlet, revenge! 1937
3 Lament for a maker 1938
4 Stop press 1939
5 There came both mist and snow 1940
6 The secret vanguard 1940
7 Appleby on Ararat 1941
8 The daffodil affair 1942
9 The weight of the evidence 1944
10 Appleby's end 1945
11 From London far 1946
12 What happened at Hazelwood 1947
13 A night of errors 1948
14 Operation Pax 1951
15 A private view 1952
16 Appleby talking 1954
17 Appleby talks again 1956
18 Appleby plays chicken 1956
19 The long farewell 1958
20 Hare sitting up 1959
21 Silence observed 1961
22 A connoisseur's case 1962
23 Money from Holme 1964
24 The bloody wood 1966
25 A change of heir 1966
26 Appleby at Allington 1968
27 A family affair 1969
28 Death at the chase 1970
29 An awkward lie 1971
30 The open house 1972
31 Appleby's answer 1973
32 Appleby's other story 1974
33 The Appleby file 1975
34 The gay phoenix 1976
35 The Ampersand papers 1978
36 Sheiks and adders 1982
37 Appleby and Honeybath 1983
38 Carson's conspiracy 1984
39 Appleby and the Ospreys 1986
HONEYBATH SERIES:
1 The mysterious commission 1974
2 Honeybath's haven 1977
3 Lord Mullion's secret 1981
4 Appleby and Honeybath 1983

INSIGHT, J.
1 I turned my collar round
2 I am the vicar 1956
3 Country parson 1961
4 I am a guienea pig 1964
N.F. Autobiography

IRISH, L.
COLONIAL TRILOGY:

1 And the wild birds sing 1984
2 The place of the swan 1986
3 The house of O'Shea 1990

IRVINE, L.
1 Runaway 1986
2 Castaway 1983
N.F. Autobiography

IRVING, L.
1 Henry Irving 1968
2 The successors 1969
3 The precarious crust 1971
N.F. A trilogy on the lives of the
author's ancestors and a picture of the
English stage from Victorian times

IRWIN, G.
1 Least of all saints 1957
2 Andrew Connington 1958

IRWIN, M.
1 Royal flush: the story of Minette 1932
2 The proud servant: the story of
Montrose 1934
3 The stranger prince: the story of Rupert
of the Rhine 1937
4 The bride: the story of Louise and
Montrose 1939
'Four books about certain people in the
17th century whose lives were linked
together'

***

1 Young Bess 1945
2 Elizabeth, captive princess 1948
3 Elizabeth and the Prince of Spain 1960
Fictionalised biography of Elizabeth I

ISON, G.
DET. CHIEF SUPT. JOHN GAFFNEY:
1 Cold light of dawn 1988
2 Confirm or deny 1989
3 A damned serious business 1990
DET. CHIEF SUPT. TOMMY FOX:
1 The Home Secretary will see you now
1989
2 Lead me to the slaughter 1990

ISRAEL, P.
B. F. CAGE SERIES:
1 Hush money 1975
2 The French kiss 1977
3 The stiff upper lip 1979

JACK, D.
THE JOURNALS OF BARTHOLOMEW DANDY:
1 Three cheers for me 1973
2 That's me in the middle 1974
3 It's me again
4 Me Dandy, you Cissie
5 Me too 1984

JACKMAN, S.
1 The Davidson affair 1973
2 Slingshot 1974
The story of Jesus transferred to a modern setting

JACKSON, A.
1 Tales from a country practice 1986
2 More tales from a country practice 1987
N.F. Memoirs of a Suffolk G.P.

JACKSON, B.
AIR DETECTIVE:
1 Crooked flight 1985
2 Spy's flight 1986
3 Terror flight 1988

JACKSON, G.
1 Soledad brother 1968
2 Blood in my eye 1972
N.F. Autobiography

JACKSON, R.
1 Before the storm 1972
2 Storm from the skies 1974
N.F. A history of the strategic air offensive against Germany
HURRICANE SQUADRON:
1 Yeoman goes to war 1978
2 Squadron scramble 1978
3 Target Tobruk 1979
4 Malta victory 1980
5 Mosquito squadron 1981
6 Operation diver 1981
7 Tempest squadron 1981
8 The last battle 1982
9 Operation Firedog 1982
10 Korean combat 1983
11 Venom squadron 1983
12 Hunter squadron 1984
SAS:
1 Desert Commando 1986
21 Partisan! 1987
3 Attack at night 1988
4 Wind of death 1990

JACKSON, S.
1 Life among the savages 1953

2 Raising demons 1956
N.F. Autobiography

JACOB, N.
THE GOLLANTZ SAGA:
1 The founder of the house 1936
2 The wild lie 1940
3 Young Emmanuel 1932
4 Four generations
5 Private Gollantz
6 Gollantz
7 London, Paris, Milan
8 Gollantz and partners 1957
1-6 reissued in two volumes as 'The Gollantz saga'
***
1 Time piece 1936
2 Fadeout 1937
***
1 Susan Crowther 1948
2 Honour's a mistress 1949
The action in 1 takes place in World War 1, in 2 in World War II.
***
1 Me 1933
2 Me again 1937
3 More about me 1939
4 Me in wartime 1943
5 Me in the Mediterranean 1946
6 Me over there 1947
7 Me and mine 1949
8 Me - looking back 1950
9 Robert, Nana and me 1952
10 Me - likes and dislikes 1954
11 Me - yesterday and today 1957
12 Me - and the swans 1961
13 Me - and the stags 1963
14 Me - thinking things over 1964
N.F. Autobiography
TALES OF THE BROAD ACRES:
1 Sally Scarth 1948
2 The loaded stick
3 Roots
Regarded by the author as connected by their locality - Yorkshire

JACOBS, T. C. H.
TEMPLE FORTUNE SERIES:
1 Red eyes of Kali 1955
2 Good night sailor 1956
3 Death in the mews 1957
4 Final payment 1962
5 Sweet poison 1966
6 Ashes in the cellar 1966
7 Death of a scoundrel 1967
8 Wild weekend 1967
9 House of horror 1969

10 The black devil 1969

JAFFE, R.
1 Class reunion
2 After the reunion 1985

JAGGER, B.
BARFORTH FAMILY:
1 The clouded hills 1980
2 Flint and roses 1981
3 The sleeping sword 1982

JAHN, M.
BLACK SHEEP SQUADRON:
1 Devil in the slot
2 The hawk flies on Sunday
Paperback

JAHVDA, G.
1 The loving maid 1961
2 Delilah's mountain 1964
*Connected but not sequels. 1 deals with
the Bickley family in East Anglia. 2
with a member of the family in West
Virginia in the 18th century.*

JAKES, J.
1 North and South 1983
2 Love and war 1985
3 Heaven and hell 1987
*A family chronicle set in the American
Civil War*
KENT FAMILY CHRONICLES:
1 The bastard
2 The rebels
3 The seekers
4 The warriors
5 The titans 1990
6 The furies 1990
7 Lawless 1990
8 Americans 1990
1-4 published in paperback
BRAK THE BARBARIAN:
1 Brak the barbarian
2 The sorcerers
3 The mark of the demons
Paperback fantasy

JAMES, B.
DET. CHIEF SUPT. COLIN HARPUR:
1 You'd better believe it 1985
2 The Lolita man 1986
3 Halo parade 1987
4 Protection 1988
5 Come clean 1989
6 Take 1990
7 Club 1991

JAMES, E.
1 Life class 1990
2 Life lines 1991
3 Lovers and friends 1991

JAMES, J.
PHOTINUS THE GREEK:
1 Votan 1966
2 Not for all the gold in Ireland 1968
*The fringes of the Roman Empire in
the 2nd century A.D.*

JAMES, M.
LAWRENCE FAMILY:
1 A touch of earth 1988
2 Fortune's favourite child 1989
3 The treasures of existence 1989

JAMES, P. D.
SUPT. ADAM DALGLEISH:
1 Cover her face 1967
2 A mind to murder 1963
3 Unnatural causes 1970
4 Shroud for a nightingale 1971
5 The black tower 1975
6 Death of an expert witness 1977
7 A taste for death 1986
8 Devices and Desires 1990
CORDELIA GRAY:
1 An unsuitable job for a woman 1972
2 The skull beneath the skin 1982

JAMES, PETER
MAX FLYNN:
1 Dead letter drop 1981
2 Atom bomb angel 1982

JAMES, W. M.
APACHE SERIES:
1 The first death
2 Knife in the night
3 Duel to the death
4 Death train
5 Fort Treachery
6 Sonora slaughter
7 Blood line
8 Blood on the trail
9 The naked and the savage
10 All blood is red
11 The cruel trail
Paperback Westerns

JAMESON, D.
1 Touched by angels 1989
2 Last of the hot metal men 1990
N.F. Autobiography

JEFFREY, E.
CHISWELL FAMILY:
1 Stranger's Hall 1988
2 Gin and gingerbread 1989
A family saga set in Essex and the oyster trade

JARMAN, R. H.
1 We speak no treason 1970
2 The King's grey mare 1972
3 The courts of illusion 1983
Novels about Richard III and the Wars of the Roses

JEFFRIES, I.
SARGEANT CRAIG SERIES:
1 Thirteen days 1959
2 Dignity and purity 1960
3 It wasn't me 1961

JEFFRIES, M.
LOREMASTERS OF ELUNDIUM:
1 The road to Underfall 1987
2 Palace of kings 1988
3 Shadowlight
Fantasy. No. 3 in paperback only
THE HEIRS TO GNARLSMYRE:
1 Glitterspike Hall
2 Hall of whispers

JEFFRIES, R.
INSPECTOR ALVAREZ:
1 Mistakenly in Mallorca 1973
2 Two-faced death 1975
3 Troubled deaths 1977
4 Murder begets murder 1979
5 Just desserts 1980
6 Unseemly end 1981
7 Deadly petard 1983
8 Three and one make five 1984
9 Layers of deceit 1985
10 Almost murder 1986
11 Relatively dangerous 1987
12 Death trick 1988
13 Dead clever 1989
14 Too clever by half 1990
15 Murder's long memory 1991

JENKINS, G.
COMMANDER GEOFFREY PEACE:
1 Twist of sand
2 Hunter-killer 1964

JEPSON, S.
EVE GILL SERIES:
1 Man running 1948
2 The golden dart 1949
3 The hungry spider 1950

4 Man dead 1951
5 The black Italian 1954
6 The laughing fish 1960

JETER, K. W.
1 Dr. Adder
2 The glass hammer
3 Death arms 1987

JEVONS, M.
PROF. HENRY SPEARMAN:
1 Murder at the margin 1978
2 The fatal equilibrium 1985

JEWELL, D.
1 Come in, Number one your number is up 1972
2 Sellout 1973

JOHN, SIR A.
1 Chiaroscuro
2 Finishing touches
N.F. Autobiography

JOHN, O.
HAGGAI GODIN SERIES:
1 Thirty days hath September 1966
2 The disinformer 1967
3 A beam of black light 1968
4 Dead on time 1969

JOHNSON, B. F.
1 Delta blood
2 Homeward winds the river
3 The heirs of love
A paperback saga set in the Deep South

JOHNSON, D. MCINTOSH
1 A doctor regrets 1948
2 Bars and barricades 1952
3 A doctor returns 1956
4 A doctor in Parliament 1958
5 A Cassandra in Westminster 1967
6 A doctor reflects 1975
N.F. Autobiography

JOHNSON, E., *see* HOMER

JOHNSON, P. H.
HELENA TRILOGY:
1 Too dear for possessing 1940
2 Avenue of stone 1947
3 A summer to decide 1952

***

1 The unspeakable Skipton 1960
2 Night and silence, who is here 1963
1 is a fictional version of part of the life

of *Frederick Rolfe*, but one character
Matthew Pryar, is the hero of *2*.
3 Cork St., next the hatters 1965
Reintroduces characters from 1 and 2
★★★
1 The good listener 1975
2 The good husband 1978

JOHNSTON, B.
1 It's been a lot of fun 1976
2 It's a funny game 1976
3 It's been a piece of cake 1989
*N.F. Cricket and broadcasting
reminiscences*

JOHNSTON, G.
SILBER:
1 The claws of the scorpion
2 The two kings

JOHNSTON, GEORGE
DAVID MEREDITH TRILOGY:
1 My brother Jack 1967
2 Clean straw for nothing 1969
3 A cartload of clay 1971
*The story of an Australian writer. 3 was
unfinished*

JOHNSTON, R.
JAMES BRUCE:
1 Disaster at Dungeness 1965
2 The angry ocean 1967

JOHNSTONE, N.
1 Hotel in Spain
2 Hotel in flight
N.F. Autobiography

JOLLEY, E.
1 My father's moon 1989
2 Cabin fever 1991

JON, M.
STEVEN KALE:
1 The Wallington case 1981
2 A question of law 1981

JONES, B.
CLAUD RAVEL SERIES:
1 The Hamlet problem 1961
2 The crooked phoenix 1962
3 Tiger from the shadows 1963
4 Death on a pale horse 1963
5 Private vendetta 1965
6 The embers of hate 1966
7 Testament of evil 1967
8 A den of savage men 1967
9 The deadly trade 1968

JONES, ELWYN
CHIEF INSPECTOR BARLOW:
1 Barlow 1972
2 Barlow in charge 1973
3 Barlow comes to judgement 1974
4 The Barlow casebook 1975
5 Barlow exposed 1976
6 Barlow down under 1978

JONES, G.
1 Lord of misrule 1983
2 Noble savage 1985

JONES, I. H.
1 Sister 1987
2 Senior sister 1988
Novels about hospital life

JONES, JACK
1 Unfinished journey 1937
2 Me and mine 1946
3 Give me back my heart 1950
N.F. Autobiography

JONES, JENNY
FLIGHT OVER FIRE:
1 Fly by night 1990
2 The edge of vengeance 1991
Fantasy

JONES, JOANNA
NURSE JONES:
1 Nurse is a neighbour
2 Nurse on the district 1958
N.F. Autobiography

JONES, SIR L. E.
1 A Victorian boyhood
2 An Edwardian yooth
3 Georgian afternoon
4 I forgot to tell you
N.F. Autobiography
FATHER LASCAUT:
1 Trepidation in Downing St. 1962
2 Father Lascaut hits back 1964
*Collections of short stories, each
containing some stories about this
character*

JONES, R.
1 The age of wonder 1967
2 The tower ise 1971

JONES, R. W.
INSPECTOR EVANS & SGT. BEDDOES:
1 Saving Grace 1986
2 Cop out 1987
3 The green reapers 1988

JONES, T.
1 A steady trade 1982
2 Heart of oak 1984
3 The incredible voyage 1977
4 Ice 1979
5 Saga of a wayward sailor 1980
6 Adrift 1981
7 A star to steer her by 1985
8 The improbable voyage 1986
N.F. Autobiography of a yachtsman

JONES, W. GLYNNE-
1 Farewell innocence
2 Ride the white stallion

JONG, E.
ISADORA WING:
1 Fear of flying 1975
2 How to save your own life 1977
3 Parachutes and kisses 1985

JORDAN, J.
THE VAUGHANS:
1 A good weekend for murder 1987
2 Murder under the mistletoe 1988

JORDAN, M.
TYLER BROTHERS:
1 Brigham's way 1976
2 Jacob's road 1976

JORDAN, R.
THE WHEEL OF TIME:
1 Eye of the world 1990
2 The great hunt 1991
Fantasy

JOSEPH, M.
DAISY PENNY:
1 A better world than this 1987
2 A world apart 1988

JOYCE, C.
GREG ALLARD:
1 Errant witness 1981
2 Errant target 1982
3 Errant sleuth 1983
INSPECTOR PAT STOCKTON:
1 Run a golden mile 1978
2 Sentence suspended 1979
3 A hitch in time 1980
4 Death of a left-handed woman 1980
5 Calculated risk 1981
6 A bullet for Betty 1981
7 From the grave to the cradle 1982
8 Murder is a pendulum 1983

JOYCE, J.
1 Portrait of the artist as a young man
2 Ulysses
Connected by the character Stephen Dedalus
3 Leopold, by P. Costello 1981

JOYCE, S.
1 My brother's keeper
2 The Dublin diary of Stanislaus Joyce
N.F. Autobiography

JOYNSON, C.
1 In spite of Henry
2 In search of Henry
3 Yes, Henry 1964
N.F. Autobiography

KAHN, J.
NEW WORLD TRILOGY:
1 World enough and time
2 Time's dark laughter
Paperback science fiction

KALLEN, L.
C. B. GREENFIELD:
1 Introducing C. B. Greenfield 1979
2 C. B. Greenfield and the tanglewood murder 1980
3 C. B. Greenfield: lady in the house 1982
4 C. B. Greenfield: the piano bird 1984
5 A little madness 1986

KALMAN, Y.
YARDLEY FAMILY:
1 Greenstone land 1982
2 Juliette's daughter 1983
3 Riversong 1985
A family saga set in New Zealand
MORGAN AND RENNIE FAMILIES:
1 Mists of heaven 1988
2 After the rainbow 1989

KAMADA, A.
1 A love so bold 1980
2 Richer than a crown 1981
Novels set in 11thC England

KAMINSKY, S. M.
INSPECTOR PORFIRY ROSTNIKOV:
1 Rostnikov's corpse 1981
2 Black Knight in Red Square 1988
3 Cold red sunrise 1990
4 The man who walked like a bear 1991
TOBY PETERS:
1 The Howard Hughes affair 1980
2 Bullet for a star 1981

3 Murder on the Yellow Brick Road 1981
4 High midnight 1982
5 Buried Caesars 1990

KANE, H.
PETER CHAMBERS SERIES:
1 A halo for nobody
2 Armchair in hell
3 Hang by your neck
4 Report for a corpse
5 A corpse for Christmas
6 Trinity in violence
7 Trilogy in jeopardy
8 Death on the double
9 The narrowing lust
10 Sweet Charlie
11 Triple terror
12 The dangling dean
13 Nirvana can also mean death
14 Death of a flack
15 Death of a hooker
16 Death of a dastard
17 Killer's kiss
18 Dead in bed
19 Snatch an eye
20 Nobody loves a loser
21 Murder for the millions
22 Devil to pay 1966
MARLA TRENT:
1 Killer's kiss
2 Private eyeful

KANTOR, M.
BUGLE ANN, FOXHOUND:
1 The voice of Bugle Ann 1950
2 The daughter of Bugle Ann 1953

KAPP, C.
CAGEWORLD:
1 Search for the sun
2 The lost world of Cronos
3 The tyrant of Hades
4 Star search
Paperback science fiction

KAPP, Y.
ELEANOR MARX:
1 Family life 1855-83 1972
2 The crowded years (part one) 1976
N.F. Autobiography

KARLSSON, E.
1 Mother sea 1964
2 Pully-haul 1966
3 Cruising off Mozambique 1969
N.F. Autobiography and sea voyaging

KARTUN, D.
ALFRED BAUM:
1 Beaver to fox 1983
2 Flittermouse 1984
3 Megiddo 1987
4 Safe house 1989

KATZ, H. W.
1 The Fishmans
2 No. 21 Castle Street

KAUFMAN, P.
1 Shield of three lions 1986
2 Banners of gold 1987
Historical novels set in the reign of Richard I

KAVANAGH, D.
DUFFY:
1 Duffy 1980
2 Fiddle City 1981
3 Putting the boot in 1985
4 Going to the dogs 1987

KAVANAGH, P. J.
1 Perfect stranger 1966
2 Finding connections 1990
N.F. Autobiography of a poet

KAY, G. G.
THE FIONAVAR TAPESTRY:
1 The summer tree 1985
2 The wandering fire 1986
3 The darkest road 1987
Fantasy

KAYE, B.
DUCKETTS GREEN:
1 Black market green
2 Rebellion on the green

KAYE, J. LISTER-, *see* MAXWELL, G.

KAYE, M. M.
1 Later than you think 1957
2 House of shade 1959
(reprinted as 'Death in Zanzibar', 1983)

KAZAN, E.
1 America, America 1969
2 The Anatolian 1983

KAZANTAS, N. *see* HOMER

KEAST, F.
DARRYL KRUSTOV:
1 Sunburst
2 Cloudburst 1986

KEATING, H. R. F.

INSPECTOR GHOTE SERIES:
1 The perfect murder 1964
2 Inspector Ghote's good crusade 1966
3 Inspector Ghote caught in meshes 1967
4 Inspector Ghote hunts the peacock 1968
5 Inspector Ghote plays a joker 1969
6 Inspector Ghote breaks an egg 1970
7 Inspector Ghote goes by train 1971
8 Inspector Ghote trusts the heart 1972
9 Bats fly up for Inspector Ghote 1974
10 Filmi, filmi Inspector Ghote 1976
11 Inspector Ghote draws a line 1979
12 Go West, Inspector Ghote 1981
13 The Sheriff of Bombay 1984
14 Under a monsoon cloud 1986
15 The body in the billiard room 1987
16 Dead on time 1988
17 The iciest sin 1990

KEE, R.

SIMON BROADSTROP:
1 Sign of the times 1955
2 Private eyefull 1958

KEENAN, W.

NO. 1 AREA CRIME SQUAD:
1 Lonely beat 1968
2 Mosaic of death 1969
3 Murder in melancholy 1970

KEILLOR, G.

LAKE WOBEGONE:
1 Lake Wobegone days 1986
2 Leaving home 1988
Humorous short stories set in an imaginary Mid-Western town

KEITH, A.

1 Land below the wind
2 Three came home 1948
3 White man returns
4 Bare feet in the palace 1956
N.F. Autobiographical account of life in Borneo, including experiences as a prisoner during Japanese occupation

KELLERMAN, J.

ALEX DELAWARE:
1 Shrunken heads 1985
2 Blood test 1985
3 Silent partner 1989
4 Time bomb 1990

KELLEY, L. P.

LUKE SUTTON:
1 Outlaw 1981

2 Gunfighter 1982
3 Indian fighter 1983
4 Avenger 1984
5 Outrider 1986
6 Bounty hunter 1991
7 Hired gun 1991

KELLOGG, M. B. & ROSSOW, W. B.

LEAR'S DAUGHTERS:
1 The wave and the flame 1987
2 Reign of fire 1988
Fantasy

KELLS, S.

LAZENDER FAMILY:
1 A crowning mercy 1983
2 The fallen angels 1984

KELLY, MARY

DET-INSPECTOR NIGHTINGALE SERIES:
1 A cold coming 1956
2 Dead man's riddle 1957
3 The Christmas egg 1958

KELLY, SHEELAGH

FEENEY FAMILY:
1 A long way from heaven 1985
2 For my brother's sins 1986
3 Erin's child 1987
4 Dickie 1989

KELLY, SUSAN

DET. INSPECTOR NICK TREVELYAN:
1 Hope against hope 1989
2 Time of hope 1990

KELLY, T.

1 FEPOW 1985
2 The Genki boys 1967
N.F. Experiences of POWs in Japanese prison camps. Listed in chronological order

KEMAL, Y.

SLIM MEHMED:
1 Mehmed, my hawk 1971
2 They burn the thistles 1973
Stories of a 'Robin Hood' in Anatolia in the 'thirties
***
1 Wind from the plain 1972
2 Iron earth, copper sky 1974
3 The undying grass 1977
Not precisely sequels, but characters from 1 reappear in 2 and 3

KEMELMAN, H.
RABBI DAVID SMALL SERIES:
1 Friday the Rabbi slept late 1966
2 Saturday the Rabbi went hungry 1967
3 Sunday the Rabbi stayed home 1969
4 Monday the Rabbi took off 1972
5 Tuesday the Rabbi saw red 1974
6 Wednesday the Rabbi got wet 1976
7 Thursday the Rabbi walked out 1979
8 Some day the Rabbi will leave 1985
9 One fine day the Rabbi bought a cross 1988

KEMP, P.
1 Mine were of trouble 1958
2 No colours of crest 1960
3 Alms for oblivion 1961
N.F. Autobiography

KEMP, S.
DR. TINA MAY:
1 No escape 1985
2 The lure of sweet death 1986
3 What dread hand? 1987

KENDRICK, B.
DUNCAN MACLAIN SERIES:
1 Blind man's bluff
2 Death knell
3 Out of control
4 You die today
5 Reservations for death
6 Clear and present danger 1958
7 The whistling hangman 1959

KENNEALY, P.
THE KELTIAD:
1 The copper crown
2 The throne of Scone
Paperback fantasy:

KENNEDY, A.
BRADSHAW TRILOGY:
1 No place to cry 1986
2 The fires of summer 1987
3 All dreams denied 1988
KINCAID TRILOGY:
1 Passion never knows 1990
2 Dancing in the shadows 1991

KENNEDY, W.
ALBANY CYCLE:
1 Legs 1975
2 Billy Phelan's greatest game 1978
3 Ironweed 1983
4 Quinn's book 1988

KENNELLY, A.
1 The peaceable kingdom 1949
2 Up home Houghton 1955
A chronicle of Mormon life in the 19th century

KENNETH, C.
1 The love riddle 1963
2 May in Manhattan 1963

KENT, A.
RICHARD BOLITHO:
1 Richard Bolitho - Midshipman (1772)
2 Midshipman Bolitho and the 'Avenger' (1773) 1971
3 Stand into danger (1774) 1980
4 In gallant company (1777) 1977
5 Sloop of war (1778) 1972
6 To glory we steer (1782) 1967
7 Command a King's ship (1789) 1973
8 Passage to mutiny (1789) 1976
9 With all despatch (1792) 1988
10 Form line of battle (1793) 1969
11 Enemy in sight (1794) 1970
12 The flag captain (1795) 1971
13 Signal - close action (1798) 1974
14 Inshore squadron (1800) 1978
15 A tradition of victory (1801) 1981
16 Success to the brave (1802) 1983
17 Colours aloft (1803) 1986
18 Honour this day (1804-5) 1987
19 The only victor (1806) 1990
The author's chronological order of reading

KENT, L. A.
1 Mrs. Appleyard's year 1941
2 With kitchen privileges 1953

KENWORTHY, C.
MATTHEW AND SON:
1 In the dark of the moon 1981
2 Ride a dark tide 1982
3 A storm in the dark 1983
4 Against a dark shore 1985
Sea stories set in the 19thC

KENYON, F. W.
1 Eugenie 1964
2 Imperial courtesan 1967
Linked novels about Napoleon III, his wife and his mistress who helped him to the throne
JOHN CHURCHILL, DUKE OF MARLBOROUGH:
1 The seeds of time 1961
2 Glory o' the dream 1963

KENYON, M.

HARRY PECKOVER:
1 The rapist 1979
2 Zigzag 1981
3 The God squad bod 1982
4 A free range wife 1983
5 A healthy way to die 1986
6 Peckover holds the baby 1988
7 Kill the butler 1991

KERNER, A.

1 Woman detective
2 Further adventures of a woman
detective
N.F. Autobiography

KEROUAC, J.

THE STORY OF JACK DULUOZ:
1 One the road 1957
2 The Dharma bums 1958
3 The subterraneans 1958
4 The lonesome traveller 1960
5 Big Sur 1962

KERR, K.

DEVERRY:
1 Daggerspell 1987
2 Darkspell 1988
3 Dawnspell; the bristling wood 1989
4 Dragonspell; the Southern sea 1990
Fantasy

KERR, R.

JAMIE STUART:
1 The Stuart legacy 1973
2 The black pearls 1975
3 The dark lady 1975

KERRIGAN, J.

SBS;
1 Fireball 1983
2 Bluebeard 1984
3 Watchdog 1984

KERSH, C.

1 The aggravations of Minnie Ashe 1975
2 Minnie Ashe at war 1979

KERSHAW, H.

CORONATION STREET:
1 Early days 1975
2 Trouble at 'The Rovers' 1976
3 Elsie Tanner strikes back 1977

KESEY, K.

1 One flew over the cuckoo's nest
2 Sometimes a great notion

KESSLER, L.

COSSACKS SERIES:
1 Black Cossacks
2 Sabres of the Reich
3 The mountain of skulls
4 Breakthrough
OTTO STAHL:
1 Otto's phoney war 1981
2 Otto's blitzkrieg 1982
3 Otto and the Reds 1982
4 Otto and the Yanks 1983
5 Otto and the SS 1984
6 Otto and the Himmler loveletters 1984
REBEL:
1 Cannon fodder 1986
2 The die-hards 1987
3 Death match 1987
4 Breakout 1988
ROMMEL:
1 Ghost division 1981
2 Massacre
*Most are in Paperback only, but some
have been published in hardback.*
SEA WOLVES:
1 Sink the Scharnhorst 1982
2 Death to the Deutschland 1982
STORM TROOP:
1 Storm troop 1983
2 Blood mountain 1983
3 Valley of the assassins 1984
4 Red assault
5 Himmler's gold
6 Fire over Kabul 1982
7 Wave of terror 1983
8 Fire over Africa 1984
STUKA SQUADRON:
1 The black knights 1983
2 The hawks of death 1983
3 The tank busters 1984
4 Blood mission 1984
SUBMARINE:
1 The wolf pack 1985
2 Operation deathwatch 1985
3 Convoy to catastrophe 1986
4 Fire in the west 1986
5 Flight to the Reich 1987
WOTAN/PANZER DIVISION:
1 SS Panzer Battalion 1975
2 Death's Head 1978
3 Claws of steel 1978
4 Guns at Cassino 1978
5 The march on Warsaw 1988
6 Hammer of the Gods 1979
7 Forced march 1979
8 Blood and ice 1977
9 Sand panthers 1977
10 Counter attack 1979
11 Hell Fire 1978

12 Panzer hunt 1979
13 Slaughter ground 1980
14 Flash point 1980
15 Cauldron of blood 1981
16 Schirmer's head hunters 1981
17 Whores of war 1982
18 Schirmer's death legions 1983
19 Slaughter at Salerno 1985
20 Death ride
21 The Hess assault 1987
22 March or die
All the Kessler series were originally published in paperback. Dates given are for hardback eds.

KETTLE, J.
1 The Athelsons 1973
2 A gift of onyx 1974
Family history. 1 is at a later period than 2.

KEYES, F. P.
1 Christian Marlowe's daughter 1933
2 The great tradition 1939

***

1 The river road 1945
2 Vail D'Alvery 1947

***

1 Steamboat Gothic 1952
2 Larry Vincent 1953
2 deals with descendants of Clyde Batchelor of 1.

***

1 Dinner at Antoine's 1948
2 Royal box 1954
Joe Racina reporter, and his wife Judith are in both novels.
CAROLINA TRILOGY:
1 Honour bright 1936
2 Blue camellia 1957
3 The gold slippers 1958

KHANNA, B.
1 Nation of fools 1984
2 Sweet chillies 1991

KIENZLE, W. X.
FATHER KOESLER SERIES:
1 The rosary murders 1978
2 Death wears a red hat 1980
3 Mind over murder 1981
4 Shadow of death 1984
5 Sudden death 1986

KILLILEA, M.
1 Karen - the story of a family 1963

2 With love from Karen 1964
N.F. Autobiography

KIM, R. E.
1 The martyred 1967
2 The innocent 1969
Two novels about modern Korea

KING, A.
1 Mine enemy grows older 1958
2 May this house be safe from tigers 1960
3 I should have kissed her more 1961
4 Is there a life after birth 1962
N.F. Autobiography

KING, B.
THE BEAUFORT FAMILY:
1 Lady Margaret 1961
2 Captive James 1966
3 Lord Jasper 1967
4 The King's mother 1969
Historical novels
NORDIC TRILOGY:
1 Starkadder 1985
2 Vargr moon 1986
Fantasy
MASTERFUL INVENTION:
1 The destroying angel
2 The time-fighters
3 Skyfire

KING, F.
INSPECTOR GLOOM:
1 The case of the painted girl
2 Green gold
DORMOUSE SERIES:
1 Enter the dormouse
2 The dormouse-undertaker
3 The dormouse has nine lives
4 The dormouse peacemaker
5 Dough for the dormouse
6 This doll is dangerous
7 They vanished at night
8 What price doubloons
9 Crook's cross
10 Gestapo dormouse
11 Sinister light
12 Catastrophe club
13 Operation halter
14 Operation honeymoon
15 Big blackmail
16 Crook's caravan 1955
17 The case of the strange beauties
Continued as 'The Conrad detective agency' (also 'The Dormouse')
18 That charming crook 1958
19 The two who talked 1958
20 The case of the frightened brother 1959

KING, L. W.
1 The day we were mostly butterflies 1963
2 The velocipede handicap 1965
Characters in 2 reappear from 1. A collection of stories

KING, ROBIN
1 No paradise
2 Sailor in the east
3 The angry sun
N.F. Autobiography

KING, S.
THE DARK TOWER:
1 The gunslinger 1988
2 The drawing of the three 1989

KINGSTON, B.
EASTER EMPIRE:
1 Tuppenny times 1988
2 Fourpenny flier 1989
3 Sixpenny stalls 1990

KINGSTON, G.
1 A wing and a prayer
2 Main force
3 The boys of Coastal
Paperback novels about the RAF in WW2

KIPLING, R.
1 Kim
2 The Imperial agent, by T. N. Murari 1987
3 The last victory, by T. N. Murari 1988
Continues the story of Kim as a man

KIRKBRIDE, R.
1 Wind blows gently
2 Spring is not gentle

KIRKUP, J.
1 The only child 1957
2 Sorrows, passions and alarms 1959
3 I, of all people 1988
4 A poet could not but be gay 1991
N.F. Autobiography

KIRST, H. H.
ZERO EIGHT–FIFTEEN: A TRILOGY OF GERMAN ARMY LIFE:
1 The strange mutiny of Gunner Asch 1955
2 Gunner Asch goes to war 1956
3 The return of Gunner Asch 1958
4 What became of Gunner Asch? 1964
A pendant to the trilogy

MUNICH TRILOGY:
1 A time for scandal 1972
2 A time for truth
3 A time for payment 1976

KIRSTEN, A.
RALPH WHITGIFT:
1 Young Lucifer 1984
2 Satan's child 1985

KITCHEN, P.
1 Lying-in 1968
2 A fleshly school 1970
3 Linsey-Woolsey 1971
4 Paradise 1972
A quartet of novels on relationships between staff and students at an art school

KITCHIN, C. H. B.
MALCOLM WARREN SERIES:
1 Death of my aunt 1929
2 Crime at Christmas 1934
3 Death of his uncle 1939
4 The Cornish fox 1949

KLEIN, N.
1 Sunshine 1983
2 The sunshine years 1984

KLINGER, H.
SHOMRI SHOMAR SERIES:
1 Wanton for murder
2 Murder off Broadway
3 Essence of murder
Originally paperback. Repub. in one vol. 1968. Not pub. in U.K.

KNAAK, R.
DRAGONREALM:
1 Firedrake
2 Ice dragon

KNEALE, N.
1 The Quatermass experiment
2 Quatermass II
3 Quatermass 1979

KNEF, H.
1 The gift horse 1974
2 The verdict 1976
N.F. Autobiography

KNIGHT, A.
INSPECTOR JEREMY FARO:
1 Enter second murderer 1988
2 Blood line 1989
3 Deadly beloved 1989

4 Killing cousins 1990
5 A quiet death 1991
Detective stories set in 19th C. Edinburgh

KNIGHT, B.
1 The sword between 1971
2 Prisoner of the past
Ireland in the early 19th century. Not strictly sequels but characters reappear
***
1 Walking the whirlwind
2 The piping on the wind
Early settlers in South Africa
***
1 Old Amsterdam 1955
2 I shall maintain
The story of a Dutch Financier in the 16th century, Peter Van Breda. 2 continues the story in the person of his daughter, Helene
***
1 The house of the swan 1961
2 The house of the bird of Paradise 1962

KNOTT, T. S.
1 Fools rush in
2 Keep it clean
N.F. Autobiography

KNOWLES, A.
1 Matthew Ratton 1979
2 The raven tree 1981
***
1 Single in the field 1984
2 An ark on the flood 1985
Novels about a woman vet in the Cotswolds

KNOX, B.
THANE AND MOSS:
1 Deadline for a dream 1957
2 Death department 1958
3 Leave it to the hangman 1959
4 Little drops of blood 1960
5 Sanctuary Isle 1961
6 The man in the bottle 1962
7 Taste of proof 1965
8 Deep fall 1966
9 Justice on the rocks 1967
10 The tallyman 1969
11 Children of the mist 1970
12 To kill a witch 1971
13 Draw batons 1973
14 Rally to kill 1975
15 Pilot error 1976

16 Live bait 1978
17 A killing in antiques 1981
18 The hanging tree 1983
19 The crossfire killings 1986
20 The interface man 1989
WEBB CARRICK, FISHERY PROTECTION:
1 The scavengers 1964
2 Devilweed 1965
3 Blacklight 1966
4 The Klondyker 1968
5 Blueback 1969
6 Seafire 1970
7 Stormtide 1972
8 Whitewater 1974
9 Hellspout 1976
10 Witchrock 1977
11 Bombship 1979
12 Bloodtide 1982
13 Wavecrest 1985
14 Dead man's mooring 1987
15 The drowning nets 1991

KNOX-MAWER, J.
1 The sultans came to tea 1961
2 A gift of islands 1984
N.F. Life in the South Seas

KOESTLER, A.
1 Arrow in the blue 1969
2 The invisible writing 1954
3 Stranger in the square 1984
N.F. Autobiography
***
1 The gladiators 1939
2 Darkness at noon 1940
3 Arrival and departure 1943
Although widely separated in time and subject, the author regarded this as a trilogy on the conflict between ends and means

KONRAD, K.
RUSSIAN SERIES:
1 First blood 1981
2 March on Moscow 1981
3 Front swine 1982

KONSALIK, H.
LOVE ON THE DON:
1 Deep waters 1979
2 Against the tide 1980

KOSTOV, K. N.
PUNISHMENT BATTALION:
1 Baptism of blood
2 The Gulag rats
3 Blood on the Baltic

4 The Steppe wolves
Paperback war stories

KRASNEY, S. A.
LIEUT. ABE LASEN SERIES:
1 Death dies in the street 1957
2 Homicide West 1962
3 Homicide call 1963

KRAVCHENKO, V.
1 I chose freedom
2 I chose justice
N.F. Autobiography

KRUGER, P.
PHIL KRAMER:
1 Weep for Willow Green 1966
2 Weave a wicked web 1967
3 If a shroud fits 1969

KRUK, Z.
1 Taste of fear
2 Taste of hope
N.F. Autobiography

KURTZ, K.
DERYNI:
1 Deryni rising
2 Deryni checkmate
3 High Deryni 1986
4 Deryni archives
Fantasies, mainly paperback
THE HISTORIES OF KING KELSON:
1 The Bishop's heir
2 The King's justice 1986
3 The quest for Saint Camber 1987
Fantasy. No. 1 in paperback only
THE LEGENDS OF CAMBER OF CULDI:
1 Camber of Culdi 1986
2 Saint Camber
3 Camber the heretic
*Paperback fantasies. No. 1 now in
hardback*

LACEY, P.
"MAUDIE" MORGAN
1 The limit 1988
2 The bagman 1989

LACY, E.
TOUSSAINT MOORE SERIES:
1 Room to swing 1964
2 Moment of untruth 1965

LADD, J.
ABILENE:
1 The peacemaker 1989

2 The sharpshooter
3
4 The night riders 1989
5 The half-breed 1990

LAGERKVIST, P.
TOBIAS TRILOGY:
1 Death of Ahaseuras 1963
2 Pilgrim at sea 1964
3 The holyland 1965
*The theme of another novel 'The Sybil'
is linked to this series, but is not part of
it.*

LAINE, A.
THE EARL OF MORISTON:
1 The reluctant heiress 1980
2 The melancholy virgin 1981
Regency romances

LAING, K.
ROLLING STONE:
1 Malignant snowman 1950
2 No man's laughter 1951

LAKER, R.
EASTHAMPTON:
1 Warwyck's wife 1978
2 Claudine's daughter 1979
3 The Warwycks of Easthampton 1980

LAMB, L.
1 Death of a dissenter 1968
2 Worse than death 1971
3 Picture frame 1972
4 Man in a mist 1974
*Detective stories set in the East Anglian
village of Fleury Feverel. Supt. Quill
and Inspector Glover are featured in 3
and 4.*

LAMBERT, D.
1 He must so live
2 No time for sleeping
***
1 Angels in the snow
2 The red house

LAMBERT, E.
1 The 20,000 thieves
2 The veterans
The Australian army in World War II

LAMBOURNE, J.
1 The kingdom that was
2 The second leopard

LAMONT, M.
1 Nine moons wasted 1977
2 Horns of the moon 1979

L'AMOUR, L.
SACKETT:
1 Sackett's land 1964
2 To the far blue mountains 1975
3 The warrior's path 1975
4 Jubal Sackett 1986
5 Ride the river
6 The daybreakers
7 Sackett
8 Lando
9 Mojave crossing
10 The Sackett brand
11 The lonely men
12 Treasure mountain
13 Mustang men
14 Galloway
15 The sky-liners
16 The man from Broken Hills
17 Ride the dark trail
18 Lonely on the mountain
THE CHANTRY FAMILY:
1 Fair blows the wind 1985
2 Over on the dry side 1988

LAMPITT, D.
SUTTON PLACE:
1 Sutton Place 1983
2 The silver swan 1984
3 Fortune's soldier 1985
4 Zachary 1990

LANCASTER, O.
1 All done from memory 1965
2 With an eye to the future 1967
N.F. Autobiography

LANCING, G., *pseud.* (LAN TSO CHI)
TZU HSI, EMPRESS OF CHINA:
1 Imperial motherhood
2 The mating of the dragon
3 Dragon in chains
4 Phoenix triumphant

LANDSBOROUGH, G.
DESERT COMMANDOS:
1 The glasshouse gang 1976
2 Desert marauders 1976
3 The Benghazi breakout 1977
4 Dead commando 1977

LANE, JANE
1 King's critic 1935
2 England for sale 1943
3 Gin and bitters 1945

2 and 3 are sequels. The main character's father is the hero of 1
TRILOGY ON CHARLES I:
1 The young and lonely king 1969
2 The questing beast 1970
3 A call of trumpets 1971

LANE, K.
1 Diary of a medical nobody 1982
2 West country doctor 1984
N.F. Autobiography

LANE, MARGARET
1 A night at sea 1963
2 A smell of burning 1965
1 describes a shipwreck and the events leading up to it, while 2 continues the story of the survivors

LANE, MAXIE
1 Running 1977
2 Sea running 1978
N.F. Autobiography

LANG, F.
GILLONNE DE BEAUREGARD:
1 The well wisher 1966
2 The duke's daughter 1967
3 The malcontent 1968

LANG, M.
PUCK BURE AND CHRISTOPHER WICK:
1 Wreath for the bride 1965
2 No more murders 1966
3 Death awaits thee 1967

LANGTON, J.
HOMER KELLY:
1 Emily Dickinson is dead 1989
2 The Memorial Hall murder 1990
3 The Dante game 1991

LAPIERRE, J.
MEG HALLORAN:
1 Unquiet grave 1988
2 Children's games 1990
3 The cruel mother 1991

LARKIN, R.
1 Mistress of desire
2 Harvest of desire
3 Torches of desire
Paperback bodice rippers

LARSON, C.
NILS BLIXEN:
1 Matthew's hand 1977
2 Muir's blood 1978

LARSSON, G.
1 Our daily bread
2 Fatherland, farewell!

LARTGUY. J.
1 The Centurions 1962
2 The Praetorians 1963
Novels of the French army in Algeria

LASGARN, H.
1 A vet for all seasons 1986
2 Vet in a storm 1987
3 Vet in a storm 1987
4 Vet in the village 1988
N.F. Experiences of a vet

LASH, J. C.
1 Eleanor and Franklin 1971
2 Eleanor: the years alone 1972
N.F. Biography of Eleanor Roosevelt

LASSWELL, M.
MRS. FEELEY SERIES:
1 Suds in your eye 1942
2 High time 1947
3 One in the house 1949
4 Wait for the wagon 1951
5 Tooner schooner 1953
6 Let's go for broke 1962

LATHEN, E.
JOHN THATCHER SERIES:
1 Banking on death 1962
2 A place for murder 1963
3 Accounting for murder 1965
4 Murder makes the wheels go round 1966
5 Death shall overcome 1967
6 Murder against the grain 1967
7 A stitch in time 1968
8 When in Greece 1969
9 Come to dust 1970
10 Murder to go 1970
11 Pick up sticks 1971
12 Ashes to Ashes 1971
13 The longer the thread 1972
14 Murder without icing 1973
15 Sweet and low 1974
16 By hook or by crook 1975
17 Double, double, oil and trouble 1979
18 Going for gold 1981
19 Green grow the dollars 1982
20 Something in the Air 1988

LAUBEN, P.
HOMER CLAY:
1 A nice sound alibi 1981
2 A surfeit of alibis 1982

3 A sort of tragedy 1985

LAUMER, K.
MR. CURLON:
1 Worlds of the Imperium 1968
2 The other side of time 1969
3 Assignment in nowhere 1971
RETIEF:
1 Envoy to new worlds 1963
2 Retief and the Warlords
3 Retief's war 1965
4 Retief's ransome 1971
5 Retief of the CDT 1971
LAFAYETTE O'LEARY:
1 The tune bender 1975
2 The world bender 1973
3 The shape changer 1977
Science fiction

LAUNAY, D.
ADAM FLUTE SERIES:
1 She modelled her coffin 1961
2 New shining white murder 1962
3 Corpse in camera 1963
4 Death and still life 1964
5 Two-way mirror 1965
6 The scream 1966

LAURENCE, J.
DARINA LISLE:
1 A deep coffyne 1989
2 A tasty way to die 1990
3 Hotel morgue 1991

LAW, J.
ANNA PETERS:
1 The big payoff 1978
2 The Gemini trip 1979
3 Under Orion 1980
4 The shadow of the palms 1981
5 Death under par 1983

LAWHEAD, S.
DRAGON KING SAGA:
1 In the hall of the Dragon King
2 The warlords of Nin
3 The sword and the flame
EMPYRION:
1 Search for Fierra
2 The siege of Dome
THE PENDRAGON CYCLE:
1 Taliesin
2 Merlin
3 Arthur
Paperback fantasies

LAWRENCE, H.
MARK EAST SERIES:

1 Blood upon the snow
2 Death of a doll
3 A time to die

LAWRENCE, L.
THE SEED:
1 Morning, noon and night
2 Out of the dust
3 Old father Antic
4 The hoax
5 The sowing

LAYBERRY, L. G. J.
OAKLEIGH FARM:
1 Hayseed 1980
2 Gleanings 1981
3 To be a farmer's girl 1982
4 A pocket full of rye 1984
5 Tangled harvest 1984
6 The last mophrey 1987
7 As long as the fields are green 1987
8 A new earth 1988
Novels about a farming family in Derbyshire. The last three titles in the series were published later, and by a different publisher

LEADER, C.
RIC MCADDEN:
1 The golden lure 1967

LEAHY, S.
1 Family ties 1983
2 Family truths 1985

LEASOR, J.
DR. JASON LOVE:
1 Passport to oblivion 1965 (Where the spies are)
2 Passport to peril 1966 (Spylight)
3 The Yang meridian 1966
4 Passport in suspense 1967
5 Passport for a pilgrim 1968
6 A week for love 1969
7 Love-all 1971
8 Love and the land beyond 1979
9 Frozen assets 1989
ARISTO MOTORS:
1 They don't make them like that any more 1969
2 Never had a spanner on her 1970
3 Host of extras 1973 (Also features Dr. Love)
        ★★★
1 Follow the drum 1972
2 Mandarin Gold 1973
3 The Chinese widow 1975

4 Jade gate 1976

LEATHER, E.
RUPERT CONWAY:
1 The Vienna elephant 1977
2 The Mozart score 1979
3 The Duveen collection 1980

LE BRETON, A.
1 Rififi 1947
2 Rififi in New York 1970

LE CARRE, J.
GEORGE SMILEY:
1 Murder of quality 1962
2 Call for the dead 1961
3 The spy who came in from the cold 1963
4 The looking glass war 1965
5 Tinker, tailor, soldier, spy 1974
6 The honourable schoolboy 1977
7 Smiley's people 1980
8 The secret pilgrim 1990
1 and 2 reissued in one volume as 'The Incongruous spy' 1964 (U.S.A.) Smiley is only a minor character in 4. 'The Quest for Carla', 1982 contains 5, 6 and 7.

LEDUC, V.
1 La Batarde 1960
2 Mad in pursuit 1971
N.F. Autobiography

LEDWITH, F.
1 The best of all possible Worlds 1987
2 Ships that go bump in the night 1974
3 Ships afloat in the city 1977
N.F. Autobiography. Listed in chronological order

LEE, A.
MISS HOGG SERIES:
1 Sheep's clothing
2 Call in Miss Hogg
3 Miss Hogg and the Bronte murders 1956
4 Miss Hogg and the squash club murder 1957
5 Miss Hogg and the dead dean 1957
6 Miss Hogg flies high 1958
7 Miss Hogg and the Covent Garden murders 1960
8 Miss Hogg and the missing sisters 1961
9 Miss Hogg's last case 1963

LEE, J.
1 The unicorn quest 1987

2 The unicorn dilemma 1989

LEE, L.
1 Cider with Rosie 1959
2 As I walked out one mid summer morning 1969
3 A moment of war 1991
4 I can't stay longer 1976
N.F. Autobiography

LEE, S.
OWEN LIGHTBRINGER:
1 Quest for the sword of infinity
2 The land where the serpents rule
3 The path through the circle of time
Fantasy

LEE, T.
BIRTHGRAVE SERIES:
1 Birthgrave
2 The storm cloud
3 Shadow fire
4 Quest for the white witch
Paperback fantasy
THE SECRET BOOKS OF PARADYS:
1 The book of the damned 1988
2 The book of the beast 1988
Fantasy

LEEMING, J. F.
1 It always rains in Rome
2 A girl like Wigan
3 Arnaldo my brother

LEES, D.
JEFF PLUMMER SERIES:
1 The rainbow conspiracy 1971
2 Zodiac 1972
3 Rape of a quiet town 1973
4 Elizabeth R.I.P. 1974
CONSTABLE CRAIG:
1 Our man in Morton Episcopi 1979
2 Mayhem in Morton Episcopi 1980

LEES-MILNE, J.
1 Ancestral voices 1975
2 Prophesying peace 1977
3 Caves of ice 1983
4 Midway on the waves 1985
N.F. Autobiography

LEGAT, M.
1 The silk maker 1985
2 The cast iron man 1987

LEHMANN, J.
1 The whispering gallery 1955
2 I am my brother 1959

3 The ample proposition 1966
N.F. Autobiography

LEIBER, F.
SWORDS SERIES:
1 Swords and diviltry
2 Swords against death
3 Swords in the mist
4 Swords against wizardry
5 Swords of Lankhmar
6 Swords and ice magic
7 The Knight & Knave of Swords
Paperback fantasy

LEIGH, H.
THE VINTAGE YEARS:
1 The grapes of Paradise
2 Wild vines
3 Kingdoms of the vine
Paperback novels about a family vineyard

LEIGH, M.
1 Highland homespun
2 Harvest of the moor
3 My kingdom for a horse
4 Spade among rushes
5 Fruit in the seed
N.F. Autobiography

LEIGH, P.
1 Garnet 1978
2 Coral 1979
3 Rosewood 1979

LEIGH, R.
SAM CARROLL:
1 The cheap dream 1982
2 The girl with the bright head 1982

LEITCH, D.
1 God stand up for bastards 1973
2 Family secrets 1984
N.F. The author's search for his real family

LEJEUNE, A.
1 Professor in peril 1987
2 Key without a door 1988

LEMARCHAND, E.
DET. SUPT. TOM POLLARD:
1 Death of an old girl 1967
2 The Affacombe affair 1968
3 Alibi for a corpse 1969
4 Death on doomsday 1970
5 Cyanide with compliments 1972

6 Let or hindrance 1973
7 Buried in the past 1974
8 A step in the dark 1976
9 Unhappy returns 1977
10 Suddenly, while gardening 1978
11 Change for the worse 1980
12 Nothing to do with the case 1981
13 Troubled waters 1982
14 The wheel turns 1983
15 Light through glass 1984
16 Who goes home? 1986
17 The Glade Manor murder 1988

LENTON, A.
GRAHAM DARREN:
1 Murder beat
2 Murder city

LEONARD, H.
1 Home before night 1979
2 Out after dark.

LEROUX, E.
THE WELGEVONDEN TRILOGY:
1 Seven days at the Silbersteins
2 One for the devil 1969
3 The third eye 1970

LESLIE, A.
1 The gilt and the gingerbread 1981
2 A story half told 1983
N.F. Autobiography

LESLIE, C.
HOUSE OF GODWIN:
1 A farrago of foxes 1975
2 Feud royal 1977

LESLIE, D.
1 Folly's end
2 The Peverills
3 A young wife's tale 1971
*3 is about the daughter and grand-
daughter of the heroine of 2*

LESLIE, DAVID STUART
1 Snap, crackle, pop 1970
2 Bad medicine 1971
The story of a pop singer

LESLIE, R.
VICTORY TRILOGY:
1 Dawn readiness 1984
2 The raging skies 1985
3 The hunters 1986
HERACLES TRILOGY:
1 Trouble in the wind 1984
2 The fateful dawn 1984

3 Under a shrieking sky 1984

LESSING, D.
CHILDREN OF VIOLENCE:
1 Martha Quest 1952
2 A proper marriage 1956
3 A ripple from the storm 1958
4 Landlocked 1965
5 The four-gated city 1966
*Volumes 1 and 2 republished in one
volume 1965*
CANOPUS IN ARGOS:
1 Shikasta 1979
2 The marriages between Zones 3, 4 & 5
1980
3 The Sirian experiments 1981
4 The making of the representative for
Planet 8 1983
5 Documents relating to the sentimental
agents in the Volyen Empire 1983
Science fiction

LESTER, F.
GEOFFREY SLADE SERIES:
1 The corpse wore rubies 1958
2 Death and the south wind 1958
3 The golden murder 1959

LETT, G.
1 Rossano
2 The many-headed monster 1957
*The Italian Resistance and its post-war
effects*

LEVENE, P.
AMBROSE WEST:
1 Ambrose in London 1959
2 Ambrose in Paris 1960

LEVERSON, A.
EDITH OTTLEY TRILOGY:
1 Love's shadow
2 Tenterhooks
3 Love at second sight
*Reprinted in 1962 in one volume 'The
little Ottley's' with an introduction by
Colin McInnes. 'In her own right and
by her own achievement a very great
artist indeed.'*

LEVI, P.
1 If this is a man 1947
2 The Truce 1963
*N.F. Autobiography. Experiences of a
concentration camp and after*
BEN JONSON:
1 Grave witness 1985
2 Knit one, drop one 1987

LEWERTH, M.
ROUNDTREE SERIES:
1 The Roundtree women
2 Claudia
Paperback

LEWIN, M. Z.
ALBERT SAMSON & DET. LT. POWDER:
1 Ask the right question 1972
2 The enemies within 1973
3 The way we die now 1974
4 The silent salesman 1976
5 Night cover 1976
6 Missing woman 1982
7 Hard line 1983
8 Out of time 1984
9 Late payments 1986
10 Child proof 1988

LEWIS, C.
HOWARD HAYES:
1 The golden grin
2 Acid test
3 Hot rain

LEWIS, HILDA
MARY TUDOR TRILOGY:
1 I am Mary Tudor 1971
2 Mary the queen 1973
3 Bloody Mary 1974
MARY OF ENGLAND:
1 Rose of England 1977
2 Heart of a rose 1978

LEWIS, N.
1 Dragon apparent 1951
2 Golden earth 1952
N.F. Travel

LEWIS, O.
THE SANCHEZ FAMILY:
1 The children of Sanchez 1968
2 A death in the Sanchez family 1970

LEWIS, R.
ARNOLD LANDON:
1 A gathering of ghosts 1983
2 Most cunning workmen 1984
3 A trout in the milk 1986
4 Men of subtle craft 1987
5 The devil is dead 1989
6 A wisp of smoke 1991
ERIC WARD:
1 A certain blindness 1980
2 Dwell in danger 1982
3 A limited vision 1983
4 Once dying, twice dead 1984
5 A blurred reality 1985

6 Premium on death 1986
7 The salamander chill 1988
8 A necessary dealing 1989
INSPECTOR CROW:
1 A lover too many 1967
2 Wolf by the ears 1970
3 Error of judgement 1971
4 A secret singing 1972
5 Blood money 1973
6 A part of virtue 1976
7 A question of degree 1976
8 Nothing but foxes 1977
9 A relative distance 1981

LEWIS, R. H.
MATTHEW COLL:
1 A cracking of spines 1980
2 The manuscript murders 1981
3 A pension for death 1983
4 Where agents fear to tread 1984
5 Death in Verona 1989
Thrillers about an antiquarian bookseller

LEWIS, T.
1 Jack's return home 1971
2 Jack Carter's law 1974
3 Jack Carter and the Mafia pigeon 1977

LEWIS, W. H.
1 The splendid century
2 The sunset of the splendid century
N.F. Life and times of Louis XIV

LEY, A. C.
THE EVERSLEY FAMILY:
1 The clandestine betrothal
2 The toast of the town
JUSTIN & ANTHEA RUTHERFORD:
1 A fatal assignation 1987
2 Masquerade of vengeance 1989
Romantic thrillers set in the Regency period

LIDDELL, R.
1 Kind relations 1939
2 Stepsons 1969
CHARLES HARBORD:
1 Unreal city 1952
2 The rivers of Babylon 1959
3 An object for a walk 1966

LIDE, M.
ANN OF CAMBRAY:
1 Ann of Cambray
2 Gifts of the Queen
3 Hawks of Sedgemont
Paperback historical romance

LIND, J.
1 Counting my steps 1970
2 Numbers 1972
N.F. Autobiography

LINDBERGH, A. M.
1 Bring me a unicorn 1972
2 Hour of gold, hour of lead 1973
3 Locked rooms and open doors 1974
N.F. Autobiography

LINDHOLM, M.
1 The reindeer people 1987
2 Wolf's brother 1989

LINDOP, A. E.
1 The singer not the song 1954
2 The Judas figures 1956

LINDSAY, JACK
THE BRITISH WAY:
1 Betrayed spring
2 Rising tide
3 Moment of choice
4 A local habitation 1957
5 Choice of times 1963
Novels of post-war Britain, linked by theme, not characters

★★★
1 Rome for sale
2 Caesar is dead
3 Last days of Cleopatra
A trilogy on the last days of the Roman Republic

★★★
1 Life rarely tells
2 The roaring twenties
3 Franfrolics and after
N.F. Autobiography

LINDSAY, JOAN
1 Time without clocks
2 Facts soft and hard
N.F. Autobiography
1 Picnic at Hanging Rock 1968
2 The secret of Hanging Rock 1987

LINDSAY, K.
1 Enchantress of the Nile 1964
2 Queen of the mirage 1966
Two novels about Cleopatra

LINDSAY, P.
SUSSEX SERIES:
1 Devil comes to Winchelsea 1956
2 Bells of Rye 1957
3 Sister of Rye 1959

★★★
1 He rides in triumph
2 Wither shall I wander?
Two novels about 15th century London. The same characters appear in both, there is a gap in time between 1 and 2

LINDSAY, R.
1 The falcon and the snowman 1980
2 The flight of the falcon 1985
N.F. Exploits of a spy

LINDSEY, D. L.
1 Cold mind 1984
2 Heat from another sun 1985
3 Spiral 1987

LININGTON, E., (A. BLAISDELL, L. EGAN, D. SHANNON, *pseuds.)*
LUIZ MENDOZ SERIES:
1 Extra kill 1962
2 The ace of spades 1963
3 Knave of hearts 1963
4 Death of a busybody 1963
5 Double bluff 1964
Nos. 6 onwards were published under the name of Dell Shannon

LINKLATER, E.
1 Man on my back 1941
2 A year of space 1953
3 Fanfare for a tin hat 1970
N.F. Autobiography

★★★
1 Juan in America 1931
2 Juan in China 1937

LINSCOTT, G.
BIRDY AND NIMUE HAWTHORN:
1 A healthy body 1984
2 Murder makes tracks 1985
3 A whiff of sulphur 1987

LINZEE, D.
INQUIRIES INC.:
1 Discretion 1981
2 Belgravia 1982

LISTER, S.
SAINTE MONIQUE SERIES:
1 Mistral Hotel
2 Sunset of France
3 Peace comes to Saint Monique
4 Marise
5 Miss Sainte Monique
6 Delorme in deep water

7 Sainte Monique roundabout 1967
8 Sainte Monique unlimited 1968
9 Broom 1969
10 The empty valley 1971
11 Hungarian roulette 1972
12 Tycoon in Eden 1973
13 A smell of brimstone 1974
14 The dog that never was 1975
15 Becky 1976
16 The abominable goat 1977
Not strictly sequels but connected by
the re-appearance of the same
characters, particularly Father
Delorme. No. 12 is a sequel to
'Everything smelt of kippers', which is
not in the Sainte Monique sequence

LITCHFIELD, M.
DET. SUPT. FERGUS MCQUEEN:
1 See how they run 1984
2 Murder circus 1985

LITVINOFF, E.
FACES OF TERROR:
1 A death out of season 1973
2 Blood on the snow 1975
3 The force of terror 1978
A trilogy about the Russian Revolution

LIVINGS, H.
RAVENSGILL:
1 Pennine tales 1983
2 Flying eggs and things 1986
Humorous short stories set in the
Pennines

LIVINGSTON, J.
JOE BINNEY:
1 A piece of the silence 1983
2 Die again, Macready 1984
3 The nightmare file 1987

LIVINGSTON, N.
MACKIE FAMILY:
1 The far side of the hill 1987
2 The land of our dreams 1989
MR. PRINGLE:
1 The trouble at Aquitaine 1985
2 Fatality at Bath and Wells 1986
3 Incident at Parga 1987
4 Death in a distant land 1988
5 Death in close-up 1989
6 Mayhem in Parva 1990
7 Unwillingly to Vegas 1991

LLEWELLYN, R.
1 How green was my valley 1939
2 Up into the singing mountain 1963

3 Down where the moon is small 1966
4 Green, green my valley now 1975
Series about a Welsh mining town.
Readers should note that though there
is no sequel to 'None but the lonely
heart', the revised edition, 1970,
contains 14 new chapters and completes
the story
EDMUND TROTHE:
1 The end of the rug 1969
2 But we didn't get the fox 1970
3 White horse to Banbury Cross 1972
4 The night is a child 1974

LLEWELLYN, S.
CHARLIE AGUTTER:
1 Dead reckoning 1987
2 Blood orange 1988
Thrillers set in the world of yacht
racing
GURNEY:
1 Gurney's revenge 1977
2 Gurney's reward 1978
3 Gurney's release 1979
Sea stories

LLOYD, A. R.
THE KINE SAGA:
1 Marshworld (Kine) 1982
2 Witchwood 1989
3 Dragonpond 1990

LLOYD, J.
1 The further adventures of Capt.
Gregory Dangerfield 1975
2 The continuing adventures of Capt.
Gregory Dangerfield 1979
Comedy thrillers

LLOYD-JONES, B.
1 The animals came in one by one 1966
2 Come into my world 1972
N.F. Autobiography of a vet

LLYWELYN, M.
THE ODYSSEY OF THE IRISH:
1 Lion of Ireland 1980
2 The horse goddess 1983
3 Bard 1985

LOBSANG RAMPA, T.
1 The third eye
2 Doctor from Lhasa
3 The Rampa story
N.F. Autobiography

LOCHTE, D.
SERENDIPITY DALHQUIST:

1 Sleeping dog 1987
2 Laughing dog 1988

LOCKLEY, R. M.
1 Island days 1934
2 Inland farm 1943
3 The island farmers 1947
4 Golden year 1948
5 The island 1969
6 Orielton 1977
7 Myself when young 1980
N.F. Autobiography

LOCKRIDGE, F. *and* R.
MR. AND MRS. NORTH SERIES:
1 Mr. and Mrs. North
2 The Norths meet murder 1940
3 Murder out of turn 1941
4 Hanged for a sheep
5 Death takes a bow 1945
6 Killing the goose 1947
7 A pinch of poison 1948
8 Death on the aisle 1949
9 Death of a tall man 1949
10 Pay off for the banker 1949
11 Murder within murder 1950
12 Murder is served 1950
13 Dishonest murderer 1951
14 Murder in a hurry 1952
15 Untidy murder 1953
16 Murder comes first 1954
17 Death has a small voice 1955
18 Dead as a dinosaur 1956
19 Curtain for a jester 1956
20 Death of an angel 1957
21 Voyage into violence 1958
22 The long skeleton 1958
23 Murder is suggested 1961
24 The judge is reversed 1961
25 Murder has its points 1962
26 The ticking clock 1963
27 Murder by the book 1964
CAPTAIN HEIMRICH SERIES:
1 I want to go home 1948
2 Spin your web, lady 1949
3 Foggy foggy death 1953
4 Client is cancelled 1955
5 Stand up and die 1955
6 Death by association 1957
7 Death and the gentle bull 1957
Continued under the name of Francis Richards
8 Burnt offering 1959
9 Let dead enough alone 1959
10 Practise to deceive 1959
11 Accent on murder 1960
12 Show red for danger 1961
13 No dignity in death 1962

14 First come first kill 1963
15 The distant clue 1964
16 Murder can't wait 1965
17 Murder roundabout 1967
18 With option to die 1968
19 A risky way to kill 1970
Continued under the name of Richard Lockridge
20 Inspector's holiday 1972
21 Not I said the sparrow 1974
Under the name of Francis Richards:
NATHAN SHAPIRO SERIES:
1 Catch as catch can 1960
2 The innocent house 1961
3 Four hours to fear 1964
4 Murder for art's sake 1968
5 Die laughing 1970
Continued under the name of Richard Lockridge
6 Preach no more 1972
7 Write murder down 1974
8 The old die young 1981
ASST. D. A. BERNIE SIMMONS SERIES:
1 Squire of death 1966
2 A plate of red herrings 1969
Continued under the name of Richard Lockridge
3 Twice retired 1971
4 Something up a sleeve 1974
The pseudonym Francis Richards was used in U.K. only for a period, and since 1970 all books have been published under the name of Richard Lockridge, and reprints are also under this name. Richard Lockridge was originally joint-author with his wife

LODGE, D.
1 Changing places 1975
2 Small world 1984

LODI, M.
1 Charlotte Morel 1963
2 The dream 1968
3 The seige 1970
A trilogy of historical novels about the Second Empire in France

LOFTHOUSE, J.
1 Lancashire countrygoer
2 Countrygoer in the Dales

LOFTS, N.
1 The silver nutmeg 1947
2 Scent of cloves 1957
Indonesia in the 18th century
★★★

1 Bless this house 1955
2 Afternoon of an autocrat 1956
Story of an 18th century village
SUFFOLK TRILOGY:
1 Town house 1959
2 House at Old Vine 1961
3 The house at sunset 1963
***
1 Knight's Acre 1974
2 The homecoming 1975
3 The lonely furrow 1976
A trilogy set in 15th century Suffolk
***
1 Gad's Hall 1977
2 The haunted house 1978

LOGAN, M.
NICK MINETT:
1 Tricoleur 1976
2 Guillotine 1976
3 Brumaire 1978
Spy stories set in the time of the French Revolution

LONG, E. L.
FLYNN SERIES:
1 Young Flynn
2 The fortunes of Flynn
3 Captain Flynn
4 The vengeance of Flynn
5 Flynn of the *Martagon*
6 Flynn, A. B.
7 Son of Flynn
8 Flynn's sampler
9 Lieut. Flynn, R.N.
10 Capt. Flynn (ret'd)
11 Ould Flynn
12 The blindness of Flynn
13 Captain Flynn, sheriff 1961
SIMPSON SERIES:
1 Seconds and thirds
2 Trials of the *Phidias*
LIZZIE COLLINS SERIES:
1 Port of destination
2 Purser's mate
3 Unhappy ship

LONG, M.
LIZ PARROTT SERIES:
1 Here's blood in your eye 1946
2 Vicious circle 1946
3 Bury the hatchet 1949
4 Short shrift 1949
5 Dull thud 1950
6 Savage breast 1951

LONGFORD, F. A. PAKENHAM, Earl

of *see* **PAKENHAM, F. A., Earl of Longford**

LONGHURST, H.
1 It was good while it lasted 1941
2 I wouldn't have missed it 1946
3 You never know till you get there 1950
N.F. Autobiography

LONGMATE, N.
DET. SGT. RAYMOND SERIES:
1 Death won't wash 1957
2 A head from death 1958
3 Strip death naked 1958
4 Vote for death 1960

LONGSTREET, S.
THE PEDLOCK FAMILY:
1 The Pedlocks 1967
2 Pedlock and sons 1969
3 Pedlock saint. Pedlock sinner 1970
4 The Pedlock inheritance 1971
5 The strange case of Sarah Pedlock 1977
FIORE FAMILY:
1 All or nothing 1984
2 Our father's house 1986

LONGSTRETCH, T. M.
1 The scarlet Force
2 The Force carries on
N.F. History of the Royal Canadian Mounted Police

LORAC, E. C. R.
INSPECTOR MACDONALD SERIES:
1 Murder on the burrows 1931
2 Affair on Thor's head 1932
3 Greenwell mystery 1932
4 Murder in St. John's Wood 1934
5 Murder in Chelsea 1934
6 Affair of Colonel Marchand
7 Death on the Oxford Road
8 The organ speaks
9 Death of an author
10 Crime counter crime
11 Post after post mortem
12 A pall for a painter
13 Bats in the belfry
14 The devil and the C.I.D.
15 These names make clues
16 Slippery staircase
17 John Brown's body
18 Black beadle
19 Death at Dyke's corner
20 Tryst for a tragedy
21 Case in the clinic
22 Rope's end rogue's end
23 The sixteenth stair

24 Death came softly
25 Checkmate to murder
26 Fell murder
27 Murder by matchlight
28 Fire in the thatch
29 The theft of the iron dogs
30 Relative to poison
31 Death before dinner
32 Part of a poisoner (Place for a poisoner)
33 Still waters
34 Policemen in the precinct (And then put out the light)
35 Accident by design
36 Murder of a martinet (I could murder her)
37 The dog it was that died
38 Murder in the millrace (Speak justly of the dead)
39 Crook O'Lune (Shepherd's crook)
40 Shroud of darkness 1954
41 Ask for a policeman
42 Murder in Vienna 1956
43 Dangerous domicile 1957
44 Murder on a monument 1958
45 Death in triplicate 1959
46 Dishonour among thieves 1960
There is an interior sequence by place 'Lunesdale', in some novels - 'Fell murder', 'Crook O'Lune', 'Theft of the iron dogs', and 'Dishonour among thieves', with many minor characters recurring

LORRIMER, C.
1 Mavreen 1977
2 Tamarisk 1978
3 Chantal 1980
ROCHFORD FAMILY:
1 The Chatelaine 1981
2 The wilderling 1982

LOTT, S. M.
STEPHEN RINGWAY SERIES:
1 Twopence for a rat's tail 1947
2 The judge will call it murder 1951

LOUVISH, S.
AVRAM BLOK:
1 The therapy of Avram Blok 1985
2 City of Blok 1988
3 The last trump of Avram Blok 1990

LOVELL, M.
APPLETON PORTER:
1 The spy game 1981
2 The spy with his head in the clouds 1982

LOVESEY, P.
SERGEANT CRIBB AND CONSTABLE THACKERAY:
1 Wobble to death 1969
2 The detective wore silk drawers 1971
3 Abracadaver 1972
4 Mad hatter's holiday 1973
5 Invitation to a dynamite party 1974
6 A case of spirits 1975
7 Swing, swing together 1976
8 Waxwork 1978
Detective stories set in Victorian times
DETECTIVE MEMOIRS OF KING EDWARD VII:
1 Bertie and the tin man 1987
2 Bertie and the seven bodies 1990

LOW, O.
ARVO LAURILA:
1 To his just deserts 1986
2 Murky shallows 1987

LOWREY, M.
1 Under the volcano 1967
2 Dark as the grave wherein my friend is laid 1969
Two novels about Mexico. Companion novels rather than sequels

LUDLUM, R.
BOURNE:
1 The Bourne identity 1980
2 The Bourne supremacy 1986
3 The Bourne ultimatum 1990

LUMLEY, B.
NECROSCOPE:
1 Necroscope
2 Wamphyri
3 The source
4 Deadspeak
5 Deadspawn
Paperback horror stories

LUTYENS, M.
RUSKIN, MILLAIS AND EFFIE GRAY:
1 Effie in Venice 1965
2 Millais and the Ruskins 1967
3 The Ruskins and the Grays 1972
A narrative using contemporary letters to tell the true story of Effie's unfortunate marriage to John Ruskin, her divorce, and marriage to Millais

LUTZ, G.
PANZER PLATOON:
1 Invade Russia
2 Blood and ice

3 Blitz Krieg
4 Support Rommel
5 Death ride
6 Attack Anzio
1-3 also in hardback
NAZI PARATROOPER:
1 Storm Belgium
2 Crete must fall
3 Cassino corpse factory

LUTZ, J.
FRED CARVER:
1 Tropical heat 1986
2 Scorcher 1988
3 Kiss 1989
4 Flame 1990
5 Blood fire 1991

LYALL, F.
SUPT. MASON:
1 A death in time 1987
2 Death and the remembrancer 1988
3 The croaking of the raven 1990

LYALL, G.
1 The wrong side of the sky 1961
2 The most dangerous game 1964
HARRY MAXIM:
1 The secret servant 1980
2 The conduct of Major Maxim 1982
3 The crocus list 1985
4 Uncle Target 1988

LYNN, E. A.
CHRONICLES OF TORNOR:
1 Watchtower
2 The dancers of Arun
3 The Northern girl
Paperback fantasy

LYONS, A.
JACOB ASCH:
1 The dead are discrete 1977
2 All God's children 1977
3 The killing floor 1977
4 Dead ringer 1983
5 Castles burning 1983
6 Hard trade 1984
7 Three with a bullet 1987
8 Other people's money 1990
9 Fast fade 1990

LYONS, G.
1 Slievelea 1985
2 The green years 1987

LYTTLETON, H.
1 I play as I please 1954

2 Second chorus 1958
3 Take it from the top 1975
N.F. Autobiography

MACAULAY, R.
1 Letters to a friend
2 Last letters to a friend
N.F. Autobiography

MACAVOY, R. A.
DAMIANO TRILOGY:
1 Damiano
2 Damiano's Lute
3 Raphael
Paperback fantasy

MCBRAIN, E.
MATTHEW HOPE:
1 Goldilocks 1978
2 Rumpelstiltskin 1981
3 Beauty and the beast 1982
4 Jack and the beanstalk 1984
5 Snow White and the rose red 1985
6 Cinderella 1986
7 Puss in boots 1987
8 The house that Jack built 1988
9 Three blind mice 1991
THE 87TH PRECINCT:
1 Cop hater 1956
2 The mugger 1956
3 The pusher 1956
4 The con man 1957
5 Killer's choice 1958
6 Killer's payoff 1958
7 Lady killer 1958
8 Killer's wedge 1959
9 'Til death 1959
10 King's ransom 1959
11 Give the boys a great big hand 1960
12 The heckler 1961
13 See them die 1961
14 Lady, lady I did it 1961
15 The empty hours 1962
16 Like love 1962
17 Ten plus one 1963
18 Axe 1964
19 He who hesitates 1964
20 Doll 1965
21 Eighty million eyes 1966
22 Fuss 1968
23 Shotgun 1969
24 Jigsaw 1970
25 Hail, hail the gang's all here 1971
26 Sadie when she died 1972
27 Let's hear it for the deaf man 1972
28 Hail to the chief 1973
29 Bread 1974

30 Blood relatives 1975
31 So long as you both shall live 1976
32 Long time no see 1977
33 Calypso 1979
34 Ghosts 1980
35 Heat 1981
36 Ice 1983
37 Lightning 1984
38 Eight black horses 1985
39 Poison 1987
40 Tricks 1987
41 McBain's ladies: women of the 87th
  Precinct 1988
42 Lullaby 1989
43 McBain's ladies, too 1990
44 Vespers 1990
45 Widows 1991

MACCAFFREY, A.
PERN AND THE RED PLANET:
1 Dragonsdawn 1988
2 Dragonflight 1971
3 Dragonquest 1973
4 Dragonsong 1974
5 Dragonsinger 1977
6 The white dragon 1979
7 Dragondrums 1979
8 Moreta, Dragonlady of Pern 1983
9 The renegades of Pern 1990
10 All the weyrs of Pern 1991
  2, 3 and 5, and 4, 6 and 7 are trilogies

1 Crystalsinger 1982
2 Killashandra 1986

MCCARRY, C.
PAUL CHRISTOPHER:
1 The Miernik dossier 1974
2 Tears of autumn 1975
3 Secret lovers 1977
4 The better angels 1979
5 The last supper 1983
6 Second sight 1991

MCCAUGHREN, T.
1 Run with the wind 1983
2 Run to earth 1984

MCCLOY, H.
BASIL WILLING SERIES:
1 Design for dying 1938 (Dance of death)
2 The man in the moonlight 1940
3 The deadly truth 1940
4 Who's calling 1942
5 Cue for murder 1942
6 The goblin market 1943
7 The one that got away 1956
8 Through a glass, darkly

9 Alias Basil Willing
10 The long body
11 Two-thirds of a ghost 1957
12 Mr. Splitfoot 1969
13 Burn this 1980
  *This is Miss McCloy's own list, order of
  publication is U.S.A. There is a Basil
  Willing short story, 'The singing
  diamonds', in the volume of that title,
  U.S.A., but 'Surprise, surprise!' in the
  English edition.*

MCCLURE, J.
LIEUT. KRAMER AND SGT. ZONDI:
1 The steam pig 1970
2 The caterpillar cop 1972
3 Four and twenty virgins 1973
4 The gooseberry fool 1974
5 Snake 1976
6 Killers 1976
7 The Sunday hangmen 1977
8 The blood of an Englishman 1980
9 The Artfall egg 1984

MACCOLLUM, W.
1 Antares passage 1989
2 Antares dawn 1989

MACCRONE, G.
THE MOORHOUSE FAMILY:
1 Antimacassar city
2 The Philistines
3 The Puritans
4 Aunt Bel 1949
5 The Hayburn family 1952
  *The first three were published as one
  volume under title 'Wax fruit' ('Red
  plush'). 1947*

MCCUTCHAN, P.
CAMERON:
1 Cameron, Ordinary Seaman 1979
2 Cameron comes through 1980
3 Cameron of the 'Castle Bay' 1981
4 Lt. Cameron, RNVR 1981
5 Cameron's convoy 1982
6 Cameron in the gap 1982
7 Orders for Cameron 1983
8 Cameron in command 1983
9 Cameron and the Kaiserhof 1984
10 Cameron's raid 1985
11 Cameron's chase 1986
12 Cameron's troop lift 1987
13 Cameron's commitment 1988
COMMANDER SHAW:
1 Gibraltar Road 1960
2 Redcap 1961
3 Bluebolt one 1961

4 The man from Moscow 1962
5 Warmaster 1963
6 The Moscow coach 1964
7 Deadline 1965
8 Skyprobe 1966
9 The screaming red balloons 1968
10 The bright red businessmen 1969
11 The all-purpose bodies 1969
12 Hartinger's mouse 1970
13 This Drakotny... 1971
14 Sunstrike 1979
15 Corpse 1980
16 Werewolf 1982
17 Rollerball 1984
18 Greenfly 1987
19 The boy who liked monsters 1989
20 The spatchcock plan 1990
JOHN MASON KEMP:
1 The convoy Commodore 1986
2 Convoy north 1987
3 Convoy south 1988
4 Convoy east 1989
5 Convoy of fear 1990
LIEUT. HALFHYDE:
1 Beware, beware the Bright of Benin 1974
2 Halfhyde's island 1975
3 The guns of arrest 1976
4 Halfhyde to the narrows 1977
5 Halfhyde for the Queen 1978
6 Halfhyde ordered south 1979
7 Halfhyde and the Flag Captain 1980
8 Halfhyde on the Yangtze 1981
9 Halfhyde on Zanatu 1982
10 Halfhyde outward bound 1983
11 The Halfhyde line 1984
12 Halfhyde and the chain-gang 1985
13 Halfhyde goes to war 1986
14 Halfhyde on the Amazon 1987
15 Halfhyde and the Admiral 1990
16 Halfhyde and the Fleet Review 1991
SIMON SHARD:
1 Call for Simon Shard 1973
2 A very big bang 1975
3 Blood runs East 1976
4 The Eros affair 1977
5 Blackmail north 1979
6 Shard calls the tune 1980
7 The hoof 1983
8 Shard at bay 1985
9 The executioners 1986
10 Overnight express 1988
11 The Logan file 1991

MCCUTCHEON, H.
ANTONY HOWARD:
1 The angel of light 1951
2 Cover her face 1955

RICHARD LOGAN:
1 To dusty death 1962
2 Suddenly, in Vienna 1963
JIMMY CARROLL SERIES:
1 Treasure of the sun 1964
2 Black attendant 1965
3 Scorpion's nest 1967
4 Hot wind from hell 1968
5 Something wicked 1970

MCDERMID, V.
LINDSAY GORDON:
1 Report for murder 1987
2 Common murder 1989
3 Final edition 1991

MACDONALD, B.
1 The egg and I
2 The plague and I
3 Anybody can do anything 1991 (rep.)
4 Onions in the stew
N.F. Autobiography. 'Who me?' is a selection from the above made into a connected autobiography.

MACDONALD, D.
TOMMY BRIGGS SERIES:
1 Briggs investigates 1968
2 No judges' rules 1969
3 The organiser 1970
4 The Ryan affair 1970
5 Two kinds of murder 1971
6 Two bullets for Briggs 1971

MACDONALD, F. J.
1 Crowdie and cream 1982
2 Crotal and white 1983
N.F. Autobiography

MCDONALD, GREGORY
FLETCH:
1 Fletch won 1985
2 Fletch, too 1987
3 Fletch and the Widow Bradley 1981
4 Fletch 1975
5 Confess, Fletch 1977
6 Fletch forever 1978
7 Fletch's fortune 1979
8 Fletch's Moxie 1983
9 Fletch and the man who 1984
10 Carioca Fletch 1984
Listed in chronological order
INSPECTOR FLYNN:
1 Flynn 1976
2 Snatched 1980
3 The buck passes Flynn 1982
4 Flynn's Inn 1985
Flynn also appears in some of the

Fletch series

MCDONALD, J. D.
TRAVIS MCGEE:
1 The deep blue goodbye 1965
2 Nightmare in pink 1966
3 A purple place for dying 1966
4 The quick red fox 1967
5 A deadly shade of gold 1967
6 Bright orange for the shroud 1967
7 Darker than amber 1968
8 One fearful yellow eye 1968
9 Pale grey for guilt 1969
10 The girl in the pale brown wrapper 1969
11 Dress her in indigo 1971
12 Flash of green 1972
13 The long lavender look 1972
14 A tan and sandy silence 1973
15 McGee 1974
16 The scarlet ruse 1975
17 The turquoise lament 1975
18 The dreadful lemon sky 1976
19 Dead low tide 1976
20 Murder for the bride 1977
21 You live once 1978
22 The empty copper sea 1979
23 The green ripper 1980
24 Free fall in crimson 1982
25 Cinnamon skin 1982
26 The lonely silver rain 1985

MACDONALD, M.
STEVENSON FAMILY:
1 The world from rough stones 1975
2 The rich are with you always 1977
3 Sons of fortune 1978
4 Abigail 1979

MACDONALD, PETER
BEN HART:
1 The hope of glory 1980
2 Wide horizons 1980
3 One way street 1981
4 Exit 1983
5 Dead end 1986
Novels about the British Army after WW2

MACDONALD, ROSS
LEW ARCHER SERIES:
1 The moving target 1949
2 The three roads 1950
3 The way some people die 1953
4 The ivory grin 1953
5 The drowning pool 1955
6 Experience with evil 1955 (Meet me at the morgue)

7 Find a victim 1955
8 The barbarous coast 1957
9 The doomsters 1958
10 The Galton Case 1960
11 The Ferguson affair 1961
12 The Wycherly woman 1962
13 The chill 1963
14 The zebra stiped hearse 1963
15 The far side of the dollar 1964
16 Black money 1966
17 Instant enemy 1967
18 The goodbye look 1968
19 The underground man 1971
20 Sleeping beauty 1973
21 The blue hammer 1976
Early titles in this series were published under the name of John Macdonald or John Ross Macdonald. The order given above is of U.S.A. publications, but the dates are first English publication. There is one title, 'Archer in Hollywood', which appears to be U.S.A. only, but may be an alternative title to 'The goodbye look'. There is also 'The name is Archer', U.S.A. paperback only. Many of the titles were first published in paperback.

MACDONALD, W. C.
THREE MESQUITEERS SERIES:
1 Restless guns
2 Law of the forty-five
3 Riders of the whistling skull
4 The singing scorpion
5 Powdersmoke range
6 Roarin' lead
7 Ghost-town gold
8 Bullets for Buckaroos
9 The three mesquiteers
10 Bad man's return
11 Mesquiteer mavericks
12 Galloping ghost
CALIPER AND NOGALES:
1 Punchers of Phantom pass
2 Riddle of Ramrod Ridge
GREGORY QUIST:
1 Destination danger
2 The Osage bow 1964

MCDONELL, J. E.
JIM BRADY TRILOGY:
1 Jim Brady, leading seaman 1954
2 Commander Brady 1956
3 Subsmash 1960
A trilogy of novels about the career of an Australian naval officer

MACENROE, R. S.

FAR STARS AND FUTURE TIMES:
1 The shattered stars
2 Flight of honour
3 Skinner
Paperback science fiction

MCGIRR, E.

PIRON SERIES:
1 The funeral was in Spain 1966
2 Here lies my wife 1967
3 A hearse with horses 1967
4 The lead lined coffin 1968
5 An entry of death 1969
6 Death pays the wages 1970
7 No better fiend 1971
8 Bardel's murder 1973
9 A murderous journey 1974

MCGREGOR, B.

1 The Liffey runs black 1978
2 The uncertain trumpet 1980
Ireland during the political disturbances

MACGOWAN, R.

SHANE MACKENZIE:
1 Monopoly to murder
2 Barracuda

MCGOWN, J.

INSPECTOR LLOYD AND SERGEANT HILL:
1 A perfect match 1987
2 Redemption 1988
3 Death of a dancer 1989
4 Murder movie 1990
5 The murders of Mrs. Austin and Mrs. Beale 1991

MACGREGOR, A. A.

1 Auld Reekie 1943
2 Vanished waters 1942
3 The goat-wife 1939
4 Turbulent years 1945
5 Go not, happy day
6 The golden lamp 1964
7 Land of the mountain and the flood 1965
N.F. Autobiography

MACHEN, A.

1 Far off things
2 Things near and far
N.F. Autobiography. Republished in one volume. 1974.

MCHUGH, A.

1 A banner with a strange device 1964

2 The seacoast of Bohemia 1965
Two novels about young people in Boston. Sally Brimmer, the heroine of 1, is an important character in 2.

MCILVANNEY, W.

LAIDLAW:
1 Laidlaw 1980
2 The papers of Tony Veitch 1983
3 Strange loyalties 1991

MCINERNY, R.

FATHER DOWLING SERIES:
1 Her death of cold 1977
2 The seventh station 1978
3 Bishop as pawn 1979
4 Lying there 1980
5 Second Vespers 1981
6 Thicker than water 1982
7 Getting a way with murder 1987
8 Sleight of body 1989

MACINNES, C.

LONDON SERIES:
1 City of Spades 1957
2 Absolute beginners 1958
3 Mr. Love and justice 1960
Later published in one vol. 'Visions of London'.
Although there is no continuity of plot or characters, there is a trilogy in scene, time and purpose.

MCINNES, G.

1 The road to Gundagai 1965
2 Humping my bluey 1966
3 Finding a father 1967
4 Goodbye Melbourne town 1968
N.F. Autobiography. Also contains some interesting biographical material on his mother, Angela Thirkell, the novelist.

MACINNES, H.

ROBERT RENWICK:
1 The hidden target 1981
2 The cloak of darkness 1982

MACINTOSH, J. T.

AMBROSE AND DOMINIQUE:
1 Take a pair of private eyes 1969
2 A coat of blackmail 1970

MACINTYRE, L.

CHRONICLES OF INVER NEVIS:
1 Cruel in the shadow 1979
2 The blind bend 1981

MACKAY, AMANDA
1 Death is academic 1976
2 Death on the river 1983

MACKEN, W.
MACMAHON FAMILY:
1 Seek the fair land 1960
2 The silent people 1962
3 The scorching wind 1964
A trilogy of novels on the foundation of the Irish Republic.

MACKENZIE, SIR C.
HIGHLAND SERIES:
1 Monarch of the glen 1951
2 Keep the Home Guard turning
3 Whisky galore (Tight little island) 1947
4 Hunting for fairies 1949
5 The rival monster 1952
6 Ben Nevis goes east 1954
7 Rockets galore 1957
8 The stolen soprano 1965
These novels are not strictly sequels but the same characters recur in all.
OLIVER HUFFNAM:
1 The red tapeworm 1958
2 Paper lives 1966

MACKENZIE, D.
1 Fugitives
2 Gentleman at crime
N.F. Autobiography

MACKENZIE, DONALD
RAVEN:
1 Raven in flight 1976
2 Raven and the ratcatcher 1976
3 Raven and the Kamikaze 1977
4 Deep, dark and dead 1977
5 Raven settles a score 1978
6 Raven feathers his nest 1979
7 Raven and the paper-hangers 1980
8 Raven's revenge 1982
9 Raven's longest night 1984
10 Raven's shadow 1985
11 Nobody here by that name 1986
12 A savage state of grace 1988
13 By any illegal means 1990
14 Loose cannon 1991

MACKENZIE, LEE
EMMERDALE FARM:
1 The legacy
2 Prodigal's progress
3 All that a man has
4 Lover's meeting
5 A sad and happy summer
6 A sense of responsibility

7 Nothing stays the same
8 The couple at Demdyke Row
9 Whispers of scandal
10 Shadows of the past
11 Lucky for some
12 Face value
13 Good neighbours
14 Innocent victim
15 False witness
16 The homecoming
17 Old flames
18 New beginnings
19 Family feuds
20 Young passions
21 Another door opens 1986
22 A friend in need, by James Ferguson
23 Divided loyalties, by James Ferguson
24 Wives and lovers, by James Ferguson

MCKEOWN, J.
1 Back crack boy
2 Liam at large
Paperback novels about Liverpool in the 1930s.

MCKIE, C. STEWARTS OF BADENOCH:
1 The wolf 1978
2 Mariota 1981
3 Blood of the wolf 1980

MCKILLIP, P. A.
CHRONICLES OF MORGAN, PRINCE OF HED:
1 Riddlemaster of Hed 1979
2 Heir of sea and fire 1979
3 Harpist in the wind 1979

MACKINNON, C.
A SCOTTISH CHRONICLE:
1 A house at war 1973
2 The years beyond 1974
3 To whom the glory 1975
4 The house remains 1977

MACKINTOSH, I.
TIM BLACKGROVE SERIES:
1 Slaying in September 1970
2 Drug called power 1971
3 The brave cannot yield 1973
WARSHIP:
1 Warship 1973
2 HMS *Hero* 1976
3 Holt R.N. 1977

MACKINTOSH, M.
LAURIE GRANT SERIES:
1 Appointment in Andalusia 1971
2 A king and two queens 1973

3 The Sicilian affair 1974

MCLAGEN, J.
HERNE THE HUNTER:
1 White death
2 River of blood
3 Black widow
4 Shadow of the vulture
5 Apache squaw
6 Blood ties
7 Death rites
8 Cross draw
9 Massacre
10 Vigilante
11 Silver threads
12 Sundance
13 Bill the Kid
14 Death school
15 Till death
16 Geronimo
17 The hanging
18 Dying ways
19 Blood line
20 Hearts of gold
21 Pony Express
Paperback Westerns

MACLAINE, SHIRLEY
1 Don't fall off the mountain 1972
2 You can get there from here 1975
3 Out on a limb 1983
4 Dancing in the light 1985
5 It's all in the playing 1987
6 Going within 1989
N.F. Autobiography and personal philosophy

MACLAUGHLIN, W. R. D.
1 Antarctic raider 1961
2 So thin the line 1963
N.F. Story of the whaling fleet during World War II.

MACLEAN, A.
1 The guns of Navarone 1957
2 Force ten from Navarone 1968

MACLEAN, N.
1 The former days
2 Set free
3 The years of fulfilment
N.F. Autobiography of Moderator of Church of Scotland.

MCLEAVE, H.
BRODIE AND SHANE:
1 A borderline case 1979
2 Double exposure 1980

3 The Icarus threat 1984
4 Under the icefall 1987
GREG MACLEAN:
1 Second time around 1984
2 Death masque 1985

MACLEOD, A.
TOM VAUGHAN:
1 The trusted servant 1966 (The Hireling)
2 No need of the sun 1969 (City of light)
Venice and Geneva in the 16th century.

MACLEOD, C.
PETER SHANDY:
1 Rest you merry 1980
2 The luck runs out 1981
3 Wrack and rune 1982
4 Something the cat dragged in 1984
5 The corpse in Oozak's pond 1986
6 Vane pursuit 1989
7 An owl too many 1991
Thrillers set in an American agricultural college.
SARAH KELLING:
1 The family vault 1980
2 The withdrawing room 1981
3 The palace guard 1982
4 The Bilbao looking glass 1983
5 The convivial codfish 1984
6 The plain old man 1985
7 The recycled citizen 1987
8 The silver ghost 1987
9 The Gladstone bag 1989

MACLEOD, L.
1 Years of peace
2 The crowded hill

MACLEOD, R.
TALOS CORD SERIES:
1 Drum of power 1965
2 Cave of bats 1966
3 Luke of fury 1967
4 Isle of dragons 1968
5 Place of mists 1969
6 Path of ghosts 1970
7 Nest of vultures 1973
JOHATHAN GAUNT:
1 A property in Cyprus 1970
2 A killing in Malta 1972
3 A burial in Portugal 1973
4 A witch dance in Bavaria 1975
5 A pay-off in Switzerland 1977
6 Incident in Iceland 1979
7 A problem in Prague 1981
8 A legacy from Tenerife 1984
9 The money mountain 1987

10 Spanish maze game 1990
ANDREW LAIRD SERIES:
1 All other perils 1974
2 Dragonship 1976
3 Salvage job 1978
4 Cargo risk 1980
5 Mayday from Malaga 1983
6 A cut in diamonds 1985
7 Witchline 1988

MACMILLAN, H.
1 Winds of change, 1914-1939 1966
2 The blast of war, 1939-1945 1967
3 Tides of fortune, 1945-1955 1969
4 Riding the storm, 1955-1959 1970
5 Pointing the way, 1959-1961 1972
6 At the end of the day 1973
N.F. Autobiography

MCMILLAN, J.
1 The way we were, 1900-1914 1978
2 The way it was, 1914-1934 1979
3 The way it happened, 1935-1950 1980
N.F. Social history, based on the files of the 'Daily Express'.

MCMULLEN, J.
1 My small country living 1984
2 The wind in the ashtree 1988
3 A small country living goes ever on 1990
N.F. Autobiography of a smallholder in Wales.

MCMURTY, L.
1 The last picture show 1966
2 Texasville 1987

1 All my friends are going to be strangers
2 Some can whistle 1990

MCNAB, C.
CAROL ASHTON:
1 The Shipley report 1990
2 Death down under 1991

MACNAGHTEN, P.
1 The car that Jack built 1964
2 The right line 1966
Stories of a racing car.

MCNALLY, C.
GHOST HOUSE:
1 The ghost house 1979
2 The ghost house revenge 1987
Horror stories.

MCNAMARA, J. D.
1 The first directive
2 Fatal command 1988

MCNEIL, D.
JAMES OGILVIE SERIES:
1 Drums along the Khyber 1968
2 Lieutenant of the line 1970
3 Sadhu of the mountain peak 1971
4 The gates of Kunarja 1972
5 The red Daniel 1973
6 Subaltern's choice 1974
7 By command of the Viceroy 1975
8 Mullah from Kashmir 1976
9 Wolf in the fold 1977
10 No charge cowardice 1978
11 Restless frontier 1979
12 Cunningham's revenge 1980
13 The train at Bundarbar 1981
14 A matter for the Regiment 1982
Novels about the British army, mainly in India.

MCNEISH, J.
1 Mackenzie 1970
2 The Mackenzie affair 1973
1 is a novel. 2 is the fact behind the novel - the 'Clearances' in the Highlands of Scotland and the settling in Australia and New Zealand in the 1850's.

MCPHERSON, W.
1 Testing the current 1986
2 To the Sargasso Sea 1988
Not strictly sequels, but some characters appear in both books.

MACVICAR, A.
REV. P. J. MACPHARLANE SERIES:
1 The temple falls 1935
2 The purple rock 1939
3 The crouching spy 1941
★★★
1 Salt in my porridge 1972
2 Heather in my ears 1974
3 Rocks in my scotch 1976
4 Silver in my sporran 1980
5 Bees in my bonnet 1982
6 Golf in my gallowses 1983
7 Gremlins in my garden 1985
8 Capers in the Kirl 1987
N.F. Autobiography
BRUCE MCLINTOCK:
1 The golden Venus affair 1972
2 The painted doll affair 1973

MAGUIRE, M.
SIMON DRAKE:
1 Shot silk 1975
2 Slaughter horse 1975
3 Scratchproof 1976

MAHFOUZ, N.
CAIRO TRILOGY:
1 Palace walk 1990
2 Place of desire 1991

MAINE, C. E.
MIKE DELANEY SERIES:
1 The isotope man 1962
2 Subterfuge 1963
3 Never let up 1964

MAIR, G.
1 Doctor goes east
2 Doctor goes north
3 Doctor goes west
***
1 Confessions of a surgeon 1974
2 Escape from surgery 1975
N.F. Autobiography

MAIR, G. B.
DAVID GRANT SERIES:
1 Death's foot forward 1963
2 Miss Turquoise 1964
3 Live, love and cry 1965
4 Kisses from Satan 1966
5 The girl from Peking 1967
6 Black champagne 1968
7 Goddesses never die 1969
8 A wreath of camellias 1970
9 Crimson jade 1971
10 Paradise spells danger 1972

MAIS, S. P. B.
1 All the days of my life 1937
2 Buffets and rewards 1952
3 These I have loved 1935
N.F. Autobiography

MAISKY, I.
1 Before the storm 1944
2 Journey into the past 1960
3 Who helped Hitler? 1962
4 Spanish notebooks 1962
N.F. Autobiography

MAKEPEACE, J.
1 Divine son of Ra
2 Daughter of Isis

MALCOLM, A.
DAUGHTERS OF CAMERON:
1 The taming 1982
2 Ride out the storm 1982

MALCOLM, J.
TIM SIMPSON:
1 A back room in Somers Town 1983
2 The Godwin sideboard 1984
3 The Gwen John sculpture 1985
4 Whistler in the dark 1986
5 Gothic pursuit 1987
6 Mortal ruin 1987
7 The wrong impression 1989
8 Sheep, goats and soap 1991

MALING, A.
BROCK POTTER:
1 Schroeder's game 1977
2 Lucky devil 1978
3 The Rheingold route 1979
4 The Koberg link 1980
5 A taste of treason 1983

MALLOCH, P.
DAVE NORTON:
1 Blood on pale fingers 1969
2 The slugger 1971

MALLOY, L.
MARTIN MOON:
1 JoJo and the private eye 1980
2 The happiest ghost in town 1981
3 Beware the yellow Packard 1982
4 So help me Hannah 1982
5 The bullet proof toga 1984

MALPASS, E.
PENTECOST FAMILY:
1 Morning's at seven 1966
2 At the height of the moon 1967
3 Fortinbras has escaped 1970
4 Oh, my darling daughter 1973
WILLIAM SHAKESPEARE:
1 Sweet Will 1972
2 The Cleopatra boy 1974
3 House of women 1975

MANDLSTAM, N.
1 Hope against hope 1971
2 Hope abandoned 1973
N.F. Autobiography

MANN, J.
TAMARA HOYLAND:
1 Funeral sites 1981
2 No man's island 1983
3 Grave goods 1984

4 A kind of healthy grave 1986
5 Death beyond the Nile 1988
6 Faith, hope and homicide 1991

MANN, P.
THE STORY OF THE GARDENER:
1 Master of Paxwax 1986
2 The fall of the families 1987

MANNERS, A.
THE ISLAND:
1 Echoing yesterday
2 Karran Kinrade 1986
3 The red bird 1987
No. 1 in paperback only.

MANNIN, E.
1 Cactus 1935
2 The pure flame 1936

***

1 Confessions and impressions 1930
2 Privileged spectator 1939
3 Brief voices 1959
4 Stories from my life 1973
*N.F. Autobiography. 1 and 2 are direct
sequels, 3 and 4 later recollections.*

MANNING, O.
A BALKAN TRILOGY:
1 The great fortune 1960
2 The spoilt city 1962
3 Friends and heroes
*The setting is Romania and Greece as
they became involved in World War II.
Published in one volume. 1987.*
LEVANT TRILOGY:
1 The danger tree 1977
2 The battle lost and won 1978
3 The sum and things 1980
*The Middle East and Egypt during
World War II.*

MANNING, V.
1 Falcon Queen 1974
2 Fertility Queen
Set in Scandinavia in the 9th century.

MANOR, J.
STEVE SUMMERS SERIES:
1 Too dead to run
2 Red Jaguar
3 Pawns of fear
4 The tramplers 1956

MANTELL, L.
STEVEN ARROW:
1 Murder in fancy dress 1978

2 A murder or three 1980
3 Murder and chips 1981
4 Murder to burn 1983
5 Murder in vain 1984
Thrillers set in New Zealand

MARCUS, D.
1 A land not theirs 1986
2 A land in flames 1987
Novels about Ireland

MARCUS, J. *pseud.* (**Lucilla Andrews**)
1 A few days in Endel 1979
2 Marsh blood 1980
Mysteries set on Romney Marsh

MARKHAM, R. *pseud.* (**Kingsley Amis**)
see **Fleming, I.**

MARLOW, J.
WHITWORTH FAMILY:
1 Kessie 1985
2 Sarah 1988
3 Anne 1989

MARLOW, L.
1 Swan's mild
2 Forth, beast
N.F. Autobiography

MARLOWE, P.
FRANK DRURY SERIES:
1 Loaded dice
2 The double thirteen 1961
3 The dead don't scare 1963
4 The man in her death 1964
5 Promise to kill 1965
6 A knife in your heart 1966
7 Hire me a hearse 1968
8 Cash my chips croupier 1969

MARLOWE, S.
CHESTER DRUM SERIES:
1 Second longest night 1966
2 Trouble is my name 1967
3 Danger is my line 1968

MARON, M.
LT. SIGRID HAROLD;
1 One coffee with 1988
2 Death of a butterfly 1988
3 Death in blue folders 1989

MARQUAND, J. P.
MR. MOTO SERIES:
1 No hero 1935 (Your turn Mr. Moto)
2 Thank you Mr. Moto 1937
3 Think fast Mr. Motto 1937

4 Mr. Moto takes a hand 1940
5 Mr. Moto is so sorry 1940
6 Last laugh Mr. Moto 1943
7 Stopover Tokyo 1957 (Last of Mr. Moto)

MARQUEZ, G. G.
1 One hundred years of solitude 1968
2 No one writes to the colonel 1970
Macondo is also the setting for the title story of 'Leaf storm and other stories' 1973

MARQUIS, M.
GENERAL HOSPITAL:
1 The caretakers 1976
2 A matter of life 1977

MARRIC, J. J., *pseud.*, see CREASEY, J.

MARS, A.
1 Unbroken
2 H.M.S. *Thule* intercepts
N.F. Autobiography of war experiences.

MARSH, J.
RAY FELTON SERIES:
1 Murderer's maze
2 Operation snatch 1958
3 City of fear 1958
4 Small and deadly 1960
SIMON LUCK:
1 The reluctant executioner 1959
2 Girl in the net 1962

MARSH, N.
INSPECTOR ALLEYN SERIES:
1 A man lay dead 1934
2 Enter a murderer 1935
3 Death in ecstasy 1937
4 Vintage murder 1937
5 Artists in crime 1938
6 Death in a white tie 1938
7 Overture to death 1939
8 Death at the bar 1940
9 Death and the dancing footman 1942
10 Died in the wool 1945
11 Surfeit of lampreys 1941
12 Colour scheme 1943
13 Final curtain 1947
14 Swing brother swing 1948 (Wreath for Riviera)
15 Opening night (Night at the Vulcan) 1951
16 Spinsters in jeopardy 1953
17 Scales of justice 1954
18 Off with his head 1957
19 Singing in the shrouds 1959

20 False scent 1960
21 Hand in glove 1962
22 Dead water 1964
23 Death at the Dolphin 1967
24 Cluster of constables 1968
25 When in Rome 1970
26 Tied up in tinsel 1972
27 Black as he's painted 1974
28 Last ditch 1977
29 Grave mistake 1978
30 Photo finish 1980
31 Light thickens 1982

MARSHALL, ALAN
1 I can jump puddles
2 This is the grass
3 In mine own heart
N.F. Autobiography

MARSHALL, B.
1 The bishop 1970
2 Urban the ninth 1972
3 Marx the first 1975
4 Peter the second 1976

MARSHALL, C.
1 A man called Peter
2 To live again
N.F. Biography of Peter Howard of Moral Re-armament

MARSHALL, L.
SUGAR KANE SERIES:
1 Sugar for the lady 1955
2 Sugar on the target 1958
3 Sugar cuts the corners 1958
4 Sugar on the carpet
5 Sugar on the cuff 1960
6 Sugar on the kill 1961
7 Sugar on the loose 1962
8 Sugar on the prowl 1963
9 Ladies can be dangerous 1974
10 Murder is the reason 1964
11 Death strikes in darkness 1965
12 The dead are silent 1966
13 The dead are dangerous 1967
14 Murder of a lady 1968
15 Blood on the blotter 1968
16 Money means murder 1969
17 Death is for ever 1969
18 Murders out of season 1970
19 Murders just for cops 1971
20 Death casts a shadow 1972
21 Moment of murder 1973
22 Loose lady death 1973

MARSHALL, MAY
1 Mulberry leaf

2 Youth storm in 1955

MARSHALL, W. L.
1 The age of death 1968
2 The middle kingdom 1971
The first two novels in a trilogy about modern China
YELLOWTHREAD STREET:
1 Yellowthread Street 1975
2 The hatchet man 1976
3 Gelignite 1976
4 Thin air 1977
5 Skulduggery 1979
6 Sci Fi 1981
7 Perfect end 1981
8 War machines 1982
9 The faraway man 1984
10 Roadshow 1985
11 Head first 1986
12 Frogmouth 1987
MANILA BAY MYSTERIES:
1 Manila Bay 1986
2 Whisper 1988

MARSTON, E.
NICHOLAS BRACEWELL:
1 The Queen's Head 1988
2 The merry devils 1989
3 The nine giants 1991
Mysteries set in Elizabethan times

MARTIN, B.
1 Miracle of Carville
2 No one must ever know
N.F. Autobiography

MARTIN, K.
1 Father figures, 1879-1931 1966
2 Editor, 1931-1945 1968
N.F. Autobiography. There are further autobiographical essays in 'Kingsley Martin: portrait and self portrait', ed. Mervyn Jones, 1969

MARTIN, L.
DEB RALSTON;
1 Too sane a murder 1987
2 A conspiracy of strangers 1988
3 Murder at the Blue Owl 1989

MARTIN, M.
1 O rugged land of gold
2 Home in the bear's domain
N.F. Autobiography

MARTIN, R.
1 Gallows wedding 1978
2 The unicorn summer 1984

Not direct sequels, but two of the same characters appear

MARTIN, S.
PROFESSOR CHALLIS SERIES:
1 Twelve girls in a garden 1957
2 The man made of tin 1958
3 The Saracen shadow 1957
4 The myth is murder 1959

MARVIN, J. W.
CROW:
1 The red hills
2 Worse than death
3 Tears of blood
4 The black trail
5 Bodyguard
6 The sisters
7 One-eyed death
8 A good day
Paperback Westerns

MASON, F. VAN W.
AMERICAN WAR OF INDEPENDENCE SERIES:
1 Three harbours (1774-1775) 1938
2 Stars of the sea (1776-1777) 1940
3 Rivers of glory (1778-1779) 1942
4 Eagle in the sky (1780-1781) 1948
Different phases of the war, but not with the same characters
COL. NORTH SERIES:
1 The Vesper service murders
2 The branded spy murders
3 The yellow arrow murders
4 The Budapest parade murders
5 The seven seas murders
6 Sulu sea murders
7 Fort terror murders
8 Shanghi bund murders
9 Washington Legation murders
10 Hong Kong air base murders
11 Singapore exile murders
12 The Cairo garter murders
13 The Bucharest ballerina murders
14 Forgotten fleet mystery
15 Rio Casino intrigue
16 Dardanelles derelict
17 Saigon singer
18 Himalayan assignment
19 Two tickets to Tangiers 1955
20 The gracious lily affair 1958
21 Secret mission to Bangkok 1960
22 Trouble in Burma 1961
23 Zanzibar intrigue 1964
24 Maracaibo mission 1966
25 The deadly orbit mission 1968
***

1 Proud new flags 1954
2 Blue hurricane 1956
3 To whom be glory 1957
(The valiant few)
*Novels of the naval action in the
American Civil War*

MASON, H.
THE SPENCER FAMILY:
1 Fool's gold 1961
2 Our hills cry woe 1963

MASSIE, A.
THE EMPERORS:
1 Augustus 1986
2 Tiberius 1990

MASTERS, A.
MINDER:
1 Minder 1984
2 Minder - back again 1985
3 Minder - yet again 1986
Based on the TV series

MASTERS, J.
THE SAVAGE FAMILY:
1 Coromandel (Jason Savage, 1622-1640) 1955
2 The deceivers (William Savage, 18th century) 1952
3 Night Runners of Bengal (Indian mutiny, 1857. Rodney Savage 1) 1951
4 The lotus and the wind (Robin Savage, Afghan Wars, 1879-1881) 1953
5 Far, far the mountain peak (Peter Savage, 1902-1921) 1957
6 Bhowani Junction (Indian independence, 1945. Rodney Savage II) 1954
7 To the coral strand (Rodney Savage II, 1945-1950) 1962
*The story of British rule in India as
shown in the lives of successive
generations of an English family. The
series was intended to comprise about
30 novels but none have been published
for some years. List above is in
chronological order, not order of
publication, 6 and 7 are direct sequels.*

1 Bugles and a tiger 1959
2 The road past Mandalay 1961
3 Pilgrim son 1972
N.F. Autobiography
LOSS OF EDEN TRILOGY:
1 Now God be thanked 1979
2 Heart of war 1980
3 By the green of the spring 1981

MASTERS, S.
TARGET:
1 The men they once were
2 The bronze heist
Based on the TV series

MASTERTON, G.
1 The Manitou
2 Revenge of the Manitou
Supernatural stories

MASUR, H. Q.
SCOTT JORDAN SERIES:
1 Suddenly a corpse 1950
2 You can't live forever 1951
3 So rich, so lovely and so dead 1953
4 The big money 1955
5 Tall, dark and deadly 1957
6 The last breath 1958 (The last gamble or Murder on Broadway)
7 Send another hearse 1960
8 Bury me deep 1961
9 The name is Jordan 1962
10 Making a killing 1964
11 The legacy lenders 1967

MATHER, B.
ROBINSON FAMILY SERIES:
1 Through the mill
2 Left foot forward

MATHER, BERKELEY
JAMES WAINWRIGHT AND ISWAL REES:
1 The pass beyond Kashmir 1964
2 The springers
3 The break in the line 1970
4 The terminators 1971
*The two do not appear together in all
the novels but are members of the same
organisation*
STAFFORD FAMILY:
1 The pagoda tree 1979
2 The midnight gun 1981
3 Hour of the dog 1982

MATHESON, H.
GEOFFREY BRANSCOMBE:
1 The third force 1960
2 The balance of fear 1961

MATHEW, D.
1 Mango on the Mango tree 1950
2 In Valambrosa 1951
3 Prince of Wales' feathers 1953

MATTHEW, C.
SIMON CRISP:
1 Diary of a somebody 1978

2 Loosely engaged 1980
3 The crisp report 1981
4 Family matters 1986

MAUGHAN, A. M.
1 Young Pitt
2 The King's malady 1978

MAUPIN, A.
1 Tales of the city 1978
2 More tales of the city 1980
3 Further tales of the city 1982
4 Babycakes 1986
5 Significant others 1988
6 Sure of you 1990
First three published as an omnibus vol. in 1989

MAURIAC, C.
LE DALOGUE INTERIEUR:
1 Toutes les femmes sont fatales 1957
2 Le diner en ville 1959
3 La marquise sortit á cinq heures 1961
4 L'angrandissement 1963
Only 2 and 3 have been translated unde the titles 'Dinner in town' and 'The Marquis went out at five', 1966

MAXWELL, G.
1 Ring of bright water 1962
2 The rocks remain 1963
N.F. Autobiography and natural history
1 Raven seek thy brother 1965
2 The white island by J. Lister-Kay 1972
N.F. The story of Kyleakin Island in the West of Scotland. 'The house of Elrig' 1965 is the story of the author's childhood

MAY, J.
THE EXILES:
1 The many coloured land 1985
2 The golden torc 1985
3 The non-born king 1985
4 The adversary 1985
Fantasy
Publ. as 1 vol. 1985 'The Phiocene Companion'

MAYNARD, K.
LIET. LAMB:
1 Lieutenant Lamb 1984
2 First Lieutenant 1985
3 Lamb in command 1986
4 Lamb's mixed fortunes 1987
Novels about the Royal Navy in the 18thC.

MAYNARD, N.
1 This is my street 1971
2 A crumb for every sparrow 1974
SCARLETT SISTERS:
1 Wayward flesh 1974
2 A grief ago 1976

MAYO, J.
CHARLES HOOD SERIES:
1 Hammerhead 1964
2 Let sleeping girls lie 1965
3 Shame, lady 1966
4 Once in a lifetime 1968
5 The man above suspicion 1969
6 Asking for it 1971

MAYOR, A.
LT. JOE GUNTHER:
1 Open season 1990
2 Borderlines 1991

MAYS, S.
1 Reuben's corner 1969
2 Fall out the officers 1970
3 No more soldiering for me 1971
4 Last post 1973
5 The band rats 1976
6 Return to Anglia 1986
N.F. Autobiography

MAZZETTI, L.
1 The sky falls 1963
2 Rage 1964

MEACHAM, E. K.
CAPT. PERCEVAL MEREWETHER:
1 The East Indiaman 1969
2 On the company's service 1972
3 For king and company 1977

MEADE, R.
JOHN ALLISON:
1 Beyond the Danube 1967
2 One round high explosive 1969

MEADOWS, R.
1 The show must go on 1969
2 A bouquet of brides 1970
3 Pretty maids all in a row
4 Slander most savage
Historical novels about the problems of the succession to George III

MECK, G. VON
1 As I remember them 1973
2 The alien years, 1942-1948 1976
N.F. Autobiography

MEEK, M. R. D.
LENNOX KEMP:
1 Hang the consequences 1983
2 The sitting ducks 1984
3 The split second 1985
4 In remembrance of Rose 1986
5 A worm of doubt 1987
6 A mouthful of sand 1988
7 A loose connection 1989
8 This blessed plot 1990

MEEK, V.
1 Cops and robbers
2 The coppering lark
N.F. Autobiography

MEHTA, V.
1 Face to face
2 Walking the Indian streets
N.F. Autobiography
1 Daddiji 1977
2 Mamaji 1979
3 Vedi 1983
4 The ledge between the streams 1984
5 Sound shadows of the New World 1986
6 The stolen light 1989
N.F. Autobiography of an Indian

MELLY, G.
1 Scouse mouse 1984
2 Rum, bum and concertina 1977
3 Owning up 1965
N.F. Autobiography, in chronological order

MELVILLE, A.
LORIMER SAGA:
1 The Lorimer line 1977
2 Lorimer legacy 1979
3 Lorimers at war 1980
4 Lorimers in love 1981
5 The last of the Lorimers 1983
6 Lorimer loyalties 1984
THE HOUSE OF HARDIE:
1 The House of Hardie 1987
2 Grace Hardie 1988
3 The Hardie inheritance 1990

MELVILLE, JAMES
SUPT. OTANI:
1 The wages of Zen 1978
2 The chrysanthemum chain 1980
3 A sort of Samurai 1981
4 The ninth netsuke 1982
5 Sayonara sweet Amaryllis 1983
6 Death of a Diamyo 1984
7 The death ceremony 1985
8 Go gently Gaijin 1986

9 Kimono for a corpse 1987
10 The reluctant ronin 1988
11 A Haiku for Hanae 1989
12 Bogus Buddha 1990

MELVILLE, JENNIE
CHARMIAN DANIELS:
1 Come home and be killed 1962
2 Burning is a substitute for loving 1963
3 Murderer's houses 1964
4 There lies your love 1965
5 Nell alone 1966
6 A different kind of summer 1967
7 A new kind of killer, an old kind of death 1970
8 Murder wears a pretty face 1981
9 Windsor red 1987
10 A cure for dying 1989
11 Witching murder 1990
12 Footsteps in the blood 1990

MELVILLE-ROSS, A.
TRELAWNEY SERIES:
1 Blindfold 1977
2 Two faces of Nemesis 1979
3 Tightrope 1981
HARDING:
1 Shadow 1984
2 Trigger 1983
3 Talon 1983
4 Command 1985
Novels about submarines in WW2.

MEMMI, A.
1 The pillar of salt
2 Strangers

MENZIES, SIR R.
1 Afternoon light 1967
2 Measure of the years 1970
N.F. Autobiography

MEREDITH, R. C.
TIMELINE TRILOGY:
1 At the narrow passage
2 No brother, no friend
3 Vestiges of time
Paperback science fiction

METALIOUS, G.
1 Peyton Place
2 Return to Peyton Place
Continued by Roger Fuller
3 Again Peyton Place
4 Carnival at Peyton Place
5 Pleasures of Peyton Place

METCALFE, T. W.
SANTA ANNA TRILOGY:
1 One night in Santa Anna
2 Life and adventures of Aloysius B.
   Callaghan
3 Fare you well my shining city

MEYER, N.
SHERLOCK HOLMES & DR. WATSON:
(created by Sir A. C. Doyle)
1 The seven per cent solution 1974
2 The West End horror 1976

MEYNELL, L. W.
1 Bluefeather 1928
2 Odds on Bluefeather 1935
HOOKY HEFFERMAN:
1 Death by arrangement 1972
2 The fatal flaw 1973
3 The thirteen trumpeters 1973
4 The fairly innocent little man 1974
5 Don't stop for Hooky Hefferman 1975
6 Hooky and the crock of gold 1975
7 The lost half-hour 1976
8 Hooky gets the wooden spoon 1977
9 Hooky and the villainous chauffer 1979
10 Hooky and the prancing horse 1980
11 Hooky goes to blazes 1981
12 The open door 1984
13 The affair at Barwold 1985
14 Hooky catches a tartar 1986
15 Hooky on loan 1987
16 Hooky hooked 1988

MEYRICK, BETTE
PEMBROKESHIRE FAMILY::
1 Behind the stream 1973
2 Behind the light 1975

MICHAEL, J.
1 Chokra 1957
2 Chokra and Tags 1958

MICHAELS, B.
GREYHAVEN MANOR:
1 Black rainbow 1982
2 Someone in the house 1981

MICHAELS, F.
TEXAS:
1 Texas rich 1988
2 Texas heat 1989

MILES, K.
ALAN SAXON:
1 Bullet hole 1986
2 Double eagle 1987
3 Green murder 1990

4 Flagstick 1991

MILES, R.
EDEN:
1 Bitter legacy 1985
2 Return to Eden 1986

MILLAR, G.
1 Maquis
2 Horned pigeon
N.F. Autobiography
***
1 Isobel and the sea
2 A white boat from England
N.F. Travel

MILLAR, M.
TOM ARAGON:
1 Ask for me tomorrow 1976
2 The murder of Miranda 1979
3 Mermaid 1982

MILLER, H.
THE MACBAIN FAMILY:
1 The open city 1973
2 Kingpin 1974

MILLER, HUGH
DISTRICT NURSE:
1 The District Nurse 1986
2 Snow on the wind
   Based on the TV series.
EASTENDERS:
1 Home fires burning 1986
2 Swings and roundabouts 1986
3 Good intentions 1986
4 The flower of Albert Square 1986
5 Blind spots 1986
6 Hopes and horizons 1987
7 The baffled heart 1987
8 Growing wild 1987
9 A place in life 1988
10 A single man 1988
11 Taking chances 1988
12 Elbow room 1988
   Novels about the early lives of
   characters in the TV series.
DET. INSPECTOR MIKE FLETCHER:
1 Echo of justice 1990
2 Skin deep 1991

MILLER, J.
CALLAGHAN BROTHERS:
1 Gone to Texas 1984
2 War clouds 1984
3 Comanche trail 1988
4 Riding shotgun 1988

MILLIGAN, S.

1 Adolph Hitler: my part in his downfall 1971
2 Rommel! Gunner who? 1973
3 Monty: his part in my victory 1976
4 Mussolini: his part in my downfall 1978
5 Where have all the bullets gone? 1985
6 Goodbye soldier 1986
N.F. Humorous war memoirs.

MILLIN, S. G.

1 The dark river 1920
2 Middle class 1921
3 Adam's rest 1922
4 The Jordans 1923

★★★

1 The night is long 1941
2 World blackout 1944
3 The reeling earth 1945
4 The pit of the abyss 1946
5 The sound of the trumpet 1947
6 Fire out of heaven 1948
7 The seven thunders 1948
8 Measure of my days 1955
N.F. Diary of World War II.

MILLS, A. R.

1 The Victorian girls 1966
2 The Halls of Ravenswood 1967
3 Two Victorian ladies 1969
N.F. Biography of Emily and Ellen Hall. No. 1 was by O. A. Sherrard, and ed. by A. R. Mills.

MILLS, O.

SUPERINTENDENT ALCOCK SERIES:
1 Misguided missile
2 No match for the law
3 The case of the flying fifteen
4 Unlucky break
5 Stairway to murder 1960

MILNE. C.

1 The enchanted places
2 The path through the trees
3 The hollow hill 1982
N.F. Autobiography of the original Christopher Robin.

MILNE, J.

JIMMY JENNER:
1 Dead birds 1986
2 Shadow play 1987
3 Daddy's girl 1988

MILNE, S.

DET. SERGEANT STEYTLER:

1 The hammer of justice 1963
2 False witness 1964

MILSTED, D.

1 The chronicles of Craigfieth 1988
2 Market forces 1989

MINTON, M.

1 Yesterday's road 1986
2 The marriage bowl 1987
3 The weeping doves 1987
Novels about a Midlands family.

MISHIMA, YUKIO

THE SEA OF FERTILITY:
1 Spring snow 1971
2 Runaway horses 1973
3 The temple of dawn 1974
4 The decay of the angel 1975

MITCHELL, A.

1 Harley Street hypnotist
2 Harley Street psychiatrist
N.F. Autobiography

MITCHELL, G.

DAME BEATRICE BRADLEY:
1 Speedy death 1929
2 Mystery of a butcher's shop
3 The longer bodies
4 The Saltmarsh murders
5 Death at the opera
6 The devil at Saxon Wall
7 Dead men's Morris 1936
8 Come away death 1937
9 St. Peter's finger 1938
10 Printer's error 1939
11 Brazen tongue 1940
12 Hangman's curfew 1940
13 When last I died 1941
14 The greenstone griffins 1983
15 Laurels are poison 1942
16 The worsted viper 1942
17 Sunset over Soho 1943
18 My father sleeps 1944
19 The rising of the moon 1945
20 Here comes a chopper 1946
21 Death and the maiden 1947
22 The dancing druids 1948
23 Tom Brown's body 1949
24 Groaning spinney 1950
25 The devil's elbow 1951
26 The echoing strangers 1952
27 Merlin's furlong 1953
28 Faintly speaking 1954
29 Watson's choice 1955
30 Twelve horses and the hangman's noose 1956

31 The twentythird man 1957
32 Spotted hemlock 1958
33 The man who grew tomatoes 1959
34 Say it with flowers 1960
35 The nodding canaries 1961
36 My bones will keep 1962
37 Adders on the heath 1963
38 Death of a delft blue 1964
39 Pageant of murder 1965
40 The croaking raven 1966
41 Skeleton island 1966
42 Three quick and five dead 1968
43 Dance to your daddy 1969
44 Gory dew 1970
45 Lament for Leto 1971
46 A hearse on Mayday 1972
47 The murder of busy Lizzie 1973
48 A javelin for Jonah 1973
49 Winking at the brim 1974
50 Convent on styx 1975
51 Late, late in the evening 1976
52 Fault in the structure 1977
53 Noonday and night 1977
54 Wraiths and changelings 1978
55 Mingled with venom 1978
56 Nest of vipers 1979
57 The mudflats of the dead 1979
58 Uncoffined clay 1980
59 The whispering knights 1980
60 The death-cap dancers 1981
61 Here lies Gloria Mundy 1982
62 Death of a burrowing mole 1982
63 Cold, lone and still 1983
64 The hangman's noose 1983
65 No winding sheet 1984
66 The Crozier pharaohs 1984
*Dame Beatrice is assisted by Laura
Gavin after 14.*

MITCHELL, I. L., see **GIBBON, L. G.**
pseud.

MITCHELL, J.
CALLAN SERIES:
1 A magnum for Schneider 1969
2 Venus in plastic 1970
3 Red file for Callan 1971
4 Russian roulette 1973
5 Death and bright water 1974
WHEN THE BOAT COMES IN:
1 When the boat comes in 1976
2 The hungry years 1976
3 Upward and onward 1977
JOE CAVE:
1 Dead Ernest 1986
2 KGB kill 1987
3 Dying day 1988

RON HOGGET:
1 Sometimes you could die 1985
2 Dead Ernest 1986

MITCHELL, S.
BROCK DEVLIN SERIES:
1 Some dames play rough 1963
2 Sables spell trouble 1963
3 Deadly persuasion 1964
4 The lovely shroud 1965
5 Come sweet death 1965
6 Double bluff 1966
7 A knife-edged thing 1969
8 You'll never get to heaven 1971
9 Haven for the damned 1971
10 Rage in Babylon 1972
11 The girl in the wet look bikini 1973
12 Dead on arrival 1974
13 Nice guys don't win 1974
14 Over my dead body 1974
15 Death's busy crossroads 1975
16 Obsession 1976

MITCHINSON, N.
1 Small talk 1973
2 All change here 1975
3 You may well ask 1981
N.F. Autobiography

MITFORD, N.
1 The pursuit of love 1945
2 Love in a cold climate 1949
*These are parallel stories rather than
sequels. The narrator and many of the
characters are the same, but the central
characters differ.*
3 Don't tell Alfred 1960
*In this the narrator of 1 and 2 becomes
the principal character.
'The blessing' is not part of the series
but many of its characters appear again
in no. 3. Readers of the novels should
also read 'Hons and rebels' by Jessica
Mitford, which gives the factual
background to many of the characters
and situations.*
1 The ladies of Alderley 1966
2 The Stanleys of Alderley 1968
*N.F. 19th century letters, edited by
Nancy Mitford.*

MITTELHOLZER, E.
A SERIES OF NOVELS ON COLONIAL LIFE
IN THE WEST INDIES:
1 Children of Kaywana
2 Kaywana heritage
3 Kaywana blood 1957
4 Kaywana stock 1958

*1 and 3 and 4 are direct sequels, telling
the story of the Van Groemwegel family.*
LEITMOTIVE TRILOGY:
1 Latticed echoes
2 Thunder returning 1961
The author died before completion.

MOBERG, V.
THE EARTH IS OURS:
1 Memory of youth
2 Sleepless nights
3 The earth is ours
***
1 The emigrants 1955
2 Unto a good land 1959
3 The last letter home
*A trilogy on the struggles of a group of
Swedish emigrants to U.S.A. in the
19th century.;*

MOFFAT, G.
1 Space below my feet 1961
2 On my home ground 1968
3 Survival count 1972
*N.F. Autobiography and
mountaineering.*
MISS PINK:
1 Lady with a cool eye 1973
2 Deviant death 1974
3 The corpse road 1975
4 Miss Pink at the edge of the world 1975
5 Hard option 1976
6 Over the sea to death 1976
7 A short time to live 1977
8 Persons unknown 1978
9 Die like a dog 1982
10 Last chance country 1983
11 Grizzly trail 1984
12 Snare 1987
13 The stone hawk 1989
14 Rage 1990
15 Raptor zone 1990

MOLE, W.
CASSON DUKER SERIES:
1 The Hammersmith maggot
2 Goodbye is not worthwhile 1956
3 Skin trap 1957

MOLL, L.
1 Seidman and son 1958
2 Mr. Seidman and the geisha 1963

MONACO, R.
ARTHURIAN LEGEND:
1 The Grail war
2 Parsifal

3 The final quest
Paperback

MONIG, C.
BRIAN BRETT SERIES:
1 The burned man 1957
2 Abra-Cadaver 1958
3 Once upon a crime 1960
4 The lonely graves 1961

MONSARRAT, N.
1 The tribe that lost its head 1956
2 Richer than all his tribe 1968
LIFE IS A FOUR LETTER WORD:
1 Breaking in 1966
2 Breaking out 1970
N.F. Autobiography
THE MASTER MARINER:
1 Running proud 1978
2 Darken ship 1980

MONTROSE, G.
ANGEL BROWN SERIES:
1 Angel of no mercy
2 Angel of death
3 Where Angels tread
4 Angel abroad
5 Angel of vengeance
6 Angel in Paradise 1968
7 Send for Angel 1969
8 Ask for Angel 1970
9 Angel and the Nero 1971
10 Fanfare for Angel 1972
11 Angel at arms 1972
12 Angel and the red admiral 1973

MOODY, L.
TUDOR TRILOGY:
1 The dark-eyed client 1974
2 The golden princess 1976
3 The greatest Tudor 1977

MOODY, R.
1 Little britches
2 Man of the family
3 The home ranch
N.F. Autobiography

MOODY, S.
PENNY WANAWAKE:
1 Penny black 1983
2 Penny dreadful 1984
3 Penny post 1985
4 Penny royal 1986
5 Penny wise 1988
6 Penny pinching 1989
7 Penny saving 1991

MOORCOCK, M.

1 Byzantium endures 1981
2 Laughter at Carthage 1986
KARL GLOGAUER:
1 Behold the man 1970
2 Breakfast in the ruins 1972
MICHAEL KANE SERIES:
1 The city of the beast
2 The lord of the spiders
3 Masters of the pit
*Reprinted in one volume entitled
'Warrior of Mars' 1981.*
DANCERS AT THE END OF TIME:
1 Alien heat 1974
2 The hollow lands 1975
3 The end of all songs 1976
4 Legends from the end of time 1976
5 The transformation of Miss Mavis
Ming 1977
CORUM:
1 The Knight of the swords 1971
2 The Queen of the swords 1971
3 The King of the swords 1972
4 The bull and the spear 1973
5 The oak and the ram 1973
6 The sword and the stallion 1974
ELRIC:
1 Elric of Melnibone 1972
2 Sailor on the seas of fate 1976
3 The weird of the white wolf
4 The vanishing tower
5 The bane of the black sword
6 Stormbringer
7 Elric at the end of time: short stories
8 The fortress of the pearl 1989
9 The revenge of the rose 1991
HAWKMOON:
1 The jewel in the skull 1973
2 The mad god's amulet 1973
3 The sword of dawn 1973
4 The runestaff 1974
5 Count Brass
6 The champion of Garathorm
7 The quest for Tanelorn
The last three are in paperback
JERRY CORNELIUS:
1 The final programme 1969
2 A cure for cancer 1970
3 The English assassin 1972
4 The condition of Muzak 1976
5 The life and times of Jerry Cornelius
1975
6 The entropy tango 1981
*Jerry Cornelius also appears in 'Una
Persson and Catherine Cornelius in the
20th century', and in a short story in
'The opium general', 1984*

JOHN DAKER, ETERNAL CHAMPION OF
EREKOSE:
1 The eternal champion 1970
2 Phoenix in Obsidian 1970
3 The dragon in the sword 1987
THE NOMAD OF TIME:
1 War lord of the air 1973
2 The land leviathan 1974
3 The steel Tsar 1981
VON BEK FAMILY:
1 The war hound and the world's pain
1982
2 The city in the autumn stars 1986

MOORE, D.

1 Far eastern agent
2 We live in Singapore 1953
N.F. Autobiography

MOORE, G.

1 Am I too loud? 1962
2 Farewell recital 1978
3 Furthermoore 1983
*N.F. Autobiography of the celebrated
accompanist*

MOORE, M.

DET. INSPECTOR RICHARD BAXTER:
1 Forests of the night 1988
2 Dangerous conceits 1989
3 Murder in good measure 1990
4 Fringe ending 1991

MOORE, R.

1 The French connection 1971
2 The fifth estate 1973
3 French connection II 1976
4 The terminal connection 1978
5 The New York connection 1979
PULSAR:
1 The London connection 1980
2 The Italian connection 1981

MORAY, H.

1 Untamed 1966
2 The savage earth 1968
3 Footsteps in the night 1975
4 To make a light 1977
5 Beacon of gold 1978
★★★
1 The harvest burns 1972
2 Blood on the wind 1973
★★★
1 I, Roxana 1969
2 Roxana and Alexander 1970
3 A son for Roxana 1971
A trilogy about Alexander the Great

and Roxana, wife of Darius.
DEAN BROTHERS:
1 Clear to sail 1974
2 The Ruby fleet 1976
HENRI, LADY RHONDA:
1 Four winds 1983
2 Before the dawn 1984

MORGAN, C.
LILY WALTERS:
1 Lily of the valleys 1989
2 Lily among thorns 1990
3 Comfort me with apples 1991

MORGAN, D.
RALPH DE GIRET:
1 The second son 1980
2 Kingmaker's Knight 1981
3 Sons and roses 1981
A trilogy set in 15th century England

MORGAN, G.
1 A small piece of Paradise 1966
2 A touch of magic 1968
3 A window of sky 1969
A trilogy about a young orphaned boy searching for a place in the world that seems to reject him

MORICE, A.
TESSA CRICHTON:
1 Death in the grand manor 1970
2 Murder in married life 1970
3 Death of a gay dog 1971
4 Murder on French leave 1972
5 Death and the dutiful daughter 1973
6 Death of a heavenly twin 1974
7 Killing with kindness 1974
8 Nursery tea and poison 1975
9 Death of a wedding guest 1976
10 Murder in mimicry 1977
11 Scared to death 1977
12 Murder by proxy 1978
13 Murder in outline 1978
14 Death in the round 1980
15 The men in her death 1981
16 Hollow vengeance 1982
17 Sleep of death 1982
18 Murder post-dated 1983
19 Getting away with murder 1984
20 Dead on cue 1985
21 Publish and be killed 1986
22 Treble exposure 1987
23 Design for dying 1988
24 Fatal charm 1988
25 Planning for murder 1989
The main character is the wife of Chief Insp. Price

MORLAND, N.
MRS. PYM SERIES:
1 The moon murders 1935
2 The phantom gunman 1935
3 Street of the leopard 1936
4 Clue of the bricklayer's aunt 1936
5 Clue in the mirror 1937
6 Case without a clue 1938
7 A rope for the hanging 1938
8 A knife for the killer 1938 (Murder at Radio City)
9 A gun for a god 1940
10 The clue of the careless hangman 1940
11 A corpse on the flying trapeze 1941
12 A coffin for the body 1943
13 Dressed to kill 1947
14 Lady had a gun 1951
15 Call him early for the murder 1952
16 Sing a song of cyanide 1953
17 Look in any doorway 1957
18 Death and the golden boy 1958
19 A bullet for Midas 1958
20 So quiet a death 1960
21 The concrete maze 1960
22 The dear dead girls 1961
23 Mrs. Pym and other stories 1976
ANDY MCMURDO SERIES:
1 She didn't like dying 1948
2 No coupons for a shroud 1949
3 Two dead charwomen 1950
4 The corpse was no lady 1950
5 Blood on the stars
6 He hanged his mother on Monday 1951
7 The moon was made for murder 1953
RORY LUCCAN SERIES:
1 Death when she wakes
2 A girl died singing

MORRELL, D.
ISRAEL SAUL GRISMAN:
1 The Brotherhood of the Rose 1985
2 The Fraternity of the Stone 1986
3 The League of Night and Fog 1978
RAMBO:
1 First blood 1975
2 First blood II
3 Rambo III
2 and 3 based on the films which arose from 1.

MORELL, LADY O.
1 Ottoline 1963
2 Ottoline at Garsington 1974
N.F. Memoirs of a famous literary hostess and patron of the arts

MORRIS, E.
1 Flowers of Hiroshima 1962

2 Seeds of Hiroshima 1965

MORRIS, G. H.
THE BRIGHTSIDE TRILOGY:
1 Doves and silk handkerchiefs 1986
2 Grandmother, grandmother, come and
   see 1989
3 The Brightside dinosaur 1991

MORRIS, I. J.
1 A kingdom for a song 1951
2 The witch's son 1954

MORRIS, J.
THE KERRION SAGA:
1 Dream dancer
2 Cruiser dreams
   Paperback fantasy

MORRIS, JAN
1 Traveller from Tokyo 1943
2 The Phoenix cup 1947
   N.F. Japan before and after the war
   ***
1 Heaven's command: an imperial
   progress 1973
2 Pax Britannica 1972
3 Farewell the trumpets 1978
   N.F. A trilogy on the British Empire

MORRIS, JOHN
COMMISSIONER ROBIN MCKAY OF
JAMAICA:
1 Fever grass 1967
2 The Candywine development 1970

MORRIS, W.
THE SCANLON FAMILY:
1 The field of vision 1966
2 Ceremony in Lone Tree 1960

MORTIMER, C.
1 Father Goose
2 Mediterraneo
   *Not strictly sequels, but some
   characters reappear*

MORTIMER, J.
RUMPOLE:
1 Rumpole of the Bailey
2 The trials of Rumpole
3 Regina v Rumpole 1981
4 Rumpole and the golden thread 1983
5 Rumpole a la carte 1990
   *1 & 2 published in hardback as
   'Rumpole' 1980*

THE RAPSTONE CHRONICLES:
1 Paradise postponed 1987
2 Titmuss regained 1990

MORTON, A., *pseud.*, *see* CREASEY, J.

MORWOOD, P.
ALDRIC TALVARIN:
1 The horse lord 1984
2 The demon lord 1985
3 The dragon lord 1987
4 The warlord's domain 1989
   Fantasy

MOSCO, M.
1 Almonds and raisins 1979
2 Scattered seed 1980
3 Children's children 1981
4 Out of the ashes 1989
5 New beginnings 1991
   *Novels about a Jewish family in
   Manchester*
ALISON PLANTAINE:
1 Between two worlds 1983
2 A sense of place 1984
3 The price of fame 1985

1 The waiting game 1987
2 After the dream 1988

MOSLEY, N.
1 Catastrophe practice 1979
2 Imago bird 1980
3 Serpent 1981
4 Judith 1986
5 Hopeful monsters 1990

MOSS, W. S.
1 Ill met by moonlight
2 War of shadows
   *N.F. World War II. Rendel's
   'Appointment in Crete' gives another
   angle on 1.*

MOTION, A.
FRANCIS MAYNE:
1 The pale companion 1989
2 Famous for the creatures 1991

MOTLEY, M. *pseud.*
1 Devils in waiting 1959
2 Morning glory 1961
3 Home to Nurmidia 1963
   *N.F. Autobiography. 2 describes her
   early life before the episode in 1.*

MOTLEY, W.
1 Knock on any door

2 Let no man write my epitaph 1959
The sequel is about the son of Romano who dies a the end of 1. Scene is slum area of Chicago.

MOTTRAM, R. H.
LIFE OBSERVED:
1 The window seat 1954
2 Another window seat 1956
N.F. Autobiography

MOWAT, F.
1 The people of the deer
2 The desperate people

MOXON, O.
THE MONSOON TRILOGY:
1 Bitter monsoon
2 The last monsoon
3 After the monsoon 1957
N.F. A trilogy on the war in Burma, particularly the fighting around Imphal.

MOYES, P.
INSPECTOR TIBBETT SERIES:
1 Dead men don't ski 1960
2 The sunken sailor 1961 (Down among the dead men)
3 Death on the agenda 1962
4 Murder á la môde 1963
5 Falling star 1964
6 Johnny underground 1965
7 Murder fantastical 1967
8 Death and the Dutch uncle 1968
9 Who saw him die? 1970
10 Season of snows and sons 1971
11 The black widower 1975
12 To kill a coconut 1976
13 Who is Simon Warwick? 1978
14 Angel death 1980
15 A six-letter word for death 1983
16 Night ferry to death 1985
17 Black girl, white girl 1990

MUGGERIDGE, M.
CHRONICLES OF WASTED TIME:
1 The green stick 1972
2 The infernal grove 1973
N.F. Autobiography

MUIR, J. A.
BREED:
1 Lonely hunt
2 Silent kill
3 Cry for vengeance
4 Death stage
5 Gallows tree

6 Judas goat
7 Time of the wolf
8 Blood debt
9 Bloodstock
10 Outlaws road
11 The dying and the damned
12 Killer's moon
13 Bounty hunter
14 Spanish gold
15 Slaughter time
16 Bad habits
17 The day of the gun
18 The colour of death
19 Blood valley
20 Gundown
Paperback Westerns

MUIR, T.
ROGER CRAMMOND SERIES:
1 Death in reserve 1948
2 Death in the trooper
3 Death in the lock 1949
4 Death without question 1951
5 Death below zero
6 Death under Virgo 1952
7 Death on the agenda 1953
8 Death in Soundings 1955

MULLALLY, F.
BOB SULLIVAN SERIES:
1 Danse macabre 1967
2 Munich involvement 1968
3 The Malta conspiracy 1971

MULLER, M.
ANNA AND JOHAN DE VILLIERS:
1 Green peaches ripen 1969
2 Cloud across the moon 1970
3 Stones of Africa 1972
SHARON MCCONE:
1 Edwin of the iron shoes 1981
2 Ask the cards a question 1983
3 The Cheshire Cat's eye 1984
4 Games to keep the dark away 1985

MUNNINGS, SIR A.
1 An artist's life 1950
2 Second burst 1951
3 The finish 1953
N.F. Autobiography

MUNRO, H.
CLUTHA SERIES:
1 Who told Clutha?
2 Clutha plays a hunch 1959
3 A clue for Clutha 1960
4 Clutha and the lady
5 Get Clutha 1974

6 Evil innocence 1976
7 The brain robbers 1977

MUNRO, J.
JOHN CRAIG SERIES:
1 The man who sold death 1964
2 Die rich, die happy 1965
3 The money that money can't buy 1967
4 The innocent bystanders 1968

MURARI, T. N.
KIM:
1 The Imperial agent 1987
2 The last victory 1988
Sequels to Kiplings "Kim"

MURDOCH, M. S.
THE MARTIAN WARS:
1 Rebellion 2456
2 Hammer of Mars
3 Armageddon off Vesta
Paperback science fiction

MURPHY, D.
1 Full tilt 1964
2 Tibetan freehold 1966
N.F. Travel. Journey to India by Bicycle and later voluntary work in Tibet.

MURPHY, D. J.
1 Winsome for winners
2 More winners for Winsome

MURPHY, E.
1 The land is bright 1989
2 To give and to take 1990
3 There is a Season 1991

MURPHY, H.
REUBEN FROST:
1 Murder for lunch 1986
2 Murder takes a partner 1987
3 Murders and acquisitions 1988
4 Murder keeps a secret 1989
5 Murder times two 1990
6 Murder saves face 1991

MURRAY, MARY
1 Escape 1965
2 Hunted 1967
N.F. Autobiography and war experiences of an Australian woman

MURRAY, MAX
CORPSE SERIES:
1 The queen and the corpse
2 Voice of the corpse
3 King and the corpse

4 No duty on a corpse
5 Neat little corpse
6 Right hon. corpse
7 Good luck to the corpse
8 Doctor and the corpse
9 The sunshine corpse
10 Royal bed for a corpse
11 Breakfast with a corpse
12 Wait for a corpse

MURRAY, S.
DET. INSPECTOR ALEC STAINTON:
1 A cool killing 1988
2 The noose of time 1989
3 Salty waters 1989
4 Fetch out no shroud 1990
5 Fatal opinions 1991

MURRAY, W. H.
JOHN TAUNT SERIES:
1 Five frontiers 1959
2 The spurs of Troodos

MUSIL, R.
MAN WITHOUT QUALITIES:
1 A sort of introduction 1953
2 The like of it now happens 1954
3 Into the millennium 1960 (The criminals)
A fourth volume will complete the translation

MUSKETT, N.
1 A crown of willow
2 The high fence

MUSPRATT, S.
1 My south sea island
2 Wild oats
3 Journey home
4 Fire of youth
N.F. Autobiography

MUSSELMAN, M. M.
1 I married a redhead
2 Second honeymoon
N.F. Autobiography

MYERS, A.
AUGUSTE DIDIER:
1 Murder in Pug's Parlour 1986
2 Murder in the limelight 1987
3 Murder at Plum's 1989
4 Murder at the masque 1991

MYERS, P.
MARK HOLLAND:
1 Deadly variations 1985

2 Deadly cadenza 1986
3 Deadly aria 1987
4 Deadly sonata 1987
5 Deadly score 1988
6 Deadly crescendo 1989
Thrillers about a musician

MYKLE, A.
1 Lasso round the moon 1959
2 The song of the red ruby 1961
The story of a young Norwegian schoolmaster

MYRIVILLIS, S.
1 The mermaid madonna
2 The schoolmistress with the golden eyes

NABB, M.
MARSHAL GUARNACCIA:
1 Death of an Englishman 1981
2 Death of a Dutchman 1982
3 Death in Springtime 1983
4 Death in Autumn 1984
5 The Marshal and the murderer 1987
6 The Marshal and the madwoman 1988
7 The Marshal's own case 1990
Detective stories set in Florence

NAJAFI, M.
1 Persia is my heart 1956
2 Reveille for a Persian village 1959
3 A wall and three willows 1961
N.F. Autobiography

NAPIER, E.
1 Youth is a blunder
2 Winter is in July
N.F. Autobiography

NAPIER, P.
1 The sword dance 1970
2 A difficult country 1972
3 Revolution and the Napier brothers 1973
N.F. History of the Napier family

NARAYAN, R. K.
MALGUDI SERIES:
1 Waiting for the Mahatma 1955
2 The financial expert 1952
3 Mr. Sampath 1949
4 The English teacher 1945
5 The dark room 1938
6 Swami and friends 1935
7 The guide 1958
8 The man-eater of Malgudi 1961
9 The sweet vendor 1967

10 A horse and two goats 1970
11 Malgudi days 1982
12 The tiger of Malgudi 1983
13 Under the banyan tree 1985
14 The talkative man 1986
15 The world of Nagaraj 1990
Novels and short stories about Malgudi, an imaginary town in South India

NASH, P.
GRASS:
1 Grass 1982
2 Grass's fancy 1982
3 Coup de Grass 1983
4 Grass in idleness 1983
5 Wayward seeds of Grass 1983
6 Grass and supergrass 1984
7 Grass makes hay 1985
8 Sheep grass 1986
Thrillers about a police informer

NASH, S.
INSPECTOR MONTERO AND ADAM LUDLOW:
1 Dead of a counterplot 1961
2 Killed by scandal 1962
3 Death over deep water 1962
4 Dead woman's ditch 1964
5 Unhallowed murder 1965

NATHANSON, E. M.
1 The dirty dozen 1966
2 A dirty distant war 1988

NAUGHTON, B.
1 Alfie 1968
2 Alfie darling 1970
★★★
1 On the pig's back 1987
2 Saintly Billy 1988
N.F. Autobiography

NAYLOR, G.
RED DWARF:
1 Red Dwarf 1989
2 Better than life 1990
Based on the TV series

NEAME, A.
1 The adventures of Maud Noakes 1963
2 Maud Noakes, guerilla 1965

NEAVE, A.
1 They have their exits 1964
2 Saturday at M19 1969
N.F. Escape from German prison camps

NEEL, J.
DET. CHIEF INSPECTOR JOHN MCLEISH:
1 Death's bright angel 1988
2 Death on site 1989
3 Death of a partner 1991

NEILL, R.
SIR HARRY BURNABY:
1 Crown and mitre 1971
2 The golden days 1972
3 Lillibulero 1975

NEPEAN, E. M.
TRILOGY ON CHARLES II:
1 Lanterns of horn
2 Ivory and apes
3 My two kings
Not published in this order

NEUMAN, F.
CAPT. REDDER, PSYCHIATRIST:
1 The seclusion room 1982
2 Manoeuvres 1984

NEVILLE, M.
INSPECTOR GROGAN SERIES:
1 Murder and gardenias 1946
2 Murder in Rockwater 1949
3 Murder of a nymph 1949
4 Murder in a blue moon 1949
5 Murder before marriage 1951
6 Come thick night 1951
7 The seagull said murder 1952
8 Murder of the well-beloved 1953
9 Murder of Olympia 1958
10 Murder to welcome her 1959
11 Sweet night to murder her 1959
12 Confession of murder 1960
13 Murder beyond the pale 1961
14 My bad boy 1964
15 Ladies in the dark 1965
16 Head on the sill 1966

NEVINSON, H. W.
1 Changes and chances
2 More changes and chances
3 Last changes and chances
N.F. Autobiography

NEW AVENGERS
1 House of Cards *by* P. Cave
2 Eagle's nest *by* J. Carter
3 Fighting men *by* J. Cartwright
4 To catch a rat *by* W. Harris
5 The last of the Cybernauts *by* P. Cave
6 Hostage *by* P. Cave

NEWBERRY, E.
1 Parson's daughter
2 Parson's daughter again
N.F. Autobiography

NEWBY, P. H.
1 A picnic at Sakkara 1955
2 Revolution and roses 1957
3 A guest and his going 1959
Three novels set in Egypt and London.
Not strictly sequels, but characters in 1
reappear in 2 and 3
HESKETH AND JANE OLIPHANT:
1 A step to silence
2 The retreat

NEWMAN, A.
1 A bouquet of barbed wire 1969
2 Another bouquet... 1984
FELIX CRAMER:
1 A sense of guilt 1988
2 A gift of poison 1991

NEWMAN, B.
PONTIVY SERIES:
1 Maginot line murder 1939
2 Death to the spy 1939
3 Siegfried spy 1940
4 Death to the fifth column
5 Secret weapon
6 Black market
7 Second front - first spy
8 Spy catchers 1945
9 Spy in the brown derby 1945
10 Dead man murder 1946
11 Moscow murder 1948
12 Flying saucer
13 The double menace 1954
See also **BETTERIDGE, D.** *pseud.*

NEWMAN, G. F.
1 Sir, you bastard 1971
2 You nice bastard 1972
3 You flash bastard 1977
LAW AND ORDER TRILOGY: 1981
1 A prisoner's tale
2 A detective's tale
3 A villain's tale
JACK BENTHAM:
1 Set a thief 1985
2 The testing ground 1987

NEWMAN, S.
ARTHURIAN SERIES:
1 Guinevere 1985
2 The chessboard queen 1985
3 Guinevere evermore 1986
Fantasies, based on Arthurian legend

NEWTON, W.
JOEY BINNS:
1 Someone has to take the fall 1979
2 The smell of money 1980
3 The set-up 1981
4 The Rio contract 1982

NICHOLAS, J.
BILL ANSTRUTHER SERIES:
1 Widow's peak 1947
2 Asbestos mask 1948
3 Whispering steel
4 Deirdre

NICHOLLS, W. B.
HENRY VIII:
1 A wonder for wise men
2 Torryzany

NICHOLS, B.
1 25 1926
2 All I could never be 1949
★★★
1 Down the garden path 1932
2 Thatched roof 1933
3 Village in a valley 1934
★★★
1 Merry Hall 1951
2 Laughter on the stairs 1953
3 Sunlight on the lawn 1956
4 The unforgiving minute 1978
*All these books are autobiographical,
but the author agrees with the above
division. A condensed version of the
Merry Hall trilogy was published in
1972 as 'The gift of a home'*
MR. GREEN SERIES:
1 No man's street 1954
2 Moonflower 1955
3 Death to slow music 1956
4 The rich die hard 1958
5 Murder by request 1959

NICOL, J.
1 Hotel Regina 1967
2 Home is the hotel 1976
3 Bertioni's Hotel 1984

NICOLE, C.
AMYOT FAMILY:
1 Amyot's cat 1963
2 Blood Amyot 1964
3 The Amyot crime 1965
*A series of novels on the history of the
Bahamas*
HILTON FAMILY:
1 Caribee 1974

2 The devil's own 1975
3 Mistress of darkness 1976
4 Black dawn 1977
5 Sunset 1978
HAGGARD:
1 Haggard 1980
2 Haggard's inheritance 1981
3 The young Haggards 1982
ANDERSON LINE:
1 The seas of fortune 1984
2 The rivals 1985
BLACK MAJESTY:
1 Seeds of rebellion 1984
2 Wild harvest 1985
*Novels about Henri Christophe and
Haiti*
CHINA TRILOGY:
1 The crimson pagoda 1984
2 The scarlet princess 1985
3 Red dawn 1985
JAPANESE TRILOGY:
1 The sun rises 1985
2 The sun and the dragon 1986
3 The sun on fire 1987
KENYAN TRILOGY:
1 The high country 1988
2 The happy valley 1989
MCGANN FAMILY:
1 Old Glory 1986
2 The sea and the sand 1986
3 Iron ships, iron men 1987
4 Wind of destiny 1987
5 Raging sea, searing sky 1988
6 The passion and the glory 1988
ROYAL WESTERN DRAGOON GUARDS:
1 The Regiment 1988
2 The Command 1989
3 The triumph 1989
SINGAPORE:
1 Pearl of the Orient 1988
2 Dragon's blood 1989
3 Dark sun 1990
RICHARD BRYANT:
1 Sword of fortune 1990
2 Sword of Empire 1991

NICOLSON, R.
THE LIFE OF MRS. ROSS:
1 Mrs. Ross 1965
2 A flight of steps 1966

NIELSON, H.
SIMON DRAKE SERIES:
1 After midnight 1967
2 A killer in the street 1967
3 Darkest hour 1969
4 The severed key 1973
5 The brink of murder 1976

NILES, D.
FORGOTTEN REALMS:
1 Darkwalker on Moonshae
2 Black wizards
3 Darkwell
Paperback fantasy

NIN, A.
1 ladders to fire 1946
2 Children of the albatross 1947
3 The four chambered heart 1959
4 Spy in the house of love 1954
5 Seduction of the minotaur 1961
*Published under the general title,
'Cities of the interior', No. 5 in the
U.S.A. edition is entitled 'Solar
barque'.*

NIVEN, D.
1 The moon's a balloon 1971
2 Bring on the empty horses 1975
N.F. Autobiography

NIVEN, L.
1 Ringworld 1971
2 Ringworld engineers 1980
***
1 The integral trees 1984
2 The smoke ring 1987
Science fiction

NIXON, A.
LARRY MAVER:
1 Item 7 1970
2 The attack on Vienna 1971

NOBBS, D.
1 The death of Reginald Perrin 1975
2 The return of Reginald Perrin 1977
3 The better world of Reginald Perrin
1978
HENRY PRATT:
1 Second from last in the sack race 1983
2 Pratt of the Argus 1988
*Tragi-comic novels about a young
journalist*
1 A bit of a "do" 1989
2 Fair do's 1990

NOLAN, F.
A CALL TO ARMS:
1 A promise of glory 1983
2 Blind duty 1984
Novels about the American Civil War
LT. PETROSINO:
1 No place to be a cop 1974
2 Kill Petrosino! 1975

THE GARRETT DOSSIER:
1 Sweet Sister Death 1989
2 Alert State Black 1990
3 Designated assassin 1990

NOLAN, W. F.
1 Logan's run
2 Logan's world
3 Logan's search
Science fiction

NORMAN, B.
PAUL BAKER:
1 A matter of mandrake 1967
2 Hounds of Sparta 1968

NORMAN, D.
HENRY II:
1 The morning gift 1985
2 Fitzempress' law 1980
3 King of the last days 1981
Listed in order of reading

NORMAN, F.
1 Bang to rights
2 Stand on me 1960
3 The Guntz 1962
4 Banana boy 1964
N.F. Autobiography
ED NELSON:
1 The dead butler caper 1978
2 Too many crooks spoil the caper 1979
3 The Baskerville caper 1982

NORMAN, J.
GOR:
1 Tarnsman of Gor
2 Outlaw of Gor
3 Priest kings of Gor
4 Nomads of Gor
5 Assassin of Gor
6 Raiders of Gor
7 Captive of Gor
8 Hunters of Gor
9 Marauders of Gor
10 Tribesmen of Gor
11 Slave girl of Gor
12 Beasts of Gor
13 Explorers of Gor
14 Fighting slave of Gor
15 Rogue of Gor
16 Guardsman of Gor
17 Savages of Gor
18 Bloodbrothers of Gor
19 Kajira of Gor
20 Players of Gor
21 Dancer of Gor
22 Mercenaries of Gor

23 Renegades of Gor
24 Vagabonds of Gor
Paperback fantasy

NORTH, G.
SERGEANT CLUFF SERIES:
1 Sergeant Cluff stands firm 1960
2 The methods of Sergeant Cluff 1961
3 Sergeant Cluff goes fishing 1962
4 More deaths for Sergeant Cluff 1963
5 Sergeant Cluff and the madmen 1964
*Contains two stories 'Blindness of
Sergeant Cluff ' and 'Sergeant Cluff
laughs last'.*
6 Sergeant Cluff and the price of pity
1965
7 The confounding of Sergeant Cluff
1966
8 Sergeant Cluff and the day of reckoning
1967
9 The procrastination of Sergeant Cluff
1969
10 No choice for Sergeant Cluff 1971
11 Sergeant Cluff rings true 1972

NORTON, A.
JANUS:
1 Judgment on Janus
2 Victory on Janus
Paperback science fiction
ROSS MURDOCK:
1 The tune traders 1979
2 Galactic derelict 1979
3 The defiant agents 1979
4 Key out of tune 1979
WITCH WORLD:
1 Witch World
2 Web of Witch World
3 Three against Witch World
4 Warlock of Witch World
5 Sorceress of Witch World
6 Year of the Unicorn
7 Spell of Witch World
8 Trey of Swords
9 Ware Hawk
Paperback fantasy

OAKES, P.
1 From middle England 1980
2 Dwellers all in time and space 1981
3 At the Jazz Band Ball 1983
N.F. Autobiography

OATES, J. C.
1 A garden of earthly delights 1968

2 Them 1971
*A trilogy in progress, set in Detroit over
the last forty years*

O'BRIAN, P.
JACK AUBREY:
1 Master and Commander 1969
2 Post Captain 1972
3 HMS Surprise 1973
4 The Mauritius command 1977
5 Desolation Island 1978
6 Fortune of war 1979
7 The surgeon's mate 1980
8 The Ionian mission 1982
9 Treason's harbour 1983
10 The far side of the world 1985
11 The reverse of the medal 1986
12 The letter of Marque 1988
13 The thirteen gun salute 1989
14 Nutmeg of consolation 1990
*Novels about the British Navy in
Napoleonic times*

O'BRIEN, E.
1 The country girls 1962
2 The lonely girl 1963
3 Girls in their married bliss 1964
*The recurring character is an Irish girl,
Cathleen, in Dublin and London.
Published in one vol. with an epilogue
1987*

O'BRINE, P. M.
MICHAEL O'KELLY SERIES:
1 Dodoes don't duck 1950
2 Killers must eat 1951
3 Corpse to Cairo 1952
4 Deadly interlude 1954
5 Passport to treason 1955
6 The hungry killer 1956
7 Daggar before me 1957
MILLS, SECRET AGENT:
1 Mills 1973
2 No earth for foxes 1974

O'CASEY, S.
1 I knock at the door
2 Pictures in the hallway
3 Drums under the window
4 Inishfallen fare thee well
5 Rose and crown
6 Sunset and evening star
7 The green crow

O'CONNOR, E.
1 Steak for breakfast 1968
2 Second helping 1969
N.F. Autobiography

O'CONNOR, F.
1 An only child 1961
2 My father's son
N.F. Autobiography

O'CONNOR, PATRICK
1 Down the Bath rocks 1973
2 In a marmalade saloon 1974
Planned as a series of autobiographical novels set in Glasgow

O'DONNELL, L.
MICI ANHALT:
1 Leisure dying
2 Falling star 1981
3 Wicked designs 1983
NOARAH MULCAHANEY:
1 The phone calls 1972
2 Don't wear your wedding ring 1973
3 Dial 577 R.A.P.E. 1975
4 Aftershock 1977
5 No business being a cop 1980
6 The children's zoo 1982

O'DONNELL, PETER
MODESTY BLAISE:
1 Modesty Blaise 1965
2 Modesty Blaise and Sabre Tooth 1966
3 I, Lucifer 1967
4 A taste for death 1969
5 The impossible virgin 1971
6 The silver mistress 1973
7 Last day in Limbo 1976
8 The dragon's claw 1978
9 The Xanadu talisman 1981
10 The night of Morningstar 1982
11 Dead man's handle 1985

OELLRICHS, I.
MATT WINTER SERIES:
1 Kettel Mill mystery 1940
2 Death of a white witch 1953
3 And die she did 1953
4 Murder comes at night 1955
5 Murder makes us gay 1956
6 Death in a chilly corner 1964
Some not published in U.K.

O'HARA, K.
CHICO BRETT SERIES:
1 Customer's always wrong 1951
2 Exit and curtain 1952
3 Sing, clubman, sing 1952
4 Always tell the sleuth 1954
5 Keep your fingers crossed 1955
6 If anything should happen 1956
7 It leaves them cold 1956
8 Women like to know 1957

9 Danger, women at work 1958
10 And here is the noose 1959
11 Well, I'll be hanged 1960
12 Take life easy 1961
13 Don't tell the police 1963
14 Don't neglect the body 1966
15 It's your funeral 1966

OLBRICH, F.
INSPECTOR DESOUZA:
1 Desouza pays the price 1978
2 Sweet and deadly 1979
3 Desouza in stardust 1980
Thrillers about the Bombay CID

OLDENBOURG, Z.
1 The awakened 1957
2 Chains of love 1959
The story of two lovers in Paris before and after World War II
***
1 The world is not enough 1948
2 Corner-stone 1955
Two novels of France in the 13th century

OLDFIELD, P.
FOXEARTH TRILOGY:
1 Green harvest 1983
2 Summer songs 1984
3 Golden tally 1985
Novels about a family of hop-growers 1900-1930
THE HERON SAGA:
1 The rich earth 1982
2 This ravished land 1982
3 After the storm 1982
4 White water 1983
Set ion 16th C Devon and Kent

OLINTO, A.
1 The water house 1985
2 The King of Ketu 1987

OLIVER, A.
1 The Pew Group 1980
2 Property of a lady 1983
3 The Ehlberg collection 1985
4 Cover-up 1987
Thrillers set in the world of antiques

OMEN
1 The Omen, by David Deltzer
2 Damien, by Joseph Howard
3 The final conflict, by Gordon McGill
4 Armageddon 2000, by Gordon McGill

5 The abomination by Gordon McGill
Based on the horror film's 'Omen' and 'Omen 2'

OMMANEY, F. D.
1 The house in the park 1964
2 The river bank 1966
N.F. Autobiography

O'NEILL, D.
BRIAN SAGA:
1 Crucible 1986
2 Of Gods and men 1987
3 Sons of death 1988

ONSTOTT, K.
FALCONHURST:
1 Mandingo 1960
2 Drum 1963
3 Master of Falconhurst 1964
4 Falconhurst fancy 1966
5 The mustee 1968
6 Heir to Falconhurst 1968
7 Flight to Falconhurst 1970
8 Mistress of Falconhurst 1973
9 Taproots of Falconhurst 1979
10 Scandal of Falconhurst 1980
11 Rogue of Falconhurst 1983
12 Miz Lucretia of Falconhurst 1985
13 Falconhurst fugitive 1988
Novels about a slave estate in Louisiana. 5-10 are written by Lance Horner, and 11-13 by Ashley Carter

ORAM, N.
THE WARP:
1 The storms howling through Tiflis
2 Lemmings on the edge
3 The balustrade paradox
Paperback fantasy

ORDE, L.
DANIEL KERR:
1 The lion's way 1985
2 The lion's progress 1987
TIGER'S HEART:
1 The tiger's heart 1987
2 The tiger's claw 1988

ORLOVITZ, G.
1 Milkbottle H. 1969
2 Ice never F. 1970
The first volumes of a trilogy about a Jewish family in Philadelphia

ORMEROD, R.
MALLIN & COE SERIES:
1 A time to kill 1974

2 The silence of the night 1974
3 Full fury 1975
4 A spoonful of Luger 1975
5 Sealed with a loving kill 1976
6 The colour of fear 1976
7 A glimpse of death 1976
8 Too late for the funeral 1977
9 This murder come to mind 1977
10 A dip into murder 1978
11 The weight of evidence 1978
12 The bright face of danger 1979
13 The amnesia trap 1979
14 Cart before the hearse 1980
15 More dead than alive 1980
16 Double take 1980
17 One deathless hour 1981
18 Face value 1983

ORUM, POUL
INSP. MORCK:
1 The whipping boy 1975
2 Nothing but the truth 1976

OSBORNE, D.
1 Voyage of the *Girl Pat*
2 Voyage of the *Victory*
3 Adventurer in chains
N.F. Autobiography

OSBORNE, G.
JAMES DINGLE AND GLYN JONES SERIES:
1 The power bug 1968
2 Balance of fear 1968
3 Traitor's gait 1969
4 Checkmate for China 1969
5 Death's no antidote 1971

OSBORNE, H.
1 White poppy 1977
2 The joker 1978

OSBOURNE, I.
1 The mango season 1985
2 Prodigal 1987

O'SULLIVAN, J. B.
STEVE SILK SERIES:
1 I die possessed 1953
2 Nerve beat 1953
3 Don't hang me too high 1954
4 The stuffed man 1955
5 Someone walked over my grave 1958
6 Gale fever 1959
7 The long spoon 1960
8 Number proof 1961

OWEN, A.
1 Gentlemen of the West 1984

2 Like birds in the wilderness 1987

OWEN, H.
JOURNEY FROM OBSCURITY:
1 Childhood 1962
2 Youth 1964
3 War 1965
N.F. Chronicles of the Owen family, largely devoted to the story of Wilfred Owen

OWEN, J.
HAGGAI GODIN:
1 Thirty days hath September 1965
2 The disinformer 1967

OWEN, R.
1 Green heart of heaven 1954
2 Worse than wanton 1956
Two novels about the south seas

PAASSEN, P. VAN
1 Days of our years
2 That day alone
N.F. Autobiography

PACKER, J.
1 Pack and follow 1945
2 Grey mistress 1949
3 Apes and ivory 1953
4 Home from sea 1963
N.F. Autobiography of a naval wife

PADFIELD, J.
GUY GREVILLA:
1 The lion's claw 1978
2 The unquiet gods 1980
3 Gold chains of Empire 1982

PAGE, E.
DET. CHIEF INSPECTOR KELSEY:
1 Every second Thursday 1981
2 Last walk home 1982
3 Cold light of day 1983
4 Scent of death 1985
5 Final moments 1986
6 A violent end 1988
7 Deadlock 1991

PAIGE, F.
MCGRATH FAMILY:
1 The Sholtie burn 1986
2 Maeve's daughter 1987
3 The distaff side 1988
4 Men who march away 1989
5 Sholtie flyer 1990

PAKENHAM, F. A., EARL of LONGFORD
1 Born to believe 1953
2 Five lives 1964
3 A grain of wheat 1974
N.F. Autobiography

PALEY, G.
1 The little disturbances of men 1959
2 Enormous changes at the last minute 1974
3 Later the same day 1985
Volumes of short stories, in which the same characters appear.

PALMER, J.
GUY PLANT AND FREYA MATTHEWS:
1 Above and below 1966
2 So much for Gennaro 1968

PALMER, M.
THE LOVELL FAMILY:
1 The white boar 1971
2 The wrong Plantagenet 1972

PALMER, S.
MISS H. WITHERS SERIES:
1 Penguin pool murder 1932
2 Murder on wheels 1932
3 Puzzle of the pepper tree 1934
4 Murder on a honeymoon
5 The briar pipe 1936 (Case of the red stallion)
6 Puzzle of the silver Persian 1935
7 Puzzle of the blue banderilla 1937
8 No flowers by request 1937
9 Death in grease paint 1946
10 Miss Withers regrets 1947
11 Four lost ladies 1950
12 At one fell swoop 1951 (The green ace)
13 Nipped in the bud 1952
14 Exit laughing 1954

PAPE, R.
1 Boldness be my friend
2 Sequel to boldness
N.F. Autobiography

PARETSKY, S.
VIC WARSHAWSKI:
1 Indemnity only 1982
2 Deadlock 1984
3 Killing orders 1986
4 Bitter medicine 1987
5 Toxic shock 1988
6 Burn marks 1990

PARGETER, E.
1 The eighth champion of Christendom: lame crusade 1945
2 Reluctant odyssey 1946
3 Warfare accomplished 1947
***
1 The heaven tree 1961
2 The green branch 1962
3 The scarlet seed 1963
A trilogy about medieval Wales
BROTHERS OF GWYNEDD:
1 Sunrise in the West 1974
2 Dragon at noonday 1975
3 Hounds at sunset 1976
4 Afterglow and nightfall 1977
See also **PETERS, ELLIS**

PARK, R.
1 Missus 1985
2 The harp in the south 1948
3 Poor man's orange 1949
Although 1 was written last, it precedes the others

PARKER, F. M.
1 Coldiron
2 Shadow of the wolf
Paperback Westerns

PARKER, J.
1 The village cricket match 1978
2 Test time at Tillingfold 1979
3 Tillingfold's tour 1986

PARKER, M.
JOHN PICKERING:
1 Which Mrs. Torr? 1952
2 Invisible red 1954

PARKER, R. B.
SPENSER:
1 The Godwolf manuscript 1973
2 God save the child 1975
3 Mortal stakes 1976
4 Promised land 1977
5 The Judas goat 1982
6 Looking for Rachel Wallace 1982
7 A savage place 1982
8 Ceremony 1983
9 A Catskill eagle 1986
10 Valediction 1986
11 Taming a seahorse 1987
12 Early autumn 1987
13 Pale kings and princes 1988
14 Crimson joy 1989
15 Playmates 1990
16 The widening gyre 1991

17 Pastime 1991

PARKES, R.
DET. INSPECTOR TAFF ROBERTS:
1 Riot 1987
2 An abuse of justice 1988
3 Gamelord 1990

PARKIN, R.
1 Out of the smoke 1960
2 Into the smother 1961
3 The sword and the blossom 1968
N.F. The personal story of a prisoner of war of the Japanese

PARKINSON, C. N.
RICHARD DELANCEY:
1 The Guernseyman 1982
2 Devil to pay 1973
3 Fireship 1974
4 Touch and go 1977
5 Dead reckoning 1978
6 So near, so far 1981

PARKINSON, R.
1 Peace for our time 1970
2 Blood, toil, tears and sweat 1972
3 A day's march nearer home 1974
N.F. History of World War II

PARKS, J.
1 Runs in the sun 1963
2 Time to hit out 1967
N.F. Autobiography and cricket history

PARLAND, O.
RIKI:
1 The year of the bull 1991
2 The enchanted way 1991

PARRISH, F.
DAN MALLETT:
1 Fire in the barley 1977
2 Sting of the honeybee 1978
3 Snare in the dark 1982
4 Bait on the hook 1983
5 Face at the window 1984
6 Fly in the cobweb 1986
7 Caught in the birdlime 1987

PARRY, L.
1 Fullback
2 The big game

PARTRIDGE, F.
1 A pacifist's war 1978
2 Everything to lose 1985
N.F. Autobiography

PASSMORE, R.
1 Blenheim boy 1981
2 Moving tent 1982
N.F. The author's experiences in World War II

PATON, A.
1 Towards the mountain 1980
2 Journey continued 1988
N.F. Autobiography of the South African novelist

PATTERSON, H.
NICK MILLER:
1 The graveyard shift 1964
2 Brought in dead 1967

PATTINSON, J.
HARVEY LANDON SERIES:
1 Contact Mr. Delgado 1960
2 The liberators 1961
3 The last stronghold 1962
4 The sinister stars 1964

PAUL, ERNEST
GEORGE BARCLAY:
1 Jewels in jeopardy 1966
2 Konespi affair 1967
3 Curtains for Konespi 1968
4 The golden fleece 1969
5 The silent murder 1970
6 The reluctant cloak and dagger men 1971

PAUL, L.
1 Living hedge 1946
2 Angry young man 1951
3 The boy down Kitchener street 1957
N.F. Autobiography

PAUSTOVSKY, K.
STORY OF A LIFE:
1 Childhood and schooldays 1964
2 Slow approach of thunder 1965
3 In that dawn 1967
4 Years of hope 1968
5 Southern adventure 1969
6 The restless years 1974
N.F. Autobiography

PAXSON, D. I.
WESTRIA:
1 Lady of light, lady of darkness
2 Silverhair the warrior
3 The earthstone
4 The sea star
Paperback fantasy

PAYNE, L.
JOHN TIBBETT:
1 Spy for sale 1969
2 Even my foot's asleep 1971
DET. INSPECTOR SAM BIRKETT:
1 The nose on my face 1961
2 Too small for his shoes 1962
3 Deep and crisp and even 1963
MARK SAVAGE:
1 Take the money and run 1982
2 Malice in camera 1983
3 Vienna blood 1985
4 Dead for a ducat 1985
5 Late knight 1987

PEAKE, M.
1 Titus Groan 1946
2 Gormenghast 1950
3 Titus alone 1964
A new edition of 3 was published in 1970, with a number of changes

PEARCE, M.
MAMUR ZAPT:
1 The Mamur Zapt and the return of the carpet 1988
2 The Mamur Zapt and the night of the dog 1989
3 The Mamur Zapt and the donkey-vous 1990
4 The Mamur Zapt and the men behind 1991
Detective stories set in Egypt in the early 20th C

PEARCE, M. E.
APPLETREE SAGA:
1 Apple tree lean down 1975
2 Jack Mercybright 1976
3 The sorrowing wind 1977
4 The land endures 1979
5 Seedtime and harvest 1980

PEARS, I.
JONATHAN ARGYLL:
1 The Raphael affair 1990
2 The Titian committee 1991

PEARSALL, R.
OAKWOOD SAGA:
1 Tides of war 1977
2 The iron sleep 1979

PEARSON, D.
1 The marigold field 1969
2 Sarah Whitman 1971

PECK, W.
1 A little learning
2 Home for the holidays
N.F. Autobiography

PEGRAM, L.
1 Blood and fire 1978
2 A day among many 1955
3 A long way from home 1986

PELL, S.
LOUIS XIV:
1 Shadow of the sun 1978
2 The sun princess 1979

PELLOW, J.
1 Pastor's green 1980
2 Parson's progress 1981
3 Parson's princess 1983
Novels about a village parson

PENN, J.
INSPECTOR THORNE AND SGT. ABBOT:
1 Notice of death 1982
2 Deceitful death 1983
3 Will to kill 1983
4 Mortal term 1984
5 A deadly sickness 1985
6 Unto the grave 1986
7 Barren revenge 1986
8 Accident prone 1987
CHIEF INSPECTOR TANSEY:
1 Outrageous exposures 1988
2 A feast of death 1989
3 A killing to hide 1990
4 A knife ill-used 1991
5 Death's long shadow 1991

PENN, M.
THE STORY OF HILDA BURTON:
1 Manchester fourteen miles
2 The foolish virgin
3 Young Mrs. Burton

PENTECOST, H.
JOHN JERICHO SERIES:
1 Hide her from every eye 1966
2 Sniper 1967
3 The creeping hours 1968
4 Dead woman of the year 1969
5 The girl with six fingers 1970
6 A plague of violence 1971
JULIAN QUIST:
1 Don't drop dead tomorrow 1972
2 The champagne killer 1974
3 The beautiful dead 1975
4 The Judas freak 1976
5 Honeymoon with death 1977

6 Die after dark 1978
7 The steel palace 1978
8 Deadly trap 1979
9 The homicidal horse 1980
10 Death mask 1981
11 Sow death, reap death 1982
12 Past, present and murder 1983
13 Murder out of wedlock 1985
14 The substitute victim 1986
15 The party killer 1987
16 Kill and kill again 1988
PIERRE CHAMBRUN:
1 The cannibal who over-ate 1963
2 The shape of fear 1964
3 The evil that men do 1966
4 The golden trap 1967
5 The gilded nightmare 1969
6 Girl watcher's funeral 1970
7 The deadly joke 1971
8 Birthday, deathday 1975
9 Walking dead man 1975
10 Bargain with death 1976
11 Time of terror 1977
12 The 14 dilemma 1978
13 Death after breakfast 1979
14 Random killer 1980
15 Beware young lovers 1981
16 Murder in luxury 1981
17 With intent to kill 1983
18 Murder in high places 1983
19 Remember to kill me 1985
20 Nightmare time 1987
21 Murder goes round and round 1989
UNCLE GEORGE:
1 The price of silence 1981
2 The copycat killers 1984
3 Death by fire 1991
4 Murder sweet & sour 1991
5 Pattern for terror 1991

PERHAM, M.
1 Lugard, the years of adventure 1959
2 Lugard, the years of authority 1960
N.F. Biography
***
1 African apprenticeship 1929
2 East African jouney 1976
N.F. Travel

PEROWNE, B., see **HORNUNG, E. W.**

PEROWNE, S.
1 The life and times of Herod the Great 1956
2 The later Herods 1958
N.F. History

PERRY, A.
THOMAS AND CHARLOTTE PITT:
1 Silence in Hanover Close 1989
2 Cardington Crescent 1990
3 Death in the Devil's Acre 1991
4 Bethlehem Road 1991
Detective stories set in Victorian London

PERRY, S.
THE MATADOR TRILOGY:
1 The man who never missed
2 Matadora
3 The Machiavelli interface

PERRY, R.
PHILIS SERIES:
1 The fall guy
2 Nowhere man
3 Ticket to ride 1973
4 Holiday with vengeance 1974
5 One good death deserves another 1976
6 Dead end 1977
7 Dutch courage 1978
8 Bishop's pawn 1979
9 Grand slam 1980
10 Fool's mate 1981
11 Foul up 1985
12 Kolwezi 1986

PETERS, ELIZABETH
AMELIA PEABODY:
1 Crocodile on the sandbank 1976
2 The curse of the Pharaohs 1982
3 The mummy case 1986
4 Lion in the valley 1987
5 The deeds of the disturber 1989
Thrillers featuring a 19th C lady archaeologist
VICKY BLISS:
1 Silhouette in scarlet 1984
2 Street of the Five Moons 1988
3 Borrower of the night 1974
4 Trojan gold 1987
Listed in chronological order
JACQUELINE KIRBY:
1 The murders of Richard III 1989 (1974 in US)
2 Naked once more 1990

PETERS, ELLIS
CHIEF INSPECTOR GEORGE FELSE SERIES:
1 Flight of a witch 1964
2 A nice derangement of epitaphs 1965
3 Piper on the mountain 1966
4 Black is the colour of my true love's heart 1966
5 Grass widow's tale 1967

6 The house of green turf 1967
7 Mourning raga 1969
8 The knocker on death's door 1970
9 Death to the landlords 1972
These are rather more than detective stories, since they concern social problems, and the Felse family is also concerned. Dominic Felse, son of George Felse, appears in no. 4, and is the leading character in no. 7 and no. 9. Bunty Felse, George Felse's wife appears in no. 5. Swami Remandatha appears in nos. 7 and 9
BROTHER CADFAEL:
1 A morbid taste for bones 1977
2 One corpse too many 1979
3 Monk's wood 1980
4 Saint Peter's Fair 1981
5 The leper of St. Giles 1981
6 The virgin in the ice 1982
7 The sanctuary sparrow 1983
8 The devil's novice 1983
9 Dead man's ransom 1984
10 The pilgrim of hate 1985
11 An excellent mystery 1985
12 The raven in the foregate 1986
13 The rose rent 1986
14 The hermit of Eyton Forest 1987
15 The confession of Brother Haluin 1988
16 The heretic's apprentice 1989
17 The Potters Field 1989
18 The summer of the Danes 1991
Detective stories whose hero is a 12thC monk 'A rare Benedictine' (1988) was an illustrated gift book, about the early life of Brother Cadfael

PETERS, G.
INSPECTOR TREVOR NICHOLLS AND SGT. TOM BUXTON SERIES:
1 The claw of the cat 1963
2 The eye of a serpent 1964
3 The whirl of a bird 1965
4 The twist of a stick 1966
5 The flick of a fin 1967
6 The mark of a buoy 1967
7 The chill of a corpse 1968
Setting is Australia

PETERS, L.
IAN FIRTH SERIES:
1 Two sets to murder 1963
2 Out by the river 1964
3 Two after Malic 1966
4 Riot 71 1967

PETERS, M.
MALONE FAMILY:

1 Tansy 1975
2 Kate Alanna 1975
3 A child called Freedom 1976
***
1 The vinegar seed 1986
2 The vinegar blossom 1986
3 The vinegar tree 1987

PETRIE, G.
MYCROFT HOLMES:
1 The Dorking Gap affair 1989
2 The monstrous regiment 1991
The adventures of Sherlock Holmes's brother

PETRIE, R.
INSPECTOR MACLURG SERIES:
1 Death in Deakins Wood 1963
2 Murder by precedent 1964
3 Running deep 1965
4 Dead loss 1966
5 Maclurg goes west 1968
NASSIM PRIDE:
1 Foreign bodies 1967
2 Despatch of a dove 1968

PETROCELLI, O. R.
1 The pact 1974
2 Olympia's inheritance 1975

PETSCHEK, J.
1 The silver bird
2 Silver dreams

PEYREFITTE, R.
1 Diplomatic diversions
2 Diplomatic conclusions

PHELAN, J.
1 Criminals in real life
2 Fetters for twenty

PHELPS, H.
1 Just across the fields 1976
2 Just over yonder 1977
3 Just where we belong 1978
N.F. Autobiography

PHILBIN, T.
PRECINCT SIBERIA:
1 Precinct Siberia
2 Under cover
3 Cop killer
Paperback thrillers

PHILBY, H. ST. J.
1 Arabian days

2 Forty years in the wilderness
N.F. Autobiography

PHILIPS, J.
PETER STYLES SERIES:
1 The laughter trap 1963
2 The black glass city 1964
3 The twisted people 1965
4 The wings of madness 1967
5 Thursday's folly 1967
6 Hot summer's killing 1969
7 Nightmare at dawn 1971
8 Escape a killer 1972
9 The vanishing senator 1973
10 The larkspur conspiracy 1974
11 The power killers 1975
12 Walk a crooked mile 1976
13 Backlash 1977
14 Five roads to death 1978
15 A murder arranged 1979
16 Why murder 1980
17 Death is a dirty trick 1981
18 A target for tragedy 1983

PHILLIPS, S.
MATTHEW FURNIVAL SERIES:
1 Down to earth 1967
2 Hidden wrath 1968
3 Death in Arcady 1969
4 Death makes the scene 1970
5 Death in sheep's clothing 1971

PICKARD, N.
JENNY CARIN:
1 Dead crazy 1989
2 Generous death
3 Marriage is murder
4 No body 1986
5 Say no to murder
6 Crossbones 1990
2 and 5 published in US

PICKLES, W.
1 Between you and me 1949
2 Sometime never 1951
N.F. Autobiography

PIKE, C.
FINAL FRIENDS:
1 The party 1991
2 The dance 1991
3 The graduation 1991
Horror stories

PIKE, C. R.
JUBAL CADE:
1 The killing trial
2 Double cross

3 The hungry gun
4 Killer silver
5 Vengeance hunt
6 The burning man
7 The golden dead
8 Death wears grey
9 Days of blood
10 The killing ground
11 Brand of vengeance
12 Bounty road
13 Ashes and blood
14 The death pit
15 Angel of death
16 Mourning is red
17 Bloody Christmas
18 Time of the damned
19 The waiting game
20 Spoils of war
21 The violent land
22 Gallows bait
Paperback Westerns, some of which are also published in large print

PIKE, R. L.
THE 52ND PRECINCT:
1 Mute witness 1965
2 The quarry 1964
3 Police blotter 1966
No. 2 not published in U.K.

PILCHER, R.
1 The shell seekers 1988
2 September 1990

PILGRIM, D.
1 No common glory
2 The grand design

PILKINGTON, R.
1 Small boat through Belgium 1960
2 Small boat through Holland 1960
3 Small boat to the Skagerrak 1961
4 Small boat through Sweden 1961
5 Small boat to Alsace 1962
6 Small boat through France 1963
7 Small boat through Germany 1963
8 Small boat through Southern France 1964
9 Small boat on the Meuse 1964
10 Small boat to Luxembourg 1965
11 Small boat on the Moselle 1965
12 Small boat on the Thames 1966
13 Small boat to Elsinore 1969
14 Small boat to Northern Germany 1970
15 Small boat on the upper Rhine 1971
16 Small boat on the lower Rhine 1971
N.F. Travel

PINNEY, P.
1 Dust on my shoes
2 Who wanders alone
3 Anywhere but here
N.F. Autobiography

PIPER, W.
1 New lives (The son of John Wintringham)
2 Full flower (The sun in his own house)
These are modernised sequels to 'Pride and Prejudice', by Jane Austen.

PLAGEMANN, B.
THE WALLACE FAMILY:
1 Father to the man 1964
2 The best is yet to be 1966
3 A world of difference 1969

PLAIDY, J.
LUCREZIA BORGIA SERIES:
1 Madonna of the seven hills 1958
2 Light on Lucrezia 1958
ISABELLA OF CASTILE AND FERDINAND OF ARAGON:
1 Castile for Isabella 1960
2 Spain for the sovereigns 1960
3 Daughters of Spain 1961
TRILOGY ON CATHERINE DE MEDICI:
1 Madame Serpent 1951
2 The Italian woman 1952
3 Queen Jezebel 1953
KATHERINE OF ARAGON SERIES:
1 Katherine, the virgin widow 1961
2 The shadow of the pomegranate 1962
3 The king's secret matter 1962
MARY QUEEN OF SCOTS:
1 The Royal road to Fotheringay 1966
2 The captive Queen of Scots 1969
TRILOGY ON CHARLES II:
1 The wandering prince 1956
2 A health unto his majesty 1956
3 Here lies our sovereign lord 1956
LOUIS XV SERIES:
1 Louis the well-beloved 1959
2 The road to Compiegne 1959
SPANISH INQUISITION:
1 The rise of the Spanish Inquisition 1959
2 The growth of the Spanish Inquisition 1960
3 The end of the Spanish Inquisition 1962
N.F. History
WILLIAM AND MARY TRILOGY:
1 The three crowns 1965
2 The haunted sisters (Mary and Anne) 1966

3 The queen's favourites (Anne) 1966
THE GEORGIAN SAGA:
1 Princess of Celle 1967
2 Queen in waiting 1967
3 Caroline the Queen 1968
4 Prince and the Quakeress 1968
5 The third George 1969
6 Perdita's prince 1969
7 Sweet lass of Richmond Hill 1970
8 Indiscretions of the Queen 1970
9 The Regents daughter 1971
10 Goddess of the green room 1971
11 Victoria in the wings 1972
QUEEN VICTORIA:
1 The captive of Kensington Palace 1972
2 The Queen and Lord M. 1973
3 The Queen's husband 1973
4 The widow of Windsor 1974
NORMAN TRILOGY:
1 The bastard king 1975
2 The lion of justice 1975
3 The passionate enemies 1976
PLANTAGENET SAGA:
1 Plantagenet prelude 1976
2 Revolt of the eaglets 1977
3 Heart of the lion 1977
4 Prince of darkness 1978
5 The battle of the Queens 1978
6 The Queen from Provence 1979
7 Edward Longshanks 1979
8 The follies of the King 1980
9 The vow on the heron 1980
10 Passage to Pontefract 1981
11 The star of Lancaster 1981
12 Epitaph for three women 1981
13 Red rose of Anjou 1982
14 The sun in splendour 1982
QUEENS OF ENGLAND:
1 Myself my enemy (Henrietta Maria) 1983
2 Queen of this realm (Elizabeth I) 1984
3 Victoria victorious 1985
4 Lady in the Tower (Anne Bolyn) 1986
5 The courts of love (Eleanor of Aquitaine) 1987
6 The Queen's secret (Catherine de Valois) 1989
7 Reluctant Queen (Anne Neville) 1990

PLAIN, B.
1 Evergreen 1984
2 The golden cup 1986
3 Tapestry 1988

PLANTE, D.
FRANCOEUR FAMILY:
1 The family 1978
2 The country 1981

3 The woods 1982
4 The native 1987
Published in one vol. 'The Francoeur Family' 1984

PLATER, A.
1 The Beiderbecke affair 1985
2 The Beiderbecke tapes 1986
3 The Beiderbecke connection

PLIVIER, T.
TRILOGY ON WORLD WAR II:
1 Moscow 1953
2 Stalingrad 1948
3 Berlin 1956
Documentary novels on the Eastern Campaign

PLOMER, W.
1 Double lives
2 At home
N.F. Autobiography

PLOWDEN, A.
1 The young Elizabeth 1972
2 Danger to Elizabeth 1973
3 Marriage with my Kingdom
4 Elizabeth Regina 1980
N.F. History

PLOWMAN, S.
THE HAMILTON FAMILY:
1 Three lives for the Czar 1969
2 My kingdom for a grave 1970

PLUMB, J. H.
1 Sir Robert Walpole: the making of a statesman 1956
2 Sir Robert Walpole: the King's minister 1960
N.F. Biography

PLUMMER, T. A.
FRAMPTON SERIES:
1 Shadowed by the C.I.D. 1932
2 Shot at night 1934
3 Frampton of the Yard 1935
4 Dumb witness 1936
5 Was the Mayor murdered? 1936
6 Death symbol 1937
7 Man they put away 1938
8 Five were murdered 1938
9 Man they feared 1939
10 Two men from the East 1939
11 Muse theatre murder 1939
12 Melody of death 1940
13 Black ribbon murders 1940
14 Crime at 'Crooked Gables' 1941

15 Fool of the Yard 1942
16 Devil's tea party 1942
17 Man who changed his face 1943
18 Murder limps by 1943
19 Murder by an idiot 1944
20 Simon takes the 'rap' 1944
21 Murder in the village 1945
22 The strangler 1945
23 Man with the crooked arm 1945
24 J. for Jennie murders 1945
25 The Barush mystery 1946
26 The pierced ear murders 1947
27 Who fired the factory 1947
28 The silent four 1947
29 Hunted! 1948
30 Strychnine for one 1949
31 Death haunts the repertory 1950
32 Yellow disc murders 1950
33 Murder of Doctor Gray 1950
34 Murder through room 45 1952
35 Frampton sees red 1953
36 Murder at Marlington 1953
37 The Westlade murders 1953
38 Murder in Windy Coppice 1954
39 A scream at midnight 1954
40 The black rat 1955
41 Where was Fruit murdered? 1955
42 Murder in the surgery 1955
43 Pagan Joe 1956
44 Condemned to live 1956
45 Murder at Lantern Corner 1958
46 The elusive killer 1958
47 The hospital thief 1959
48 The vestry murder 1959
49 The spider man 1960
50 Murder at Brownhill 1962

PODNAISKY, A.
1 My dancing white horses
2 My horses, my teachers
   *N.F. Story of the famous white horses
   of Vienna*

POE, E. A.
1 Fall of the House of Usher
2 Usher's passing by Robert McCammon
   1989

POHL, F.
HEECHEE:
1 Gateway 1978
2 Beyond the Blue Event horizon 1980
3 Heechee rendezvous 1984
4 The annals of Heechee 1987
   Science fiction
SPACE MERCHANTS:
1 Space merchants 1985

2 The merchants' war 1985
   Science fiction

POHL, F. and WILLIAMSON, J.
1 The reefs of space 1964
2 Starchild 1966
   Science fiction

JACK EDEN:
1 Undersea quest 1964
2 Undersea fleet 1968
3 Undersea city 1969

POLNAY, PETER de
1 Death and tomorrow
2 Fools of choice
   N.F. Autobiography

PONSONBY, D. A.
THE JASPARD FAMILY:
1 The general 1958
2 The fortunate adventure 1959
3 The Bristol cousins 1961

POOK, P.
POOK SERIES:
1 Banking on form 1961
2 Pook in boots 1962
3 Pook in business 1963
4 Pook Sahib 1964
5 Bwana Pook 1965
6 Professor Pook 1966
7 Banker Pook confesses 1966
8 Pook at college 1968
9 Pook's tender years 1969
10 Pook and partners 1969
11 Playboy Pook 1970
12 Pook's class war 1971
13 Pook's tale of woo 1972
14 Pook's Eastern promise 1972
15 Beau Pook proposes 1973
16 Pook's tours 1974
17 The teachers hand Pook 1975
18 Gigolo Pook 1976
19 Pook's lovenest 1976
20 Pook's china doll 1977
21 Pook's curiosity shop 1977
22 Marine Pook, Esq. 1978
23 Pook's Viking virgins 1979

POPE, D.
EDWARD YORKE:
1 Convoy 1979
2 Decoy 1983
NED YORKE:
1 Buccaneer 1981
2 Admiral 1982
3 Galleon 1986

4 Corsair 1987
Set in the Caribbean in the days of the pirates Ned Yorke is an ancestor of Edward Yorke
RAMAGE:
1 Ramage 1966
2 Ramage and the drum beat 1967
3 Ramage and the free-booters 1969
4 Governor Ramage, RN 1972
5 Ramage's prize 1974
6 Ramage and the guillotine 1975
7 Ramage's diamond 1976
8 Ramage's mutiny 1977
9 Ramage and the rebels 1978
10 The Ramage touch 1979
11 Ramage's signal 1980
12 Ramage and the renegades 1981
13 Ramage's devil 1982
14 Ramage's trial 1984
15 Ramage's challenge 1985
16 Ramage at Trafalgar (1805) 1986
17 Ramage and the Saracens 1988
18 Ramage and the Dido 1989
Novels set in the Napoleonic Wars

POPE, R.
1 Strosa light 1965
2 Salvage from Strosa 1967

PORTER, H.
1 The watcher on the cast-iron balcony 1963
2 The paper chase 1965
N.F. Autobiography

PORTER, J.
EDDIE BROWN SERIES:
1 Sour cream with everything 1968
2 The chinks in the curtain 1969
3 Neither a candle nor a pitchfork 1970
4 Only with a bargepole 1971
HON. CONSTANCE MORRISON BURKE SERIES:
1 Rather a common sort of crime 1970
2 The meddler and her murder 1972
3 The package included murder 1975
4 Who the heck is Sylvia? 1977
5 The cart before the crime 1979
DET. CHIEF INSPECTOR DOVER:
1 Dover one 1964
2 Dover two 1965
3 Dover three 1965
4 Dover and the unkindest cut of all 1966
5 Dover goes to Pott 1968
6 Dover strikes again 1970
7 It's murder with Dover 1973
8 Dover and the claret tappers 1977
9 Dead easy for Dover 1978

10 Dover beats the band 1980

PORTER, R.
1 Summer driftwood
2 Winter fire

POSEY, C. A.
STEVEN BORG:
1 Kiev footprint 1983
2 Prospero drill 1984

POTOK, C.
REUVEN AND DANNY:
1 The chosen 1968
2 The promise 1970

POTTER, J.
INSPECTOR HISCOCK SERIES:
1 Death in office 1965
2 Foul play 1967
3 Dance of death 1968
4 Trail of blood 1970

POTTER, J. H.
PILGRIM:
1 Call me Pilgrim 1981
2 Pilgrim's trail 1981
3 Young Joe Pilgrim 1982
4 Pilgrim's blood 1982
5 Bounty for Pilgrim 1983
6 Requiem for Pilgrim 1983
7 The Pilgrim raid 1983
8 A coffin for Pilgrim 1984
9 The Pilgrim kill 1984
10 Pilgrim's revenge 1990
Westerns

POURNELLE, J.
JANISSARIES:
1 Janissaries
2 Clan and crown
3 Storms of victory
Paperback science fiction

POWE, R.
1 Possessed 1990
2 Possessed II 1991

POWELL, A.
THE MUSIC OF TIME:
1 A question of upbringing 1951
2 A buyer's market 1952
3 The acceptance world 1955
Published 1962 in one volume, 'A dance to the music of time'
4 At Lady Molly's 1957
5 Casanova's Chinese restaurant 1960

6 The kindly ones 1962
  These form a second trilogy in the
  series
7 The valley of bones 1964
8 The soldier's art 1966
9 The military philosophers 1968
  The third trilogy in the series, set
  during World War II
10 Books do furnish a room 1971
11 Temporary kings 1973
12 Hearing secret harmonies 1975
TO KEEP THE BALL ROLLING:
1 Infants of the Spring 1976
2 Messengers of the day 1978
3 Faces in my time 1980
4 The strangers all are gone 1982
N.F. Autobiography

POWELL, J., see **Family at War** *and* **Sam**

POWELL, L.
PHILLIP ODELL SERIES:
1 A count of six 1948
2 Shadow play 1949
3 Spot the lady 1950
4 Still of night 1952
5 The black casket 1955

POWELL, M.
1 Below stairs 1968
2 Climbing the stairs 1969
3 The treasure upstairs 1970
4 The London season 1971
5 My mother and I 1972
6 Margaret Powell in America 1973
7 Albert, my consort 1975
8 My children and I 1977
N.F. Autobiography

POWER, M. S.
CHILDREN OF THE NORTH:
1 The killing of yesterday's children 1985
2 Lonely the man without heroes 1986
3 Darkness in the eye 1987
Novels set in contemporary Northern
Ireland

POYER, J.
A TIME OF WAR:
1 The transgressors 1984
2 Come evil days 1985

PRATCHETT, T.
DISCWORLD:
1 The colour of magic
2 The light fantastic
3 Equal rites 1986
4 Mort 1987

5 Sorcery 1988
6 Wyrd sisters 1988
7 Pyramids 1989
8 Guards! Guards! 1989
9 Eric 1990
10 Moving pictures 1990
11 Reaper man 1991
Fantasy

PRATHER, R. S.
SHELL SCOTT:
1 Kill the clown 1967
2 Vanishing beauty 1968
  Others published only in U.S.A. in
  paperback, including 'Shell Scott's
  seven slaughters', 'The cockeyed
  corpse', and 'Three's a shroud'

PRENDERGAST, W.
Z CARS:
1 Z car detective
2 Calling all Z cars
  Adapted from the TV Series

PRENTIS, E.
1 A nurse in time 1978
2 Nurse in action 1979
3 Nurse in parts 1980
4 A nurse nearby 1981
5 A turn for the nurse 1982
N.F. Autobiography

PRESCOT, J.
CASE BOOKS:
1 Both sides of the case
2 The case continued 1959
3 The case proceeding 1960
4 Case for the accused 1961
5 Case for trial 1962
6 Case for hearing 1963
7 Case for court 1964
8 The case re-opened 1965
9 Case counterfeit 1967

PRESCOTT, H. F. M.
PILGRIMAGES OF FRIAR FELIX FABIO:
1 Jerusalem journey (Friar Felix at large)
  1955
2 Once to Sinai 1957

PRESTON, F.
1 Harvest of daring
2 Great refusals 1958
  Novels of a New Zealand family

PREUSSLER, O.
1 Robber Hotzenplotz 1970

2 Further adventures of Robber Hotzenplotz 1973

PRICE, A.
DR. DAVID AUDLEY:
1 44 vintage 1977
2 A new kind of war 1987
3 The labyrinth makers 1970
4 Alamut ambush 1971
5 Colonel Butler's wolf 1972
6 October men 1973
7 Other paths to glory 1974
8 Our man in Camelot 1975
9 War game 1976
10 Tomorrow's ghost 1979
11 The Old Vengeful 1982
12 Gunner Kelly 1983
13 Sion Crossing 1984
14 Here be monsters 1985
15 For the good of the state 1986
16 A prospect of vengeance 1988
17 The memory trap 1989

PRICE, E.
ST. SIMONS TRILOGY:
1 The lighthouse 1972
2 New moon rising 1973
3 The beloved invader 1974
★★★
1 Savannah 1986
2 To see your face again 1987
3 Before the darkness falls 1988
4 Stranger in Savannah 1990

PRICE, R.
THE MUSTIAN FAMILY:
1 A long and happy life 1962
2 Generous man 1967

PRICHARD, K. S.
AUSTRALIAN TRILOGY:
1 The roaring nineties 1946
2 Golden miles 1948
3 Winged seeds 1950

PRIESTLEY, J. B.
THE IMAGE MEN:
1 Out of town 1968
2 London end 1968
★★★
1 Midnight on the desert 1937
2 Rain upon Godshill 1939
3 Margin released 1962
4 Instead of the trees 1977
N.F. Autobiography

PRIOR, A.
1 The sky cage 1967
2 Mirror image 1969

THE PRISONER
1 The prisoner *by* T. L. Disch
2 A day in the life *by* H. Stine
3 Who is No. 2? *by* H. Stine
Based on the TV series

PRITCHETT, V. S.
1 A cab at the door 1968
2 Midnight oil 1971
N.F. Autobiography

PRITT, D. N.
1 From right to left: 1887-1941
2 Brasshats and bureaucrats: 1941-1950 1966
3 The defence accuses 1966
N.F. Autobiography

PROCTER, M.
CHIEF INSPECTOR MARTINEAU SERIES:
1 No proud chivalry 1946
2 Each man's destiny 1947
3 The end of the street 1948
4 Hurry the darkness 1952
5 Rich is the treasure 1952
6 Hell is a city 1953 (Somewhere in the city)
7 I will speak daggers 1956 (The ripper)
8 Man in ambush 1957
9 The midnight plumber 1957
10 Killer at large 1958
11 Three at the Angel 1958
12 The pub crawler 1958
13 Devil's due 1960
14 The devil was handsome 1961
15 The spearhead death 1961
16 A body to spare 1962
17 The devil in moonlight 1962
18 The moonlight flitting 1963
19 Two men in twenty 1964
20 Death has a shadow 1964
21 The graveyard rolls 1964
22 His weight in gold 1965
23 Rogue running 1967
24 Exercise hoodwink 1967
25 Hideaway 1968
26 The dog man 1969

PROFESSIONALS
1 Where the jungle ends
2 Long shot
3 Stake-out
4 Hunter-hunted
5 Blind run

6 Fall girl
7 Hiding to nothing
8 Dead reckoning
9 No stone
10 Cry wolf
11 Spy probe
12 Fox hole
13 The untouchables
14 Operation Susie
15 You'll be all right
Paperbacks based on the TV series

PROLE, L.
TUDOR TRILOGY:
1 The ghost that haunted a king 1963
2 The ten day queen 1973
3 Consort to the queen (n.d.)

PRONZINI, B.
THE NAMELESS DETECTIVE:
1 The snatch 1974
2 The vanished 1975
3 Undercurrent 1975
4 Blowback 1978
5 Two spot 1980
6 Labyrinth 1981
7 Hoodwink 1981
8 Scattershot 1982
9 Dragonfire 1983
10 Casefile 1983
11 Bindlestaff 1984
12 Quicksilver 1984
13 Nightshades 1986
14 Jackpot 1991

PUNSHON, E. R.
BOBBY OWEN SERIES:
1 Information received 1933
2 Death among the sunbathers 1934
3 Crossword mystery 1934
4 Mystery villa 1934
5 Death of a beauty queen 1935
6 Death comes to Cambers 1935
7 The Bath mysteries 1936
8 Mystery of Mr. Jessop 1937
9 The dusky hour 1937
10 Dictator's way 1938
11 Comes a stranger 1938
12 Suspects nine 1939
13 Murder abroad 1939
14 Four strange women 1940
15 Ten star clues 1941
16 The dark garden 1941
17 Diabolical candelabra 1942
18 Conqueror inn 1943
19 Night's cloak 1944
20 Secrets can't be kept 1944
21 There's a reason for everything 1945

22 It might lead anywhere 1946
23 Helen passes by 1947
24 Music tells all 1948
25 The house of Godwinsson 1948
26 So many doors 1949
27 Everybody always tells 1950
28 The secret search 1951
29 The golden dagger 1951
30 The attending death 1952
31 Strange ending 1953
32 Brought to light 1954
33 Dark is the clue 1955
34 Six were present 1956
CARTER AND BELL SERIES:
1 Unexpected legacy 1929
2 Proof counterproof 1931
3 Cottage murder 1931
4 Genius in murder 1932
5 Truth come out 1932

PURSER, P.
COLIN PANTON SERIES:
1 The twentymen 1968
2 Peregrination 22 1969
3 The Holy Father's navy 1971

PUTZ, H., see HASEK, J.

PUZO, M.
1 The Godfather 1969
2 Godfather II
3 The Sicilian 1985

QUANTRILL, M.
THE GOTOBED TRIPTYCH:
1 Gotobed Dawn 1959
2 Gotobedlam 1961
3 John Gotobed alone 1963

QUARTERMAIN, H.
RAVEN SERIES:
1 The diamond hook 1970
2 The man who walked in diamonds 1971
3 Rock of diamond 1972
4 The diamond hostage 1975

QUEEN, E.
1 The Roman hat mystery 1929
2 The French powder mystery 1930
3 The Dutch shoe mystery 1931
4 The Greek coffin mystery 1932
5 The Egyptian cross mystery 1932
6 The American gun mystery 1933
7 The Siamese twin mystery 1933
8 Adventures of Ellery Queen 1934
9 The Chinese orange mystery 1934

10 The Spanish cape mystery 1935
11 Halfway house 1936
12 Door between 1937
13 Devil to pay 1938
14 The four of hearts 1938
15 The dragon's teeth 1939
16 The new adventures of Ellery Queen
   1940
17 Calamity town 1942
18 There was an old woman 1943
19 The murderer is a fox 1945
20 Cat of many tails 1949
21 Casebook of Ellery Queen
22 Ten days wonder 1948
23 Double double
24 Origin of evil 1931
25 The king is dead
26 The scarlet letters 1953
27 Adventures of Ellery Queen
28 New adventures of Ellery Queen
29 Inspector Queen's own case 1956
30 The finishing stroke 1957
31 Queen's Bureau of investigation 1954
32 The player on the other side 1963
33 And on the eighth day 1964
34 Queen's full 1966
35 Face to face 1967
36 The house of brass 1968
37 Q.E.D. - Queen's experiments in
   deduction 1969
38 When fell the night 1970
39 The last woman in his life 1970
40 A fine and private place 1971
41 Dead man's tale 1977
   *There is an inner sequence in the novels
   set in Wrightsville - 'Calamity Town',
   'Murderer is a fox', 'Ten days wonder'
   and 'The Wrightsville heirs' (a story in
   No. 34)*

QUENNELL, P.
1 Byron: the years of fame
2 Byron in Italy
N.F. Autobiography
1 The marble foot 1976
2 The wanton chase 1980
3 Customs and characters 1982
N.F. Autobiography

QUENTIN, P.
PETER DULUTH SERIES:
1 Puzzle for fools
2 Puzzle for players
3 Puzzle for puppets
4 Puzzle for wantons
5 Puzzle for fiends
6 Puzzle for pilgrims
7 Run to death

8 Fatal woman (Black widow)
9 The follower
10 The wife of Ronald Sheldon
11 The man in the net 1956
12 Highly suspicious circumstances 1957

QUEST, E.
DET. CHIEF INSPECTOR KATE MADDOX:
1 Death walk 1989
2 Cold coffin 1990
3 Model murder 1991

QUINAIN, P.
1 Country beat
2 Policeman on the green
N.F. Autobiography of a policeman

QUINN, P.
PETE RILEY SERIES:
1 Once upon a private eye 1968
2 Twice upon a crime 1969
3 Thrice upon a killing spree 1970
4 The big game 1971
5 The fatal complaint 1972

QUEST, R.
PETER QUENTIN SERIES:
1 The Cerberus murders 1969
2 Murder with a vengeance 1970
3 Death of a sinner 1971

QUIGLEY, J.
1 King's Royal 1976
2 Queen's Royal 1977
*Novels about a family of whisky
distillers*

QUOGAN, A.
MATTHEW PRIOR:
1 The fine art of murder 1989
2 The touch of a vanished hand 1990

RADFORD, E. M. and A.
DR. MANSON SERIES
1 Inspector Manson's success
2 Murder jigsaw
3 Crime pays no dividends
4 John Kyeling died
5 Who killed Dick Whittington?
6 Murder to live
7 Murder isn't cricket
8 Look in on murder 1955
9 The heel of Achilles 1956
10 Death on the Broads 1958
11 Death of a frightened editor 1959
12 Death at the Chateau Noir 1959

13 Murder on my conscience 1960
14 Death's inheritance 1960
15 Death takes the wheel 1961
16 From information received 1962
17 A cosy little murder 1963
18 Murder of three hosts 1963
19 The hungry killer 1964
20 Mask of murder 1965
21 Murder magnified 1965
22 Death of a 'gentleman' 1966
23 Nor reason for murder 196?
24 Jones's little murders 1967
25 Middlefold murders 1967
26 Safety first murders 1968
27 Trunk call for murder 1968
28 Death of an ancient Saxon 1968
29 Death of a peculiar rabbit 1969
30 Two ways to murder 1969
31 Murder is a ruby red 1969
32 The greedy killers 1970
33 Dead water 1971
34 Death has two faces 1972
SUPT. CARMICHAEL
1 Look in on murder 1955
2 Married to murder 1959
1 is also Dr. Manson

RADLEY, S.
DET. SUPT. QUANTRILL:
1 Death and the maiden 1980
2 The Chief Inspector's daughter 1981
3 A talent for destruction 1982
4 Blood on the happy highway 1984
5 Fate worse than death 1985
6 Who saw him die? 1987
7 This way out 1989

RAINE, K.
1 Farewell, happy fields 1973
2 The land unknown 1975
3 The lion's mouth 1977
N.F. Autobiography

RAMSAY, D.
LIEUTENANT MEREDITH SERIES:
1 Deadly discretion 1971
2 A little murder music 1972
3 No cause to kill 1973
4 You can't call it murder 1977

RANDALL, A. A.
ROGER PATTEN:
1 Ride a tiger 1965
2 Flashpoint 1966

RANDALL, R.
1 The Drayton legacy 1986
2 The potter's niece 1987

3 The rival potters 1990

RANDISI, R. J.
MILES JACOBY, PRIVATE EYE:
1 Eye in the ring
2 The Steinway collection
3 Full contact 1986

RANKIN, I.
DET. INSPECTOR JOHN REBUS:
1 Knots and crosses 1990
2 Hide and seek 1991

RANKIN, R.
ARMAGEDDON:
1 Armageddon 1990
2 They came and ate us 1991
BRENTFORD TRILOGY:
1 The anti-Pope
2 The Brentford triangle
3 East of Ealing
Paperback only

RANKINE, J.
FLETCHER SERIES:
1 Interstellar 2-5 1969
2 One is one 1970
3 The Plantos affair 1971
4 The ring of Garamas 1972
5 The Bromium phenomenon 1976
Science fiction
SPACE CORPORATION:
1 Never the same door
2 Moon of Triopus
3 The Fingalnan conspiracy 1973
Science fiction
See also **Space 1999**

RANSOME, S.
SCHUYLER COLE SERIES:
1 False bounty 1948
2 The deadly Miss Ashley 1950
3 Lilies in her garden grew 1951
4 Tread lightly, angel 1952
5 Drag the dark 1953
6 Deadly bedfellows 1955
7 The tragic aquittal 1955
8 Night drop 1956
9 So deadly my love 1958
10 The men in her death 1959
11 I'll die for you 1959

RASMUSSEN, A. H.
1 Sea fever
2 China trader
3 Return to the sea
N.F. Autobiography

RATHBONE, J.
COLONEL NUR ARSLAN SERIES:
1 Diamonds bid 1969
2 Handout 1970
3 Trip trap 1972
JAN ARGAND:
1 The Eurokillers 1979
2 Base case 1981
3 Watching the detectives 1983

RATTRAY, S., *pseud* (E. Trevor)
HUGO BISHOP SERIES:
1 Knight sinister 1951
2 Queen in danger 1952
3 Bishop in check 1953
4 Dead silence 1954
5 Dead circuit 1955
   These stories were re-published under
   another pseudonym, Adam Hall, (q.v.)
   and the titles of nos. 4 and 5 were
   changed to 'Rook's gambit' and 'Pawn
   in jeopardy' respectively.

RAVEN, S.
ALMS FOR OBLIVION:
1 The rich pay late 1964
2 Friends in low places 1965
3 The Sabre squadron 1966
4 Fielding Gray 1967
5 The Judas boy 1968
6 Places where they sing 1970
7 Sound the retreat 1971
8 Come like shadows 1972
9 Bring forth the body 1974
10 The survivors 1976
THE FIRST BORN OF EGYPT:
1 Morning star 1984
2 The face of the waters 1985
3 Before the cock crow 1986
4 New seed for old 1988
5 Blood of my bone 1989
6 In the image of God 1990
   ★★★
1 The old gang 1988
2 Is there anyone there? 1990
N.F. Autobiography

RAWN, M.
DRAGON PRINCE:
1 Dragon prince 1989
2 The star scroll 1990
Fantasy

RAYMOND, A.
FLASH GORDON:
1 The witch queen of Mongo
2 The war of the Cybernauts

3 The time trap of Ming XIII
4 The space circus
5 The lion men of Mongo
6 The plague of sound
Paperback science fiction

RAYMOND, D.
FACTORY SERIES:
1 He died with his eyes open 1984
2 The devil's home on leave 1985
3 How the dead live 1986
4 I was Dora Suarez 1990

RAYMOND, E.
A LONDON GALLERY:
1 We, the accused 1935
2 The marsh 1937
3 Gentle Greaves 1949
4 The witness of Canon Welcome 1950
5 A chorus ending 1951
6 The Kilburn tale 1947
7 Child of Norman's End 1934
8 For them that trespass 1944
9 Was there love once?
10 The corporal of the guard 1943
11 A song of the tide 1940
12 The chalice and the sword 1952
13 To the wood no more 1954
14 The Lord of Wensley 1956
15 The old June weather 1957
16 The city and the dream 1958
17 Our late member 1972
   A series of novels portraying the variety
   of London life over the last half
   century. Not otherwise connected.
   ★★★
1 Daphne Bruno 1926
2 The fulfilment of Daphne Bruno 1926
   ★★★
1 A family that was 1929
2 The jesting army 1930
3 Mary Leith 1931
   ★★★
1 Story of my days, 1888-1922 1968
2 Please you, draw near, 1922-28 1969
3 Good morning, good people, 1928-1970
N.F. Autobiography

RAYNER, C.
POPPY CHRONICLES:
1 Jubilee 1978
2 Flanders 1988
3 Flapper 1989
4 Blitz 1990
5 Festival 1991
THE PERFORMERS:
1 Gower Street 1973

2 The Haymarket 1974
3 Paddington Green 1975
4 Soho Square 1976
5 Bedford Row 1977
6 Long Acre 1978
7 Charing Cross 1979
8 The Strand 1980
9 Chelsea Reach 1982
10 Shaftesbury Avenue 1983
11 Piccadilly 1985
12 Seven dials 1986
A family saga set in 19th and 20th centuries.

RAYNER, W.
1 The bloody affair at Riverside Drive 1972
2 The trail to Bearpaw mountain 1974
Complementary novels rather than sequels. The central character of 2 is Sir Richard Burton, who becomes associated with the hero of no. 1.
THE DEVIL'S PICTURE BOOK:
1 Wheels of fortune 1979
2 Knave of swords 1980
No. 3 was abandoned before publication.

READ, MISS
1 A fortunate grandchild 1982
2 Time remembered 1986
N.F. Autobiography
FAIRACRE:
1 Village school 1954
2 Village diary 1956
3 Storm in the village 1960
4 Miss Clare remembers 1962
5 Over the gate 1964
6 Village Christmas 1966
7 Fairacre festival 1969
8 Tyler's Row 1972
9 Further afield 1974
10 No holly for Miss Quinn 1976
11 Village affairs 1977
12 The white robin 1979
13 The village centenary 1980
14 Summer at Fairacre 1984
15 Mrs. Pringle 1989
16 Changes at Fairacre 1991
'Chronicles of Fairacre' 1989 and 'Christmas at Fairacre' 1991 are omnibus volumes
THRUSH GREEN:
1 Thrush Green 1960
2 Winter in Thrush Green 1961
3 News from Thrush Green 1970
4 Battles at Thrush Green 1975
5 Return to Thrush Green 1978

6 Gossip from Thrush Green 1981
7 Affairs at Thrush Green 1983
8 At home in Thrush Green 1985
9 The school at Thrush Green 1987
10 Friends at Thrush Green 1990
CAXLEY SERIES:
1 The market square 1966
2 The Howards of Caxley 1967
3 Emily Davis 1971

REEMAN, D.
BLACKWOOD FAMILY:
1 Badge of glory 1982
2 The first to land 1984

REES, D., *pseud., see* **DANIEL, G.**

REES, G.
1 A bundle of sensations 1960
2 A chapter of accidents 1971
N.F. Autobiography

REEVE, D.
1 Smoke in the lanes
2 No place like home

REEVE, L-D.
ANNE BOLEYN:
1 The early years 1980
2 The royal suitor 1981

REID, P. R.
1 The Colditz story 1953
2 The latter days 1955
3 Colditz: the full story 1984
4 Colditz: the German story, by R. Eggers 1961
5 The diggers of Colditz, by J. Champ & C. Burgess 1985
6 Padre at Colditz, by J. E Platt 1985
7 Tunnelling into Colditz, by J. Rogers 1986
8 Colditz last stop, by J. Pringle 1988
N.F. War stories about the prison camp. 1 & 2 were published in one volume, 'Colditz' in 1962

REILLY, H.
INSPECTOR MCKEE SERIES:
1 McKee of Centre St. 1934
2 Dead man control 1937
3 All concerned notified 1939
4 Dead can tell 1940
5 Murder in Shinbone Alley 1940
6 Death demands an audience 1940
7 Mourned on Sunday 1941
8 Opening door
9 Murder on Angler's Island 1948

10 Silver leopard 1949
11 The farm house 1950
12 Staircase 4 1950
13 Murder at Arroways 1952
14 The velvet hand 1955
15 Not for me Inspector 1960
16 Murder rides the express 1964
   (Compartment K)
17 Follow me 1961
18 The day she died 1963

RENAULT, M.
1 The King must die 1960
2 The bull from the sea 1962
   The story of Theseus
ALEXANDER THE GREAT:
1 Fire from heaven 1971
2 The Persian boy 1972
3 Funeral games 1981
   Alexander also makes a brief
   appearance in 'The mask of Apollo', by
   the same author

RENDELL, R.
INSPECTOR WEXFORD:
1 From Doon with death 1965
2 A new lease of death 1967
3 Wolf to the slaughter 1968
4 The best man to die 1969
5 A guilty thing surprised 1970
6 No more dying then 1971
7 Murder being once done 1972
8 Some lie and some die 1973
9 Shake hands for ever 1975
10 A sleeping life 1978
11 Make death love me 1979
12 Put on by cunning 1981
13 The speaker of Mandarin 1983
14 An unkindness of ravens 1985
15 The veiled one 1988

REVELLI, G.
1 Commander Amanda Nightingale 1969
2 Resort to war 1970

REYNOLDS, W. J.
NEBRASKA:
1 Nebraska quotient 1986
2 Moving targets 1987
3 Money trouble 1988
4 Things invisible 1989
5 Naked eye 1990

RHEA, N.
1 Constable on the hill 1979
2 Constable on the prowl 1980
3 Constable around the village 1981
4 Constable across the moors 1982

5 Constable in the dale 1983
6 Constable by the sea 1985
7 Constable along the lane 1986
8 Constable through the meadow 1988
9 Constable in disguise 1989
10 Constable among the heather 190
   N.F. Autobiography of a Yorkshire
   policeman

RHODE, J.
DR. PRIESTLEY SERIES:
1 The Paddington mystery
2 Dr. Priestley's quest
3 The Ellerby case
4 The Davidson case
5 Tragedy on the line
6 The hanging woman
7 Mystery at Greycombe farm
8 Dead men at the folly
9 Motor rally mystery
10 The Claverton mystery
11 Death in the hopfields
12 Invisible weapons
13 Bloody tower
14 Death on Sunday
15 Death pays a dividend
16 Death on the boat train
17 Murder at the cottage
18 Death at the helm
19 They watched the night
20 The fourth bomb
21 Death on the track
22 Men die at Cypress Lodge
23 Death invades the meeting
24 Vegetable duck
25 Bricklayer's arms
26 The lake house
27 Death in Harley St.
28 Nothing but the truth
29 Death of an author
30 The telephone call
31 Blackthorn house
32 Up the garden path
33 The two graphs
34 Family affairs
35 Dr. Goodwood's locum
36 The secret meeting
37 Death in Wellington Road
38 Death at the dance
39 By registered post
40 Death at the inn
41 The Davidson murders
42 Death on the lawn 1954
43 The domestic agency 1955
44 Death of a godmother 1955
45 Open verdict 1956
46 An artist dies 1956
47 Death of a bridegroom 1957

48 Robbery with violence 1957
49 Murder at Derivale 1958
50 Death takes a partner 1958
51 Licensed for murder 1959
52 Three cousins die 1959
53 Twice dead 1960
54 The fatal pool 1960
55 The vanishing diary 1961
Inspector Waghorn is also a major character in the later novels.

RHODES, D.
GUILHELM de COURDEVAL:
1 Next, after Lucifer 1988
2 Adversary 1989

RHODES, E.
1 Madeleine 1989
2 The house of Bonneau 1990

RHYS, J., *see* BRONTE, C.

RICE, A.
CHRONICLES OF THE VAMPIRES:
1 Interview with the vampires 1985
2 The vampire Lestat 1987
3 The Queen of the damned 1989

RICE, C.
1 Innocent bystander
2 My kingdom for a hearse 1959

RICH, L. D.
1 We took to the woods
2 Happy the land
3 My neck of the woods
4 Innocence under the elms
N.F. Autobiography

RICH, N.
ADAM HOOD:
1 The Blane document
2 Spy now, pay later

RICHARDS, A.
1 Ennal's Point 1977
2 Barque whisper 1979
Set in a South Wales fishing village.

RICHARDS, F., *pseud.*, *see* LOCKRIDGE, F. *and* R.
This was a pseudonym used in U.K. only; recent novels have been under the name of Richard Lockridge, but have been retained under the original joint authors for convenience.

RICHARDS, J.

1 The donkey walk 1968
2 Donkey in danger 1970
A modern version of 'Travels with a donkey'

RICHARDSON, D. M.
PILGRIMAGE:
1 Pointed roofs 1915
2 Backwater 1916
3 Honeycombe 1917
4 The tunnel 1919
5 Interim 1919
6 Deadlock 1921
7 Revolving lights 1923
8 The trap 1925
9 Oberland 1928
10 Dawn's left hand 1931
11 Clear horizon 1935
12 Dimple hill 1960
Later collected in four volumes with a hitherto unpublished book 'March moonlight' which is a key to the whole work.

RICHARDSON, R.
AUGUSTUS MALTRAVERS:
1 The Latimer Mercy 1987
2 Bellringer Street 1988
3 The book of the dead 1989
4 The dying of the light 1990
5 Sleeping in the blood 1991

RICHMOND, SIR A.
1 Twenty-six years (1879-1905)
2 Another sixty years 1965
N.F. Autobiography

RICHTER, C.
AMERICAN PIONEER TRILOGY:
1 The trees 1940
2 The fields 1946
3 The town 1950

RIDLEY, S.
1 Nurse in danger 1963
2 Nurse in doubt 1964
3 Nurse in the South Seas 1965
4 Nurses and ladies 1967
5 Nurse in the mutiny 1970

RIETZ, D.
1 Commando
2 Trekking on
3 No outspan
N.F. Autobiography

RIFKIN, S.
MCQUAID:

1 McQuaid
2 The snow rattlers
3 McQuaid in August

RIGBY, R.
PRIVATE JOHNNY JACKSON:
1 Jackson's war 1967
2 Jackson's peace 1974
3 Jackson's England

★★★

1 The hill
2 Hill of sand 1981

RILEY, J. M.
MARGARET OF ASHBURY:
1 A vision of light 1990
2 In pursuit of the green lion 1991

RIPLEY, M.
FITZROY MACLEAN ANGEL:
1 Just another angel 1988
2 Angel touch 1989
3 Angel hunt 1990
4 Angels in arms 1991

RIPPON, M.
INSPECTOR YGREC:
1 Behold the druid weeps 1972
2 The ninth tentacle
3 The hand of Solange 1985

RIVERS, C.
1 Virgins 1984
2 Girls forever brave and true 1986

RIVKIN, J. F.
SILVERGLASS:
1 Silverglass
2 Web of wind
Paperback fantasy

RIX, B.
1 My farce from my elbow 1974
2 Farce about face 1989
N.F. Autobiography

ROBARDS, K.
1 Island flame 1985
2 Sea fire 1986
Bodice rippers

ROBBINS, H.
HOLLYWOOD TRILOGY:
1 The dream of merchants 1951
2 The carpetbaggers 1956
3 The inheritors 1964
Connection is by theme, not continuing characters.

ROBERSON, J.
CHRONICLES OF CHEYSULI:
1 Shapechangers
2 The song of Homana
3 Legacy of the sword
4 Track of the white wolf
5 A pride of princes
6 Daughter of the lion
Paperback fantasy

ROBERTS, A. V.
1 Louisa Elliott 1989
2 Liam's story 1991

ROBERTS, C.
1 Victoria fourthirty 1937
2 They wanted to live 1938

★★★

1 Pilgrim cottage 1933
2 The guests arrive 1934
3 Volcano 1935

★★★

1 Spears against us 1932
2 Pamela's spring song 1929

★★★

1 Gone rustic 1934
2 Gone rambling
3 Gone afield 1935

★★★

1 And do to Bath 1940
2 And so to America 1946

★★★

1 Halfway 1931
2 One year of life 1952
N.F. Autobiography:

★★★

1 The growing boy (1892-1908) 1967
2 The years of promise (1908-1919) 1968
3 The bright twenties (1920-1929) 1970
4 Shunshine and shadow (1930-1946) 1972
5 The pleasant years (1947-1972) 1974
N.F. Autobiography. The two earlier volumes are episodes and alluded to in the full autobiography.

ROBERTS, C. S.
1 The running tide 1987
2 Upon stormy downs 1988
3 A wind from the sea 1989
4 A seagull crying 1989

ROBERTSON, C.
PETER GAYLEIGH SERIES:
1 The temple of dawn 1940
2 The amazing corpse 1941

3 Zero hour 1942
4 Alibi in black 1945
5 Explosion 1945
6 Two must die
7 Dark knight 1946
8 Devil's lady
9 Knaves' castle 1948
10 Call Peter Gayleigh 1948
11 Sweet justice 1949
12 Death wears red shoes
13 Dusky limelight 1950
14 Peter Gayleigh flies high 1957
15 Demon's moon
16 The tiger's claw 1951
17 Smuggler's moon 1954
18 A lonely place to die
DETECTIVE SUPERINTENDENT BRADLEY
SERIES:
1 Time to kill 1961
2 Conflict of shadows 1962
3 The frightened widow 1963
4 Dead on time 1964
5 Sinister moonlight 1965
6 Killer's mask 1966
7 Double take 1967
8 Twice dead 1968
9 The devil's cloak 1969
10 The green diamonds 1970
ALAN STEEL:
1 Clash of steel
2 The Judas spies
3 Project X
VICKY MACBAIN SERIES:
1 The tiger's claws 1951
2 Venetian mask 1954
3 The Eastlake affair 1956
4 Who rides a tiger 1957
5 The golden triangle 1959
6 Night trip 1960
7 You can keep the corpse 1961
8 Murder sits pretty 1961
EDWARD NORTH SERIES:
1 Dusky limelight
2 North for danger
3 Lady take care
4 No trial - no error

ROBERTSON, D.
BELGATE TRILOGY:
1 The land of lost content 1985
2 A year of winter 1987
3 Blue remembered hills 1987
*Published in one vol. under the first
title 1988*

ROBERTSON, J.
1 Any fool can be a pig farmer 1975
2 Any fool can be a dairy farmer 1980

3 Any fool can be a countryman 1983
4 Any fool can be a villager 1984
5 Any fool can be a yokel 1985
6 Any fool can be a country lover 1986
7 Any fool can keep a secret 1987
8 Any fool can see a vision 1988
9 Any fool can be independent 1989
N.F. Autobiography

ROBINS, P.
DICK AND TAMILY TRILOGY:
1 The long wait 1964
2 The constant heart 1965
3 The uncertain joy 1966

ROBINSON, D.
1 The Elderado network
2 Artillery of lies 1991

ROBINSON, PETER
INSPECTOR BANKS:
1 Gallows view 1988
2 A dedicated man 1989
3 A necessary end 1989
4 The hanging valley 1990

ROCHE, E.
FORTUNE AND POWER:
1 The Berg family fortune 1985
2 New money 1986

ROCHE, R. FRISON-
THE STORY OF SIMON SOKKI:
1 The raid 1964
2 The last migration 1967
Two novels about Lapland
★★★
1 The last crevasse
2 Return to the mountains

ROCK, P.
1 Passing bells 1981
2 Circles of time 1982
3 A future arrived 1985

RODNEY, B.
THE OWL SERIES:
1 The Owl hoots 1945
2 The Owl meets the Devil 1949
3 The Owl flies home 1952

ROE, C. F.
DR. JEAN MONTROSE:
1 The Lumsden baby 1989
2 Death by fire 1990
3 Bad blood 1991
4 Deadly partnership 1991

ROGERS, R.
1 Sweet savage love 1982
2 Dark fires 1982
3 Lost love, last love 1981

ROHAN, M. S.
THE WINTER OF THE WORLD:
1 The anvil of ice 1986
2 The forge in the forest 1987
3 The hammer of the sun 1988

ROHMER, S.
1 Tales of secret Egypt
2 Brood of the witch queen
FU-MANCHU SERIES:
1 The mysterious Dr. Fu-Manchu 1913
2 The devil doctor
3 The Si-Fan mysteries
4 Daughter of Fu-Manchu
5 Return of Dr. Fu-Manchu
6 Insidious Dr. Fu-Manchu
7 Hand of Dr. Fu-Manchu
8 Mask of Fu-Manchu
9 The bride of Fu-Manchu
10 President Fu-Manchu
11 The drums of Fu-Manchu
12 The island of Fu-Manchu
13 Shadow of Fu-Manchu
14 Emperor Fu-Manchu
15 Re-enter Dr. Fu-Manchu 1957
16 The wrath of Fu-Manchu 1973
    (previously uncollected short stories)
    SUMURU SERIES:
1 Sins of Sumuru
2 Slaves of Sumuru
3 Virgin in flames
4 The moon is red
5 Sand and satin
6 Sinister Madonna 1956

ROLPH, C. H.
1 London particulars 1980
2 Further particulars 1987
    N.F. Autobiography of a ciminologist

ROMAINS, J.
MEN OF GOODWILL:
1 Book 1 Sixth of October (Le 6 Octobre)
  Book 2 Quinnette's crime (Crime de Quinnette)
2 Book 3 Childhood's love (Les amours enfantines)
3 Book 4 Eros in Paris (Eros de Paris)
4 Book 5 The proud of heart (Les superbes)
5 Book 6 The humble (Les humbles)
6 Book 7 The lonely (Recherche d'une église)

7 Book 8 Provincial interlude (Province)
8 Book 9 Flood warning (Montèe des perils
  Book 10 The powers that be (Les pouvoirs)
9 Book 11 To the gutter (Recours á l'abime)
  Book 12 To the stars (Les creàtures)
10 Book 13 Death of a world (Mission á Rome)
  Book 14 Death of a world (Le drapeau noir)
11 Book 15 Verdun. The prelude (Prelude á Verdun)
  Book 16 Verdun. The battle (Verdun)
12 Book 17 The aftermath (Vorge contre Quinette)
  Book 18 The aftermath (La douceur de la vie)
    The following are published only in U.S.A., commencing with volume 10 of the U.S.A. edition.
10 The new day
  Book 19 Promise of dawn (Cette grande lueur á l'est)
  Book 20 The world is your adventure
11 Work and play
  Book 21 Mountain days
  Book 22 Work and play
12 The wind is rising
  Book 23 The gathering of the gangs (Naissance de la bande)
  Book 24 Offered in evidence (Compurations)
13 Escape in passion
  Book 25 The magic carpet
  Book 26 Franccoise
14 Book 27 Seventh of October
    The difference in numbering of the U.K. and U.S.A. editions is due to Books, 3, 4, 5 and being separate volumes in the U.K. and in two volumes in the U.S.A. Early U.S.A. titles differ slightly. The final volume of American edition contains an index of characters.
    The titles in brackets are the original French titles, given when these were published as separate volumes.
    Book 15 was separately republished in 1958 as 'The adventurers' and Book 16 in 1962 as 'Verdun'. The title 'Verdun' could therefore be Books 15 and 16 in the first English edition, or Book 16 only in the 1962 edition.

RONALD, E. B.
RUPERT BRADLEY SERIES:
1 The cat and fiddle murders 1954

2 Death by proxy 1956
3 A sort of madness 1958

RONAN, T.
1 Deep of the sky 1962
2 Pack horse and pearling boat 1964
3 Once there was a bagman 1966
N.F. 1 is a biography of his father, 2 his own early life on his father's sheep station, in Australia.

ROOME, A.
1 A real shot in the arm 1989
2 A second shot in the arm 1990

ROOSEVELT, ELEANOR
1 On my own
2 You learn by living
N.F. Autobiography

ROOSEVELT, ELLIOTT
1 An untold story: the Roosevelts of Hyde Park
2 A rendezvous with destiny: the Roosevelts of the White House
N.F. Family history
1 Murder and the First Lady 1984
2 The Hyde Park murder 1985
3 Murder at the Palace 1987

ROSCOE, M.
JOHNNY APRIL SERIES:
1 Death is a round black ball 1954
2 Riddle me this 1955
3 A slice of hell 1955
4 One tear for my grave 1956

ROSE, A. P.
1 Room for one more
2 The gentle house
N.F. The adoption of a displaced child

ROSEN, R.
HARVEY BLISSBERG:
1 Strike three, you're dead 1985
2 Fadeaway
3 Saturday night dead 1989

ROSENBERG, J.
GUARDIANS OF THE FLAME:
1 The sleeping dragon
2 The sword and the chain
3 The silver crown
4 The heir apparent
5 The warrior lives
Paperback fantasy

ROSS, A.

MARK FARROW:
1 The Manchester thing 1970
2 The Huddersfield job 1971
3 The London assignment 1972
4 The Dunfermline affair 1973
5 The Bradford business 1974
6 The Amsterdam diversion 1974
7 The Leeds fiasco 1975
8 The Edinburgh exercise 1975
9 The Ampurias exchange 1976
10 The Aberdeen conundrum 1977
11 The Burgos contract 1978
12 The Congleton lark 1979
13 The Hamburg switch 1980
14 The Menwith tangle 1982
15 The Darlington jaunt 1985
16 The Tyneside ultimatum 1988

ROSS, C.
1 The haunted seventh
2 When the devil was sick

ROSS, CAMERON
ALISTAIR DUNCAN:
1 Case for compensation 1980
2 Villa plot, counterplot 1981
3 The scaffold 1981

ROSS, D. F.
WAGONS WEST:
1 Independence 1987
2 Nebraska 1987
3 Wyoming 1988
4 Oregon 1989
5 Texas 1990
6 California 1990
7 Colorado 1990
8 Nevada 1991
9 Washington 1991
10 Montana
11 Dakota
12 Utah
13 Idaho
14 Missouri
15 Mississippi
16 Louisiana
17 Tennessee
Dates are for hardback editions

ROSS, I.
PAUL SHAW:
1 Rocking the boat 1990
2 Beverley Hills butler 1991

ROSS, I. T.
BEN GORDON SERIES:
1 Requiem for a schoolgirl 1960
2 Murder out of school 1961

3 Old students never die 1963
4 Man who would do anything 1964
5 Teacher's blood 1965

ROSS, JEAN
1 Under a glass dome
2 The garden by the river

ROSS, JONATHAN
CHIEF INSPECTOR ROGERS:
1 The blood running cold 1968
2 Diminished by death 1968
3 Dead at first hand 1969
4 The deadest thing you ever saw 1969
5 Here lies Nancy Frail 1970
6 The burning of Billy Toper 1974
7 I know what it's like to die 1976
8 A rattling of old bones 1978
9 Dark blue and dangerous 1981
10 Death's head 1982
11 Dead eye 1983
12 Dropped dead 1984
13 Burial deferred 1985
14 Fate accomplished 1987
15 Sudden departures 1988
16 A time for dying 1989
17 Daphne dead and done for 1990

ROSS, S.
CIVIL WAR TRILOGY:
1 Vagabond treasure
2 Sword is king 1958
3 Drum and trumpet sound! 1960

ROSSITER, J.
ROGER TALLIS:
1 The murder makers 1969
2 The deadly green 1970
3 A rope for General Dietz 1972
4 The golden virgin
***
1 The manipulators 1973
2 The villains 1974
*Two novels about the workings of the
criminal courts*

ROSTEN, L., *pseud.* (L. Q. ROSS)
1 The education of Hyman Kaplan
2 The return of Hyman Kaplan
3 O Kaplan, my Kaplan 1979

ROTH, J.
1 Radetzky march
2 The Emperor's tomb 1984
*Not directly linked, but the characters
are related*

ROTH, L.
1 I'll cry tomorrow
2 Beyond my worth
N.F. Autobiography

ROTH, P.
ZUCKERMANN:
1 The ghost writer 1979
2 Zuckermann unbound 1981
3 The anatomy lesson 1984
4 The Prague orgy 1985
5 The counterlife 1987

ROTHEART, M.
HENRY V:
1 Cry 'God for Harry' 1972
2 Cry 'God for Glendower' 1973

ROTHENSTEIN, SIR J.
1 Summer's lease 1964
2 Brave day, hideous night 1966
3 Time's thievish progress 1970
N.F. Autobiography

ROTHENSTEIN, SIR W.
1 Men and memories
2 Since fifty
N.F. Autobiography

ROTHWELL, H. T.
MICHAEL BROOKS SERIES:
1 Exit a spy 1967
2 Dive deep for danger 1968
3 Duet for three spies 1968
4 No honour among spies 1969
5 No kisses from the Kremlin 1969

ROUGVIE, C.
ROBERT BELCOURT SERIES:
1 Medal for Pamplona 1963
2 Tangier assignment 1965
3 The Gredos reckoning 1966
4 When Johnny died 1967

ROWLAND, J.
INSPECTOR SHELLEY SERIES:
1 Grim souvenir 1930
2 Bloodshed in Bayswater 1935
3 Professor dies
4 Death on Dartmoor
5 Suicide alibi 1937
6 Dangerous company
7 Murder in the museum 1938
8 Slow poison
9 Cornish Riviera mystery 1939
10 Crooked house
11 Spy with a scar 1940
12 Gunpowder alley

13 Death of Neville Norway 1942
14 Death beneath the river
15 Puzzle in pyrotechnics 1947
16 The orange tree mystery 1949
17 Time for killing 1950
18 Calamity in Kent 1950

ROWLANDS, B.
MELISSA CRAIG:
1 A little gentle sleuthing 1990
2 Finishing touch 1991

ROWSE, A. L.
1 The early Churchills 1957
2 The later Churchills 1958
N.F. Biography
***
1 A Cornish childhood 1942
2 A Cornishman at Oxford 1965
3 A Cornishman abroad 1979
N.F. Autobiography

ROYCE, K.
SPIDER SCOTT AND INSPECTOR BULMAN:
1 The XYY man 1970
2 The concrete boot 1971
3 The miniatures frame 1972
4 Spider underground 1974
5 Trap Spider 1974
6 The crypto man 1984
7 The Mosley receipt 1985
8 No way back 1986

ROYSTON, J.
1 The Penhale Heiress 1988
2 The Penhale Fortune 1989

RUARK, R.
1 The old man and the boy
2 The old man's boy grows older
N.F. Autobiography
***
1 Grenadine Etching 1968
2 Grenadine's spawn 1970

RUBENSTEIN, A.
1 My young years 1973
2 My many years 1980
N.F. Autobiography

RUCK, B.
1 A storyteller tells the truth
2 A smile for the past
3 A trickle of Welsh blood 1967
4 An asset to Wales 1970
5 Ancestral voices 1972

N.F. Autobiography and family chronicles

RUCK, R. J.
1 Place of stones 1970
2 Hill farm story 1966
3 Along came a llama 1978
N.F. Autobiography

RUDORFF, R. *see* STOKER, B.

RUESCH, H.
1 Top of the world 1952
2 Back to the top of the world 1974
The story of an Eskimo family

RUHEN, C.
NEIGHBOURS:
1 Neighbours
2 Indiscretions
3 Home truth 1988
4 Testing times 1989
5 Family matters 1989
6 Special friends 1989
7 Dark secrets 1989
8 Unsolved crimes 1989
9 Cover stories 1990
Based on the TV series

RUNDLE, A.
AMBERWOOD SERIES:
1 Amberwood 1973
2 Heronbrook 1975
3 Judith Lammeter 1976

RUSH, R.
1 The birthday treat 1983
2 The birthday girl 1983
Horror stories

RUSSELL, D.
THE TAMARISK TREE:
1 My quest for liberty and love 1975
2 My school and the years of war 1980
3 Challenge to the Cold War 1985
N.F. Autobiography of the wife of Bertrand Russell

RUSSELL, M.
JIM LARKIN:
1 Deadline
2 Concrete evidence
3 Crime wave 1974
4 Phantom holiday 1974
5 Murder by the mile 1975

RUSSELL, R. *see* **Family at war** *series*

RUSSELL, R.
DR. STEVEN RUSHTON:
1 Go on, I'm listening 1983
2 While you're here, Doctor 1985

RUSSO, R.
1 Mohawk 1986
2 The risk pool 1989
About a small town in New York State

RYAN, C.
1 The longest day 1960
2 The last battle 1966
3 A bridge too far 1974
N.F. A trilogy on World War II

RYAN, F.
DET. INSPECTOR SANDY WORDINGS:
1 Sweet summer 1987
2 Tiger, Tiger 1988
3 Goodbye Baby Blue 1990

RYLAND, C.
CHIEF INSPECTOR SHANNON:
1 The Notting Hill murder
2 The murders at the manor

SABBAGH, P. and GRAZIANA, A.
1 Fanina 1966
2 Fanina, child of Rome 1967

SABERHAGEN, F.
BERSERKER:
1 Berserker man
2 Brother Berserker
3 Berserker's planet
Paperback fantasy
BOOK OF SWORDS:
1 The first book of swords
2 The second book of swords
3 The third book of swords
4 The first book of lost swords:
Woundhealer's story
5 The second book of lost swords:
Sightbinders story
6 The third book of lost swords:
Stonecutter's story
Paperback fantasy

SACHS, M.
1 Witches' sabbath 1964
2 The hunt 1967

SADDLER, K. A.
DAVE STEVENS:
1 The great brain robbery 1965

220

2 Gilt edge 1966
3 Talking turkey 1967

SADLER, B.
CASCA:
1 The eternal mercenary
2 God of death
3 The war lord
Paperback fantasy

SADLER, G.
JUSTUS:
1 The lash
2 Bloodwater
3 Black vengeance
Paperback slave saga

SADLER, J.
ANDERSON:
1 Arizona blood trail 1981
2 Sonora lode 1982
3 Tamaulipas guns 1982
4 Severo siege 1983
5 Lobo moon 1983
6 Sierra showdown 1983
7 Throw of a rope 1984
8 Manhunt in Chihuahua 1985
9 Return to Amarillo 1986
10 Montana mine 1987
11 Saltillo Road 1987
12 Long gun war 1988
13 Palomino stud 1988
14 Ghost town guns 1990

SAGAN, F.
1 Those without shadows 1959
2 Wonderful clouds 1961
Josèe and Bernard from 1 appear in 2, though they are not the main characters.
***
1 Castle in Sweden
2 Scars on the soul 1974
1 is a play, 2 a novel with the same characters

SAHGAL, N.
1 Prison and chololate cake
2 From fear set free
N.F. Autobiography

SAINT, D. J., see **READ, MISS**, *pseud.*

ST. ALBANS, DUCHESS OF
1 Mimosa and the mango 1974
2 Road to Bordeaux 1976
3 Uncertain wings 1977
N.F. Autobiography

ST. LAURENT, CECIL, *pseud.* (LAURENT-CELY)

CHERIE SERIES:
1 Caroline Cherie 1959
2 Caroline in Italy 1960
3 The loves of Caroline Cherie 1960
4 Caroline Cherie and Juan 1961
5 Intrigues of Caroline Cherie 1962

CLOTILDE:
1 Clotilde 1959
2 Encore Clotilde 1960
Although the atmosphere is romantic, the background of Vichy France in World War II is authentic.

BERNADETTE:
1 Algerian adventure
2 Toujours Bernadette

SALINGER, J. D.

THE GLASS FAMILY:
1 For Esme with love and squalor 1953
2 Franny and Zooey 1962
3 Raise high the roof beam, carpenters and Seymour 1963
This series of short stories and novels tell the story of a New York family of six precocious children. In 1, a collection of short stories, there are several allusions to them, but only one, 'A perfect day for banana fish' is a complete episode, describing the death of the eldest, Seymour. 'Franny and Zooey' consists of two short stories about the two youngest members. 'Raise high the roof beam, carpenters', tells the story of Seymour's wedding, as seen by Buddy, the second of the family, and a detailed story of Seymour.
There are six short stories leading up to 'The catcher in the rye', by the same author, concerning Vincent and Holden Caulfield. They are: 'The last day of the last furlough', 'A day in France', 'This sandwich has no mayonnaise', 'The stranger', 'I'm crazy', and 'Slight rebellion off Madison'.

SALISBURY, D.

MRS. NORRIS:
1 Death of an old sinner
2 A gentleman called

SALISBURY, R.

1 Close the door behind you 1982
2 When the boys came out to play 1984
3 Birds of the air 1988
4 Sweet Thursday 1990

SALLIS, S.

RISING FAMILY:
1 A scattering of daisies 1985
2 The daffodils of Newent 1985
3 Bluebell windows 1987
4 Rosemary for remembrance 1987

SALTER, E.

INSPECTOR HORNSLEY SERIES:
1 Death in a mist 1957
2 Will to survive 1958
3 There was a witness 1960
4 Voice of the peacock 1962
5 Once upon a tombstone 1963

SALVATORE, R. A.

FORGOTTEN REALMS:
1 The crystal shard
2 Streams of silver
3 The halfing's gem

THE DARK ELF TRILOGY:
1 Homeland 1990
2 Exile 1991
3 Sojourn 1991

SAM

1 Sam *by* Jonathan Powell 1973
2 Sam: stay single and live forever *by* Leslie Sands 1974
3 Sam: up in the world *by* Leslie Sands 1976
Based on the TV series

SAMPSON, P.

DAUGHTERS OF TINTAGEL:
1 Wise woman's telling 1989
2 White nun's telling 1989
3 Black Smith's telling 1990
4 Taliesen's telling 1991

SAMPSON, G.

PAOLA AND GEORGE:
1 Drug on the market
2 Playing with fire 1968

SANDEL, C.

1 Alberta and Jacob 1962
2 Alberta and freedom 1963
3 Alberta alone 1964

SANDERS, B.

WARD AND SALLY DIGBURN:
1 Secret dragnet 1956
2 To catch a spy 1958
3 Code to dishonour 1965
4 Feminine for spy 1967

SANDERS, J.
NICHOLAS PYM SERIES:
1 A firework for Oliver 1964
2 The hat of authority 1965
3 Without trumpet or drum 1966
4 Cromwell's cavalier 1968
5 Roundabout retreat 1971
Stories of a Cromwellian secret service agent

SANDERS, L.
PETER TANGENT:
1 Tangent objective 1977
2 Tangent factor 1978
TIMOTHY CONE:
1 The Timothy files 1987
2 Timothy's game 1988

SANDFORD, J.
LUCAS DAVENPORT:
1 Rules of prey 1989
2 Shadow prey 1990
3 Eyes of prey 1991

SANDISON, J., *pseud.* (J. DUNCAN)
AN APOLOGY FOR THE LIFE OF JEAN ROBERTSON:
1 Jean in the morning 1969
2 Jean at noon 1971
3 Jean in the twilight 1972
4 Jean towards another day 1975

SANDON, J. D.
GRINGOS:
1 Guns across the river
2 Cannons in the rain
3 Fire in the wind
4 Border affair
5 Easy money
6 Mazatlan
7 One too many mornings
8 Wheels of thunder
9 Durango
10 Survivors
Paperback Westerns

SANDSTROM, F.
1 Midwife of Pont-Clery 1954
2 The virtuous women of Pont-Clery 1956

SANDYS, O.
1 The pleasure garden
2 Old roses

SANGSTER, J.
KATY TOUCHFEATHER; AIR HOSTESS:
1 Touchfeather 1969

2 Touchfeather, too 1970
JOHN SMITH:
1 Private i
2 Foreign exchange

SANTAYANA, Y.
1 Persons and places
2 The middle span
3 My host the world
N.F. Autobiography

SAPPER, *pseud.* (H.C. McNEILE)
1 Bull-dog Drummond 1920
2 The Black gang 1922
3 The third round 1924
4 The final count 1926
5 The female of the species 1928
6 Temple Tower 1929
7 The return of Bull-dog Drummond 1934
8 Knockout 1934 (Bull-dog Drummond strikes back)
9 Bull-dog Drummond at bay
10 Challenge 1937
Continued by Gerald Fairlie
11 Bull-dog Drummond on Dartmoor 1939
12 Bull-dog Drummond attacks 1939
13 Captain Bull-dog Drummond 1945
14 Bull-dog Drummond stands fast 1947
15 Hand off Bull-dog Drummond 1949
16 Calling Bull-dog Drummond 1951
17 Return of the Black gang 1954
***
1 Jim Maitland 1932
2 The island of terror 1932
***
1 Ronald Standish 1933
2 Ask for Ronald Standish 1936

SAROYAN, W.
1 Mama, I love you 1956
2 Papa, you're crazy 1957
Two novels about the same family, told by the small daughter in 1 and by the small son in 2.

SARTRE, J. P.
THE ROADS TO FREEDOM: A TETRALOGY:
1 The age of reason 1947
2 The reprieve 1947
3 Iron in the soul 1950 (Troubled sleep)
A sequence of novels about France before, during and after World War II

SAUL, R.
FIELD:

1 The next best thing 1986
2 The paradise eater 1988

SAVA, G.
1 The healing knife 1937
2 The lure of surgery 1955
N.F. Autobiograpy
PETER SLAVINE:
1 A boy in Samarkand 1950
2 Caught by revolution
3 Flight from the palace 1953
4 Pursuit in the desert 1955

SAVARIN, J. J.
LEMMUS, A TIME TRILOGY:
1 Waiters on the dance 1972
2 Children of Lemmus 1972
3 Beyond the outer mirr 1973
GORDON GALLAGHER:
1 Waterhole 1983
2 Wolf run 1984
3 Windshear 1985
4 Naja 1986
5 The Quiraing list 1988

SAVILLE, A.
BERGERAC:
1 Bergerac and the fatal weakness
2 Bergerac and the Jersey Rose 1990 (hb)
3 Bergerac and the moving fever
4 Bergerac and the traitor's child
Paperbacks based on the TV series

SAWKINS, R.
JOHN SNOW SERIES:
1 Snow on high ground 1966
2 Snow in Paradise 1967
3 Snow along the border 1968

SAXON, P.
THE GUARDIANS SERIES:
1 Dark ways of death 1966
2 Through the dark curtain 1967
3 The curse of Rathlaw 1968
4 Vampires of Finisterre 1968
5 The killing bone 1968

SAXTON, J.
NEYLER FAMILY:
1 The pride 1983
2 The glory 1983
3 The splendour 1984
4 Full circle 1985

SAYERS, D. L.
LORD PETER WIMSEY SERIES:
1 Who's body? 1923
2 Unnatural death 1927 (The Dawson

pedigree)
3 Clouds of witness 1927
4 The unpleasantness at the Bellona Club 1928
5 Lord Peter views the body 1929
Short stories, some in series
6 Strong poison 1930
7 Five red herrings 1931 (Suspicious characters)
8 Have his carcase 1932
9 Murder must advertise 1933
10 Hangman's holiday 1933
Short stories, some in series
11 The nine Tailors 1934
12 Gaudy night 1935
13 Busman's honeymoon 1937
14 In the teeth of the evidence 1939
The original edition of no. 14 contained two Peter Wimsey stories. A new edition in 1972 contained three more, two of which, 'Striding folly', and 'The haunted policeman', were first published in 'Detective medley', ed. by John Rhode. A further story, 'Talboys', is here published for the first time, and is the final Peter Wimsey story. Nos. 6, 8, 12 and 13, form an internal sequence, being the love story of Peter Wimsey and Harriet Vane. Monatague Egg appears in short stories in nos. 5, 10 and 14.

SCANLAN, N. M.
NEW ZEALAND SERIES:
1 Top step
2 Primrose Hill
3 Pencarrow
4 Tides of youth
5 Winds of heaven
6 Ambition's harvest

SCANLON, NOEL
QUINN:
1 Quinn 1975
2 Quinn and the desert oil 1976

SCANNELL, D.
1 Mother knew best 1976
2 Dolly's war 1976
3 Dolly's mixture 1977
N.F. Autobiography
1 Polly Bright 1984
2 Jet Bright 1985

SCANNELL, V.
1 Argument of kings 1987
2 The tiger and the rose 1971

SCARBOROUGH, E.

ARGONIAN SERIES:
1 The song of sorcery
2 The unicorn creed
3 Bronwyn's bane
Paperback fantasy

SCERF, M.
MARTIN BUELL SERIES:
1 Always murder a friend 1949
2 Gilbert's last toothache 1949
3 Curious custard pie 1950
4 The elk and evidence 1952
5 Murder makes me nervous 1952
6 Green plaid pants 1952
7 Glass on the stairs 1955
8 Death of the diplomat 1964
9 Corpse in the flannel nightgown 1966
Not all published in U.K.

SCHIDDEL, E.
1 The devil in Buck's County 1962
2 Scandal's child 1963
3 Devil's summer 1965
A trilogy of novels about a country area in the U.S.A.

SCHILDT, G.
1 In the wake of Odysseus
2 In the wake of a wish
3 The sun boat
N.F. Autobiography and travel

SCHMIDT, D.
TWILIGHT OF THE GODS:
1 The first name
2 Groa's other eye
3 Three trumps sounding

SCHMITZ, J. H.
TELZEY AMBERDON:
1 The eternal frontiers 1974
2 The Telzey toy 1976
3 The lion game 1976

SCHOLEFIELD, A.
1 View of vultures 1966
2 Great elephant 1967
Novels on the early history of South Africa

SCHWEITZER, A.
1 On the edge of the primeval forest
2 More from the primeval forest
N.F. Autobiography

SCOTT, A.
1 Scott free 1986
2 Scott goes south 1988

N.F. Travel

SCOTT, B.
STEVE MACLAREN:
1 Prayer mat 1967
2 Secret of the elephant 1968
3 A hell of a spot 1971
WALT SLADE:
1 Death's harvest 1967
2 Texas death
3 Pecos law
4 Thunder trail
5 Blood on the moon
6 Six-gun fury
7 Rider of the mesquite trail
8 Curse of dead men's gold
9 Lead and flame
10 The border terror
11 Outlaw roundup
12 Red road to vengeance
13 Haunted valley
14 The sky riders 1970
15 Boom town riders
16 The river raiders 1970
Paperback only

SCOTT, SIR H.
1 Your obedient servant
2 Scotland Yard
N.F. Autobiography

SCOTT, J.
DET. INSPECTOR ROSHER:
1 The poor old lady's dead 1976
2 A better class of business 1976
3 A shallow grave 1977
4 A clutch of vipers 1979
5 The gospel lamb 1980
6 A distant view of death 1981
7 An uprush of mayhem 1982
8 The local lads 1982
9 A death in Irish Town 1983
10 All the pretty people 1983
11 A knife between the ribs 1986

SCOTT, J. M.
1 Snowstone
2 The silver land

SCOTT, M.
FREDDIE SERIES:
1 Families are fun 1963
2 No sad songs 1964
3 Freddie 1965

SCOTT, MARY
1 Breakfast at six 1955
2 Dinner doesn't matter 1957

224

3 Tea and biscuits 1962
4 A change from mutton 1965
5 Turkey at twelve 1968
6 Haven't we met before? 1970
7 If I don't, who will? 1971
8 Shepherd's pie 1972
9 Strangers for tea 1975
10 Board but no breakfast 1978
Stories of New Zealand in which characters recur

SCOTT, MICHAEL
TALES OF THE BARD:
1 Magician's law
2 Demon's law
3 Death's law
Paperback fantasy

SCOTT, P.
THE RAJ QUARTET:
1 The jewel in the crown 1966
2 The day of the scorpion 1968
3 The towers of silence 1971
4 Division of the spoils 1975
Novels about India immediately before independence. Not precisely sequels so much as the same central event and its consequences followed up, related and extended.

SCOTT, SHEILA
1 I must fly
2 On the top of the world 1973
N.F. Autobiography

SCOTT, SUTHERLAND
SEPTIMUS DODD SERIES:
1 Murder is infectious 1936
2 Influenza mystery 1938
3 Murder in the mobile unit 1944
4 Operation urgent 1946
5 Blood in their ink 1947
6 The mass radiography murders 1947
7 Tincture of murder 1951
8 Diagnosis: murder 1954
9 Doctor Dodd's experiment 1955

SCYOC, S. J.
1 Darkchild
2 Bluesong
3 Starsilk
Paperback science fiction

SEAFARER, *pseud.* (C. H. BARKER)
CAPTAIN FIREBRACE SERIES:
1 Captain Firebrace
2 Firebrace and the *Java Queen*
3 Firebrace and Father Kelly 1957

4 Smuggler's pay for Firebrace 1959

SEAGRAVE, G. S.
1 Burma surgeon
2 Burma surgeon returns
3 My hospital in the hills
N.F. Autobiography

SEATON, S.
INSPECTOR MARTIN LAIDMAN:
1 Don't take it to heart 1955
2 Dust in your eye 1957

SECOMBE, F.
1 How green was my curate 1988
2 A curate for all seasons 1990
N.F. Autobiography

SEDGES, J., *pseud.*, see BUCK, P. S.

SELA, O.
NICK MAASTEN:
1 The bearer plot 1972
2 The Portuguese fragment 1974

SEGAL, E.
1 Love story 1970
2 Oliver's story 1977

SELLERS, M.
CALOSTE FISHER:
1 Leonardo and others 1980
2 From eternity to here 1981
3 Cache on the rocks 1982

SELLWOOD, A. V.
1 Atlantic
2 Dynamite for hire
N.F. Story of a captain of a German raider in World War II and his subsequent career

SELVON, S.
THE LONELY LONDONERS:
1 The lonely Londoners 1956
2 Moses ascending 1975
3 Moses immigrating 1983

SELWYN, F.
SGT. VERITY SERIES:
1 Cracksman on velvet 1974
2 Sgt. Verity and the Imperial diamond 1975
3 Sgt. Verity presents his compliments 1977
4 Sgt. Verity and the Blood Royal 1979
5 Sgt. Verity and the swell mob 1981
Detective stories set in Victorian days

SEMYONOV, J.
1 Tass is authorised to announce 1987
2 Intercontinental Knot 1988

SENDER, R.
1 Chronicle of dawn 1945 (Cronica del
  Alba 1942)
2 Hipogripo Violento 1954
3 La Quinta Julieta 1957
*Published in one volume under title
'Before noon' (1959)*

SERAFIN, D.
SUPT. LUIS BERNAL:
1 Saturday of glory 1979
2 Madrid underground 1982
3 Christmas rising 1982
4 The body in Cadiz Bay 1985
5 Port of light 1987
6 The angel of Torremolinos 1988
Detective stories set in Spain

SERLING, R.
1 The President's plane is missing 1978
2 Air Force One is haunted 1986

SETTLE, M. L.
BEULAH QUINTET:
1 The long road to Paradise (Prisons)
  1974
2 O Beulah land 1956
3 Know nothing 1960
4 The scapegoat 1980
5 The killing ground 1983
*About the life and social change in
America from the settlers in Cromwellian
times to 1980. Reprinted in paperback in
1988, with a change of title for volume 1.*

SEUFFERT, M.
MIKE HUBBARD SERIES:
1 Hand of a killer 1967
2 Trespassers will die 1968
3 Devil at the door 1969

SEVERN, R.
JEFF CASS:
1 Stalk a long shadow
2 Game for hawks
3 The killing match

SEWART, A.
DET. INSPECTOR EVANS:
1 Loop current 1980
2 The turn up 1981
DET. SGT. CHAMBERLAYNE:
1 In that rich earth 1981
2 A romp in green heat 1981

3 Smoker's cough 1982
4 Drink! for once dead 1983
5 Dead man drifting 1984

SEYMOUR, A.
1 The land where I belong 1970
2 Fragrant the fertile earth 1971
N.F. Autobiography of a farmer

SEYMOUR, ANN
1 Maid of destiny 1970
2 The bitter chalice 1972
*History romances about Anne Boleyn
and the people around her*

SEYMOUR ARABELLA
1 The sins of Rebeccah Russell 1988
2 The end of the family 1990

SEYMOUR, JEANETTE
1 Purity's passion
2 Purity's ecstasy
3 Purity's shame
Historical romances

SEYMOUR, JOHN
1 On my own terms
2 The fat of the land
N.F. Autobiography

SHAKESPEARE, I. M.
JAMES ROSS-GILBERT:
1 Utmost good faith 1988
2 The gentleman's Mafia 1989
*Financial thrillers set in Lloyds of
London*

SHALLIT, J.
DAN MORRISON:
1 Billion dollar body 1952
2 Lady don't die on my doorstep 1952
3 Kiss the killer 1954
4 Yell ruddy murder 1958

SHAND, W.
TEMPEST:
1 A man called Tempest
2 Tempest weaves a shroud
3 Tempest in a tea-cup

SHANE, B.
1 Railhead
2 Iron rails
3 Rails west
*Westerns about the building of the first
railroads in America*

SHANNON, D.

LUIS MENDOZA:
1 Extra kill 1962
2 The ace of spades 1963
3 Knave of hearts 1963
4 Death of a busybody 1963
5 Double bluff 1964
6 Case pending 1964
7 Mark of murder 1965
8 Root of all evil 1966
9 The death-bringers 1966
10 Death by inches 1967
11 Coffin corner 1967
12 With a vengeance 1968
13 Chance to kill 1969
14 Rain with violence 1969
15 Kill with kindness 1969
16 Schooled to kill 1970
17 Crime on their hands 1970
18 Unexpected death 1971
19 Whim to kill 1971
20 The ringer 1972
21 Murder with love 1972
22 With intent to kill 1973
23 No holiday for crime 1974
24 Spring of violence 1974
25 Crime file 1975
26 Deuces wild 1976
27 Streets of death 1977
28 Cold trail 1978
29 Felony at random 1979
30 Felony file 1980
31 Murder most strange 1981
32 The motive on record 1982
33 Exploit of death 1983
34 Destiny of Death 1985
35 Chaos of crime 1986
36 Blood count 1987
Nos. 1-5 were published under the author's real name, Elizabeth Linington

SHANNON, DORIS
ROBERT FORSYTH:
1 Death for a Doctor 1986
2 A death for a dancer 1987
3 A death for a dreamer 1991

SHARAM, N.
WHITE DOG TRILOGY:
1 The white earth 1986
2 The white arrow 1987
3 White rage 1988

SHARP, A.
JOHN MOSELY TRILOGY:
1 A green tree in Gedde 1966
2 The wind shifts 1967
3 The apple pickers 1969

SHARP, M.
1 The eye of love 1961
2 Martha, in Paris 1962
3 Martha, Eric and George 1964

SHARPE, T.
1 Riotous assembly 1971
2 Indecent exposure 1972
'Black comedy' novels about South African police
WILT:
1 Wilt 1977
2 The Wilt alternative 1979
3 Wilt on high 1984
Humorous novels about a lecturer at a provincial college

SHATNER, W.
1 Tekwar 1990
2 Teklords 1991

SHAW, B.
1 The ragged astronauts 1986
2 The wooden spaceships 1988
ORBITSVILLE:
1 Orbitsville
2 Orbitsville departure 1983
3 Orbitsville judgement 1990

SHAW, I.
JORDACHE FAMILY:
1 Rich man, poor man 1970
2 Beggerman, thief 1977

SHEA, R.
SHIKE:
1 Time of the dragons 1981
2 Last of the Zinja 1982
Set in Japan during the war against the Khans

SHEA, R. and WILSON, R. A.
ILLUMINATUS:
1 Eye of the pyramid
2 The golden apple
3 Leviathan
Paperback science fiction

SHEARS, S.
FRANKLIN FAMILY:
1 The village 1984
2 Family fortunes 1985
3 The young generation 1986
4 Return to Russets 1990
THE NEIGHBOURS:
1 The neighbours 1982
2 The neighbours' children

'COURAGE' SERIES:
1 Child of gentle courage 1973
2 Courage in darkness 1974
3 Courage to serve 1974
4 Courage in war 1976
5 Courage in parting 1977
    ★★★
1 Tapioca for tea 1970
2 Gather no moss 1972
3 The seventh commandment 1973
4 Other people's children 1978
N.F. Autobiography
LOUISE:
1 Louise 1975
2 Louise's daughters 1976
3 Louise's inheritance 1977
ANNIE PARSONS:
1 Annie Parsons 1978
2 Annie's boys 1979
3 Annie's kingdom 1980
THOMAS:
1 The sisters 1988
2 Thomas 1989
3 Son of Thomas 1991

SHECKLEY, R.
HUNT:
1 Victim prime 1987
2 Tenth victim 1966
3 Hunter/victim 1988
Science fiction

SHEFFIELD, C.
HERITAGE UNIVERSE:
1 Summertide 1990
2 Divergance 1991

SHELBY, G.
1 The knights of dark renown 1968
2 The kings of vain intent 1970
Two novels about the last years of the kingdom of Jerusalem and the third Crusade
WILLIAM THE MARSHAL:
1 The devil is loose 1972
2 The wolf at the door 1975
England under Richard I and John
CANNAWAYS:
1 The Cannaways 1978
2 The Cannaways concern 1981
Novels about a family of coach builders in the 18th century

SHELDON, S.
1 The other side of midnight 1975
2 Memories of midnight 1990

SHELYNN, J.
NED PARKER:
1 A place called Purgatory 1978
2 The night marches 1978
3 The Cuoto snatch 1979
4 For a girl called Isiah 1979
5 The Judas factor 1980
6 Joker in a stacked deck 1981
SAM CLAYTON:
1 The affair of Cralla Voe 1978
2 A fall of snow 1980
3 Epilogue for Selena 1980

SHEPHARD, E. H.
1 Drawn from memory 1957
2 Drawn from life 1961
N.F. Autobiography

SHERWOOD, JOHN
MR. BLESSINGTON SERIES:
1 Disapperance of Dr. Brunderstein 1949
2 Mr. Blessington's plot 1951
3 Ambush for Anatol 1952
4 Vote for poison 1956
CELIA GRANT:
1 Green trigger fingers 1984
2 A botanist at bay 1985
3 The mantrap garden 1986
4 Flowers of evil 1987
5 Menacing groves 1988
6 A bouquet of thorns 1989
7 The sunflower plot 1990
Thrillers about a horticulturalist

SHERWOOD, V.
LOVESONG:
1 The beauty and the English lord 1987
2 The beauty and the buccaneer 1987
Bodice rippers

SHIPLEY, R.
MILLARD FAMILY:
1 Wychwood 1989
2 Echoes of Wychwood 1991

SHIPWAY, C.
1 The Paladin 1972
2 The wolf time 1973
Historical novels of Normandy in the 11th century
AGEMEMNON:
1 Warrior in bronze 1977
2 King in splendour 1979

SHORT, A.
1 The heritors 1977
2 Clatter vengeance 1979
Novels set in 18th century Scotland

CHRISTIE FAMILY:
1 The first fair wind 1984
2 The running tide 1986
3 The dragons sea 1988
Novels about the Scottish fishing industry

***

1 Silvercairns 1990
2 Rainbow Hill 1991

SHULMAN, S.
1 Francesca the Florentine 1971
2 Francesca: the Madonna of the shadows 1973

SHUPP, M.
DESTINY MAKERS:
1 With fate conspire
2 Morning of creation
3 Soldier of another fortune
4 Death's grey land

SHWARTZ, S.
HEIRS TO BYZANTIUM:
1 Byzantium's crown
2 The woman of flowers
3 Queensblade
Paperback fantasy

SIBLEY, P.
1 High wald to Wandlemere 1973
2 Ravens in winter 1974
Stories of a Devon family

SILKE, J. R.
DEATH DEALER:
1 Prisoner of the horned helmet
2 Lords of destruction
3 Tooth and claw
4 Plague of knives

SILLIPHANT, S.
JOHN LOCKE:
1 Steel tiger 1986
2 Bronze bell 1987

SILLITOE, A.
1 The death of William Posters 1965
2 A tree on fire 1967
3 The flame of life 1979
MICHAEL CULLEN:
1 A start in life 1970 (rev. ed. 1979)
2 Life goes on 1986
JOE SEATON:
1 Saturday night and Sunday morning 1958
2 Key to the door 1961
3 Open door 1989

SILONE, I., *pseud.* (S. TRANQUILLI)
1 Bread and wine
2 The seed beneath the snow

SILVERBERG, R.
MAJIPOOR:
1 Lord Valentine's castle 1981
2 Majipoor chronicles 1982
3 Valentine Pontifex 1984
NEW SPRINGTIME:
1 At winter's end 1988
2 The Queen of springtime 1989

SILVERBERG, R. & GARRETT, R.
1 The shrouded planet
2 The dawning light

SILVERMAN, D.
JOHN MUNG:
1 The fall of the Shogun 1986
2 The black dragon 1988
3 Shishi 1989
4 Tairo: the great elder 1990

SILVERWOOD, R.
SUPERINTENDENT CAWTHORNE:
1 Deadly daffodils 1968
2 Dying for a drink 1971
3 Illegitimate spy 1972

SIMENON, G.
The sequence of the 'Maigret' series in translation is difficult, since they have been produced by different publishers, and the early volumes contained two stories, usually one Maigret story and one a regional novel or thriller. The following list is a complete one of the chronological order of publication of the French titles before 1965, with the English translation. This is not necessarily the order of publication in England. Where a Maigret story is in another volume, this is indicated.
1 Pietr-le-letton. The stange case of Peter the Lett *in* Inspector Maigret investigates
2 M. Gallet, décèdè. The death of M. Gallett, *in* Introducing Inspector Maigret
3 Le Pendu de St. Pholien. The crime of Inspector Maigret *in* Introducing Inspector Maigret
4 Le Charretier de la Providence. The crime at Lock 14 *in* Triumph of Inspector Maigret
5 La Tête d'un homme. A battle of nerves *in* Patience of Inspector Maigret

Since 1964 Maigret volumes have been published separately in English. Four Maigret titles have been published in paperback under different titles. They are nos. 1, 7, 13 and 42. 'The triumph of Inspector Maigret' covering nos. 4 and 13 is not the same as 'Maigret

triumphant' 1969 which is an omnibus volume.
AFRICAN TRILOGY:
1 Talatala
2 Tropic moon
3 Aboard the Aquitaine
Set in French Equatorial Africa

SIMMONS, D.
1 Hyperion 1990
2 The fall of Hyperion 1991

SIMON, R. L.
MOSES WINE SERIES:
1 The big fix 1974
2 Wild turkey 1976
3 Peking duck 1979
About a Jewish private eye.

SIMONS, R.
INSPECTOR WACE SERIES:
1 The houseboat killings 1959
2 A frame for murder 1960
3 Murder joins the chorus 1969
4 Gamble with death 1960
5 The killing chase 1961
6 Silver and death 1963
7 Bullet for a beast 1964
8 Dead reckoning 1965
9 The veil of death 1966
10 Taxed to death 1967
11 Death on display 1968
12 Murder first class 1969
13 Reel of death 1970
14 Picture of death 1973

SIMPSON, A.
1 I threw a rose into the sea
2 Red dust of Africa
N.F. Autobiography. Not published in this order

SIMPSON, D.
INSPECTOR LUKE THANET:
1 The night she died 1980
2 Six feet under 1982
3 Puppet for a corpse 1983
4 Close her eyes 1984
5 Last seen alive 1985
6 Dead on arrival 1986
7 Element of doubt 1987
8 Suspicious death 1988
9 Dead by morning 1989
10 Doomed to die 1991

SIMS, GEORGE
NICHOLAS HOWARD SERIES:
1 The terrible door 1964

2 Sleep no more 1966
3 The last best friend 1967
4 The sand dollar 1969

SIMS, L. LANG-
1 A time to be born 1973
2 Flower in a tea cup 1974
N.F. Autobiography

SINCLAIR, A.
ALBION TRYPTYCH:
1 Gog 1967
2 Magog 1972
3 King Ludd 1988
BUMBO:
1 The breaking of Bumbo 1959
2 Beau Bumbo 1985

SINCLAIR, HAROLD
1 The horse soldiers 1956
2 The cavalryman 1958
Novels of the American army in the Civil War and shortly after. Not published in Great Britain.

SINCLAIR, JANICE
1 Warrior Queen 1977
2 Canis the warrior 1979
Novels about Queen Boadicea and the Romans in Britain

SINCLAIR, U.
NEW YORK TRILOGY:
1 The metropolis 1908
2 The money-changers 1908
3 The machine 1908
SYLVIA SERIES:
1 Sylvia 1913
2 Sylvia's marriage 1914
WORLD'S ENDS SERIES:
1 Worlds end (1913-1919) 1940
2 Between two worlds (1919-1929) 1941
3 Dragon's teeth (1929-1934) 1943
4 Wide is the gate (1934-1937) 1943
5 Presidential agent 1937-1938) 1944
6 Dragons harvest (1939-1940) 1945
7 A world to win (1940-1942) 1946
8 Presidential mission (1942-1943) 1947
9 One clear call (1943-1946) 1948
10 O shepherd speak (1945-1946) 1949
11 Return of Lanny Budd (1946-1947) 1953

SINDEN, D.
1 A touch of the memoirs 1982
2 Laughter in the second act 1985
N.F. Autobiography

SINGER, B.
1 You're wrong, Delaney 1953
2 Have patience, Delaney 1954
3 Don't slip, Delaney 1954
4 Your move, Delaney 1958

SINGER, I. B.
1 The manor 1968
2 The estate 1970
The story of a Jewish family in Poland

SITWELL, SIR O.
1 Left hand, right hand 1945
2 The scarlet tree 1946
3 Great morning 1948
4 Laughter in the next room 1949
5 Noble essences 1950
6 Tales my father taught me 1961
N.F. Autobiography. No. 5 is a series of pen portraits and no. 6 is a pendant to the series, including material omitted from the main work.

★★★

1 England reclaimed 1929
2 Wrack at Tidesend 1933
3 On the Continent 1958
N.F. A trilogy of poems

SJOWALL, M. and WAHLOO, P.
INSPECTOR MARTIN BECK SERIES:
1 Roseanna 1968
2 The man on the balcony 1969
3 The man who went up in smoke 1970
4 The laughing policeman 1971
5 The fire engine that disappeared 1972
6 Murder at the Savoy 1972
7 The abominable man 1973
8 The locked room 1974
9 Cop killer 1975
10 The terrorists 1977

SKELTON, C. L.
1 MacLarens 1979
2 Sweethearts and wives 1980
Novels about an Army family in the late 19th century
HARDACRE FAMILY:
1 Hardacres
2 Hardacres luck 1985

SKELTON, P.
1 The charm of hours 1971
2 The promise of days 1972
3 The blossom of months 1974
A series of novels on adolescence and early manhood

SKIDMORE, I.
1 Island fling 1981
2 The magnificent Evans 1984
Humorous novels about a Welsh island

SKINNER, P.
1 Ursula 1985
2 Hello Pat 1989

SKIRROW, D.
JOHN BROCK:
1 It won't get you anywhere 1966
2 I was following this girl 1967
3 I'm trying to give it up 1968

SKVORECKY, J.
DANNY SMIRICKY:
1 The engineer of human souls
2 The miracle game 1991
LIEUTENANT BORUVKA:
1 The mournful demeanour of Lieutenant Boruvka 1973
2 Sins for Father Knox 1989
3 The end of Lieutenant Boruvka 1990
4 The return of Lieutenant Boruvka 1990

SLADEN, D.
1 A Japanese marriage
2 Playing the game

SLAUGHTER, F. G.
AMERICAN CIVIL WAR:
1 In a dark garden 1946
2 The stubborn heart 1950
BIBLICAL SERIES:
1 Road to Bithynia 1951
2 The Galileans 1953
3 The song of Ruth 1954
4 The scarlet cord 1956

SLOVO, G.
KATE BAEIER:
1 Morbid symptoms 1984
2 Death by analysis 1986
3 Death comes staccato 1987

SMEETON, M.
1 A taste of the hills
2 A change of jungles
N.F. Autobiography
THE CHRONICLES OF TZU HANG:
1 Once is enough 1959
2 Sunrise to windward 1966
N.F. Sailing

SMITH, C. GIBBS-
PAUL HARVARD PSYCHOLOGIST:
1 Operation Caroline 1955

2 Escape and be secret 1957

SMITH, D.
1 No rain in these clouds
2 Same sky all over
N.F. Autobiography

SMITH, DODIE
1 Look back with love 1974
2 Look back with mixed feelings 1978
3 Look back with astonishment 1979
4 Look back with gratitude 1986
N.F. Autobiography

SMITH, D. W.
DET. CHIEF INSPECTOR HARRY FATHERS:
1 Father's law 1986
2 Serious crimes 1987
3 The fourth crow 1989

SMITH, E.
1 Memories of a country girlhood
2 Seven pennies in my hand
3 Many fingers in the pie
4 Never too late
N.F. Paperback autobiographies, set in Leicester

SMITH, E. E. 'DOC', *pseud.*
LENSMAN SERIES:
1 Triplanatary 1955
2 First lensman 1957
3 Galactic patrol 1971
4 Grey lensman 1971
5 Second stage lensman 1972
6 Children of the lens 1972
7 Masters of the vortex 1972
8 Dragon Lensman by D. E. Kyle
9 Lensman from Rigel by D. E. Kyle
SKYLARK SERIES:
1 The Skylark of Space
2 Skylark three
3 The Skylark of Valeron
4 Skylark Duquesne
LORD TEDRIC SERIES:
1 Lord Tedric
2 The Space pirates
3 The Black Knights of the Iron Sphere
4 Alien realms
FAMILY D'ALEMBERT:
1 The Imperial stars
2 Strangler's moon
3 The clockwork traitor
4 Getaway world
5 The bloodstar conspiracy
6 The purity plot
7 Plant of treachery
8 Eclipsing boundaries

9 The Omicron invasion
SUBSPACE:
1 Subspace explorers
2 Subspace encounter
Paperback science fiction

SMITH, EVELYN E.
SUSAN MELVILE:
1 Miss Melvile regrets 1987
2 Miss Melvile returns 1988

SMITH, F. E.
PERSUADERS:
1 The Persuaders 1975
2 The Persuaders - again 1976
3 The Persuaders at large 1977
SAFFRON:
1 Saffron's war
2 Saffron's army
633 SQUADRON:
1 633 Squadron 1956
2 Operation Rhine Maiden 1975
3 Operation Crucible 1977
4 Operation Valkyrie 1978
5 Operation Cobra 1981
6 Operation Titan 1982
***
1 Rage of the innocent 1987
2 In presence of my foes 1988
3 Years of the fury 1989
***
1 A meeting of stars 1986
2 A clash of stars 1987

SMITH, F. M.
1 Surgery at Aberffrwd 1981
2 A GP's progress to the Black Country 1984
N.F. Autobiography of a doctor

SMITH, G. N.
SABAT:
1 The graveyard vulture
2 The blood merchants
3 Cannibal cult
4 The druid connection
Paperback horror stories
THIRST:
1 The thirst
2 The plague
Paperback horror stories

SMITH, JOAN
1 The masculine ending 1987
2 Why aren't they screaming? 1988

SMITH, M. C.

ARKADY RENKO:
1 Gorky Park 1981
2 Polar Star 1989

SMITH, MARTIN
ROMAN GREY:
1 Gypsy in amber 1975
2 Canto for a gypsy 1975

SMITH, S.
NOREEN SPINKS:
1 Flies 1990
2 Dosh 1991

SMITH, W.
SEAN COURTNEY:
1 When the lion feeds 1965
2 The sound of thunder 1966
3 A sparrow falls 1977
South Africa and the Boer War
BALLANTYNE FAMILY:
1 A falcon flies 1980
2 Men of men 1981
3 The angels weep 1982
'The leopard hunts in darkness' is about a descendant of the family
COURTNEY FAMILY:
1 The burning shore 1985
2 Power of the sword 1986
3 Rage 1987
4 A time to die 1989
5 Golden fox 1990
About the descendants of Sean Courtney

SMYTH, SIR J.
1 Beloved cats 1963
2 Blue Magnolia 1964
3 Ming 1966
N.F. A family of Siamese cats

SMYTHE, P.
1 Jump for joy 1954
2 One jump ahead 1956
3 Jumping round the world 1962
N.F. Autobiography

SNOW, C. P., 1st BARON
STRANGERS AND BROTHERS SERIES:
1 Time of hope 1938
2 Strangers and brothers 1940
3 The conscience of the rich 1958
4 The light and the dark 1947
5 The masters 1957
6 The new men 1961
7 Homecomings 1956
8 The affair 1960
9 The corridors of power 1964

10 The sleep of reason 1968
11 Last things 1970
12 In their wisdom
A series of novels depicting various aspects of the contemporary scene in which the narrator, Lewis Eliot, takes part. In some he is the principal character, in others hardly more than a spectator. The general theme is the manifestation and corruption of power. The order given above is the chronological order of the life of Lewis Eliot. Nos. 5 and 8 are direct sequels, but the novels are generally interconnected.

SNOW, E.
1 Red star over China
2 The other side of the river 1962
N.F. Travel and politics. 1 was published in the 30's. 2 tells the story of changes since the first visit.

SNOWDEN, K.
1 King Jack
2 Jack the outlaw

SNYDER, M.
THE QUEEN'S QUARTER:
1 New moon
2 Sedar's keep

SOLZHENITSYN, A.
1 August 1917 1972
2 Lenin in Zurich 1976
Novels about the Russian Revolution
THE GULAG ARCHIPELAGO:
Vols. 1-3
N.F. Accounts of life under Soviet rule

SOMERS, D.
MAJOR JOHN FALCONBRIDGE:
1 Falcon — Queen's messenger
2 Falcon and the diamond necklace

SOMERS, J. (D. LESSING)
1 Diary of a good neighbour 1983
2 If the old could 1984
Published in one vol. 1985 as Doris Lessing

SOMERS, P.
HUGH CURTIS AND MOLLIE BROWN, REPORTERS:
1 Beginner's luck 1957
2 Operation piracy 1958
3 The shivering mountain 1959

SORIANO, O.

1 A funny dirty little war 1983
2 Winter quarters 1989

SOUBIRAN, A.
THE STORY OF JEAN NERAC:
1 The doctors 1953
2 The healing oath 1954
3 Bedlam 1956

SOUTHWORTH, L.
INSPECTOR TOM ANDERSON:
1 Felon in disguise 1967
2 Corpse on London Bridge 1969

SOYINKA, W.
1 Ake: years of childhood 1985
2 Isara: a voyage round Essay 1990
N.F. Autobiography

SPACE 1999
1 Breakaway *by* E. C. Tubb
2 Moon odyssey *by* J. Rankine
3 Space guardians *by* B. Ball
4 Collision course *by* E. C. Tubbs
5 Lunar attack *by* J. Rankine
6 Astral quest *by* J. Rankine
7 Alien seed *by* E. C. Tubb
8 Android planet *by* J. Rankine
9 Rogue planet *by* E. C. Tubb
10 Earthfall *by* E. C. Tubb
11 Mindbreaks of space *by* M. Butterworth
Based on the TV series

SPAIN, N.
MIRIAM BIRDSEYE SERIES:
1 Cinderella goes to the morgue 1950
2 R. in the month 1950
3 Not wanted on voyage 1951
4 Out damned tot 1952

SPANIER, G.
1 It isn't all mink 1968
2 And now it's sables 1970
N.F. Autobiography

SPEAKMAN, F. J.
1 A keeper's tale 1962
2 A forest by night 1965
3 Out of the wild 1967
N.F. Autobiography and country life

SPEDDING, A.
A WALK IN THE DARK:
1 The road and the hills 1988
2 A cloud over water
3 The streets of the city
Fantasy. 2 & 3 in paperback

SPENCER, C.
THE SIMPSON FAMILY:
1 Anarchists in love 1965
2 The tyranny of love 1967
3 Lovers in war 1969
4 Victims of love 1978
A quartet of novels about a London family

SPERBER, M.
1 Wind and the flame
2 To dusty death
3 The lost boy 1956
A trilogy on the Partisans in Yugoslavia

SPICER, B.
CARNEY WILDE SERIES:
1 The dark light 1949
2 Blues for the Prince 1952
3 The golden door 1952
4 Blacksheep run 1952
5 Shadow of fear 1953 (The long green)
6 Taming of Carney Wilde 1955
7 Exit, running 1960

SPICER, M.
LADY JANE HILDRETH:
1 Cotswold manners 1990
2 The Cotswold murders 1991

SPILLANE, M.
MIKE HAMMER SERIES:
1 I, the jury 1952
2 The big kill 1952
3 The long wait 1953
4 Kiss me deadly 1953
5 The snake 1964
6 The twisted thing 1966
7 The body lovers 1967
8 Survival zero 1970
9 The killing man 1990
This is not a complete list. Many Spillane stories have only been published in paperback.
'TIGER' MANN:
1 Day of the guns
2 Bloody sunrise
3 The death dealers 1965
4 By-pass control 1966

SPILLER, A.
CHIEF INSPECTOR 'DUCK' MALLARD SERIES:
1 You can't get away with murder 1948
2 And thereby hangs 1948
3 Brief candle 1949
4 Phantom circus 1950
5 Murder without malice 1954

6 Murder is a shady business 1954
7 Black cap for murder 1955
8 Brains trust for murder 1955
9 Ring twice for murder 1955
10 The black rat 1956
11 It's in the bag 1956
12 Murder on a shoestring 1958

SPRAGUE DE CAMP, L.
1 The incompleat enchanter
2 The castle of iron
3 The enchanter compleated
Paperback fantasy
THE RELUCTANT KING:
1 The goblin tower
2 The clocks of Iraz
3 The unbeheaded king
Paperback fantasy

SPRING, H.
1 Heaven lies about us 1939
2 In the meantime
3 And another thing
N.F. Autobiography
***
1 Shabby tiger 1934
2 Rachel Rosing 1935
***
1 Hard facts 1944
2 Dunkerley's 1950
3 Time and the hour 1957

SPRING, M. H.
1 Memories and gardens 1964
2 Frontispiece 1969
*N.F. Autobiography. The author was
the wife of Howard Spring, so the above
are closely connected with his own
memoirs (q.v.)*

SPRINGER, N.
THE BOOK OF ISLE:
1 The white hart 1984
2 The silver sun 1984
3 The sable moon 1985
4 The black beast 1985
5 The golden swan 1985
SEA KING TRILOGY:

1 Madbond
2 Mindbond
Fantasy

SPURLING, H.
1 Ivy when young 1974
2 Secrets of a woman's heart 1984
N.F. Autobiography of Ivy

Compton-Burnett

STABLEFORD, B.
HOODED SWAN:
1 Halcyon drift 1973
2 Rhapsody in black 1974
3 Promised land 1975
THE DAEDALUS MISSION:
1 The Florians
2 Critical threshold
3 Wildeblood's empire
4 City of the Sun
ASGARD TRILOGY:
1 Journey to the centre
2 Invaders from the centre
3 The centre almost told
***
1 The werewolves of London 1990
2 The angel of pain 1991

STACEY, R.
DOOMSDAY WARRIOR:
1 Doomsday warrior
2 Red America
3 The last American
4 Bloody America
5 America's last declaration
6 American rebellion
7 American defiance
8 American glory
Paperback

STAFFORD, A.
1 Light me a candle 1949
2 Bess
3 Great Mrs. Pennington
4 The time it takes
*Novels of Victorian and Edwardian
London*

STALL, M,
DANIEL LACEY:
1 The killing mask 1981
2 The wet job 1982

STALLMAN, R.
THE BOOK OF THE BEAST:
1 The orphan 1989
2 The captive 1989
3 The beast 1990

STAMP, T.
1 Stamp album 1987
2 Coming attractions 1988
3 Double feature 1989
N.F. Autobiography of the actor

STAND, M.
BILL RICE SERIES:
1 Murder in the camp 1963
2 Escape from murder 1964
3 Death came with darkness 1965
4 Death came with flowers 1965
5 Death came in Lucerne 1966
6 Death came with diamonds 1967
7 Diana is dead 1968
8 Death came to Lighthouse steps 1968
9 Death came in the studio 1969
10 Death came too soon 1970

STANDISH, R.
1 The three bamboos
2 The small general
Novels of China in the Civil Wars

STANFORD, J. K.
LT-COL. JAMES GORE-BUNBURY:
1 Guns wanted 1956
2 Jimmy Bundobust 1958
*A minor character in 1 is the hero of 2,
where he is trying to settle in village life
after retirement.*
THE LIFE AND DEATH OF GEORGE
PROTERON:
1 The twelfth 1944
2 Full moon at Sweatenham
*Short story
Both with further extensions, were
republished as 'The twelfth and after',
1964*

STANLEY, G.
ARAKI:
1 A death in Tokyo 1990
2 The ivory seal 1991

STANTON, M.
1 The heavenly horse from the outermost
west 1989
2 Piper of the gates of dawn 1989

STAPLEDON, O.
1 Last and first men
2 Last men in London
*The sequel is an expanded section of
the first book*

STAPLES, M. J.
1 Down Lambeth way 1988
2 Our Emily 1989
3 King of Camberwell 1990

STAR TREK:
1 Star Trek, by J. Blish
2 Star Trek 2
3 Star Trek 3
4 Star Trek 4
5 Star Trek 5
6 Star Trek 6
7 Star Trek 7
8 Star Trek 8
9 Star Trek 9
10 Star Trek 10
11 Star Trek 11
12 Star Trek 12
13 Star Trek log 1, by A. D. Foster
14 Star Trek log 2
15 Star Trek log 3
16 Star Trek log 4
17 Star Trek log 5
18 Spock must die, by J. Blish
19 Spock Messiah, by T. R. Cogswell
20 The galactic whirlpool, by D. Gerrold
21 Mudd's angels, by J. A. Lawrence
22 Planet of judgement, by J. Haldeman
23 The new voyages, by S. Marshak
24 The new voyages 2
25 Death's angels, by K. Sky
26 The entropy effect, by V. N. MacIntyre
27 The wrath of Khan, by V. N.
MacIntyre
28 Web of the Romulans by M. S.
Murdock
29 The Klingon gambit, by R. E.
Vardeman
30 The search for Spock, by V. N.
MacIntyre
31 Uhura's song, by J. Kagan
32 The covenant of the crown, by H.
Weinstein
33 Mutiny on the 'Enterprise', by R. E.
Vardeman
34 Corona, by G. Bear
35 The final reflection, by J. M. Ford
36 Dwellers in the crucible, by M. W.
Bonnano 1987
37 Mindshadow, by J. M. Dillard 1987
38 Pawns and symbols, by M. Larson
1987
39 Ishmael, by B. Hambly 1987
40 Killing time, by D. Van Hise 1987
41 The voyage home, by V. N. MacIntyre
42 The Prometheus design, by S. Marshak
and M. Culbreath 1986
43 Triangle, by S. Marshak and M.
Culbreath 1986
44 Black fire, by S. Cooper 1986
45 The abode of life, by L. Correy 1986
46 The tears of the singers, by M.
Snodgrass 1986
47 Shadow lord, by L. Yep 1987
48 Spock's world, by Diane Duane 1989
49 Rules of engagement, by P. Morewood

50 The Pandora principle, by C. Clowes
51 Metamorphis, by J. Lorrah
52 The final frontier, by J. M. Dillard 1989
53 The lost years, by J. M. Dillard 1990
54 Prime directive, by J. Reeves-Stevens 1991
55 The new generation by P. David
56 Crisis on Centaurus, by Brad Ferguson 1991
57 Boogeyman, by Mel Gilden 1991
58 Demons by J. M. Dillard 1991
59 Renegade, by Gene Deweere 1991
Mostly paperback, but some hardbacks published

STAR WARS
1 Star wars, by G. Lucas
2 Splinter of the mind's eye, by A. D. Foster
3 The empire strikes back, by D. Glut
4 Han Solo at Stars End by B. Daley
5 Han Solo's revenge, by B. Daley
6 Han Solo and the lost legacy, by B. Daley
7 Return of the Jedi, by J. Khan
8 Lando Calrissian and the Mindharp of Sharu
9 Lando Calrissian and the flame-wind of Oseon
10 Lando Calrissian and the starcave of Thonboka
8-10 are by L. N. Smith

STARK, F.
1 Traveller's prelude (1893-1927) 1950
2 Beyond Euphrates (1928-1933) 1951
3 Coast of incense (1933-1939) 1953
N.F. Autobiography
***
1 Ionia 1954
2 The Lycian shore 1956
N.F. Travel in Greece and Asia Minor

STARK, R.
ALAN GROFIELD SERIES:
1 The dame 1967
2 The damsel 1968
3 The blackbird 1970
PARKER:
1 The hunter
2 The man with the getaway face 1985
3 The outfit 1988
4 The mourner 1987
5 The score 1985
6 The jugger 1986
7 The seventh (The split)

8 The handle 1986
9 The rare coin score 1967
10 The green eagle score 1987
11 The black ice score 1986
12 The sour lemon score 1985
13 Deadly edge
14 Slayground 1969
15 Point blank 1985
16 Plunder squad 1972
17 Butcher's moon 1977
Most are published only in USA. UK dates are 1985-

STARLING, J.
1 Alice in reflection 1987
2 Emily in waiting 1988

STARR, L.
1 To please myself
2 To please myself again
N.F. Autobiography

STASHELT, C.
COSMIC WARLOCK:
1 A warlock in spite of himself
2 A wizard in Bedlam
3 King Kobold

STATHAM, F. P.
1 The Roswell women 1989
2 Roswell legacy 1990

STAYNES, J. & STOREY, M.
DET. SUPT. BONE:
1 Goodbye, Nanny Gray 1987
2 A knife at the opera 1988
3 Body of opinion 1988
4 Grave words 1991

STEED, N.
PETER MARKLIN:
1 Tin-plate 1986
2 Die-cast 1987
3 Chipped 1988
4 Wind up 1990
5 Boxed-in 1991
Thrillers about a dealer in tin-plate toys
JOHNNY BLACK:
1 Black eye 1989
2 Black mail 1990

STEEN, M
THE FLOOD TRILOGY:
1 The sun is my undoing 1941
2 Twilight on the Floods 1949
3 Phoenix rising (Jehovah blues) 1952
SPANISH TRILOGY:
1 Matador 1934

2 One-eyed moon 1935
3 The tavern 1935
　　　★★★
1 Looking glass 1966
2 Pier glass 1969
N.F. Autobiography

STEEN, S.
1 Sailor, beware!
2 Watch it, sailor! 1961

STEIN, A. M.
TIM MULLIGAN AND ELSIE HUNT:
1 Death meets 400 rabbits 1953
2 Moonmilk and murder 1955
3 Shoot me dacent 1957
MATT ERRIDGE SERIES:
1 Never need an enemy
2 Home and murder
3 Blood on the stars
4 I fear the Greeks
5 Faces of death
6 Deadly delight
7 Executioner's rest
8 Snare Andalucia
9 Kill is a four-letter word
10 Alp murder
11 The finger
12 Lock and key
13 Coffin country
14 Lend me your car
15 Body search
16 Nowhere?
17 The rolling heads
18 One dip dead
19 The cheating butcher
20 A nose for it
21 A body for a buddy 1981
22 Hangman's row 1982
23 The bombing run 1983
24 The garbage collector 1986

STEIN, S.
GEORGE THOMASSEY:
1 The magician 1983
2 Other people 1984
3 The touch of treason 1985

STEINBECK, J.
1 Cannery Row 1945
2 Sweet Thursday 1954

STEPHENS, R.
BREW GINNY:
1 The man who killed his brother 1980
2 The man who risked his partner 1985
3 The man who tries to get away 1990

STERLING, S.
FIRE MARSHAL BEN PEDLEY SERIES:
1 Where there's smoke 1946
2 Alarm in the night 1949
3 The hinges of hell 1956
4 Candle for a corpse 1958
5 Fire on Fear St. 1959
GIL VINE SERIES:
1 Alibi baby 1955
2 Dead right 1957
3 Dead to the world
4 The body in the bad 1960

STERN, G. B.
THE RAKONITZ FAMILY:
1 Tents of Israel (The matriarch) 1924
2 The deputy was king 1926
3 Mosaic 1930
4 Shining and free 1935
5 The young matriarch 1942
　　　★★★
1 Monogram 1936
2 Another part of the forest 1941
3 Trumpet voluntary 1944
4 Benefits forgot 1949
5 A name to conjure with 1953
6 All in good time 1954
7 The way it worked out 1956
N.F. Autobiography. 'The ragbag chronicles that apparently I am under complusion to write every three or four years'. From 'A name to conjure with'.

STEVENSON, D. E.
DRUMBERLEY SERIES:
1 Vittoria Cottage 1949
2 Music in the hills 1950
3 Winter and rough weather 1951
　(Shoulder the sky)
　　　★★★
1 Celia's house
2 Listening valley
　　　★★★
1 Mrs. Tim
2 Mrs. Tim carries on 1947
3 Mrs. Tim gets a job 1947
4 Mrs. Tim flies home 1952
1 was originally published as two volumes. 'Mrs. Tim of the Regiment', and 'Golden Days'
　　　★★★
1 Miss Buncle's book 1937
2 Miss Buncle married
3 The two Mrs. Abbotts
　　　★★★
1 Five windows 1953

2 The tall stranger 1957
*The first volume contains a brief
appearance of the main character
(Barbie France) in volume 2.*

***

1 Katharine Wentworth 1964
2 Katharine's marriage 1965
*One of the characters, Mac Aslan,
appears in an earlier book.
'Smouldering fire', reissued 1966.*

***

1 Amberwell 1954
2 Summerhills 1956
*Not sequels in plot, but the Ayrton
family appears in both novels.*

***

1 Sarah Morris remembers 1967
2 Sarah's cottage 1968

***

1 Gerald and Elizabeth 1969
2 The house of the deer 1970

STEVENSON, R. L.
TREASURE ISLAND:
1 Treasure Island 1883
2 The adventures of Long John Silver *by*
D. Judd 1977
3 Return to Treasure Island *by* D. Judd
4 The adventures of Ben Gunn *by* R. F.
Delderfield
5 Silver's revenge *by* R. Leeson 1978
*'The Last Will and Testament of
Robert Louis Stevenson', by S.
Llewellyn 1981 is a pendant.*

STEVENSON, ROBERT
1 Highland vet 1976
2 Vets rush in 1976
3 Vets rush out 1979
N.F. Autobiography

STEWART, A.
1 Alicella
2 Family tapestry
N.F. Autobiography

STEWART, C.
1 The residency 1962
2 Jethro's daughters 1964
Novels of Victorian India

STEWART, D.
THE SEQUENCE OF ROLES: A TRILOGY:
1 The round Mosaic 1965
2 The pyramid inch 1966
3 The mamelukes 1967
The story of the Lomax family, in a

*setting of Scotland, Ireland, Egypt and
London*

STEWART, F.
INSPECTOR NEWSOM:
1 Deadly nightcap 1966
2 Blood relations 1967

STEWART, F. L.
1 I wore my rabbit
2 Flowering in the sun
3 Bees in our bonnet 1961
N.F. Farming in Natal

STEWART, J. I. M.
A STAIRCASE IN SURREY:
1 Young Patullo 1975
2 Gaudy 1974
3 The memorial service 1976
4 The Madonna of the Astrolabe 1977
5 Full term 1978
*A series of novels about life in an
Oxford college*

STEWART, MARY
THE STORY OF MERLIN AND ARTHUR:
1 The crystal cave 1972
2 The hollow hills 1973
3 The last enchantment 1979
4 The savage day 1984

STIRLING, J.
HOLLY BECKMAN:
1 Deep well at noon 1979
2 Blue evening gone 1981
3 The gates of midnight 1983

***

1 The spoiled earth 1975
2 The hiring fair 1976
3 The dark pasture 1978
*A trilogy about a Scottish family in the
19th century*
PATTERSON FAMILY:
1 Treasures on earth 1985
2 Creature comforts 1986
3 Hearts of gold 1987
Set in 18th & 19th century Scotland
NICHOLSON FAMILY:
1 The good provider 1988
2 The asking price 1989
3 The wise child 1990
4 The welcome light 1991

STOCKS, M.
1 My commonplace book 1970
2 Still more commonplace 1973
N.F. Autobiography

STOEKL, BARONESS DE
1 Not all vanity
2 My dear Marquis
3 When men had time to love

STOKER, B.
DRACULA:
1 Dracula
2 Dracula's guest
3 The Dracula archives *by* R. Rudorff 1971
4 Dracula's diary *by* M. Geare & M. Corby 1982
5 Dracula, my love *by* P. Tremayne 1983
6 Dracula's children *by* R. Chetwynd-Hayes 1987
7 House of Dracula *by* R. Chetwynd-Hayes 1987
8 Dracula unbound *by* B. Aldiss 1991

STOKES, D.
1 Voices in my ear 1980
2 More voices in my ear 1981
3 Innocent voices in my ear 1983
4 Whispering voices in my ear 1985
N.F. Autobiography of a medium

STONIER, G. W.
1 Off the rails
2 Rhodesian Spring
N.F. Autobiography

STOREY, A.
A TRILOGY ON THE SECOND COMING:
1 The rector 1970
2 The centre holds 1973
3 The Savior 1978

STORM, J.
SARAH VANESSA SERIES:
1 Dark emerald 1951
2 Bitter rubies 1952
3 Deadly diamond 1953

STORY, J. T.
ALBERT ARGYLE:
1 Live now, pay later 1961
2 Something for nothing 1963
3 The urban district lover 1964
HORACE SPURGEON FENTON:
1 Hitler needs you 1970
2 One last mad embrace 1969
This is chronological order, not order of publication

STOTT, M.
1 Forgetting's no excuse 1973
2 Before I go 1985

N.F. Autobiography

STOUT, R.
NERO WOLFE SERIES:
1 Fer-de-Lance 1934
2 The league of frightened men 1935
3 The rubber band 1936
4 The red box 1937
5 Some buried Caesar 1939
6 Over my dead body 1940
7 Black orchids 1940
8 Where there's a will 1940
9 Not quite dead enough 1944
10 Too many cooks
11 The silent speaker 1946
12 Too many women 1947
13 More deaths than one (And be a villain)
14 Trouble in triplicate 1949
15 The second confession 1950
16 Three doors to death 1950
17 Even in the best families 1951
18 Curtains for three 1952
19 Murder by the book 1952
20 Triple jeopardy
21 Out goes she 1953 (Prisoner's base)
22 The golden spiders 1954
23 Three men out 1954
24 The final deduction 1955
25 Before midnight
26 The black mountain 1955
27 Three witnesses 1956
28 Might as well be dead 1957
29 Three for the chair 1958
30 If death ever slept 1959
31 Crime and again 1959
32 Champagne for one 1959
33 Murder in style 1960
34 Three at Wolfe's door 1960
35 Too many clients 1961
36 Homicide trinity 1962
37 Gambit 1963
38 The mother hunt 1964
39 Trio for blunt instruments 1964
40 A right to die 1965
41 The doorbell rang 1966
42 Death of a doxy 1967
43 The father hunt 1969
44 Death of a dude 1970
45 Please pass the guilt 1974
46 A family affair 1976
47 Murder in E minor *by* R. Goldsborough 1987
Nos. 14, 16, 20, 23, 27, 29, 31, 34, 36, 39, each contain three novellas.
TECUMSEH FOX SERIES:
1 Double for death 1939
2 Broken vase 1940
3 Bad for business 1941

STRAITON, E.
1 Animals are my life 1979
2 A vet at large 1982
3 Positively vetted 1983
4 A vet on the set 1985
N.F. Autobiography of a vet

STRAKER, J. F.
DAVID WRIGHT SERIES:
1 A coil of rope 1962
2 Final witness 1963
INSPECTOR PITT SERIES:
1 Postman's knock
2 Pick up the pieces
3 Ginger horse 1955
4 A gun to play with 1956
5 Good-bye Aunt Charlotte 1958
JOHNNY INCH SERIES:
1 Sin and Johnny Inch 1968
2 Tight circle 1970
3 A letter for Obi 1971
4 The goat 1972

STRANGE, O.
1 Sudden
2 Sudden gold-seeker
3 Sudden outlawed
4 Sudden makes war
5 Sudden rides again
6 Sudden takes the trail
7 Sudden plays a hand
Continued by F. H. Christian
8 Sudden strikes back
9 Sudden troubleshooter
10 Sudden at bay
11 Sudden - Apache fighter
12 Sudden - dead or alive

STRANGER, J.
1 The running foxes 1971
2 Lakeland vet 1972
*Dai Evans is a character in 1 but the
centre of 2.*
DOG SERIES:
1 Three's a pack 1980
2 Two for joy 1982
3 A dog in a million 1984
4 Dog days 1986
*N.F. The author's experiences with her
dogs.*

STRATTON, A.
1 The lady 1986
2 Gina 1988

STREATFIELD, N.
1 The vicarage family 1963
2 Away from the vicarage 1965

3 Beyond the vicarage 1971
N.F. Autobiography

STREET, PAMELA
1 The millrace 1983
2 The way of the river 1984
3 Many waters 1985
4 Unto the fourth generation 1985

STRESHINSKY, S.
1 Hers the kingdom 1981
2 Gift of the golden mountain 1989

STRONG, T.
SAS:
1 Whisper who dares 1983
2 The fifth hostage 1984

STUART, A.
VALADIMIR GULL:
1 Snap judgement 1976
2 Vicious circles 1978
3 Force play 1980
Thrillers about a Russian interpreter

STUART, I.
DAVID GRIERSON:
1 Death from disclosure 1979
2 End on the rocks 1981
3 The garb of truth 1982
4 Thrilling sweet and rotten 1983
5 A growing concern 1987

STUART, V.
COMMANDER PHILLIP HAZARD:
1 The valiant sailors 1967
2 The brave captains 1968
3 Black sea frigate 1971
4 Hazard in *Huntress* 1972
5 Hazard of *Circassia* 1973
6 Hazard: Victory at Sebastopol 1973
7 Shannon's brigade 1976
8 Sailors on horseback 1978
*Stories of the naval campaign in the
Crimean War*
CAPT. ALEX SHERIDAN:
1 Like victors and lords 1964
2 Mutiny in Meerut 1974
3 Massacre at Cawnpore 1974
4 Battle of Lucknow 1975
5 The heroic garrison 1975
THE AUSTRALIANS:
1 The exiles 1981
2 The settlers 1981
3 The traitors 1982
4 The explorers 1983
5 The adventurers 1983
6 The colonists 1984

7 The gold-seekers 1985
8 The patriots 1986
9 The empire builders 1987
10 The seafarers 1988
11 The nationalists 1989
12 The imperialists 1990

STUBBS, J.
INSPECTOR LINOTT:
1 Dear Laura 1973
2 The painted face 1974
3 The golden crucible 1976
BRIEF CHRONICLES:
1 Kit's Hill 1979
2 The ironmaster 1981
3 The Vivian inheritance 1982
4 The northern correspondent 1984

STUDLEY, E.
1 Teddy Boy's picnic
2 Life is for living
N.F. Autobiography

STUNTZ S. C. *see* CONRAD, S., *pseud.*

STURROCK, J.
THE BOW ST. RUNNER:
1 Village of rogues 1972
2 A wicked way to die 1973
3 The wilful lady 1975
4 A conspiracy of poisons 1977
5 Suicide most foul 1981
6 Captain Bolton's corpse 1982
7 The Pangersbourne murders 1984

STYLES, S.
MR. FITTON SERIES:
1 A sword for Mr. Fitton 1975
2 Mr. Fitton's commission 1977
3 Baltic convoy 1979
4 Gun-brig captain 1987
5 H.M.S. Cracker 1988

SUE, E.
MYSTERIES OF THE PEOPLE SERIES:
1 The gold sickle
2 The brass bell
3 The iron collar
4 The silver cross
5 The casque's lark
6 The poniard's hilt
7 The branding needle
8 The abbatical crosier
9 The Carlovingian coins
10 The iron arrowhead
11 The infant's skull
12 The pigrim's shell

13 The iron pincers
14 The iron trivet
15 The executioner's knife
16 The pocket bible
17 The blacksmith's hammer
18 The sword of honour
19 The galley slave's ring
A chronicle of a family from 57 B.C. to A.D. 1951

SUGERMAN, D.
1 No-one gets out of here alive 1980
2 Wonderland Avenue 1989

SUMMERS, R.
1 Killigrew clay 1986
2 Clay country 1987
3 Family ties 1988
A family saga set in the clay-mines in Cornwall

SUMNER, R.
1 Mistress of the streets 1975
2 Mistress of the boards 1977
3 Mistress of the King 1979
A trilogy about Nell Gwynn

SUTHERLAND, D.
1 The English gentleman 1978
2 The English gentleman's wife 1979
3 The English gentleman's child 1979
N.F. A satirical view of the habits of the landed gentry.

SUTHERLAND, H.
1 The arches of the years
2 A time to keep
3 In my path
N.F. Autobiography

SUTHREN, V.
PAUL GALLANT:
1 The black cockade 1979
2 A King's ransom 1980
EDWARD MAINWARING:
1 Royal Yankee 1987
2 Golden galleon 1989
3 Admiral of fear 1991

SUTTON, G.
THE FLEMING FAMILY:
1 The rowan tree
2 Shepherd's warning 1946
3 Smoke across the fell 1947
4 North star
5 Fleming of Honister
This is chronological order, not order of publication

SUTTON, J.
BEL AIR GENERAL:
1 Bel Air General 1987
2 The price of life 1988
3 Masks and faces 1988
4 Vital signs 1989
5 Critical condition 1989
Novels set in a Californian hospital

SVEVO, L., *pseud.* (ETTORE SCHNITZ)
1 Confessions of Zeno 1930
2 Further confessions of Zeno 1969
All Svevo'a novels have a connected theme, being autobiographical, but these are direct sequels.

SWANTON, E. W.
1 Sort of a cricket person 1976
2 Follow on 1977
N.F. Cricket reminiscences

THE SWEENEY
1 The Sweeney *by* I. K. Martin
2 Regan and the Manhattan pipeline *by* J. Balham
3 The Sweeney 2 *by* J. Balham
4 Regan and the deal of the century *by* J. Balham
5 Regan and the Lebonese shipment *by* J. Balham
6 Regan and the human pipeline *by* J. Balham
7 Regan and the snout who cried wolf *by* J. Balham
8 Regan and the bent stripper *by* J. Balham
9 Regan and the Venitian virgin *by* J. Balham
10 Regan and the high rollers *by* J. Balham

SWINNERTON, F.
1 The woman from Sicily 1956
2 A tigress in Prothero 1958
3 The Grace divorce 1960
3 Quadrille 1965
A sequence of novels about a family in four generations - all actors. The scene is a small country town in East Anglia
★★★
1 Background with chorus
2 Figures in the foreground
N.F. Autobiography

SWINSON, A.
SERGEANT CORK:
1 Sergeant Cork's casebook 1968

2 Sergeant Cork's second casebook 1969
The hero first appeared in a television series

SYKES, W. S.
INSPECTOR DRURY:
1 The missing money-lender
2 The harness of death

SYLVESTER, M.
WILLIAM WARNE:
1 A dangerous age 1986
2 A lethal vintage 1988
3 Rough red 1989
Thrillers about a wine merchant

SYMONS, J.
SHERIDAN HAYNES:
1 The Blackheath poisonings 1978
2 Sweet Adelaide 1980
3 The Detling murders 1982
4 A three-pipe problem
5 The Kentish Manor murders 1988

TANGYE, D.
1 A gull on the roof 1964
2 A cat in the window 1965
3 A drake at the door 1966
4 A donkey in the meadow 1967
5 Lama 1969
6 Cornish summer 1971
7 Cottage on a cliff 1973
8 A cat affair 1975
9 The way to Minack 1975
10 Sun on the lintel 1976
11 Somewhere a cat is waiting 1977
12 The winding lane 1978
13 When the winds blow 1980
14 The Ambrose rock 1982
15 A quiet year 1984
16 The cherry tree 1986
17 The evening gull 1990
N.F. Country life in Cornwall

TANNAHILL, R.
1 The world, the flesh and the devil (1400s) 1985
2 Camerons of Kinveil (1800s) 1988

TANNER, J.
HILLSBRIDGE:
1 The black mountains 1983
2 The emerald valley 1985
3 The hills and the valley 1988

TAPPLY, W. G.
BRADY COYNE:
1 Death at Charity's Point 1984

2 The Dutch Blue error 1985
3 Follow the sharks 1986
4 A rodent of doubt 1987
5 Dead meat 1987
6 The vulgar boatman 1988
7 A void in hearts 1989
8 Dead winter 1990
9 Client privilege 1991

TARGET, G. W.
1 The evangelists 1958
2 The teachers 1960
3 The missionaries 1961
4 The shop stewards 1962
5 The Americans 1964
6 The scientists 1966
A series of novels on aspects of life in post-war Britain, concerned particularly with the moral and social problems of our times. Connected only by their theme. Characters do not recur.

TARR, J.
THE HOUND AND THE FALCON:
1 The Isle of Glass 1986
2 The golden horn 1986
3 The hounds of God 1987
Fantasy
THE AVARYAN RISING:
1 The hall of the mountain king
2 The lady of Han-Gilen
3 A fall of princes

TARSIS, V.
1 The pleasure factory 1967
2 The gay life 1968
Two novels about a Black Sea resort in the Soviet Union. The author was imprisoned for his critical novels in 1962, later was released and allowed to live outside the Soviet Union.

TASAKI, H.
THE STORY OF PRIVATE TAKEO:
1 Long the imperial way 1950
2 The mountains remains 1952

TAYLOR, A.
1 To school through the fields 1990
2 Quench the lamp 1991
N.F. Autobiography life in Ireland.

TAYLOR, ANDREW
WILLIAM DOUGAL:
1 Caroline Miniscule 1983
2 Waiting for the end of the world 1984
3 Our fathers' lies 1985
4 An old school tie 1986

5 Freelance death 1987
6 Blood relation 1990

TAYLOR, DAVID
1 Zoo vet 1976
2 Doctor in the zoo 1978
3 Going wild 1980
4 Next panda, please 1982
5 The wandering whale 1984
6 Dragon doctor 1986
7 Vet on the wild side 1990.
N.F. Autobiography of a vet

TAYLOR, DAY
1 The black swan
2 Moss rose
Historical romances

TAYLOR, G.
1 Piece of cake 1969
2 Return ticket 1972
N.F. Autobiography. 2 describes a return to Germany and the prison camp where he spent part of World War II.

TAYLOR, H. B. *pseud.* (H. WAUGH)
DAVID HALLIDAY:
1 The duplicate 1964
2 The trumvirate 1966

TAYLOR, K.
BARD:
1 Bard
2 The first long ship
3 The wild sea
4 Raven's gathering

TAYLOR, P. A.
ASEY MAYO SERIES:
1 The Cape Cod mystery 1931
2 The mystery of the Cape Cod players 1933
3 Mystery of the Cape Cod tavern 1934
4 Tinkling symbol 1935
5 Sandbar majestic 1936
6 Figure away 1938
7 Octagon house 1938
8 Annulet of guilt 1939
9 Banbury bog 1939
10 Spring harrowing 1939
11 The criminal C.O.D. 1940
12 Deadly sunshade 1941
13 Perennial border 1942
14 Six iron spiders 1943
15 Going going gone 1944
16 Proof of the pudding 1945
17 Punch with care 1947
18 Diplomatic corpse 1951

TAYLOR, R.
CHRONICLES OF HAWKLAN:
1 The call of the sword
2 The fall of Fyorland
3 The waking of Orthlund
4 Into Narsindal
   Paperback fantasy

TAYLOR, S.
1 Lights across the Delaware 1954
2 Farewell to Valley Forge 1955
3 Storm the last rampart 1960
   A trilogy of the American War of
   Independence

TELSCOMBE, A.
1 Miss Bagshott goes to Moscow 1960
2 Miss Bagshott goes to Tibet 1961

TELUSHKIN, J.
RABBI DANIEL WINTER:
1 The unorthodox murder of Rabbi Moss
   1987
2 The final analysis of Dr. Stark 1988
3 An eye for an eye 1990

TEMPLE, P.
1 The Tyler mystery 1957
2 East of Algiers 1959

TEMPLE, R.
SIMON LEIGH:
1 Spy is a dirty word 1970
2 The Schulsinger affair 1971

TEMPSKI, A. VON
1 Born in paradise
2 Aloha (my love to you)
   N.F. Autobiography

TENKO
1 Tenko, by A. Masters 1981
2 Last Tenko, by M. Hardwick 1985
3 Tenko reunion, by A. Valery 1985
   Paperback. Based on the TV series

TENNANT, E.
1 A house of hospitalities 1987
2 A wedding of cousins 1988

TEPPER, S. S.
JINIAN FOOTSEER:
1 Jinian Footseer
2 Dervish daughter
3 Jinian Stareye
MARVIN MANYSHAPED:
1 The song of Marvin Manyshaped
2 The flight of Marvin Manyshaped

3 The search of Marvin Manyshaped
PETER:
1 King's blood four
2 Necromancer nine
3 Wizard's eleven
   Paperback fantasies. Each trilogy is
   linked to 'The True Game'

TERRY, C.
1 King of Diamonds 1983
2 The fortune seekers 1985

TEVIS, W.
1 The hustler 1960
2 The colour of money 1985

TEY, J.
DETECTIVE INSPECTOR GRANT SERIES:
1 The man in the queue 1927
2 A shilling for candles 1936
3 The Franchise affair 1948
4 To love and be wise 1950
5 The daughter of time 1951
6 The singing sands 1952

THANE, E.
WILLIAMSBURG SERIES:
1 Dawn's early light (American
   Revolution) 1943
2 Yankee stranger (Civil War) 1944
3 Ever after (Spanish American War)
   1945
4 The light heart (World War I) 1947
5 Kissing kin (1920-1930) 1948
6 This was tomorrow (1934-1938) 1951
7 Homing (1938-1941) 1958

THAYER, L.
PETER CLANCY SERIES:
1 The mystery of the thirteenth floor
2 The unlatched door
3 The puzzle
4 Sinister mark
5 The key
6 Poison
7 Alias Dr. Ely
8 The darkest spot
9 Set a thief
10 Dead men's shoes
11 The last shot
12 The glass knife
13 To catch a thief
14 The Scrimshaw millions
15 Hell-gate tides
16 The counterfeit bill
17 The second shot
18 The death weed
19 Red-handed

20 Murder in the mirror
21 Death in the gorge
22 Last trump
23 The man's doom
24 Ransome racket
25 The strange Sylvester affair
26 Lightning strikes twice
27 Stark murder
28 X marks the spot
29 Guilty
30 Persons unknown
31 Hallowe'en homicide
32 Murder is out
33 Murder on location
34 Accessory after the fact
35 Hanging's too good 1945
36 A plain case of murder 1945
37 Accident, manslaughter or murder 1946
38 Five bullets 1947
39 A hair's breadth 1947
40 The jaws of death 1948
41 Murder stalks the circle 1949
42 Out, brief candle 1950
43 A clue for Clancy 1947 (Pig in a poke)
44 Death within the vault 1950
45 Civil root 1951
46 Too long endured 1952
47 Clancy's secret mission 1952
48 Prisoner pleads not guilty 1954
49 No holiday for death (1954)
50 Murder on the Pacific 1955
51 Fatal alibi 1959 (Who benefits)
52 Web of hate 1959 (Still no answer)
53 Two ways to die 1960
54 Dead on arrival 1960
55 And one cried murder 1962
56 Death walks in shadow 1966 (Dusty death)

THEROUX, P.
1 The consul's file 1981
2 The London embassy 1982

THEW, I. M.
1 The pit village and the store 1985
2 From store to war 1987
   N.F. Autobiography set in a South Yorkshire mining community.

THIRKELL, A.
BARSETSHIRE SERIES:
1 High rising 1933
2 Wild strawberries 1934
3 The demon in the house 1934
4 August folly 1936
5 Summer half 1937
6 Pomfret Towers 1935
7 The Brandons 1939

8 Before lunch 1939
9 Cheerfulness breaks in 1940
10 Northbridge Rectory 1941
11 Marling Hall 1942
12 Growing up 1943
13 The headmistress 1945
14 Miss Bunting 1945
15 Peace breaks out 1946
16 Private enterprise 1947
17 Love among the ruins 1948
18 The old bank house 1949
19 Country chronicle 1950
20 Duke's daughter 1951
21 Happy returns 1952
22 Jutland cottage 1953
23 What did it mean 1954
24 Enter Sir Robert 1955
25 Never too late 1956
26 A double affair 1957
27 Close quarters 1958
28 Love at all ages 1959
29 Three score and ten (originally
   announced as 'The vicar's daughter')
   Completed by C. A. Lejeune 1961.
   Many characters recur throughout these
   novels, 'Each is a separate entity, but it
   is perhaps less confusing to read them
   in order, as it gives more clue to the
   people.' Author

THOMAS, C.
O'NEILL FAMILY:
1 Bridie 1989
2 April 1990
3 Hannah 1991

THOMAS, CRAIG
FIREFOX:
1 Firefox 1977
2 Firefox down 1983
3 Winter hawk 1987
KENNETH AUBREY:
1 The bear's tears 1985
2 All the grey cats 1988
3 The last raven 1990

THOMAS, D. M.
SERGEI ROZANOV:
1 Ararat 1983
2 Swallow 1984
3 Sphinx 1986
4 Summit 1987
5 Lying together 1990

THOMAS, DONALD
INSPECTOR SWAIN:
1 Belladonna 1984
2 The Ripper's apprentice 1986

3 Jekyll, alias Hyde 1988
Detective stories set in Victorian London

THOMAS, E. M.
1 Reindeer Moon 1987
2 The animal wife 1991

THOMAS, H.
1 As it was 1926
2 World without end 1931
3 Time and again 1978
4 Under storm's wing 1988
N.F. Autobiography of the wife of Edward Thomas, the poet

THOMAS, LESLIE
1 The virgin soldiers 1966
2 Onward, Virgin Soldiers 1971
3 Stand up, Virgin soldiers 1975
 * * *
1 This time next week 1974
2 In my wildest dreams 1984
N.F. Autobiography
DANGEROUS DAVIES:
1 Dangerous Davies 1976
2 Dangerous in love 1987

THOMAS, R.
MACCORKIE AND PADILLO:
1 The cold war swap (Spy in the Vodka)
2 Cast a yellow shadow 1971
3 The backup men 1972

THOMPSON, D.
WILDERNESS:
1 King of the mountain
2 Lure of the wild
3 Savage rendezvous
Paperback westerns

THOMPSON, E. V.
NATHAN JAGO:
1 The restles sea 1983
2 Polrudden 1985
Set in Cornwall in the 18th and 19th centuries
RETALLICK FAMILY:
1 Ben Retallick 1980
2 Chase the wind 1977
3 Harvest of the sun 1978
4 Singing spears 1982
5 The stricken land 1986
6 Lottie Trago 1990
Novels about mining in Cornwall and S. Africa

THOMPSON, GENE
DADE COOLEY:
1 Murder mystery 1981
2 Nobody cared for Kate 1983
3 A cup of death 1988

THOMPSON, GRACE
VALLEY SERIES:
1 A welcome in the valley 1989
2 Valley affairs 1990
3 The changing valley 1990
Novels set in South Wales

THOMPSON, K.
THE DERAIN FAMILY SERIES:
1 Great house 1955
2 Mandevilla 1957
3 Sugarbied 1963
4 Richard's way 1965
5 The painted caves 1968

THOMPSON, L. S.
1 Death stops the show 1946
2 Hear not my steps 1953

THOMPSON, N.
1 At their departing 1986
2 On their return 1987

THOMPSON, R.
1 No exit from Vietnam 1971
2 Peace is not at hand 1974
N.F. History of the Vietnam war

THOMPSON, D.
1 Daniel
2 Break in the sun

THOMSON, DAVID
1 Nairn in darkness and light 1987
2 Woodbrook 1974
N.F. Memories of a Scottish childhood

THOMSON, J.
CHIEF INSPECTOR FINCH:
1 Not one of us 1972
2 Death cap 1973
3 The long revenge 1974
4 Case closed 1977
5 A question of identity 1978
6 Deadly relations 1979
7 Alibi in time 1980
8 Shadow of a doubt 1981
9 To make a killing 1982
10 Sound evidence 1984
11 A dying fall 1985
12 The dark stream 1986
13 No flowers, by request 1987

14 Rosemary for remembrance 1988
15 The spoils of time 1989
16 Past reckoning 1990
17 Foul play 1991

THORNDYKE, R.
DOCTOR SYN:
1 Doctor Syn on the high seas 1936
2 Doctor Syn returns 1935
3 Further adventures of Doctor Syn 1936
4 Courageous exploits of Doctor Syn 1936
5 The amazing quest of Doctor Syn 1938
6 The shadow of Doctor Syn 1944
7 Doctor Syn 1915
Listed in chronological order of reading

THORNE, N.
ASKHAM CHRONICLES:
1 Never such innocence 1985
2 Yesterday's promises 1986
3 Bright morning 1986
4 A place in the sun 1987

THORWALD, J.
THE CENTURY OF THE DETECTIVE:
1 The marks of Cain 1965
2 Dead men tell tales 1966
3 Proof of poison 1966
N.F. Criminology
1 Century of the surgeon
2 Triumph of surgery
N.F. Medicine

THURLEY, J.
1 Household gods 1988
2 Tenements of clay 1989
Not direct sequels, but companion novels

TIBBER, R.
1 No white coat 1958
2 Love on my list 1959
3 Patients of a saint 1961
N.F. Autobiography. Story of a doctor
***
1 The general practice 1968
2 Practice makes perfect 1969
Two novels on life of a doctor

TIBBLE, A.
1 Greenhorn 1973
2 One woman's story 1976
3 Alone 1979
N.F. Autobiography

TIDYMAN, E.
JOHN SHAFT SERIES:
1 Shaft 1971
2 Shaft's big score
3 Shaft has a ball
4 Shaft's carnival of killers
5 Shaft among the Jews 1973
6 The last Shaft 1974
2-4 published in U.S.A. only

TILLEY, P.
AMTRAK WARRIORS:
1 Cloud warrior 1974
2 The first family 1985
3 Iron master
4 Blood river
5 Death bringer
6 Earth-thunder
Paperback fantasy. "Dark visions", a guide to the Amtrak Wars mission is a pendant to the series

TILMAN, H. W.
1 Mischief in Patagonia
2 Mischief among the penguins
3 Mischief in Greenland

TISLEY, F.
1 Voice of the crowd 1954
2 Brother Nap 1954

TILTMAN, M. H.
1 Quality Chase 1939
2 Quality Chase's daughter 1955
Stories of an antique dealer
COUNTRY LIFE TRILOGY:
1 Cottage pie 1940
2 Little place in the country 1944
3 The birds began to sing 1952

TIMLETT, P. V.
1 Seedbearers
2 Power of the serpent
3 Twilight of the serpent
Paperback fantasy

TIMMS, E. V.
AUSTRALIAN SAGA:
1 Forever to remain 1948
2 Pathway of the sun 1949
3 Beckoning shore 1950
4 Valleys beyond 1952
5 The challenge 1953
6 Scarlet frontier 1954
7 The fury 1955
8 They came from the sea 1956
9 Shining harvest 1957
10 Robina 1958

11 The big country 1959
   Concluded by Alma Timms
12 Time and change 1972
   *Series of novels on the development of
   Australia since 1831*

TIMPSON, J.
1 Paper trail 1990
2 Sound track 1991
   Semi-autobiographical novels

TINNISWOOD, P.
BRANDON FAMILY:
1 A touch of Daniel 1969
2 I didn't know you cared 1973
3 Except you're a bird 1974
4 Call it a canary 1985
5 Uncle Mort's North Country 1986
6 Uncle Mort's South Country 1990
THE BRIGADIER:
1 Tales from a long room 1981
2 More tales from a long room 1982
3 The Brigadier down under 1983
4 The Brigadier in season 1984
5 Tales from Witney Scrotum 1987

   ★★★

1 Hayballs 1989
2 Winston 1991

TIPPETT, G.
WILSON YOUNG:
1 Wilson's gold
2 Wilson's luck
3 Wilson's choice
4 Wilson's revenge 1983
   Westerns

TOER, P. A.
1 This earth of mankind 1979
2 Child of all nations 1980

TOLKIEN, J. R. R.
THE LORD OF THE RINGS:
1 The Hobbit 1950
2 The fellowship of the ring 1952
3 The two towers 1954
4 The return of the King 1955
5 The Silmarillion 1978
   *An allegory of a mythical world. 1
   describes the finding of the ring, the
   sequels which are a separate cycle, its
   consequences*
HISTORY OF MIDDLE EARTH:
1 The book of lost tales 1 1983
2 The book of lost tales 2 1984
3 The lays of Beleriad 1985
4 The shaping of Middle Earth 1986

5 The lost road etc. 1987
6 The return of the shadow 1988
   *A mixture of fiction and fragments
   based on Tolkien's notes for 'The Lord
   of the Rings', edited by his son*

TOLSTOY, L.
*'Count Vronsky's daughter', by C.
Salisbury is a continuation of 'War and
Peace'. 1981*

TOMALIN, R.
RALPH OLIVER:
1 The garden house 1964
2 The spring house 1968

TOMAS, ANDREW
1 We are not the first 1971
2 On the shores of endless worlds 1974
   N.F. Mysteries of the Universe

TOMKINSON, C.
1 Les girls 1956
2 African follies 1959
3 What a performance
   N.F. Autobiography

TOMS, P.
CHRONICLES OF PENNYCRESS:
1 Mrs Sherwood's summer 1965
2 Three fountains 1966
3 Cottage on the green 1967

TORR, I.
1 A time of change 1967
2 Sundown 1969
   *Two novels about the transfer of power
   in West Africa*

TORRIE, M., *pseud.* (GLADYS
MITCHELL)
TIMOTHY HERRING SERIES:
1 Heavy as lead 1966
2 Late and cold 1967
3 Your secret friend 1968
4 Churchyard salad 1969
5 Shades of darkness 1970
6 Bismark herrings 1971

TOURNEY, L.
MATTHEW STOCK:
1 The players' boy is dead 1982
2 Low treason 1984
3 Familiar spirits 1985
4 The Bartholomew Fair murders 1987
   Detective stories set in the 17th century

TOVEY, D.

THE JUNGLE NOVELS:
1 Government 1971
2 The carreta 1970
3 March to Caobaland 1961
4 Trozas
5 The rebellion of the hanged 1952
6 General from the jungle
Not all published in the U.K.

TRAVERS, B.
1 Vale of laughter 1957
2 A' sitting on a gate 1978
N.F. Autobiography

TRAVERS, H.
DOMINIQUE AUBREY:
1 Madame Aubrey and the police 1966
2 Madame Aubrey dines with death 1967

TREACY, S.
1 Shay Scally and Manny Wagstaff
2 Scallywags 1979

TREASE, G.
1 A whiff of burnt boats 1972
2 Laughter at the door 1974
N.F. Autobiography

TREGER, A.
1 Probationer nurse
2 Maternity nurse
N.F. Autobiography

TREHERNE, J.
DR. JAMES YEO:
1 The trap 1985
2 Mangrove chronicles 1986

TREMAYNE, P.
LANKERNE:
1 The fires of Lankerne 1979
2 The destroyers of Lankerne 1982
3 Buccaneers of Lankerne 1983

TRENEER, A.
1 School house in the wind 1944
2 Cornish years
3 Stranger in the Midlands 1952
N.F. Autobiography

TRENHAILE, J.
STEPAN POVIN:
1 A view from the square 1983
2 Nocturne for the general 1985

TRESILLIAN, R.
BLOODHEART:
1 Bloodheart 1986

2 Bloodheart royal 1986
3 Bloodheart feud 1987
BONDMASTER:
1 Bondmaster 1977
2 Bondmaster Buck 1984
3 Blood of the Bondmaster 1978
4 Bondmaster breed 1979
5 Bondmaster fury 1982
6 Bondmaster's revenge 1983
Novels set on a slave plantation in Dominica, listed in chronological order
FLESH TRADERS:
1 Master of Black River 1987
2 Black River affair 1987
3 Black River breed 1987

TREVANION, M.
JONATHAN HEMLOCK:
1 The Eiger sanction 1973
2 The Loo sanction 1974

TREVELYAN, R.
PENDRAGON SERIES:
1 Pendragon - late of Prince Albert's Own 1975
2 His Highness commands Pendragon 1976
3 Pendragon and the Montenegran plot 1977
4 Pendragon and the seeds of mutiny 1979
Spy stories set in Victorian times

TREVENA, J.
DARTMOOR TRILOGY:
1 Furze the cruel
2 Granite
3 Heather

TREVOR, E., *see* **HALL, A.,** *and*
RATTRAY, S., *pseuds.*

TREVOR, M.
LUXEMBOURG SERIES:
1 The fugitives 1973
2 The marked man 1974
3 The enemy at home 1974
4 The forgotten country 1975
5 The treacherous paths 1976
6 The civil prisoner 1977
7 The fortunes of peace 1978
8 Wanton fires 1979
Novels about a family in the time of the French Revolution

TREWIN, J. C.
1 Up from the lizard 1948

2 Down to the lion 1952
N.F. Autobiography

TRIPP, M.
JOHN SAMSON:
1 Obession 1973
2 The once a year man 1977
3 Cruel victim 1979
4 The wife smuggler 1978
5 A woman in bed 1976
6 Going solo 1981
7 One love too many 1983
8 Death of a man-tamer 1987
9 The frightened wife 1987
10 The cords of vanity 1989
11 Video vengeance 1990

TROW, M. J.
INSPECTOR LESTRADE:
1 The adventures of Inspector Lestrade 1985
2 Brigade 1986
3 Lestrade and the hallowed house 1986
4 Lestrade and the Leviathan 1987
5 Lestrade and the brother of death 1987
6 Lestrade and the Ripper 1988
7 Lestrade and the guardian angel 1990
8 Lestrade and the deadly game 1990
9 Lestrade and the gift of the prince 1991
10 Lestrade and the magpie 1991
   see also Doyle, A. C. Sherlock Holmes

TROY, S.
INSPECTOR SMITH SERIES:
1 Half way to murder 1955
2 Tonight and tomorrow 1957
3 Drunkard's end 1960
4 Second cousin removed 1961
5 Waiting for Oliver 1961
6 Don't play with the rough boys 1963
7 Cease upon the midnight 1964
8 No more a roving 1966
9 Sup with the devil 1968
10 Swift to its close 1969
11 Blind man's garden 1970

TROYAT, H.
SYLVIE:
1 Sylvie 1982
2 Sylvie; her teenage years 1987
3 Happiness 1989

TRUSS, E. C.
INSPECTOR GIDLEIGH SERIES:
1 In secret places 1958
2 The hidden men 1959
3 One man's death 1960 (One man's enemies)

TS'AO CHAN HSUEH CHIN
THE STORY OF THE STONE:
1 The golden days 1973
2 The crab-flower club 1977
3 The warning voice 1980
4 The debt of tears 1982
5 The dreamer wakes 1986

TUBB, E. C.
DUMAREST SAGA:
1 Winds of Gath
2 Derai
3 Toyman
4 Kalin
5 The jester at Scar
6 Lallia
7 Technos
8 Veruchia
9 Mayenne
10 Jendelle
11 Zenya
12 The eye of the Zodiac
13 Eloise
14 Jack of swords
15 Spectrum of a forgotten sun
16 Haven of darkness
17 Prison of night
18 Incident on Ath
19 The Quillian sector
20 Web of sand
21 Iduna's Universe
22 The terra data
23 World of promise
24 Nectar of heaven
25 The Terridae
26 The coming event
27 Earth is heaven
28 Melome
29 Angado
30 Symbol of Terra
31 The temple of truth
   Paperback science fiction 28 & 29, and 30 & 31 published as two in one vol.

TUCKER, T.
1 Woman into wolf 1969
2 The unravished bride 1970
   Historical romances about Richard II

TURNBULL, P.
GLASGOW POLICE DIVISION:
1 Deep and crisp and even 1981
2 Dead knock 1982
3 Fair Friday 1983
4 Big money 1984
5 Two way cut 1988
6 Condition purple 1989
7 And did murder him 1991

TURNER, B.
SOLDEN SERIES:
1 Bound to die 1966
2 Sex trap 1968
3 Circle of squares 1969
4 Another little death 1970
5 Solden's woman 1972

TURNER, G.
THE TREELAKE SAGA:
1 A stranger and afraid 1964
2 The cupboard under the stairs 1962
3 Waste of shame 1965
4 Lame dog man 1968
A tetralogy of novels about modern Australia

TURNER, GEORGE
1 Beloved son 1978
2 Vaneglory 1981
3 Yesterday's men 1983
Science fiction

TURNER, JAMES
RAMPION SAVAGE SERIES:
1 Murder at Landred Hall 1954
2 A death by the sea 1955
3 The dark index 1959
4 The glass interval 1961
5 The nettleshade 1962
6 The slate landscape 1964
7 The blue mirror 1965
8 Requiem for two sisters 1968
9 The stone dormitory 1970

***

1 Seven gardens for Catherine 1968
2 Sometimes into England 1970
N.F. Autobiography
THE STORY OF NICHOLAS DE LA HAYE:
1 The crimson moth 1962
2 The long avenues 1964
3 Anna Chevron 1966

TURNER, JUDY
HAISBY:
1 The arcade 1990
2 Harbour Hill 1991

TURNER, P.
1 Colonel Shepperton's clock 1964
2 The Grange at High Force 1965

TURNER, S,
1 Over the counter
2 A farmer's wife 1963
3 The farm at King's Standing 1964
N.F. Autobiography

TUROW, S
"SANDY" STERN:
1 Presumed innocent 1988
2 Burden of proof 1990

TURPIN, A.
GEOFFREY GILLIARD:
1 My flat and her apartment 1963
2 The box 1965
3 Beatrice and Bertha 1966
4 Innocent employments 1967
5 Laughing cavalier 1969

TURTLEDOVE, H.
THE VIDESSOS CYCLE:
1 The misplaced legion
2 An Emperor for the Legion
3 The Legion of Videssos
4 Swords of the Legion
Paperback fantasy

TUTE, W.
1 The Felthams
2 The younger Felthams
'TARNHAM' SERIES:
1 A matter of diplomacy 1969
2 The powder train 1970
3 The Tarnham connection 1971
4 The resident 1973
5 Next Saturday in Milan 1975

TUTTLE, W. C.
HASHKNIFE SERIES:
1 The medicine man
2 Ghost trails
3 Thicker than water
4 Morgan trail
5 Santa Dolores stage
6 Hashknife of Stormy river
7 Tumbling river range
8 The dead line
9 Arizona ways (Hashknife of Double Bar)
10 Hashknife lends a hand
11 Hashknife of the canyon trail
12 Bluffer's luck
13 Hidden blood
14 Trouble trailer
15 Shot gun gold
16 Valley of suspicion 1964
17 Double-crossers of Ghost Tree 1965
18 The payroll of fate 1966
19 The ghost busters 1968

TWAIN, M.
TOM SAWYER AND HUCKLEBERRY FINN:
1 Adventures of Tom Sawyer
2 Adventures of Huckleberry Finn

3 Tom Sawyer abroad
4 Tom Sawyer, detective
5 Tom Sawyer grows up, by C. Wood
6 Further adventures of Huck Finn, by
  G. Matthews 1982

TWEEDSMUIR, LADY see BUCHAN, S. C.

TYNDALL, J.
ROGER TURNBULL:
1 Death in the Jordan 1970
2 Death in the Lebanon 1971

UHNAK, D.
CHRISTIE OPERA SERIES:
1 The bait 1969
2 The witness 1970
3 The ledger 1971

ULASI, A. L.
1 Many things you no understand 1970
2 Many things begin for change 1971
Two novels about Nigeria in the '30s

UNDERHILL, C.
FANTOM:
1 Captain Fantom 1977
2 The forging of Fantom 1979

UNDERWOOD, M.
NICK ATTWELL:
1 The juror 1975
2 The fatal trip 1977
3 Murder with malice 1977
4 Crooked wood 1978
RICHARD MONK:
1 The man who died on Friday 1967
2 The man who killed too soon 1968
ROSA EPTON:
1 A pinch of snuff 1974
2 Anything but the truth 1978
3 Smooth justice 1979
4 Victim of circumstance 1980
5 Crime upon crime 1981
6 Double jeopardy 1981
7 Goddess of death 1982
8 A party to murder 1984
9 Death in camera 1985
10 The hidden man 1985
11 Death at Deepwood Grange 1986
12 The uninvited corpse 1987
13 The injudicious judge 1987
14 Dual enigma 1988
15 A compelling case 1989
16 Rosa's dilemma 1990
17 Dangerous business 1990
18 The seeds of murder 1991

UPDIKE, J.
1 Rabbit, run 1961
2 Rabbit redux 1972
3 Rabbit is rich 1982
4 Rabbit at rest 1990
BECH:
1 Bech: a book 1970
2 Bech is back 1983

UPFIELD, A. W.
NAPOLEON BONAPARTE SERIES:
1 The house of Cain 1928
2 The Barakee mystery 1929
3 The beach of atonement 1930
4 A royal abduction 1932
5 Gripped by drought 1932
6 Wings above the Diamantia 1936
  (Wings above the claypan *or* The
  winged mystery)
7 Mr. Jelly's business 1938 (Murder
  down under)
8 The bone is pointed 1938
9 The sands of Windee 1939
10 Winds of evil 1939
11 Bushranger of the skies 1940
12 No footprints in the bush 1944
13 Death of a swagman 1945
14 The devil's steps 1946
15 An author bites the dust 1948
16 The widows of Broome 1951
17 The mountains have a secret 1952
18 The new shoe 1952
19 Venom house 1953
20 Murder must wait 1953
21 Death of a lake 1954
22 Cake in the hatbox 1954 (Sinister
  stones)
23 The battling prophet 1956
24 The man of two tribes 1956
25 Bony buys a woman 1957 (The
  bushman who came back)
26 The bachelors of Broken Hill 1958
27 Bony and the mouse 1959 (Journey to
  the hangman)
28 Bony and the black virgin 1959
29 The mystery of Swordfish Reef 1960
30 Bony and the Kelly gang 1960 (Valley of
  smugglers)
31 Bony and the White Savage 1961
32 The will of the tribe 1962
33 Madman's bend 1962
34 The Lake Frome monster 1966
  completed by Mrs. Upfield
  *It is difficult to establish a correct order
  of reading for this series, since early
  titles were not all published in U.K.
  Heinemann published in U.K. from no.
  16 and later republished some of the*

early titles. Others were republished by the London house of Angus and Robertson, who originally published many of the early titles in Australia. This is however a complete list, except for one title, 'Lure of the bush', apparently only published in U.S.A., and which may be a variant title of another volume.

UPSTAIRS, DOWNSTAIRS SERIES:
1 Upstairs, downstairs *by* John Hawkesworth 1973
2 Rose's story *by* Terence Brady and Charlotte Bingham 1973
3 Sarah's story *by* Mollie Hardwick 1973
4 Mr. Hudson's diary *by* Michael Hardwick 1973
5 In my lady's chamber *by* John Hawkesworth 1974
6 Mr. Bellamy's story *by* Michael Hardwick 1974
7 The years of change *by* Mollie Hardwick 1974
8 Mrs. Bridges' story *by* Mollie Hardwick 1975
9 The war to end wars *by* Mollie Hardwick 1976
10 Endings and beginnings *by* Mollie Hardwick 1976
11 On with the dance *by* Mollie Hardwick 1977
12 Thomas and Sarah *by* Mollie Hardwick 1978
13 Two for a spin *by* Mollie Hardwick 1978
   The last two follow the adventures of Thomas and Sarah, after they leave the Bellamy household.
   Stories adapted from the TV series

UPWARD, E.
ALAN SEBRILL TRILOGY:
1 In the thirties 1968
2 The rotten elements 1969
3 No home but the struggle 1977

URQUHART, F.
THE STORY OF BESSIE HIPKISS:
1 The ferret was Abraham's daughter
2 Jezebel's dust

URQUHART, M.
1 Frail on the north circular 1962
2 Girl on the waterfront 1962
3 Dig the missing 1963

USHER, F.

DAYE SMITH SERIES:
1 Ghost of a chance 1956
2 The lonely cage 1956
3 Portrait of fear 1957
4 The price of death 1957
5 Death is waiting 1958
6 First to kill 1959
7 Death in error 1959
8 Dig my darling 1960
9 Shot in the dark 1961
10 The faceless stranger 1961
11 Fall into my grave 1962
12 Who killed Rosie Gray 1962
13 Stairway to murder 1964
AMANDA CURZON AND OSCAR SALLIS:
1 The man from Moscow 1967
2 No flowers in Braslov 1968
3 The Boston crab 1970

USHER, G.
DETECTIVE-SUPERINTENDENT DREXEL:
1 Death in the straw 1954
2 The Restmaster riddle 1955

VACHSS, A.
BURKE:
1 Flood 1986
2 Strega 1988
3 Blue Belle 1989
4 Hard candy 1990
5 Blossom 1991

VAIL, A.
1 Love me a little
2 The bright young things

VALENTINE, D.
KEVIN BRYCE:
1 Unorthodox methods 1988
2 A collector of photographs 1989

VALIN, J.
HARRY STONER:
1 The lime pit 1980
2 Final notice 1981
3 Dead letter 1982
4 Day of wrath 1983
5 Natural causes 1984
6 Life's work 1988
7 Fire lake 1989

VANCE, J.
DEMON PRINCES:
1 Star king 1968
2 The killing machine
3 Palace of love
4 The face 1980

5 The book of dreams 1982
Science fiction
PLANET OF ADVENTURE:
1 City of Chasch 1974
2 Servant of the Wankh 1974
3 The Dirdir 1975
4 The Pnume 1975
Science fiction
LYONESSE:
1 Lyonesse
2 The green pearl
3 Madouc 1990
Fantasy

VANCE, J. H.
SHERIFF JOE BAIN:
1 The Fox valley murders 1966
2 The Pleasant Grove murders 1968

VANDERCOOK, J. W.
BERTRAM LYNCH SERIES:
1 Murder in Trinidad 1933
2 Murder in Fiji 1936
3 Murder in Haiti 1956
4 Murder in New Guinea 1959

VANDERGRIFF, A.
DAUGHTERS OF THE SOUTH WIND:
1 Daughters of the wild country
2 Daughters of the opal skies
3 Daughters of the far islands
4 Daughters of the misty isles
Paperback fantasy

VAN DER MEERSCH, M.
1 The poor girl
2 The hour of love 1956

VAN DER POST, L.
1 A bar of shadow 1956
2 The seed and the sower 1957
3 The sword and the doll 1959
*Published in one volume in 1962,
under the title of 2. Wartime
experiences of a soldier*

***

1 The lost world of the Kalahari 1958
2 The heart of the hunter 1960
N.F. Travel

***

1 A story like the wind 1972
2 A far off place 1974

VAN DER WATER, F. F.
AMERICAN REVOLUTION SERIES:
1 Reluctant rebel 1948

2 Wings of the morning 1955
3 Day of battle 1958
4 Catch a falling star 1949
*Mainly centred on the history of the
State of Vermont*

VAN GREENAWAY, P.
INSPECTOR CHERRY:
1 The Medusa touch 1973
2 Doppelganger 1975
3 The destiny man 1977
4 'Cassandra' Bell 1981
5 The Lazarus lie 1982
6 The killing cup 1987

VAN GULIK, R.
JUDGE DEE SERIES:
1 The Chinese bell murders 1958
2 The Chinese gold murders 1959
3 The Chinese lake murders 1960
4 The Chinese nail murders 1961
5 The Chinese maze murders 1961
6 The Emperor's pearl 1962
7 The haunted monastery 1963
8 The lacquer screen
9 The red pavillion 1964
10 The willow pattern 1965
11 The monkey and the tiger 1965
12 The phantom of the temple 1966
13 Murder in Canton 1966
14 Judge Dee at work 1967
15 Necklace and calabash 1967
16 Poets and murder 1968
*An unusual series in that the scene is
medieval China. Nos. 8 and 9 are direct
sequels within the sequence*

VAN LUSTBADER, E.
SUNSET WARRIOR:
1 Sunset warrior 1979
2 The shallows of night 1980
3 Dai-San 1980
Fantasy

***

1 The Ninja 1983
2 The Miko 1984
3 White Ninja 1990
JAKE MAROC:
1 Jian 1985
2 Shan 1987

VANNER, L.
1 Rannoch Chase
2 Guardian of Rannoch 1986
Paperback

VAN SLYKE, H.
1 The heart listens 1974
2 The mixed blessing 1975

VAN VOGT, A. E.
1 The weapon shops of Isher
2 The weapon makers
Science fiction

***

1 The worlds of Null-A 1968
2 The players of Null-A 1970
Science fiction

VARDEMAN, R. E.
THE WAR OF POWERS:
1 The war of powers
2 Istu awakened
Paperback fantasy

VARLEY, J.
GAE TRILOGY:
1 Titon
2 Wizard 1981
3 Demon 1984
Paperback fantasy

VARNHAM, J.
INSPECTOR SEMLAKE SERIES:
1 Death rehearses 1950
2 Travelling dead man 1951
3 Beware of the dog 1954

VAUGHAN, A.
1 Signalman's morning 1981
2 Signalman's twilight 1983
3 Signalman's nightmare 1987
N.F. Autobiography of a railwayman

VAUGHAN, R.
1 Moulded in earth 1951
2 Son of Justin 1955
*2 is about the son of Justin Peele, main
character in 1*

VELIKOVSKY, I.
AGES IN CHAOS:
1 From the Exodus to King Akhnaton
1953
2 The time of Isaiah and Homer
3 Rameses II and his time 1979
4 Peoples of the sea 1977
N.F. Cosmography

VENTERS, A.
GIL KENNEDY:
1 Kennedy's killing 1982
2 Blood on the rocks 1983

VERNE, J.
CAPTAIN HATTERAS SERIES:
1 The English at the North Pole (At the
North Pole) 1875
2 The ice desert (The Field of ice *or* The
desert of ice) 1876
CAPTAIN NEMO SERIES:
1 20,000 leagues under the sea 1872
2 Dropped from the clouds 1875
3 Abandoned
4 The secret of the island
THE CRYPTOGRAM:
1 The conspirators of Trieste
2 The captives of Antekirtta
GIANT RAFT SERIES:
1 800 leagues of the Amazon (Down the
Amazon)
2 The crypogram
J. R. KASALLON:
1 The survivors of the Chancellor
2 Martin Paz
KEREBAN THE INFLEXIBLE:
1 Captain of the *Guidara*
2 Scarpante, the spy

***

1 From the earth to the moon 1873
2 Round the moon 1875
THE STEAM HOUSE:
1 The demon of Cawnpore
2 Tigers and traitors
THE BARSAC MISSION:
1 The city in the Sahara
2 Into the Niger bend
Both republished in 1959

***

1 Into the abyss 1963
2 Leader of the resistance 1963
*Republication in two volumes of 'A
family without a name', historical novel
on the 1987 rising in Quebec*

***

1 Anomalous phenomena
2 Homeward bound
*Reprinted in this form, 1965, but they
are parts of the novel 'Hector Servadac'*
CAPTAIN GRANT'S CHILDREN:
1 The mysterious document
2 Among the cannibals
*Published in this form, 1964. Originally
published in English as a trilogy.
'Voyage around the world'. Vol. 2 of this
is 'On the track', which in the above ed.
is divided between vols. 1 and 2*
CESAR CASCABEL:
1 The show on ice

2 The travelling circus
Published in this form 1966
THE FUR COUNTRY:
1 The sun in eclipse
2 Through the Behring strait
Published in this form 1966
NORTH AGAINST SOUTH:
1 Burbank the Northerner
2 Texas the Southerner
*The story of the American Civil War,
published in this ed. in 2 vols. 1963*
THE GOLDEN VOLCANO:
1 The claim on forty mile creek
2 Flood and flame
Published in this ed. in 2 vols. 1962
THE SURVIVORS OF THE JONATHAN:
1 The masterless man
2 The unwilling dictator
Published in this ed. in 2 vols. 1962
THE THOMSON TRAVEL AGENCY:
1 Package holiday
2 End of the journey
Published in this ed. in 2 vols. 1965
TWO YEARS' HOLIDAY:
1 Adrift in the Pacific
2 Second year ashore
Published in this ed. in 2 vols. 1964
CLIPPER OF THE CLOUDS:
1 Master of the world
2 Robur the conqueror
Published in this ed. in 2 vols. 1963

VERNER, G.
1 The cleverness of Mr. Budd 1935
2 The return of Mr. Budd 1938
3 Mr. Budd again 1939
4 Mr. Budd investigates 1963

VERNEY, J.
1 Going to the wars 1955
2 A dinner of herbs 1966
*N.F. Autobiography. In 2 the author
revisits the scene of his wartime
imprisonment and tells the story of his
escape*

VERNON, E.
1 Practice makes perfect 1971
2 Practise what you preach 1978
3 Getting into practise 1979
N.F. Autobiography of a young doctor

VERNON, F.
1 Gentlemen and players 1984
2 Privileged children 1982
3 A desirable husband 1987
Novels about Edwardian family life

VICKERS, B.
1 Fed up to the top attic 1984
2 Life golden in time 1985
N.F. Life in Victorian Bridlington

VICKERS, R.
DEAD ENDS SERIES:
1 The department of dead ends 1946
(Murder will out)
2 Eight murders in the suburbs 1954
*There is a story in this series in Ellery
Queen's 'Double dozen', 1965. Le Cour
'The murder book' states there are six
collections of 'Dead ends' stories, but
the editor has not been able to trace
them*
INSPECTOR CURWEN SERIES:
1 Gold and wine 1949
2 They can't hang Caroline 1950
3 Six came to dinner 1951
4 Murder in two flats 1952

VIDAL, GORE
1 Myra Breckinridge 1968
2 Myron 1975
WASHINGTON TRILOGY:
1 Burr 1973
2 1876 1976
3 Washington D.C. 1967
The political evolution of America

VINES, F.
1 The lonely shore 1959
2 So wild the sea 1961
Historical novels on Western Australia

VINGE, J.
1 The snow queen
2 World's end
Paperback science fiction

VINGE, V.
1 The peace war
2 Marooned in real time
Paperback science fiction

VINTER, M.
1 All these shall perish 1970
2 Rat in a trap 1971
3 The wounds of treason 1972
A trilogy of novels on espionage

VIVIAN, F.
INSPECTOR KNOLLIS SERIES:
1 Death of Mr. Lomas 1941
2 Sable messenger 1947
3 The threefold cord 1947
4 The ninth enemy 1948

5 Laughing dog 1949
6 Singing masons 1950
7 Sleeping island 1951
8 Elusive bowman 1951
9 The ladies of Locksley 1953

VOINOVICH, V.
1 Life and adventures of Private Ivan
Chomkin 1978
2 Pretender to the throne 1981
*Novels about Russia during and after
WWII*

VOSS BARK, C.
MR. HOLME SERIES:
1 Mr. Holmes at sea 1962
2 Mr. Holmes goes to ground 1963
3 Mr. Holmes and the fair Armenian
1964
4 Mr. Holmes and the love bank 1964
5 The Shepherd file 1966
6 See the living crocodiles 1967
7 The second red dragon 1968

VYVYAN, C. C.
1 Roots and stars 1962
2 Journey up the years 1966
N.F. Autobiography and gardening

WADDELL, M.
THE OTLEY QUARTET:
1 Otley 1965
2 Otley pursued 1966
3 Otley forever 1967
4 Otley victorious 1969

WADE, H.
INSPECTOR POOLE SERIES:
1 The Duke of York's steps
2 No friendly drop
3 Policeman's lot
4 Constable, guard thyself
5 Bury him darkly
6 Lonely Magdalen
7 New graves at Great Norme
8 Be kind to the killer
9 Diplomat's folly
10 Too soon to die
11 Gold was our grave
12 The Litmore snatch

WAHLOO, P.
CHIEF INSPECTOR JENSEN SERIES:
1 Murder on the 31st floor 1969
2 The steel spring 1970
See also **Sjowall, M.** *and* **Wahloo, P.**

WAIN, J.
1 Where the rivers meet 1988
2 Comedies 1990

WAINWRIGHT, J.
1 Death in a sleeping city 1966
2 Ten steps to the gallows 1966
3 Evil intent 1966
4 The crystallised carbon pig 1967
5 Talent for murder 1967
6 The worms must await 1968
7 Web of silence 1968
8 Edge of extinction 1968
9 The darkening glass 1969
10 The takeover men 1969
11 The big tickle 1969
12 Prynter's devil 1970
13 Freeze thy blood less coldly 1970
14 The last buccaneer 1971
15 Dig the grave and let him die 1971
16 Night is a time to die 1972
17 Requiem for a loser 1972
18 A pride of pigs 1973
19 High class kill 1973
20 A touch of malice 1973
21 Kill the girls and make them cry 1974
22 The hard hit 1974
23 Square dance 1974
24 Death of a big man 1975
25 Landscape with violence 1975
26 Coppers don't cry 1975
27 Acquittal 1976
28 Walther P.38 1976
29 Who goes next? 1976
30 The bastard 1976
31 Pool of tears 1977
32 A nest of rats 1977
33 The day of the peppercorn kill 1977
34 The jury people 1978
35 Thief of time 1978
36 Death certificate 1978
37 A ripple of murders 1978
38 Brainwash 1979
39 Tension 1979
40 Duty elsewhere 1979
41 Take murder 1979
42 The eye of the beholder 1980
43 Dominoes 1980
44 A kill of small consequences 1980
45 Venus fly trap 1980
46 The tainted man 1980
47 All on a summer's day 1981
48 An urge for justice 1981
49 Anatomy of a riot 1982
50 Blayde RIP 1982
51 Distaff factor 1982
52 Their evil ways 1983
53 Spiral staircase 1983

54 All through the night 1985
55 Clouds of guilt 1985
56 Forgotten murders 1987
57 A very parochial murder 1988
58 The man who wasn't there 1989
Novels about police work in the North of England
DAVIS SERIES:
1 Davis doesn't live here anymore 1970
2 The pig got up and slowly walked away 1971
3 My word you should have seen us 1972
4 My God how the money rolls in 1972
5 The devil you don't 1974
1-4 volumes in the series were published under the name of Ripley, J.

WALDER, D.
1 Bags of swank 1964
2 The short list 1965
3 The house party 1966
Political novels. The main characters are Charles Lilburne and Rupert Inglis.

WARDMAN, F.
INSP. CLOUSEAU:
1 The return of the Pink Panther 1977
2 The Pink Panther strikes again 1977

WALDRON, S.
STEVE ESSEX:
1 Leap before you look 1968
2 Hot ice 1969

WALKER, A.
MISS CELIE AND MISS SHUG:
1 The colour purple 1983
2 The temple of my familiar 1989

WALKER, D.
DOUGAL TROCHAR:
1 Winter of madness 1964
2 Black Dougal 1973
GEORDIE BLACK:
1 Geordie 1966
2 Come back Geordie 1968

WALKER, L. (D. L. Sanders, *pseud.*)
MONTGOMERIES OF PEPPER TREE BAY:
1 Six for heaven 1953
2 Shining river 1955
3 Waterfall 1956 *reissued 1971 as* The Bell branch
4 Ribbons in her hair 1957
5 Pepper Tree Bay 1959
6 Monday in summer 1961
The re-issue of 1971-2, published under the author's real name, contains

several minor amendments

WALKER, P. N.
CARNABY-KING:
1 Carnaby and the hi-jackers 1967
2 Carnaby and the jail breakers 1968
3 Carnaby and the assassins 1968
4 Carnaby and the conspirators 1969
5 Carnaby and the saboteurs 1970
6 Carnaby and the eliminators 1971
7 Carnaby and the demonstrators 1972
8 Carnaby and the infiltrators 1974
9 Carnaby and the kidnappers 1976
10 Carnaby and the counterfeiters 1980
11 Carnaby and the campaigners 1984
PANDA ONE SERIES:
1 Panda One on duty 1977
2 Panda One investigates 1978
3 Witchcraft for Panda One 1979
4 Siege for Panda One 1980

WALLACE, R.
ESSINGTON HOLT:
1 To catch a forger 1988
2 An axe to grind 1989
3 Paint out 1990
4 Finger play 1991

WALLER, L.
1 The banker 1968
2 The family 1969
3 The American 1971

WALMSLEY, L.
1 Foreigners 1935
2 Three fevers 1932
3 Sally Lunn 1938
4 Phantom lobster 1933
5 Love in the sun 1939
6 The golden waterwheel
7 The happy ending
8 Paradise Creek 1963
"Phantom lobster' was the box that held 'Three fevers', but 'Three fevers' was also to hold 'Foreigners'. 'Love in the sun' fitted over the lot, but later, I was to squeeze in a sequel to 'Three fevers', 'Sally Lunn', wherein I resolved the agelong quarrel between the Fosdycks and the Lunns."
From 'So many loves', by L. Walmsley.
6, 7 and 8 are pendants to the series

WALSH, B.
1 Live bait 1981
2 Cheat 1982

WALSH, J. M.

1 Once in Tiger Bay 1947
2 Return to Tiger Bay 1950
3 King of Tiger Bay 1952
COLONEL ORMISTON SERIES:
1 Spies are abroad 1935
2 The secret service girl 1937
3 King's messenger 1936
4 Spies in pursuit 1937
5 The man from Whitehall 1939
6 Spies never return 1937
7 The silent man
8 Tiger of the night 1937
9 The half ace 1938
10 Spies' vendetta 1938
11 Spies in Spain
'O.K.' KEENE SERIES:
1 Island of spies 1938
2 Black dragon 1939
3 Dial 999 1938
4 Bullets for breakfast 1939
5 King's enemies 1939
6 Secret weapons
7 Death at his elbow
8 Spies from the skies
9 Danger zone
10 Island alert
11 Face value
12 Whispers in the dark

WALTARI, M. T.
1 Michael the Finn (The adventurer) 1950
2 The Sultan's renegade (The wanderer) 1951

WALTON, E.
1 Prince of Annwynn
2 The children of Llyr
3 The song of Rhiannon
4 The island of the mighty
Paperback fantasy

WARBURG, F. J.
1 An occupation for gentlemen 1959
2 All authors are equal 1973
N.F. Autobiography of a publisher

WARD, E.
1 Number one boy 1969
2 I've lived like a lord 1970
N.F. Autobiography

WARD, R. H.
NEIL FALDER: VARIATIONS ON A LIFE:
1 The conspiracy 1964
2 The wilderness 1962
3 The offenders 1963
1, published last, is about Neil as a

young boy

WARNER, E. S.
1 Trial by sasswood 1956
2 The crossing fee 1968
Two novels set in East Africa

WARNER, R.
1 The young Caesar 1959
2 Imperial Caesar 1960
1 covers the period to his first Consulship; 2 to his death

WARREN, C. H.
1 Happy countryman 1939
2 England is a village 1940
3 The land is yours 1943
4 Miles from anywhere 1944
5 Adam was a ploughman 1947
6 Scythe in the apple tree 1953
7 Content with what I have 1967
N.F. Rural life in Essex

WARREN, L.
THE WHETSTONE SAGA:
1 Foundation stone 1940
2 Whetstone walls 1952

WARREN, R.
1 Where no mains flow
2 A lamb in the lounge 1959
N.F. Autobiography

WARREN, V.
BRANDON SERIES:
1 Brandon takes over 1953
2 Brandon in New York 1954
3 Brandon returns 1954
4 Bullets for Brandon 1955
5 No bouquets for Brandon 1955

WARRINER, T.
AMBO, MR. SCOTTER AND THE
ARCHDEACON SERIES:
1 Method in his murder 1950
2 Ducats in her coffin 1951
3 Death's dateless night 1952
4 The doors of sleep 1955
5 Death's bright angel 1956
6 She died, of course 1958
7 Heavenly bodies 1960

WARRINGTON, F.
BLACKBIRD SERIES:
1 A blackbird in silver
2 A blackbird in darkness
3 A blackbird in amber

4 A blackbird in twilight
Paperback fantasy

WATERHOUSE, K.
1 Billy Liar 1961
2 Billy Liar on the moon 1975

WATSON, C.
THE FLAXBOROUGH SERIES (INSPECTOR PURBRIGHT):
1 Coffin, scarcely used 1963
2 Bump in the night 1964
3 Hopjoy was here 1965
4 Lonely heart 4122 1967
5 Charity ends at home 1968
6 The Flaxborough crab 1969
7 Broomsticks over Flaxborough 1972
8 The naked nuns 1975
9 One man's meat 1977
10 Blue murder 1979
11 Plaster sinners 1980
12 Whatever's been going on at
   Mumblesby? 1982
   *'The Flaxborough chronicle' is an
   omnibus of 1-3*

WATSON, CLARISSA
PERSIS WILLUM:
1 The fourth stage of Gainsborough
   Brown 1978
2 The bishop in the back seat 1981
3 Runaway 1986

WATSON, I.
1 The book of the river 1983
2 The book of the stars 1984
3 The book of being 1985
   Science fiction

WATSON, S.
1 In the twinkling of an eye
2 The mark of the beast

WATT-EVANS, L.
LORDS OF DUS:
1 Lure of the basilisk
2 The seven altars of Dusarra
3 The sword of Bheleu
4 The book of silence
   Paperback fantasy

WAUGH, E.
BASIL SEAL:
1 Black mischief 1932
2 Put out more flags 1942
   *Basil Seal also makes a brief appearance
   in 'Work suspended'. A new short
   story, 'Basil Seal rides again', appeared*

*in the 'Sunday Telegraph' February
10th and 17th, 1963, and was later
published in a limited edition. Several
characters from other novels also
appear.*

★★★

1 A handful of dust 1934
2 Mr. Loveday's little outing 1936
   *A volume of short stories, one of which
   is an alternative last chapter to 'Handful
   of dust'*
WORLD WAR II TRILOGY:
1 Men at arms 1952
2 Officers and gentlemen 1955
3 Unconditional surrender 1961
   *A revised edition was published in 1965
   under the title 'Sword of honour'. 'The
   product is intended (as it was originally)
   to be read as a single story.' Author*

WAUGH, H.
CHIEF OF POLICE FELLOWS SERIES:
1 Road block 1960
2 Sleep long my love 1961
3 Born victim 1962
4 The late Mrs. D. 1962
5 That night it rained 1962
6 Last seen wearing 1962
7 Death and circumstance 1963
8 The missing man 1964
9 Prisoner's plea 1964
10 End of a party 1965
11 Pure poison 1966
12 The con game 1967
FRANK SESSIONS:
1 Finish me off 1969
2 The young prey 1970
   See also **Taylor, H. B.,** *pseud.*
SIMON KAYE:
1 The Glenna Powers case 1981
2 The Doria Rafe case 1982
3 The Billy Cantrell case 1982
4 The Nerissa Claire case 1983
5 The Veronica Dean case 1984
6 The Priscilla Copperthwaite case 1986

WAWN, F. T.
1 The masterdillo
2 The road to the stars

WAY, P.
CRISPIN BRIDGE:
1 Super celeste 1979
2 Icarus 1980
3 Belshazzar's feast 1982

WAYNE, J.
1 Brown bread and butter in the basement 1977
2 The purple dress 1979
N.F. Autobiography

WEALE, A.
LONGWARDEN SERIES:
1 All my worldly goods 1988
2 Time and chance 1989

WEATHERHEAD, J.
PROFESSOR DAVID CONNELL:
1 A force of innocence 1966
2 The sacred shaft 1967

WEAVER, M.
1 Wolf dreams 1987
2 Nightreaver 1988
3 Blood fang 1989

WEBB, G. *and* **MASON, E. J.**
1 The Archers of Ambridge 1955
2 The Archers intervene 1956

WEBB, J.
FATHER SHANLEY SERIES:
1 The big sin 1953
2 Such women are dangerous 1954
3 The damned lovely 1954
4 The bad blonde 1956

WEBSTER, E.
BENNI SOLDANO:
1 Cossack hide-out 1981
2 Red alert 1982
3 The Venetian spy-glass 1982
4 Madonna of the black market 1983
5 Million dollar stand-in 1983
6 The Verratoli inheritance 1983

WEBSTER, JACK
1 A grain of truth 1981
2 Another grain of truth 1988
N.F. Autobiography of a Scots journalist

WEBSTER, JAN
1 Collier's Row 1976
2 The Saturday city 1978
3 Beggarman's country 1979
A trilogy about a Scottish mining family in the 1920's

WEDGWOOD, C. V.
1 The King's peace 1955
2 The King's war
N.F. Charles I and the Civil War

WEIDMAN, J.
1 I can get it for you wholesale 1937
2 What's in it for me?
BENNY KRAMER:
1 Forth Street East 1971
2 Last respects 1972
3 Tiffany Street 1974

WEINSTEIN, H. & CRISPIN, A. C.
V:
1 V 1984
2 East Coast crisis 1985
3 The alien swordmaster, by S. Sucharitkul
4 Prisoners and pawns
Based on the TV series. 3 & 4 in paperback

WEIR, M.
1 Shoes were for Sunday 1969
2 Best foot forward 1972
3 A toe on the ladder 1973
4 Stepping into the spotlight 1975
5 Walking into the Lyon's den 1977
6 One small footprint 1980
7 Spinning like a peerie 1986
8 A gangin' fits aye getting 1988
N.F. Autobiography

WEIS, M. & HICKMAN T.
ROSE OF THE PROPHET:
1 The will of the wanderer
2 The paladin of the night
3 The prophet of Akhran
THE DARKSWORD TRILOGY:
1 Forging the darksword
2 Doom of the darksword
3 Triumph of the darksword
THE DEATH GATE CYCLE:
1 Dragon wing 1990
2 Elven star 1991
Fantasies by the creators of "Dragonlance"

WEISS, D.
1 Sacred and profane 1969
2 The assassination of Mozart 1970
Fictionalised life of Mozart

WELCOME, J.
1 Bellary Bay 1979
2 A call to arms 1985
RICHARD GRAHAM SERIES:
1 Run for cover 1959
2 Hard to handle 1964
3 Wanted for killing 1965
4 Hell is where you find it 1967
5 On the stretch 1969

6 Go for broke 1972

WELLMAN, M. W.
SILVER JOHN:
1 Who fears the devil 1975
2 The old gods waken 1979
3 After dark 1981
4 The lost and the lurking 1982
Supernatural stories

WELLMAN, P.
1 The walls of Jericho 1947
2 The chain 1949
3 Jericho's daughter 1957
Novels about the town of Jericho, Kansas

WELLS, A.
THE BOOKS OF THE KINGDOMS:
1 The wrath of Ashar
2 The usurper
3 The way beneath
Paperback fantasy

WELLS, M.
THE EXPATRIATES:
1 The expatriates 1987
2 The silk king 1987
3 The tycoon 1988

WELLS, T.
DETECTIVE KNUT SEVERSON:
1 A matter of love and death 1966
2 What should you know of dying? 1967
3 Dead by the light of the moon 1968
4 Murder most fouled up 1968
5 Die quickly dear mother 1969
6 The young can die protesting 1970
7 Dinky died 1971
8 What to do until the undertaker comes 1972
9 Lotus affair 1973
10 How to kill a man 1973
11 A die in the country 1974
12 Brenda's murder 1974
13 Have mercy upon us 1975
14 Hark, hark the watchdogs bark 1976
15 A creature was stirring 1977

WELSH, K.
1 Hail for the hero
2 Fear for the hero

WENDORF, P.
THE PATTERAN TRILOGY:
1 Larksleve 1985
2 Blanche 1986
3 Bye bye blackbird 1987

WENSBY-SCOTT, C.
THE PERCY TRILOGY:
1 Lion of Alnwick 1980
2 Lion dormant 1983
3 Lion invincible 1984

WENTWORTH, P.
MISS SILVER SERIES:
1 Grey mask 1928
2 The case is closed 1937
3 Lonesome road 1939
4 Danger point 1942 (In the balance)
5 The Chinese shawl 1943
6 Miss Silver intervenes 1944
7 The clock strikes twelve 1945
8 The key 1946
9 The traveller returns 1948 (She came back)
10 Pilgrim's rest 1948
11 Latter end 1949
12 Spotlight 1949 (Wicked uncle)
13 Eternity ring 1950
14 The case of William Smith 1950
15 Miss Silver comes to stay 1951
16 The catherine wheel 1952
17 The Brading collection 1952
18 Through the wall 1952
19 The ivory dagger 1953
20 Anna where are you? 1953 (Death at the deep end)
21 The watersplash 1953
22 Ladies' bane 1954
23 Out of the past 1955
24 Vanishing point 1955
25 The silent pool 1955
26 The Benevent treasure 1956
27 Poison in the pen 1956
28 The listening eye 1957
29 The gazebo 1957
30 The fingerprint 1958
31 Alington inheritance 1959
32 The girl in the cellar 1960
33 Miss Silver detects 1961
THE WAVENEYS:
1 A little more than kin
2 Anne Belinda

WESCHBERG, J.
1 Looking for a bluebird
2 Sweet and sour
3 Blue trout and black truffles
Autobiographical sketches and stories

WEST, E.
1 Hovel in the hills 1977
2 Garden in the hills 1980
N.F. Describes how the author created

a house and garden in a remote part of
Wales

WEST, J.
JESS AND ELIZA BIRDWELL:
1 The friendly persuasion 1946
2 Except for me and thee 1969
A Quaker family in the 19th century
U.S.A.

WEST, M.
VATICAN TRILOGY:
1 The shoes of the fisherman 1963
2 Clowns of God 1981
3 Lazarus 1990

WEST, P.
ALLEY JAGGERS:
1 Alley Jaggers 1970
2 I'm expecting to live quite soon 1971
3 Bela Lugosi's white Christmas 1971

WEST, R.
AUBREY FAMILY:
1 The fountain overflows 1957
2 This real night 1984
3 Cousin Rosamund 1985
A family saga, of which the third
volume was published after the author's
death

WESTHEIMER, D.
1 Von Ryan's express 1969
2 Von Ryan's return 1979

WESTLAKE, D. E.
JOHN DORTMUNDER:
1 Hot rock 1969
2 Bank shot 1972
3 Jimmy the kid 1975
4 Nobody's perfect 1978
5 Why me?
6 Good behaviour 1987

***

1 The fugitive pigeon 1965
2 The busy body 1966
3 The spy in the ointment 1967
Humorous detective stories.
Characters recur in both series

WESTON, C.
KRUG AND CASEY:
1 Poor, poor Ophelia 1973
2 Susannah screaming 1975
3 Rouse the demon 1976

WETERING, J. VAN DE

ADJUTANT GRIJPSTRA AND SGT. DE GIER:
1 Outsider in Amsterdam 1976
2 Tumbleweed 1976
3 Corpse on the dyke 1977
4 Death of a hawker 1977
5 The Japanese corpse 1978
6 The blond baboon 1978
7 The Maine massacre 1979
8 The mind murders 1981
9 The streetbird 1984
10 The rattle-rat 1986
11 Hard rain 1987
12 The Adjutant's cat and other stories
1988
Detective stories set in Holland

WHALLEY, P.
HARRY SOMMERS:
1 Robbers 1986
2 Bandits 1986
3 Villains 1987

WHARTON, M.
1 The missing Will 1984
2 A dubious codicil 1991
N.F. Autobiography

WHEATLEY, D.
ROGER BROOK SERIES:
1 Launching of Roger Brook 1947
2 Shadow of Tyburn tree 1948
3 The rising storm 1952
4 The man who killed the king 1953
5 Dark secret of Josephine 1958
6 The rape of Venice 1959
7 The sultan's daughter 1963
8 The wanton princess 1966
9 Evil in a mask 1969
10 The ravishing of Lady Mary Ware 1970
11 The Irish witch 1973
12 Desperate measures 1974
DUC DE RICHLIEU SERIES:
1 Three inquisitive people 1931
2 The forbidden territory 1933
3 The devil rides out 1935
4 The golden Spaniard 1938
5 Strange conflict 1941
6 Code-word golden fleece 1946
7 The second seal 1944
8 Dangerous inheritance 1965
9 Gateway to hell 1970

***

The earlier adventures of Duc di
Richlieu are told in:
1 Prisoner in the mask 1957
2 Vendetta in Spain 1961

JULIAN DAY SERIES:
1 The quest of Julian Day 1939
2 The sword of fate 1944
3 Bill for the use of a body 1964
GREGORY SALLUST SERIES:
1 The scarlet imposter 1942
2 Faked passports 1943
3 The black baroness 1944
4 V for vengeance
5 Come into my parlour
6 The island where time stands still 1954
7 Traitor's gate 1958
8 They used dark forces 1964
9 The white witch of the South Seas 1967
*Gregory Sallust also appears in 'Black
August' and 'Contraband', but these are
not part of the same series*
THE TIME HAS COME:
1 The young man said 1978
2 Drink and ink 1979
3 My secret war 1980
N.F. Autobiography

WHEELER, D.
EDWIN MOULD:
1 Mould 1967
2 An unimpeachable source 1970
*Novels about an extraordinary
journalist*

WHEELER-BENNETT, SIR J.
1 Knaves, fools and heroes 1974
2 Special relationships 1975
N.F. Autobiography

WHELPTON, E.
1 The making of a European 1974
2 The making of an Englishman 1976
N.F. Autobiography

WHIPPLE, D.
1 The other day 1956
2 Random commentary 1966
*N.F. Autobiography. 2 is compiled
from notebooks kept from 1925 and
may be regarded as a supplement*

WHITAKER, B.
JOHN ABBOT SERIES:
1 Of mice and murder 1968
2 A matter of blood 1969
3 The chained crocodile 1970
4 The man who wasn't there 1971

WHITE, A.
AYSGILL FAMILY:
1 The homeward tide 1981
2 The vanishing land 1982

3 The years of change 1983
COMMANDO SERIES:
1 The long day's dying 1965
2 The long night's walk 1966
3 The long watch 1968
4 The long drop 1969
5 The long midnight 1972
6 The long fuse 1973
7 The long summer 1975
8 The long silence 1976
*A series of novels about commando
exploits in World War II*
INSPECTOR ARMSTRONG:
1 Armstrong 1973
2 Death in duplicate 1974
3 Death in darkness 1975
RAVENSWYKE:
1 Ravenswyke 1979
2 The homeward tide 1981

WHITE, ANTONIA
1 The lost traveller
2 The sugar house
3 Beyond the glass
*'Frost in May' should be considered as
part of the series, since the central
character is the same, though under a
different name*
***

1 Minka and Curdy 1957
2 Living with Minka and Curdy 1970
N.F. Cats

WHITE, EDMUND
1 A boy's own story 1985
2 The beautiful room is empty 1988

WHITE, J.
BEN ESCOBIE:
1 The Persian oven 1987
2 California exit 1987

WHITE, J. D.
SEBASTIAN KETTLE:
1 The Leipzig affair 1974
2 The Salzburg affair 1977
3 The Brandenburg affair 1979
ROGER KELSO SERIES:
1 Young Mr. Kelso 1963
2 Brave Captain Kelso 1959
3 Kelso of the *Paragon* 1969
4 Captain of marine 1960
5 The princess of Persia 1961
6 Commodore Kelso 1967
7 Fair wind to Malabar 1978
8 A wind in the rigging 1973
9 A spread of sail 1975

This is in chronological order of Kelso's career

WHITE, JAMES
SECTOR GENERAL:
1 Ambulance ship 1986
2 Major operation 1986
3 Star surgeon 1987
4 Hospital station 1987
5 Sector General 1988
6 Star healer 1989
7 Futures past 1989
8 Code blue emergency 1990
Science fiction. 3 is in paperback

WHITE, S.
PENHALIGON:
1 The English Captain 1976
2 Clear for action 1977
3 His majesty's frigate 1979
Sea stories set in the period of the Napoleonic Wars

WHITE, T. H.
1 Earth stopped
2 Gone to ground

★★★

1 Age of scandal
2 The scandal monger
N.F. 18th century essays
THE ONCE AND FUTURE KING, AN ARTHURIAN EPIC:
1 The sword in the stone 1939
2 The witch in the wood 1939
3 The ill-made knight 1940
4 The candle in the wind
5 The book of Merlyn 1977
Republished in one volume See also
Swift, J.

WHITEHEAD, B.
YORK CYCLE OF MYSTERIES:
1 Playing God 1988
2 The girl with red suspenders 1990
3 The Dean it was that died 1991

WHITING, C.
DESTROYERS:
1 Operation Afrika 1974
2 Operation Stalag 1974
3 Operation Caucasian Fox 1974
4 Operation Il Duce 1974
5 Operation Kill Ike 1975
6 Operation Werewolf 1976
T-FORCE:
1 The big breakout 1978
2 Massacre at Metz 1979

3 Highway through hell 1979
MAJOR JOHN BOLD:
1 Bugles at dawn 1990
2 Sabres in the sun 1991

WHITMAN, C.
INSPECTOR LINDON AND SERGEANT GRAY:
1 Doctor Death 1969
2 Death out of focus 1970
3 Death suspended 1971

WHITTAKER, J.
1 The raking of the embers 1982
2 The flame in the morning 1984
Novels set in 19th C Australia

WHITTEMORE, E.
JERUSALEM QUARTET:
1 Sinai tapestry 1978
2 Jerusalem poker 1978
In progress

WHITTLE, T.
QUEEN VICTORIA TRILOGY:
1 The young Victoria 1971
2 Albert's Victoria 1972
3 The window of Windsor 1973

★★★

1 Bertie 1974
2 Edward 1975
Novels about Edward VII

WHYTE, B.
1 Yellow on the broom 1979
2 Red rowane and wild honey 1990
N.F. Autobiography set in Scotland

WIAT, P.
BLACK BOAR SAGA:
1 Raven in the wind 1978
2 Lord of the Black Boar 1975
3 Sword of Woden 1975
4 Tree of Vortigern 1976
5 The Atheling 1977
6 Westerfalca 1979
7 Lord of the wolf 1980
WYATT SAGA:
1 Master of Blandeston Hall 1973
2 The heir of Allington 1973
3 Sound now the passing bell 1973
4 Knight of Allington 1974
5 Rebel of Allington 1977
6 My lute be still 1977
HOWARD SAGA:
1 Maid of gold 1971
2 Like as the roaring waves 1972

3 Wear a green kirtle 1987
4 The Queen's fourth husband 1976
5 Lion without claws 1976
6 Yet a lion 1978
WILMINGTON NOVELS:
1 The fourposter 1979
2 Shadow of Samain 1980
CHARLTON MEAD:
1 The mistletoe bough 1981
2 Bride of darkness 1982
3 Wychwood 1982
EDWARD III TRILOGY:
1 Queen gold 1985
2 The grey goose-wing 1985
3 The whyte swan 1986
GREY FAMILY:
1 Five gold rings 1982
2 Children of the spring 1983

WIBBERLEY, L.
1 Beware of the mouse 1958
2 The mouse that roared 1959
Stories about the mythical Duchy of Grand Fenwick. 1 is in medieval times, 2 is contemporary

WIDEMAN, J. E.
1 Damballah 1984
2 Hiding place 1984
3 Sent for you yesterday 1984
Novels set in a Black ghetto in Pennsylvania

WIESEL, E.
1 Night
2 Dawn
N.F. Autobiography

WIGG, T. I. G.
1 For the sons of gentlemen 1960
2 A job with the boys 1959
Autobiographical novels on teaching

WIGHTMAN, F.
THE VOYAGES OF 'WYLO':
1 The wind is free
2 My way leads me seaward
N.F. Travel

WILCOX, C.
LIEUT. FRANK HASTINGS:
1 The lonely hunter 1971
2 The disappearance 1972
3 Dead aim 1972
4 Hiding place 1973
5 Long day down 1974
6 Aftershock 1974
7 The watcher 1977

8 Power plays 1981
9 Mankiller 1982
10 Victims 1986
11 Swallow's fall 1987

WILCOX, J.
1 Modern Baptists 1984
2 North Gladiola 1985
3 Miss Undine's living room 1987
Novels set in Tula Springs, Louisiana

WILDE, J.
1 Love's tender fury 1982
2 Love me Marietta 1983
Bodice rippers

WILES, J.
1 The grand trunk road 1972
2 Delhi is far away 1974
N.F. Travel

WILHELM, K.
CHARLIE MEIKLEJOHN & CONSTANCE LEIDL:
1 The Hamlet trap 1987
2 Smart house 1989
3 The dark door 1990
4 Sweet, sweet poison 1991

WILKINS, V.
1 And so Victoria 1936
2 Husband for Victoria 1958

WILKINSON, B.
GEOFFREY MILDMAY SERIES:
1 Proceed at will 1949
2 Run, mongoose 1951
3 Last clear chance 1954
4 Night of the short knives 1965

WILLARD, B.
1 Proposed and seconded
2 Echo answers

WILLEFORD, C.
HOKE MOSELEY:
1 Miami blues 1985
2 New hope for the dead 1987
3 Sideswipe 1988

WILLEY, B.
1 Spots of time, 1987-1920 1965
2 Cambridge and other memories, 1920-1953 1968
N.F. Autobiography

WILLIAMS, A.
RUPERT QUINN:

1 The long run south 1960
2 Barbouze 1962

***

1 The Beria papers 1972
2 Gentlemen traitor 1974

WILLIAM, B. A.
1 Come spring
2 Thread of scarlet
3 Strange woman
4 Time of peace
THE CURRAIN FAMILY:
1 House divided 1947
2 The unconquered 1953
Two novels of a southern family in the Civil War

WILLIAMS, D.
FIGHTER:
1 Bluebirds over 1982
2 Vendetta 1982
MARK TREASURE:
1 Unholy writ 1974
2 Treasure by degrees 1977
3 Treasure up in smoke 1978
4 Murder for Treasure 1979
5 Copper, gold and Treasure 1982
6 Treasure preserved 1983
7 Advertise for Treasure 1984
8 Wedding Treasure 1985
9 Murder in Advent 1985
10 Treasure in roubles 1986
11 Divided Treasure 1987
12 Treasure in Oxford 1988
13 Holy Treasure! 1989
14 Prescription for murder 1990
15 Treasure by post 1991
TANK:
1 Tank 1985
2 Fortress Eagle 1986
3 Sugar sugar 1987
War stories set in North Africa

WILLIAMS, E. M.
1 Pig in paradise 1966
2 Valley of animals 1967
3 The Pant Glas story 1970
N.F. Wild life preservation

WILLIAMS, EMLYN
1 George 1961
2 Emlyn 1973
N.F. Autobiography

WILLIAMS, G.
AMAZING CHRONICLES OF THE
MICRONAUTS:

1 Micronaut world
2 Revolt of the Micronauts
Paperback science fiction

WILLIAMS, L.
LEGENDARY MURDERS:
1 A copper snare 1981
2 The murder triangle 1982
3 Images of death 1984
4 Portrait of the dead 1985

WILLIAMS, M.
1 Carnecrane 1980
2 Return to Carnecrane 1981
Gothic romances set in Cornwall

WILLIAMS, P.
1 I am Canute
2 God's warrior

WILLIAMS, P. O.
PELBAR:
1 The ends of the circle
2 The breaking of North Wall
3 The dome in the forest
4 The fall of the shell
Paperback fantasy

WILLIAMS, R.
1 Border country 1962
2 Second generation 1964
3 Fight for manhood 1979
PEOPLE OF THE BLACK MOUNTAINS:
1 The beginning 1989
2 Eggs of the eagle 1990

WILLIAMS, TAD
MEMORY, SORROW AND THORN:
1 The dragonbone chair 1989
2 Stone of farewell 1990

WILLIAMS, TIMOTHY
COMMISSARIO TROTTI:
1 Converging parallels 1982
2 The puppeteer 1985
3 Persona non grata 1987

WILLIAMSON, AUDREY
DET. SUPT. YORK:
1 Funeral march for Siegfried 1979
2 Death of a theatre filly 1980

WILLIAMSON, H.
THE FLAX OF DREAM:
1 Beautiful years 1921
2 Dandelion days 1922
3 Dream of fair women 1924
4 The pathway 1928

5 The star-born 1930
*5 is not part of the tetrology but is a
pendant to it. 'Dark lantern' starts a
new series on Philip Maddison, cousin
of Willie Maddison of 'Flax of dream'*
A CHRONICLE OF ANCIENT SUNLIGHT:
1 Dark lantern 1951
2 Donkey boy 1952
3 Young Philip Maddison 1953
4 How dear is life 1954
5 Fox under my cloak 1957
6 The golden virgin 1957
7 Love and the loveless 1958
8 A test of destruction 1960
9 The innocent moon 1961
10 It was the nightingale 1962
11 The power of the dead 1963
12 The phoenix generation 1965
13 A solitary war 1966
14 Lucifer before sunrise 1967
15 The gale of the world 1969
*Chronicle of a family from Victorian
times to World War II*

WILLIAMSON, H. R.
CATHERINE DE MEDICI TRILOGY:
1 The Florentine woman 1969
2 The last of the Valois 1970
3 Paris is worth a Mass 1971
PASSING OF THE PLANTAGENETS:
1 The butt of Malmsey (1459-1478) 1967
2 The marriage made in blood
(1478-1522) 1968
3 A matter of martyrdom (1522-1541)
1969
4 The Cardinal in exile (1541-1553) 1969
5 The Cardinal in England (1553-1558)
1970

WILLIS, F.
1 101, Jubilee Road 1948
2 Peace and dripping toast
3 London journal
*N.F. A trilogy of life in Edwardian
London*

WILLIS, T., LORD
DIXON OF DOCK GREEN:
1 The devil's churchyard 1957
2 Seven gates to nowhere 1958
ROSIE CARR:
1 Spring at the 'Winged Horse' 1983
2 The green leaves of summer 1988
3 The bells of Autumn 1991

WILLIS, W.
1 The seven little sisters 1960
2 An angel on each shoulder 1963

3 Hundred lives of the ancient mariner
1967
N.F. Autobiography

WILLS, C. M.
SUPERINTENDENT BOSCOBELL SERIES:
1 Author in distress (No. 18)
2 Death at the Pelican
3 The chamois murder
4 Death treads...
5 Then came the police
6 Defeat of a detective
7 Fatal accident
8 On the night in question
9 A body in the dawn
10 The case of the Calabar bean
11 The case of the R.E. pipe
*This introduces a new main character,
Roger Ellerdine*
12 The clue of the lost hour
Mainly Roger Ellerdine
ROGER ELLERDINE AND SERGEANT
BLOSSOM SERIES:
1 The clue of the golden earring
2 Who killed Brother treasurer?
3 What say the jury?
4 The dead voice
5 It pays to die
6 Death in the dark 1955
7 The dyer strikes again 1956
8 Mere murder 1959
9 Case of the empty bee hive 1959
10 Death of a best seller 1959

WILMOT, R. P.
STEVE CONSIDINE:
1 Blood in your eye 1954
2 Death rides a painted horse 1955

WILMOTT, P.
1 Growing up in a London village 1979
2 A green girl 1983
N.F. Autobiography

WILSON, A. N.
1 Unguarded hours 1978
2 Kindly light 1979
Humorous novels about a young priest
LAMPITTS:
1 Incline our hearts 1989
2 Bottle in the smoke 1990
3 Daughters of Albion 1991

WILSON, B.
PAM NILSEN:
1 Murder in the collective 1986
2 Sisters of the road 1987
3 The dog collar murders 1989

WILSON, C.

GERALD SORME SERIES:
1 Ritual in the dark 1960
2 Man without a shadow 1963
3 The god of the labyrinth 1970

***

1 An encyclopedia of murder
2 A casebook of murder
3 Order of assassins 1972
N.F. A trilogy of books about murder
CHIEF INSPECTOR GREGORY SALTFLEET:
1 The school murder case 1974
2 The Janus murder case 1984
SPIDER WORLD:
1 The tower 1987
2 The delta 1987
Science fiction

WILSON, D.

ROBERT DUDLEY:
1 Bear's whelp 1979
2 Bear rampant 1981

WILSON, F. P.

1 The keep 1981
2 Reborn 1990
Horror stories

WILSON, G. M.

INSPECTOR LOVIK SERIES:
1 Murder on Monday 1963
2 Shot at dawn 1964
3 The devil's skull 1965
4 The headless man 1966
5 Cake for Caroline 1967
6 Do not sleep 1968
7 Death is buttercups 1969
8 A deal of death caps 1970
9 The bus ran late 1971
10 She kept on dying 1972

WILSON, I.

GREGORY FLAMM SERIES:
1 But not for love 1962
2 That feeds on men 1963
3 Lilies that fester 1964
4 Empty tigers 1965

WILSON, J.

ISLAND CHRONICLE:
1 Weep in the sun 1976
2 Troubled heritage 1977
3 Mullatto 1978
Set in the West Indies in the 18th century

WILSON, R.

SCHRODINGER'S CAT:
1 The universe next door
2 The trick top hat
3 Homing pigeons
Paperback science fiction

WILSON, SANDRA

LADY CICELY PLANTAGENET TRILOGY:
1 Less fortunate than fair 1970
2 The Queen's sister 1973
3 The Lady Cicely 1974

WILSON, STEVE

1 Dealer's move 1979
2 Dealer's war 1980
3 Dealer's wheels 1982

WILSON, T. E.

BIG TOM HOLDER:
1 The newcomers 1981
2 Yellow fever 1982
3 Harvest of gold 1983
Set in New Zealand

WILSON, T. R.

1 Master of Morholm 1986
2 The ravished earth 1988
3 Straw tower 1990

WILTZ, C.

NEAL RAFFERTY:
1 The killing circle 1981
2 A diamond before you die 1988

WINGATE, J.

1 Frigate 1980
2 Carrier 1981
3 Submarine 1982
Novels about the Royal Navy in a Third World War

WINGFIELD, R. D.

INSPECTOR JACK FROST:
1 Frost at Christmas 1989
2 A touch of Frost 1990

WINGFIELD-STRATFORD, E.

1 Charles, King of England 1949
2 King Charles and King Pym 1949
3 King Charles the martyr 1950
N.F. Biography of Charles I

WINGROVE, D.

CHUNG KUO:
1 The middle kingdom 1989
2 Broken wheel 1990

WINGS, M.

b 'Enter Psmith' is the second part of 'Mike'
c 'Mike' is now published in two parts, 'Mike at Wrykyn' and 'Mike and Psmith'
PSMITH SERIES:
1 *See above*
2 Psmith in the city 1910
  This also completes the story of Mike
3 Psmith journalist 1915
4 Leave it to Psmith 1923
  This is also the second of the Blandings Castle series.
BLANDINGS CASTLE SERIES:
1 Something fresh 1915 (Something new)
2 Leave it to Psmith
3 Blandings Castle 1935
  (Short stories, chronologically placed here though published later)
4 Summer lightning 1929 (Fish preferred)
5 Heavy weather 1933
6 Lord Emsworth and others 1927 (Crime wave at Blandings)
  (Only one story in this series)
7 Full moon 1947
8 Pigs have wings 1952
9 Service with a smile 1962
  (also features Uncle Fred)
10 Galahad at Blandings 1965
11 A pelican at Blandings 1969 (No nudes is good news)
12 Sunset at Blandings 1977
  Uncompleted
  'Plum pie', 1966, contains a Blandings story
UNCLE FRED, EARL OF ICKENHAM:
1 Uncle Fred flits by *(a story in* Young men in spats, 1936)
2 Uncle Fred in the spring time 1930
  (also features Blandings Castle)
3 Uncle dynamite 1948
4 Cocktail time 1958
UKRIDGE:
1 Love among the chickens 1906
2 Ukridge 1924
  There are 3 Ukridge stories in 'Lord Emsworth and others', 3 in 'Eggs, beans and crumpets', 1940, and one each in 'Nothing serious', 1950, 'A few quick ones', 1959, and 'Plum pie', 1966
OLDEST MEMBER SERIES:
1 The clicking of Cuthbert 1922
2 The heart of a goof 1926
3 Nothing serious 1950
  (contains 5 stories)
MR. MULLINER SERIES:
1 Meet Mr. Mulliner 1927

2 Mr. Mulliner speaking 1929
3 Mulliner nights 1933
  There are five Mulliner stories in 'Blandings Castle', 3 in 'Young men in spats', 1936, and 1 each in 'Lord Emsworth and others', 'Eggs, beans and crumpets', and 'A few quick ones'. A Mulliner story, 'Pudding at Xmas', appeared in the 'Sunday Telegraph', December 22nd, 1968.
MONTY BODKIN:
1 The luck of the Bodkins 1935
2 Pearls, girls and Monty Bodkin 1972
IVOR LLEWELEYN:
1 The luck of the Bodkins 1935
2 Bachelors anonymous 1973
  The hero is a minor character in 1
THE DRONES CLUB:
1 Young men in spats 1936
2 Eggs, beans and crumpets 1940
3 A few quick ones 1959
  The Drones club and its members feature in many Wodehouse novels and short stories; but the above collections each contain several stories about eventful days there. The above lists are based on the main character, but Wodehouse characters recur in many of the novels and short stories - Sir Roderick Glossop Per, Bingo Little, Percy Pilbeam, Freddie Widgeon and others are much more than minor characters. For a complete bibliography and descriptions of characters, 'A bibliography and reader's guide to the first editions of P. G. Wodehouse', by D. A. Jasen, 1971, is invaluable. 'Wooster's World' by G. Jaggard, 1967, is a guide to the Wooster-Jeeves-Drones Club saga. 'Wodehouse at work', by R. Usborne, 1961, is a general study, but also identifies many minor characters.

***
1 Performing flea 1953
2 Over seventy 1957
  N.F. Autobiography

WOGAN, C.
SEBASTION STOLE SERIES:
1 Horror at warden's Hall
2 Cyanide for the chorister
3 Hangman's hands

WOIWODE, I.
1 Beyond the bedroom wall 1975
2 Born brothers 1990
  Companion volumes

WOLFE, G.
THE BOOK OF THE NEW SUN:
1 Shadow of the torturer 1980
2 The claw of the conciliator 1981
3 The sword of the Lictor 1982
4 The citadel of the Autarch 1983
5 The urth of the New Sun 1987

1 Soldier of the mist 1986
2 Soldier of Arete 1990

WOLFE, H.
1 Now a stranger
2 Upward anguish
N.F. Autobiography

WONGAR, B.
1 Walg 1987
2 Karan 1987
3 Gabo Djara 1988
A trilogy about Australian Aborigines

WOOD, B.
1 Minstrel's lute 1987
2 Satanic lute 1987

WOOD, C.
1 John Adam - samurai 1971
2 John Adam in Eden 1972

WOOD, CHRISTOPHER
1 Taiwan 1983
2 A dove against death 1983

WOOD, J.
1 Northern mission
2 Great river
Stories of Ian Ross and ex-service
associates
JAMES FRAZER SERIES:
1 The sealer 1960
2 The Liza Bastian 1962
3 Bay of seals 1963
4 Fire Rock 1965
5 The Friday run 1966
6 Three blind mice 1968
Stories of a Scottish trawler

WOOD, JAMES
INSP. JUMBO COLLINS:
1 North beat 1973
2 North kill 1975

★★★

1 Tipple in the deep
2 Beer for Christmas
3 A drop of himself
N.F. Autobiography

WOOD, R. S.
1 The Riding Officer 1987
2 The rose of St. Keverne 1989
Novels about smuggling in Cornwall

WOOD, T.
REID BENNETT:
1 Dead in the water 1984
2 The killing cold 1984
3 Dead centre 1985
4 Fool's gold 1986
5 The killing cold 1987
6 Corkscrew 1988
7 When the killing starts 1989
8 On the inside 1990

WOODARD, C.
1 A doctor heals by faith
2 A doctor's faith holds fast
3 A doctor's faith is challenged
N.F. Autobiography

WOODBERRY, J.
1 Rafferty takes to fishing 1959
2 Floodtide for Rafferty 1960
3 Rafferty rides a winner 1961
4 Rafferty makes a landfall 1962

WOODHOUSE, M.
GILES YEOMAN SERIES:
1 Treefrog 1970
2 Rock baby 1971
3 Mama doll 1972
4 Blue bone 1973
5 Moon hill 1975

WOODHOUSE, M. and ROSS, R.
1 The Medici guns 1974
2 The Medici emerald 1975
3 The Medici hawks 1977
Thrillers set in Renaissance Italy

WOODHOUSE, S.
DR. ALEXANDER FRENCH:
1 Season of mists 1984
2 The peacock's feather 1988
3 Native air 1990
Novels set in 18th century Norfolk

WOODMAN, R.
NATHANIEL DRINKWATER:
1 An eye of the fleet (1780) 1981
2 A King's cutter (1797) 1983
3 A brig of war (1798) 1983
4 Bomb vessel (1801) 1984
5 The corvette (1803) 1985
6 1805 1985
7 Baltic mission (1807) 1986

3 House of the wolf
Paperback fantasy
CONAN FLAGG:
1 Curiosity didn't kill the cat 1975
2 A multitude of sins 1976
3 Oh, bury me not 1978
4 Nothing's certain but death 1978
5 Wake up darlin' Corey. 1984

WRIGHT, A. T.
ISLANDIA:
1 Islandia 1942
2 The Islar, by M. Saxton 1969
3 The two kingdoms
4 Havoc in Islandia, by M. Saxton 1984
Fantasy

WRIGHT, B.
1 The world's my football pitch
2 Captain of England
3 Football is my passport
4 One hundred caps and all that
N.F. Autobiography

WRIGHT, E.
CHARLIE SALTER:
1 The night the gods smiled 1983
2 Smoke detector 1984
3 Death in the old country 1985
4 A single death 1986
5 A body surrounded by water 1987
6 A question of murder 1988
7 A sensitive case 1989
8 Final cut 1991

WRIGHT, L. R.
KARL ALBERG:
1 The suspect
2 Sleep while I sing
3 Chill rain in January 1990

WRIGHT, P.
1 I am England 1987
2 That near and distant place 1988

WRIGHT, W.
BART CONDOR SERIES:
1 Suddenly you're dead 1964
2 Blood in the ashes 1964
3 A hearse waiting 1965
4 Until she dies 1965
5 Blonde target 1966
6 Two faces of death 1967
PAUL CAMERON:
1 Shadows don't bleed 1967
2 The sharp edge 1968

WRIGHTSON, P.
THE BOOK OF WIRRUN:
1 The ice is coming 1977
2 The dark bright water 1979
3 Behind the wind 1981
Fantasy. Published in one vol. 1987

WURTS, J.
CYCLE OF FIRE:
1 Stormwarden 1989
2 Keeper of the keys 1989
3 Shadowfane 1990

WYLIE, I. A. R.
1 Towards morning
2 Brodie and the deep sea

★★★

1 The undefeated
2 Home are the hunted 1959

WYLIE, J.
SERVANTS OF ARK:
1 The first named
2 Centre of the circle
3 The mage-born child
Paperback fantasy
THE UNBALANCED EARTH:
1 Dreams of stone
2 The lightless kingdom
3 The age of chaos
Fantasy, originally in paperback, but published as one hardback volume in 1991

WYLIE, P.
CRUNCH AND DES SERIES:
1 The big ones get away!
2 Salt water daffy
3 Fish and tin fish
4 Crunch and Des
Short stories about deep sea fishing. Selection published under title 'The best of Crunch and Des'

WYLLIE, J.
DR. QUARSHIE:
1 The killer breath 1980
2 Skull still bone 1975
3 The butterfly flood 1977
4 To catch a viper 1978
5 Death is a drum 1979
6 A pocketful of death 1979
7 A tiger in red weather 1981
8 The long dark night of Baron Samedi 1982

WYNDHAM, J.
1 Love is blue 1986

2 Love lessons 1984
N.F. Autobiography

YARDLEY, J.
KISS AND ANGUS FANE:
1 Kiss the boys and make them die 1969
2 A kiss a day keeps the corpses away 1971

YARROW, A.
1 Softly, softly casebook 1975
2 Softly, softly murder casebook 1976

YATES, D.
BERRY SERIES:
1 Brother of Daphne 1914
2 Courts of idleness 1920
3 Berry and Co. 1921
4 Jonah and Co. 1922
5 Adele and Co. 1933
6 And Berry came too 1936
7 The house that Berry built 1945
8 The Berry scene 1947
9 As Berry and I were saying 1952
10 B-Berry and I look back 1958
No. 10 is autobiographical, but contains many sidelights on the series

***

1 Anthony Lyveden
2 Valerie French
RICHARD CHANDOS SERIES:
1 Blind corner 1927
2 Perishable goods 1930
3 Blood royal 1934
4 Fire below (By royal command) 1934
5 She fell among thieves 1937
6 Gale warning 1939
7 An eye for a tooth 1943
8 Red in the morning 1946
9 Cost price 1949
10 Ne'er do well 1954
Jonathan Mansel, though not the main character, occurs in all the 'Berry' series and in other books as follows: 'Blind corner', 'Perishable goods', 'Gale warning', 'Shoal water', 'An eye for a tooth', 'Red in the morning'.
John Bagot is the hero of 'Gale warning', and appeared in 'Red in the morning'.
Richard Chandos and Jonathan Mansel appear in 'Ne'er do well', but do not play an active part.

YEH, CHUN-CHAN
QUIET ARE THE MOUNTAINS:

1 The mountain village 1988
2 The open fields 1988
3 A distant journey 1989

YERBY, F.
1 The man from Dahomey
2 The darkness at Ingraham Crest 1981

YORK, A.
JONAS WILDE SERIES:
1 The eliminator 1965
2 The co-ordinator 1966
3 The predator 1968
4 The deviator 1969
5 The dominator 1970
6 The infiltrator 1970
7 The expurgator 1971
8 The assassinator 1972
9 The captivator 1973
10 The fascinator 1975
JONATHAN ANDREWS:
1 The doom fishermen 1969
2 Man hunt for a general 1970
MUNROE TALLENT:
1 Tallent for trouble 1976
2 Tallent for disaster 1978

YORKE, K.
1 A woman's place 1983
2 The pair bond 1984

YORKE, M.
DR. PATRICK GRANT SERIES:
1 Dead in the morning
2 Silent witness 1971
3 Grave matters 1973
4 Mortal remains 1974
5 Cast for death 1976

YOUNG, A.
1 A prospect of flowers
2 A retrospect of flowers
N.F. Botany

YOUNG, GAVIN
1 Slow boats to China 1981
2 Slow boats home 1985
N.F. Travel

YOUNG, S.
1 So red the rose
2 Feliciana

YUILL, P. B.
JAMES HAZELL:
1 Hazell plays Solomon 1974
2 Hazell and the three-card trick 1975
3 Hazell and the menacing jester 1976

YUKIO MISHIMA, *see* **MISHIMA YUKIO**

title 'Winifred'
Order given is chronological of events not order of publication

Z CARS
1 Z Cars *by* Troy Kennedy Martin 1975
2 Z Cars again *by* Allan Prior 1976

ZELAZNY, R.
THE KINGDOM OF AMBER:
1 Nine princes in amber 1973
2 The guns of Avalon 1974
3 The sign of the Unicorn 1977
4 The hand of Oberon 1978
5 The courts of chaos 1979
6 Knight of shadows 1991
CHANGELING SAGA:
1 Changeling
2 Madwind
Science fiction

ZILAHAY, L.
THE DUKAY FAMILY:
1 The donkeys 1949
2 The angry angel 1953
3 A century in scarlet 1966
The story of an aristocratic Hungarian family in two world wars

ZINKIN, T.
1 Odious child 1970
2 Weeds grow fast 1973
N.F. Autobiography

ZUIKERMAN, S.
1 From apes to war lords 1978
2 Monkeys, men and missiles 1988
N.F. Autobiography of Chief Scientific Adviser to H. M. Government

ZWEIG, A.
Sequence of novels about Germany before and during World War I in which the characters Werner Bertin and Lenote Wahl appear:
1 The time is ripe 1962 (Die Zeit it reif 1957)
2 Young woman of 1914 1932 (Junge frau von 1914 1931)
3 Education before Verdun 1936 (Erziehung vor Verdun 1935)
4 The case of Sergeant Grischa 1928 (Der Streit um den Sergeanten Grischa 1927)
5 Die Feuerpause 1954 (Not yet translated)
6 The crowning of a king 1938 (Einsetzung eines Königs 1937) U.S.A.

INDEX OF SERIES AND CHARACTERS

Titles of the most popular series and names of leading characters are listed alphabetically in this index. The list is by no means comprehensive, but it may serve to answer many of the routine enquiries about fictional characters or novels based on television series. The detail of individual volumes in the series are given in the main text under the author's name, which appears in the right hand column.

Title/character	Author	Title/character	Author
Accursed King Series	Druon, M.	Black Boar Series	Wiat, P.
Adkins, Harry	Foxall, R.	Blackoaks Series	Carter, A.
Alexandria Quartet	Durrell, L.	Black Widowers	Asimov, I.
Alleyn *Inspector*	Marsh, N.	Blackshirt	Graeme, B.
Alms for Oblivion	Raven, S.	Blackstone	Falkirk, R.
Alvarez, *Inspector*	Jeffries, R.	Blade	Chisholm, M.
Angel	Ripley, M.	Blair, Peter	Anderson, J.R.L.
Angel, Frank	Christian, F.H.	Blaise, Modesty	O'Donnell, P.
Angelique	Golon, S.	Blake, Jonathon	Chance, J.N.
Apache	James, W.M.	Bliss, Vicky	Peters, E.
Appleby, *Sir* John	Innes, M.	Blue Bicycle	Deforges, H.
Appletree Saga	Pearce, M.	Blue Pete	Allan, L.
Apprentice Adept	Anthony, P.	Bognor, Simon	Heald, T.
Archer, Lew	MacDonald, R.	Bolitho, Richard	Kent, A.
Argand, Jan	Rathbone, J.	Bonaparte, *Inspector*	Upfield, A.W.
Arnold, *Inspector*	Burton, M.	Bond, James	Flemming, I.
Arrow, Steve	Mantell, L.	Bondmaster Series	Tresillian, R.
Arthurian Trilogy	Canning, V.	The Book of Isle	Springer, N.
Arthurian Trilogy	Gloag, R.	Borges, *Inspector*	Bonett, J. & E.
Arthurian Trilogy	Stewart, M.	Bostock Family	Darby, C.
Asch, Gunner	Kirst, H.H.	Bourne	Ludlum, R.
Askham Chronicles	Thorne, N.	Bowman, Glenn	Howard, H.
Aubrey, Jack	O'Brian, P.	Bradley, *Dame*	
Audley, *Doctor*	Price, A.	Beatrice	Mitchell, G.
Austin, Steve	Caidin, M.	Brandon Family	Tinniswood, P.
The Australians	Stuart, V.	Brandsetter, Dave	Hansen, J.
Aveyard, Supt.	Fraser, J.	Breakenridge Series	Cleary, D.
Aysgill Family	White, A.	Breckland Series	Home, M.
Bailey, Bill	Cookson, C.	Breed	Muir, J.A.
Bailey, Hogleg	Borg, J.	Bridges over time	Anand, V.
Balkin Trilogy	Manning, O.	Brissac Family	Banis, V.J.
Banks, *Inspector*	Robinson, P.	Brogan, Jerry	Breen, J.
The Barclays	Elder, M.	Brothers of	
Barforth Family	Jagger, B.	Gwynnedd	Pargeter, E.
Barlow, *Chief Supt.*	Jones, E.	Brook Roger	Wheatley, D.
The Baron	Creasey, J.	Brown, Dagobert	Ames, D.
Barsetshire Series	Thirkell, A.	Brunt, *Sergeant*	Hilton, J.B.
Basnett, Andrew	Ferrars, E.	Mr. Bunting	Greenwood, R.
Bawtry, Sam	Enefer, D.	Burke, *Hon.*	
Bebb, Leo	Buechner, F.	Constance	Porter, J.
Beef, *Sgt.*	Bruce, L.	Burmann, Cheviot	Cobb, B.
Bel Air General	Sutton, J.	Cable, Brevet	Callison, B.
The Belgariad	Eddings, D.	Cadfael, *Brother*	Peters, E.
Belgate Trilogy	Robertson, D.	Calder, Keith	Hammond, G.
Bencolin, Henri	Carr, J.D.	Callaghan, Slim	Cheyney, P.
Bennet, Reid	Wood, T.	Cameron, R.N.	McCutchan, P.
Beulah Land	Coleman, L.	Camillo, Don	Guareschi, G.
Bindle Series	Jenkins, H.	Campion, Albert	Allingham, M.
Birthgrave Series	Lee, T.	Cannaway Family	Shelby, G.

Title/character	Author	Title/character	Author
Canopus in Argus	Lessing, D.	Cuddy, J.F.	Healy, J.
Capricorn Merlin	Winslow, P.G.	Craig, Peter	Benton, K.
Carlyle, Carlotta	Barnes, L.	Craigallan, Rob	Barclay, T.
Carmichael, Nurse	Cohen, A.	Crawford of	
Carnaby Series	Walker, P.N.	Lymond	Dunnett, D.
Carrick, Webb	Knox, B.	Cribb, *Sergeant*	Lovesey, P.
Carver, Rex	Canning, V.	Crichton, Tessa	Morice, A.
Caspian, *Doctor*	Burke, J.	Crook, Arthur	Gilbert, A.
Casteel Family	Andrews, V.	Crossroads Motel	Hulke, M.
Cassidy, Horatio	Crosby, J.	Crow, *Inspector*	Lewis, R.
Castang, Henri	Freeling, N.	Crowther Family	Armstrong, T.
Castle Rising	Cradock, F.	Dalgleish, *Supt.*	James, P.D.
Catherine	Benzoni, J.	Dallas	Hirschfield, B.
The Cedar Tree	Hardwick, M.	Dalziel, *Supt.*	Hill, R.
Cellini, *Doctor*	Creasey, J.	Dancers at the End of	
Challenger, *Professor*	Doyle, A.C.	Time	Moorcock, M.
Chambrun, Pierre	Pentecost, H.	Dancing Gods	Chalker, J.L.
Chan, David	Leader, C.	Dando	Clive, W.
Charles I	Beardsworth,	Daniels, Chaimian	Melville, J.
	M.M.	Darkover Series	Bradley, M.Z.
Charlie's Angels	see title	De Silva, Jose	Fish, R.L.
Chelmarsh, Dorian		Davy, Captain	Bray, D.
Fairweather	Hardwick, M.	Dawlish, Patrick	Creasy, J.
Cherry, *Inspector*	Van Greenaway, P.	Daughters of England	Carr, P.
Cheyney, *Colonel*	Cosgrave, P.	Dax, Saturnin	Cumberland, M.
Children of the north	Powers, M.S.	Death Merchants	Rosenberger, J.
Children of Violence	Lessing, D.	Deene, Carolus	Bruce, L.
Chronicles of an		Delancey, Richard	Parkinson, C.N.
Age of Darkness	Cook, H.	Department Z	Creasey, J.
Chronicles of		Derain Family	Thompson, K.
Ancient Sunlight	Williamson, H.	Derben, *Inspector*	Foxall, P.A.
Chronicles of		Desert Commandos	Landsborough, G.
Hawklan	Taylor, R.	Destroyers	Whiting, C.
Chronicles of		Destiny of Eagles	Carnegie, S.
Invernevis	MacIntyre, L.	Deutsch, Richard	Christian, J.
Chronicles of		Deventer, Piet	Anderson, J.R.L.
Prydain	Alexander, L.	Devlin, Brock	Mitchell, S.
C.I.D. Room	Alding, P.	Devlin, Liam	Higgins, J.
Clachan Series	Armstrong, S.	Dexter, Paul	Hackforth-Jones,
Claudia Series	Franken, R.		G.
Claudine Series	Colette	Discworld	Pratchett, T.
Cluster Series	Anthony, P.	Dollengager Family	Andrews, V.
Clutha	Munro, N.	Dorsai Trilogy	Dickson, G.R.
Cody	Brierley, D.	Dover, *Ch. Inspector*	Porter, J.
Coffin, *Inspector*	Butler, G.	Dowling, *Father*	McInerny, R.
Conan	Howard, R.G.	Dragonlance Chronicles	Weis, M. &
Conquest, Norman	Gray, B.		Hickman, T.
Cooperman, Benny	Engel, H.	Dragon Series	McCaffrey, A.
Cornelius, Jerry	Moorcock, M.	Dragon Prince	Rawn, M.
Coronation Street,	Kershaw, H.	Dragonard Series	Gilchrist, R.
Corridon	Chase, J.H.	Drinkwater, Nathaniel	Woodman, R.
Courage Series	Shears, S.	Drummond, Bulldog	Sapper
Courtney Family	Smith, W.	Duchess of Duke St.	Hardwick, M.
Coyne, Brady	Tapply, W.G.	Duddleswell, *Father*	Boyd, N.
Craddocks of	Delderfield,	Duffy	Kavanagh, D.
Shallowford	R.F.	Dumarest Saga	Tubb, E.C.

Title/character	Author	Title/character	Author
Dune	Herbert, F.	Gideon, *Commander*	Creasey, J.
Durrell, Sam	Aarons, S.	Girland, Mark	Chase, J.H.
Eastenders	Miller, H.	Gollantz Saga	Jacob, N.
Easthampton Series	Laker, R.	The Good Life	Esmonde, B.
Edge the Loner	Gilman, G.G.	Goodey	Alverson, C.
87th Precinct Series	McBain, E.	Gor Series	Norman, J.
Eisengrin Trilogy	Davies, P.	Gordon, Flash	Raymond, A.
Elenium	Eddings, D.	Gorodish and Alba	Delacorta
Eliot Family	Goudge, E.	Gotobed Trilogy	Cuddon, J.A.
Emmerdale Farm	Mackenzie, L.	Grafton, Jake	Coonts, S.
Epton, Rosa	Underwood, M.	Graham, Davina	Anthony, E.
Erridge, Matt	Stein, A.M.	Grants of Rothiedrum	Fraser, C.S.
Everard, Nick	Fullerton, A.	Greystone Series	Bronte, L.
Fairacre Series	Miss Read	Gunslinger	Garrett, C.G.
Falcon Family	Darby, C.	Gurney	Llewellyn, S.
Falcon Series	Benzoni, J.	Habsburg Series	Hamilton, J.
Falconhurst Series	Onstott, K.	Haggard Series	Nicole, C.
Falkenstein, Jesse	Egan, L.	Halfhyde Series	McCutchan, P.
Family D'Alambert	Smith, E.E.	Hallam, *Det. Supt.*	Douglas, G.
Fansler, Kate	Cross, A.	Haller, Mike	Byrd, M.
Faraday, Mike	Cooper, B.	Halley, Sid	Francis, D.
Farne, Max	Butler, R.	Halliday, Willie	Fredman, M.
Farrow, Mark	Ross, A.	Halloran, Meg	LaPierre, J.
Fell, Gideon	Carr, J.D.	Hamilton	Cookson, C.
Fen, Gervase	Crispin, E.	Hannay, Richard	Buchan, J.
Finch, *Inspector*	Thomson, J.	Harding	Melville-Ross, A.
Finch, Septimus	Erskine, M.	Hardwick Family	Heath-Miller, M.
Mr. Finchley	Canning, V.	Harpur, Colin	James, B.
The First Born of		Mrs. Harris	Gallico, P.
Egypt	Raven, S.	Harris, Paul	Black, G.
Mr. Fitton	Styles, S.	Harris, Sam	Cronin, M.
Flagg, *Ch. Inspector*	Cassells, J.	Havoc	Healey, B.
Flandry, *Lieut.*	Anderson, P.	Hawk	Brady, W.S.
Flashman	Fraser, G.M.	Hawkmoon	Moorcock, M.
Flax of Dream Series	Williamson, H.	Hawkwood, *Sir*	
Flaxborough		John	Cole, H.
Chronicles	Watson, C.	Hawksmoor Series	Armitage, A.
Fletch	MacDonald, G.	Hazard, Commander	Stuart, V.
Flynn Family	Glover, J.	Hazell, James	Yuill, P.B.
Flynn, *Inspector*	MacDonald, G.	Hedley, Paul	Healey, B.
Flynn, Xavier	Braine, J.	Hefferman, Hooky	Meynell, L.
Forsyte Saga	Galsworthy, J.	Helliconia Trilogy	Aldiss, B.
Mr. Fortune	Bailey, H.C.	Helm, Matt	Hamilton, D.
Fortune, Dan	Collins, M.	Herne the Hunter	McLaglen, J.
Foundation Series	Asimov, I.	Heron Saga	Oldfield, P.
Four Winds of Love	MacKenzie, C.	Hilton Family	Nicole, C.
Foxearth Trilogy	Oldfield, P.	Miss Hogg	Lee, A.
Frazer, Tim	Durbridge, F.	Holland, Mark	Myers, P.
Freer, Felix	Ferrars, E.	Holmes, Sherlock	Doyle, A.C.
French, *Inspector*	Crofts, F.W.	Honeybath	Innes, M.
Gaunt, Jonathan	MacLeod, R.	Hope, Matthew	McBain, E.
Gautier, *Inspector*	Grayson, R.	Hopewell Saga	Campbell, D.
Gently, *Ch. Inspector*	Hunter, A.	Hornblower Series	Forrester, C.S.
Gently, Dirk	Adams, D.	Horne, Adam	Hill, P.
Gerard, *Brigadier*	Doyle, A.C.	Horowitz, Jacob &	
Ghote, *Inspector*	Keating, H.R.F.	Helen	Delman, D.

Title/character	Author	Title/character	Author
Horseclans	Adams, R.	Lorrimer Family	Melville, A.
Hoskins, Sam	Dacre, R.	Louise	Shears, S.
A House for the Season	Chesney, M.	Love, Jason	Leasor, J.
Howard Saga	Wiat, P.	Lovejoy	Gash, J.
Howarths of Kit's Hill	Stubbs, J.	Lucia	Benson, E.F.
Howton Series	Haworth, E.	Lugh the Harper	Finney, P.
Hoyland, Tamara	Mann, J.	Lynley, Thomas	George, E.
Hurricane Squadron	Jackson, R.	McAllister	Chisholm, M.
Illuminatus	Shea, R.	McCall, Andrew	Carrel, M.
Incarnations of		McCunn, Dick	Buchan, J.
Immortality	Anthony, P.	McGarr, *Ch. Inspector*	Gill, B.
Jalna Series	De la Roche, M.	McGee, Travis	MacDonald, J.D.
Jury, *Chief Inspector*	Grimes, M.	McGlusky Series	Hales, A.G.
Kai Lung Series	Bramah, E.	McGuire, Kelly	Hennessey, M.
Kane, Sugar	Marshall, L.	M.A.S.H.	Hooker, R.
Kaplan, Hyman	Rosten, L.	Maddox, *Sergeant*	Blaisdell, A.
Kaywana Series	Mittelholzer, E.	Maigret, *Inspector*	Simenon, G.
Keegan	Ball, B.	Maitland, Anthony	Woods, S.
Kelling, Sarah	MacLeod, C.	Majipoor Series	Silverberg, R.
Kelly, Homer	Langton, J.	Malcolm, Solo	Graham, N.
Kelsey, *Detective*		Mallen Family	Cookson, C.
Chief Inspector	Page, E.	Mallett, Dan	Parrish, F.
Kelso, Roger	White, J.D.	Mallin & Coe	Ormerod, R.
Kemp, Lennox	Meek, M.R.D.	Malloreon	Eddings, D.
Kenworthy, *Supt.*	Hilton, J.B.	Mamur Zapt	Pearce, M.
Keyon, *Inspector*	Crisp, N.J.	Manning, *Supt.*	Cobb, B.
Kerry, Don	Ashford, J.	March, Milo	Chaber, M.E.
Kessler, *Sergeant*		Margery Family	Bassett, R.
Rolf	Hutson, S.	Marianne	Benzoni, J.
Kettle, *Captain*	Hyne, C.J.	Marlowe, Philip	Chandler, R.
Kildare, *Doctor*	Brand, M.	Miss Marple	Christie, A.
Kincaid Family	Kennedy, A.	Martian Series	Burroughs, E.R.
Kingdom of Amber	Zelazny, R.	Mary Ann Series	Cookson, C.
Kinsfolk	Cowper, R.	Mason, Perry	Gardner, E.S.
Kirk, *General*	Blackburn, J.	Masters, *Ch. Inspector*	Clark, D.
Kent Family	Jakes, J.	Masuto, Masao	Cunningham. E.V.
Koesler, Father	Kienzle, W.	Mather, *Det. Sergeant*	Graeme, B.
Kramer, *Lieut.*	MacClure, J.	Matthew and Son	Kenworthy, C.
Kruger, Herbie	Gardner, J.	Maxim, Harry	Lyall, G.
Lampitts	Wilson, A.N.	McGann Family	Nicole, C.
Landon, Arnold	Lewis, R.	Men at War	Baldwin, A.
Landover Series	Brooks, T.	Mendoza, Luis	Shannon, D.
Larkin Family	Bates, H.E.	Merivale, *Sir* Henry	Dickson, C.
Lavette Family	Fast, H.	Miami Vice	Grave, S.
Leaphorn and Chee	Hillerman, T.	Minder	Masters, A.
Leithen *Sir* Edward	Buchan, J.	Mission Earth	Hubbard, L.R.
Lensman Series	Smith, E.E.	Mongo Mysteries	Chesbro, G.C.
Leric, *Det. Sergeant*	Busby, R.	Montgomery Family	Deveraux, J.
Lestrade, *Inspector*	Trow, M.J.	Montrose, Doctor Jean	Roe, C.F.
Levant Trilogy	Manning, O.	Moorhouse Family	McCrone, G.
Lewker, Abercrombie	Carr, G.	Morgan, Rain	Grant-Adamson, L.
Lightbringer Trilogy	Lee, S.	Morse, *Det. Ch.*	
Lisle, Darina	Laurence, J.	*Inspector*	Dexter, C.
Littlejohn, *Det. Insp.*	Bellairs, G.	Mortdecai, Charlie	Bonfiglioli, K.
Lomax, Jacob	Allegretto, M.	Mosely, *Detective*	
Longarn Series	Evans, T.	*Inspector*	Greenwood, J.

Title/character	Author	Title/character	Author
Muffin, Charlie	Freemantle, B.	Poirot, Hercule	Christie, A.
Mulcahaney, Norah	O'Donnell, L.	Poldark Series	Graham, W.
Murder League Series	Fish, R.L.	Pollard, *Det. Supt.*	Lemarchand, M.
The Music of Time	Powell, A.	Mrs. Pollifax	Gilman, D.
Myth	Asprin, R.	Polonsky Family	Angoff, C.
Nash, *Captain*	Butler, R.	Poppy Chronicles	Rayner, C.
Necroscope	Lumley, B.	Porridge	Clement, D.
Neighbours	Ruhen, C.	Potter, Brock	Maling, A.
New Avengers	see title	Preston, Mark	Chambers, P.
Neyler Family	Saxton, J.	Mr. Pringle	Livingston, N.
Nighthawk	Horler, S.	Probyn, Julia	Bridge, A.
Noon, Ed	Avallone, M.	Mrs. Pym	Morland, N.
Nugent Family	Burton, B.	Quantrill, *Detective*	
Oakes, Blackford	Buckley, W.F.	*Superintendent*	Radley, S.
Oakes, Boysie	Gardner, J.	Quartermain, Allan	Haggard, H.R.
Ogilvie, James	MacNeil, D.	Quatermass	Kneale, N.
Omaran Saga	Cole, A.	Quiller	Hall, A.
Omen Series	Howard, J.	Quintain, Richard	Baker, W.H.
Onedin Line	Abrahams, C.	Quist, Julian	Pentecost, H.
Otani, *Supt.*	Melville, J.	Rackstraw	Hardwick, M.
Palfrey, *Doctor*	Creasey, J.	Raffles	Hornung, E.W.
Palmer-Jones, George	Cleeves, A.	Rainwood Family	Bromige, I.
M. Pamplemousse	Bond, M.	Raj Quartet	Scott, P.
Panda One Series	Walker, P.N.	Ramage	Pope, D.
Panzer Platoon	Lutz, G.	Rambo	Morrell, D.
Mrs. Pargeter	Brett, S.	Ramsay, *Inspector*	Cleeves, A.
Paris, Charles	Brett, S.	Raven	Mackenzie, D.
Parker	Stark, R.	Raven, Richard	Griffin, J.
Parson, Annie	Shears, S.	Raynes of Rayleigh	Heath-Miller, M.
Pascoe, *Sergeant*	Hill, R.	Reachfar Series	Duncan, J.
Pasquier Series	Duhamel, G.	Reamer, D. *Supt.*	Duncan, W.M.
Paton, Crispin	Draper, A.	Rebel	Kessler, L.
Peabody, Amelia	Peters, E.	Resnick, Charlie	Harvey, J.
Peacock Series	Gordon, K.	Rhanna	Fraser, C.M.
Peckover, Harry	Kenyon, M.	Rhodenbarr, Bernie	Block, L.
Pel, *Inspector*	Hebden, M.	Richlieu, *Duc de*	Wheatley, D.
Pellucidar Series	Burroughs, E.R.	Riftwar Saga	Feist, R.E.
Pendragon Series	Trevelyan, R.	Rimrunners	Chandler, B.
Penhaligon Series	White, S.	Rings of the Master	Chalker, J.L.
Pentecost Family	Malpass, E.	Ripley	Highsmith, P.
Percy Trilogy	Wensby-Scott, C.	Rivers, Julian	Carnac, C.
The Performers	Rayner, C.	Riverworld Saga	Farmer, P.J.
Peroni, *Inspector*	Holme, T.	Rogers, *Ch. Inspector*	Ross, J.
Perrin, Reginald	Nobbs, D.	Rolfe, Helga	Chase, J.H.
Peters, Anna	Law, J.	Roper, *Det. Supt.*	Hart, R.
Peters, Toby	Kaminsky, S.	Roselynde Chronicles	Gellis, R.
Philis	Perry, R.	Rowan Series	Darby, C.
Pibble, *Det. Supt.*	Dickinson, P.	Rumpole	Mortimer, J.
Picaroon	Cassells, J.	Runestaff Series	Moorcock, M.
Pinaud, *Monsieur*	Audemars, P.	Russell, Charles	Haggard, W.
Miss Pink	Moffat, G.	S.A.S.	Albany, J.
Pink Panther	Waldman, F.	Ryan, Father	
Piper & Quinn	Carmichael, H.	"Blackie"	Greeley, A.M.
Pitt, Dirk	Cussler, C.	Sabre Series	Darby, C.
Plantagenet Saga	Plaidy, J.	Sackett	L'Amour, L.
Plantagenet Series	Dymoke, J.	The Saint	Charteris, L.

Title/character	Author	Title/character	Author
St. Ives, Philip	Bleeck, O.	Starr, David-Space	
St. Mark's Hospital	Harrison, E.	Ranger	Asimov, I.
Sainte Monique		Starskey & Hutch	Franklin, M.
Series	Lister, S.	Steele, Adam	Gilman, G.G.
Sallust, Gregory	Wheatley, D.	Stephanie	Gobineau, M.
Salter, Charlie	Wright, E.	Stevenson Family	MacDonald, M.
Sam	see title	Stoner, Harry	Valin, J.
Samson, Bernard	Deighton, L.	Storm Troop Series	Kessler, L.
Savage Family	Masters, J.	Strangeways, Nigel	Blake, N.
Savage, Mark	Payne, L.	Styles, Peter	Philips, J.
Sawyer, Pete	Albert, M.	Sudden	Strange, O.
Saxon, Ludovic	Cassells, J.	Summer Wine	
Saxon, Trilogy	Duggan, A.	Chronicles	Clarke, R.
Scamp, *Det. Sergeant*	Foxall, P.A.	The Survivalist	Ahern, J.
Scarlet Pimpernel	Orczy, Baroness	Sutton Place Series	Lampitt, D.
Schmidt, *Inspector*	Bagby, G.	Swann Saga	Delderfield, R.F.
School for Manners	Chesney, M.	The Sweeney	see title
Scudder, Matthew	Block, L.	Sweyneseye (Swansea)	Gower, I.
Scully Series	Bleasdale, A.	Syn, *Doctor*	Thorndike, R.
Sea Wolf	Bulmer, K.	T-Force	Whiting, C.
Seaton Family	Sillitoe, A.	Tallentire Family	Bragg, M.
Sector General	White, J.	Tallon, Jack	Ball, J.
Secret Army	Brason, J.	Tanner, Evan	Block, L.
Miss Seeton	Carvic, H.	Tanner, John	Greenleaf, S.
The Sensual Life	Croft-Cooke, R.	Tarzan	Burroughs, E.R.
Sidhe Legends	Flint, K.C.	Tedric, Lord	Smith, E.E.
Shaft	Tidyman, E.	Temple, Paul	Durbridge, F.
Shand, Dale	Enefer, D.	Thane & Moss	Knox, B.
Shannara Series	Brooks, T.	Thanet, *Inspector*	Simpson, D.
Shard, Simon	McCutchan, P.	Thatcher, John P.	Lathen, E.
Sharpe, Richard	Cornwell, B.	Thomas Covenant	Donaldson, S.
Shaw, *Commander*	McCutchan, P.	Thongor Series	Carter, L.
She	Haggard, H.R.	Thorn, Caleb	Coburn, W.
Sheridan, Alex	Stuart, V.	Thorndyke, *Doctor*	Freeman, R.A.
Shore, Jemima	Fraser, A.	Thorne, *Inspector*	Penn, J.
Miss Silver	Wentworth, P.	Thrush Green Series	Miss Read
Silver, Elsie	Golding, L.	Tibbett, *Inspector*	Moyes, P.
Silvertip	Brand, M.	Tibbs, Virgil	Ball, J.
633 Squadron	Smith, F.E.	Tildy Crawford	Fraser, S.
Skylark Series	Smith, E.E.	To Keep the Ball	
Slade, Anthony	Gribble, L.	Rolling	Powell, A.
Sloan, *Inspector*	Aird, C.	Tobin, Mitchell	Coe, T.
Small, *Rabbi*	Kemelman, H.	The Toff	Creasey, J.
Smiley, George	Le Carre, J.	Tramont Series	Barclay, T.
Space 1999	see title	Travers, Ludovic	Bush, C.
Spade, Sam	Hammett, D.	Treasure, Mark	Williams, D.
Spenser	Parker, R.B.	Trethowan, Perry	Barnard, R.
Squadron	Holden, M.	Triad	Cookson, C.
Stahl, Otto	Kessler, L.	Trotter, Tilly	Cookson, C.
Stainless Steel Rat	Harrison, H.	Tweed	Forbes, C.
Stainton, Alec	Murray, S.	Unwin, Miss	Hervey, E.
Standish, Tiger	Horley, S.	Urgent, Mark	Forde, N.
Star Lord Saga	Buffery, J.	Van Der Valk	Freeling, N.
Star Requiem	Cole, A.	Varallo, Vic	Egan, L.
Star Trek	see title	Verity, *Sergeant*	Selwyn, F.
Star Wars	see title	Virginian Series	Fletcher, I.

Title/character	Author	Title/character	Author
Walker, Amos	Estleman, L.D.	Wings of Gold	Cruise, T.E.
Wanawake, Penny	Moody, S.	Wintercombe	Belle, P.
Ward, Eric	Lewis, R.	Winter King's War	Dexter, S.
The Way Ahead	Briggs, V.	Winter, *Lieut.* Jason	Gaston, B.
Weatherly, Kate	Birmingham, M.	Wintringham, David	Bell, J.
Webb, *Chief Inspector*	Fraser, Anthea	The Witches	Darke, J.
Wellworld Saga	Chalker, J.L.	Witchworld	Norton, A.
Wentworth Lyon	Forrest, R.	Wolfe, Nero	Stout, R.
West, *Inspector*	Creasey, J.	World's End Series	Sinclair, U.
Wexford, *Inspector*	Rendell, R.	World of the Alfar	Boyer, E.H.
Wheel of Time	Jordan, R.	Wotan Panzer Series	Kessler, L.
When The Boat		Wyatt Saga	Wiat, P.
Comes In	Mitchell, J.	Wycliff, *Det. Supt.*	Burley, W.J.
Whiteoaks Series	De la Roche, M.	Wyndsor, *Det. Supt.*	Hill, P.
Wilchester Chronicles	Ashton, H.	Xanth	Anthony, P.
Williamsburg Series	Thane, E.	Yarrow Series	Best, R.
Willing, Basil	McCloy, H.	Yellowthread Street	Marshall, W.L.
Willows and Parker	Gough, L.	York Cycle of Mysteries	Whitehead, B.
Wimsey, *Lord* Peter	Sayers, D.L.	Yorke, Edward	Pope, D.
Windmill Hill	Evans, S.	Yorke, Ned	Pope, D.